IN
HIS
STEPS

IN HIS STEPS

Lyndon Johnson and the Kennedy Mystique

BY

PAUL R. HENGGELER

Ivan R. Dee

CHICAGO, 1991

Library of Congress Cataloging-in-Publication Data:
Henggeler, Paul R.
    In his steps : Lyndon Johnson and the Kennedy mystique / by Paul R. Henggeler.
        p.   cm.
    Includes bibliographical references and index.
    ISBN 0-929587-50-2
    1. Johnson, Lyndon B. (Lyndon Baines), 1908–1973—Friends and associates. 2. Kennedy, John F. (John Fitzgerald), 1917–1963—Influence. 3. Kennedy family. 4. United States—Politics and government—1963–1969. I. Title.
E847.2.H46   1991
973.923'092—dc20   90-20289

For Marianne

ACKNOWLEDGMENTS

In the process of writing this book I relied on the kindness of many friends and colleagues to whom I owe a great deal of gratitude.

This book was conceived originally as a dissertation and was written under the direction of my friend and teacher, Lawrence J. Friedman of Bowling Green State University. Professionally our discussions generated important concepts fundamental to this book. Personally he urged me to reach beyond myself. Larry's guidance, criticism, and confidence in me both sustained and confounded me, but always prompted me to do it right.

I extend my appreciation and affection to Bernard Sternsher, whose scholarly attendance and know-how helped instill the discipline necessary to complete this work. His insights and companionship were a source of enlightenment and support. I also deeply appreciate the efforts of Ivan R. Dee, whose critique of the original manuscript and skillful editing helped to minimize customary flaws associated with writing a first book. Similarly, my thanks to Alicia Browne, whose keen, organized mind often discovered problems that others had missed.

I am grateful also to several people and their respective departments at Bowling Green State University. I am especially appreciative of the Department of History, Gary Hess, and William Rock for their financial and academic support during my graduate studies there. Dennis Hale, director of the School of Mass Communication, encouraged an interdisciplinary approach to this study. Paul Yon and Ann Bowers of the Center for Archival Collections were kind enough to provide me with repeated funding during summers while giving me needed time to complete the work. Some of my research and travel expenses were provided by Research Services at Bowling Green State University. Outside of the university, archivists at the Lyndon Baines Johnson Library in Austin, Texas, and at the John F. Kennedy Library in Boston demonstrated considerable patience and provided me with needed assistance.

Several people contributed in more subtle ways. I am especially grateful to Beverly Ott and Dave Wilson, two strangers who befriended me in Austin and made my research experience there a pleasant surprise. Similarly,

Marian Smith, Joe and Lani Gerson, and G. J. Barker-Benfield showed that hospitality is not a trait unique to Texas. Two other "strangers," Annette Krutsch and Mary Jen Meerdink, allowed me to complete a more personal journey. And a special thanks to Frank Burdick at the State University of New York at Cortland. Fifteen years ago he infused me with the necessary skepticism and curiosity to pursue this line of work.

Finally, I owe more than I can adequately express to Marianne Emerson for her constant willingness to hit behind the runner. As my wife, friend, and editor, she provided the sacrifice, insight, patience, and faith necessary to complete this book.

P. R. H.

Bowling Green, Ohio
November 1990

CONTENTS

IN
HIS
STEPS

INTRODUCTION

In a recent poll reported by *CBS This Morning,* Americans were asked to name one president whom they felt most deserved a place on Mount Rushmore if another bust were sculpted into the monument. More than one of three people chose John Kennedy. He was followed by Ronald Reagan, Harry Truman, Franklin Roosevelt, Jimmy Carter, and Richard Nixon. Lyndon Johnson was not considered. On the twentieth anniversary of John Kennedy's death, in 1983, a *Newsweek* poll indicated that two of three people thought American society would have been different had Kennedy lived. One of three wished he were then president. Only one of every one hundred people wished the same of Lyndon Johnson. More than twenty years after their respective presidencies, John Kennedy remains a beloved figure while Lyndon Johnson is belittled. Typically, Johnson is perceived as boorish and manipulative—a sinister political animal who stopped at nothing in his ruthless pursuit of power. If polls are correct, he generates even less affection than Richard Nixon.[1]

In the popular imagination, the relationship between Johnson and the Kennedys presents a dark Macbethian image. For years rumors persisted that Johnson conspired with right-wing Texas oil moguls to kill John Kennedy because Kennedy planned to "dump" him from the 1964 ticket. Folklore has it that, after the assassination, Johnson summoned his personal advisers to the cargo section of Air Force One, hoisted himself onto Kennedy's coffin, and joyfully detailed his plans for the new administration. In 1967 the Macbeth analogy was carried to its extreme in Barbara Garson's theatrical parody *MacBird.* Recently this image has re-emerged as a result of Robert Caro's multi-volume biography of Johnson. One reviewer of Caro experienced "the sickening notion" that the author might later "attempt to prove that a Macbeth-like LBJ was behind the Kennedy assassination."[2]

As with many myths, the ones surrounding Johnson and the Kennedys have been reduced to their rawest emotional components. But simplistic popular attitudes do not explain the relationship between these diverse and powerful figures. A more realistic understanding of Johnson's reactions to

3

John and Robert Kennedy begins by delineating the circumstances that shaped his response to them.

Johnson's inability to compete with John Kennedy's appeal has been longstanding. It was early noted in November 1965 by Tom Wicker of the *New York Times,* in an article for *Esquire* entitled, "Lyndon Johnson vs. the Ghost of Jack Kennedy." Wicker, a White House correspondent during the Kennedy and Johnson administrations, lamented Johnson's failure to win the popular affection that the late president had enjoyed. In Washington, Wicker wrote, there was a feeling that the "Golden Age" had passed—"implying, perhaps believing, that the Kennedy years were a period of higher heart and broader spirit, a sort of Instant Greece when everything from art to athletics flowered, and the people rose above themselves." Few disputed that Johnson had achieved greater legislative success than Kennedy; it was the disparity in personality and style that made many people nostalgic. "It is a sad and terrible likelihood," Wicker wrote, "that Lyndon Johnson will not live down the fact that he followed John Kennedy. . . . [T]he shadow of Kennedy will fall on him all his days."

Wicker discussed the images that beleaguered Johnson: his deficient social skills and insufficient refinement; his lack of proper intellectual and artistic sophistication; his shady political reputation; and his inability to comprehend global issues the way his predecessor had and would if he were still alive. Compounding his difficulties were the "living and breathing reminders, the flesh-and-blood heirs of the Golden Age." Robert and Edward Kennedy personified what had been and what might still be—if only Johnson were removed from the presidency. The anxiety of those who yearned for a "restoration" was intensified by the knowledge that Robert had opposed Johnson's nomination for vice president in 1960 and that Johnson had denied Kennedy a spot on *his* ticket in 1964. "The net effect here," Wicker wrote, "is that the unspoken attitude toward Lyndon Johnson of many people in Washington is that he is somehow the constitutional usurper who does not belong where he is."

Appreciating Johnson's resentment, Wicker sensed that it was not so much directed against his predecessor as it was toward "Washington's unwillingness to let each claim his own greatness without comparison to the other." Kennedy had inspired style. But Johnson generated substance. Cautioning readers about the dangers of their mass fantasy, Wicker noted that the "Golden Age" was actually the "Age of the Golden Figure." "We have erected that figure into such a towering symbol," he noted, "that it diminishes all else." Those who yearned for the past were deluding themselves by refusing to accept political realities. "We remember John Kennedy for what we wanted to be," Wicker concluded, "and we do not like to admit that Lyndon Johnson takes us for what we are":

For some, that is what is too much, too hard to take—not Johnson's style, not his foreign policy, not his political maneuvers, but the fact that somehow he makes the wheels go around and the country move. To admit that is to admit that we need politicians and politics, we need manipulation, we do have ambitions and interests and weaknesses and beliefs that can ensnarl or release us—we are not golden but human.[3]

Without labeling it as such, Wicker had fairly well described the Kennedy "mystique," delineating many of its crucial elements: the fascination with the Kennedy style; the hostility toward usurpers; the attraction to myth; the anticipation that Robert Kennedy would complete John's unfinished presidency; and the desire to reside in Camelot and escape reality. Wicker also alluded to a troubling consequence of the Kennedy "mystique": its effect on the public's orientation toward the past, present, and future. The past was exalted and distorted by the notion that Kennedy's death had deprived the country of its proper destiny. The present was rendered illegitimate and absorbed in a fantasy that life would be better if only John Kennedy had lived. The future was delusional, consumed in the belief that the nation would resume its proper course only with the return of the rightful heir to the throne. The Kennedy "mystique" colored the progression of time and events.[4]

Johnson treated the "mystique" not as a single entity but as two separate forces, embodied in John and Robert Kennedy, which drew him near and pushed him away. As a nonthreatening figure from the past, John represented the "good" Kennedy—a symbol which could win Johnson vicarious public affection provided he could convincingly portray himself as its surrogate. During their careers together, Kennedy had treated Johnson fairly and had opened power to him—and he could not return from the dead to displace the new president. Attracted to John and to the power of his memory, Johnson sometimes emulated his attributes and framed his legislative agenda and foreign policies in the context of the Kennedy legacy. In contrast, Robert represented for Johnson the "bad" Kennedy—a figure of the future who could more rightfully claim the "mystique" for his own purposes and offer a restoration of his brother's presidency. Johnson responded with hostility to this element of the "mystique," engaging in aggressive political ploys and turning against those, especially in the news media, whom he believed were conspiring with Robert to dethrone him.

Johnson's ambivalence toward the Kennedys was also a product of Johnson himself. Those who knew him, and those who have studied him, agree that he was burdened by enormous insecurities. Unable to admit his own shortcomings, he lied and exaggerated to avoid blame for his failures. Despite his legislative brilliance, he felt intellectually inferior in the company of academicians. Although he was charming and an entertaining storyteller, he feared being a social outcast. He dreaded loneliness, clamored for attention, and sometimes displayed behavior that some of his closest aides called "paranoid." Seeking approval, he assimilated the behavior of others in order to be liked, and he pursued power in order to compensate for his feelings of inadequacy. Throughout his life his pattern was to serve under more powerful figures and then undermine them to create his own realm of authority.

Given the scope of Johnson's insecurities, it was not surprising that his reaction to the Kennedys was exaggerated. John and Robert Kennedy represented both opportunities and threats to his career. During the 1950s Johnson admired John Kennedy's boyish good-looks, playboy life-style, and social appeal. But he resented those same qualities when voters found them more attractive than Johnson's own political skills during the 1960s. In the powerful position of Senate Majority Leader, Johnson had handled the junior senator with relative confidence, for Kennedy needed him in order to advance his own career in the Senate. But during the 1960 campaign for the Democratic presidential nomination, Johnson was humbled and humiliated by the power of Kennedy's charisma. Defeated at the Democratic National Convention, Johnson relinquished his position as Senate Majority Leader to become Kennedy's vice president, hoping to use the position as a stepping-stone to the presidency in 1968. In the New Frontier he served loyally but was shunned politically and socially, ill-suited for the Kennedys' stylistic demands. Lacking power and influence, he withdrew into self-pity, feared he would be eliminated from the 1964 ticket, and blamed Robert Kennedy for his fate. After becoming president, Johnson was haunted by accusations that he was a usurper. He believed that those unhappy with his ascension to power would try to displace him, so he promoted himself as John Kennedy's surrogate in order to gain approval while at the same time rebelling against the Kennedy image by waging a covert political war against Robert Kennedy.

This study traces the development of Johnson's ambivalence toward the Kennedy "mystique" and the resulting consequences for his presidency. Chapters 1 through 3 focus on the period from the mid-1950s until John Kennedy's assassination in 1963. They examine Johnson's personality structure and his evolving political and personal relationship with the Kennedy brothers. Chapters 4 through 7 detail the transition year from November 22, 1963, through the fall election of 1964. Part of Johnson was determined to convey an image of continuity with the Kennedy administration, and he

6

adjusted the image and substance of his presidency accordingly. Less conspicuously, he undermined Robert's influence on his administration. Chapters 8 through 10 concern Johnson's presidency from his November 1964 victory through 1968. These years were marked by his sporadic attempts to distance himself from John Kennedy and to protect his power from Robert. Having benefited from the "mystique," he became inordinately fearful that its power might be used against him.

The general literature on the Johnson presidency has dealt with the influence of the Kennedys in only a cursory manner. The precise impact of the Kennedys on Lyndon Johnson has been obscured by broader considerations. My aim is to consider major components of the Johnson administration, including its policies, staff composition, press relations, and image-management operations, largely in the context of the Kennedys. The reader should not be misled by this concentrated approach. Although Johnson was at times obsessed with the Kennedys, the "mystique" was not the only or even the most important determinant in his decision-making process. He accepted the assumption that the federal government should take an active role in promoting the economic and social well-being of its citizens. His foreign policy was a product of a postwar philosophy that disparaged appeasement and appreciated military force as a means to contain communism. His media relations reflected trends in press-presidential relations dating back to Theodore Roosevelt's presidency. Moreover, the Kennedys were not the only political personalities that influenced Johnson. At various stages of his career, he was attracted to and emulated other popular and powerful figures, including Franklin Roosevelt, Sam Rayburn, and Richard Russell. The Kennedys were the last of a number of politicians who prompted Lyndon Johnson to adjust his behavior, appearance, and political style.

Other influences on Johnson have had their historians. William Leuchtenburg's *In the Shadow of FDR* (1983) devoted a chapter exclusively to Roosevelt's impact on Johnson. Doris Kearns's *Lyndon Johnson and the American Dream* (1976) and Robert Caro's *The Years of Lyndon Johnson: The Path to Power* (1983) concentrated largely upon cultural and psychological forces behind Johnson's political behavior, noting the broad array of people and events that influenced him.

The appropriation of presidential myths and symbols is, to be sure, longstanding. Merrill D. Peterson's *The Jefferson Image in the American Mind* (1962) traced the uses and abuses of Thomas Jefferson's ideas and doctrines by successive generations of politicians, reformers, and others who sought to exploit them for political gain. John William Ward's *Andrew Jackson: Symbol for an Age* (1955) discussed the process by which the general public made Jackson a symbol of popular values, attributing to him qualities which they admired and believed in.[5]

During his early career, Franklin Roosevelt mimicked his famous cousin, Theodore, copying his physical appearance, borrowing his rhetoric, and often reminding reporters of his connection to the popular president. Likewise, other presidents have felt intimidated by their charismatic predecessors. When aides sought to encourage Woodrow Wilson to promote personal aspects of his presidency, he protested that his "conjectural personality" would pale in comparison with Theodore Roosevelt's "vivid" character. During the early stages of the Great Depression, Herbert Hoover's media advisers wanted to offset bad news by publicizing the president's earlier military involvement in the Boxer Rebellion. "You can't make a Teddy Roosevelt out of me," Hoover lamented. Harry Truman, too, felt constrained in having to follow in the footsteps of Franklin Roosevelt.[6]

The Kennedy "mystique" is only the most recent symbolic force to prompt such heedfulness. In the 1988 presidential campaign, Gary Hart and Joseph Biden each sought to embody the "mystique" but suffered negative repercussions. Biden was criticized for plagiarizing from Robert Kennedy's speeches before his withdrawal from the Democratic primaries. Hart became a Kennedy clone, mimicking John Kennedy's mannerisms and rhetorical style (and perhaps even his promiscuity) to such an extent that he invited ridicule. According to some people close to the Hart campaign, he ignored warnings about his excessive reliance on the Kennedy image because he had supplanted his own personality with his idol's.[7]

More detached politicians have simply augmented their images by drawing from the "mystique." George McGovern selected Sargent Shriver as his running mate in 1972 in part because he was an in-law of the Kennedys. When Ronald Reagan sought to generate support for more defense spending and new tax cuts, he quoted John Kennedy more than any other president, illustrating the Republican party's desire to exploit the "mystique" for its own purposes. In 1988 Michael Dukakis evoked memories of the 1960 campaign by selecting Texas Senator Lloyd Bentsen as his vice presidential candidate and re-creating the Boston-Austin axis. And Bentsen denied Republicans access to the "mystique" by pointedly reminding Dan Quayle, "You're no Jack Kennedy."[8]

Unlike other presidential images, the Kennedy "mystique" possessed flesh-and-blood heirs to the Kennedy mantle. Robert and Edward Kennedy embodied the qualities that the public found so attractive in John. The presence of the two brothers intimidated politicians who sought to exploit those qualities for their own purposes. In 1968 Richard Nixon's staff was pleased that their candidate was popularly known among young adults as the

8

man who had lost to John Kennedy in 1960. But Nixon was also wary that year of the prospect of running against Robert Kennedy, and after the election he closely monitored Edward's behavior, fearful that the next Kennedy might challenge him in 1972. In 1976 Jimmy Carter frequently invoked John Kennedy's name during the campaign and was aware that his vague physical resemblance to the late president could attract Kennedy supporters. Privately, however, he boasted that he had won the nomination without kowtowing to the Kennedys, and he later promised to "kick" Edward Kennedy's "ass" if he challenged him in 1980.[9]

Lyndon Johnson was the "mystique's" first and perhaps cruelest victim. Assuming the role of John Kennedy's surrogate, he exalted a myth which finally overshadowed him. He exploited Kennedy's memory to move legislation and to win vicarious support, but he had to relinquish credit to his predecessor for his achievements, and he had to accept sole responsibility for his failures; John Kennedy, he was reminded, would have handled events differently. Lacking the self-assurance necessary to detach himself from the "mystique," he sometimes relied on Kennedy's image at the expense of his own unique qualities.

The story of Lyndon Johnson and the Kennedys is not a morality play. It is a tale of one man whose political and personal insecurities prevented him from effectively contending with new symbols and myths. As a "wheeler-dealer" obscured by the Camelot myth, Johnson was eclipsed by stylistic demands which he never fully understood. As a president who had hoped to be measured by his achievements, he was haunted by the public's affection for his more charismatic predecessor and the growing popularity of a similarly attractive "heir apparent." Lyndon Johnson was neither "good" nor "bad"; he was an old-style politician who confronted an unprecedented set of circumstances for which he was tragically unprepared.

I

PROLOGUE: THE JOHNSON PERSONALITY

During his presidency, Lyndon Johnson's response to the Kennedy "mystique" was given to extremes. He exalted John Kennedy's memory while deeply resenting the shadow that the Kennedy myth cast on his administration. He embraced his predecessor's agenda and ideals—but then bitterly maintained that Kennedy was all style and no substance and had unfairly escaped blame for the Vietnam War. He fondly remembered John while churning with hostility toward Robert. The Kennedys enjoyed many of the qualities Johnson envied and resented. They were handsome, cultured, educated, witty, charismatic, and beloved. In contrast, Lyndon Johnson sometimes felt like a country bumpkin. Long before he ever met a Kennedy, however, he had developed a predisposition that destined him to experience emotional difficulty in dealing with the Kennedy family. The dichotomy of his response resulted from a broad and complex array of cultural and psychological factors. The intensity of his feelings was rooted in a troubled past.

The observation that Johnson was a complex man is both a cliché and an understatement. Bill Moyers, one of Johnson's closest protégés, aptly described him as "thirteen of the most interesting and difficult men I ever met." For years administrative aides, journalists, scholars, and psychoanalysts have tried in vain to pin down his inner nature. To some he was a man who, having been raised in the destitution of the Texas hill country, understood the meaning of poverty and acted from an empathic desire to improve life for those traditionally neglected by the system. To others he was a self-serving opportunist, the consummate politician whose single-minded pursuit of power twisted his principles and warped his ambitions. These polarized perceptions are testimony to his enigmatic quality. Indeed, Paul Conkin, a recent biographer, found the task of "intellectualizing" Johnson so difficult that he abandoned and disparaged any attempt to do so.[1]

The difficulty of compartmentalizing Johnson is due in part to the subject himself. Ideally, a student of Johnson would want to examine letters, interviews, and diaries which might lend insight into his private thoughts and feelings. Unfortunately, Johnson was extremely secretive. Despite, or perhaps because of, his sensitivity to history, he left little revealing tangible evidence. Robert Caro has even accused him of conspiring to remove pages from hundreds of copies of his college yearbook in order to censor portions that reflected poorly on himself. His sense of privacy extended to an unwillingness to discuss sensitive aspects of his life. While Johnson was quick to display his emotions, he was reluctant to elaborate on his feelings. He seldom revealed his inner thoughts to friends or family members. Except through an occasional quip of self-pity, he rarely discussed or even admitted to periods of loneliness and fear.[2]

The task of delineating Johnson is further complicated by his manipulativeness. Nearly everyone who has known or written seriously about him agrees that he was, if not a compulsive liar, at least a frequent and imaginative exaggerator of the truth. He embellished recollections much in the manner of Texas tall tales. In his later life he provided gullible biographers with a collection of inaccurate anecdotes about his early days. He would also affect a wide range of emotions in order to win others' favor. If anger was required to persuade, Johnson could cue outrage. If he sought sympathy, he might manufacture a sad story and crocodile tears. His ambitions were so intense that many people suspected he could say anything to anyone at anytime to achieve his goals.[3]

The complexity of uncovering Johnson's "true" personality has not stopped writers from trying. The Johnson literature is replete with interpretations and descriptions. Aides have assessed his character with mixed conclusions. Each has offered valuable, personalized observations, but together their evidence is largely anecdotal. Scholars have produced thoroughly investigated monographs about the Johnson presidency but offer only a cursory discussion of his personality.[4]

In contrast, several researchers have considered Johnson's personality as a central theme. Doris Kearns, Robert Caro, and two medical experts, Hyman

Muslin and Thomas Jobe, have scrutinized Johnson's upbringing and applied their analyses to events in his political career. Their interpretations suffer from author's bias, flawed data, or the inadequacies of the psychological frameworks upon which they base their conclusions. Together, however, they begin to re-create fragments of Johnson's early childhood and illustrate patterns of behavior that allow for a cursory understanding of his adult personality. Looking at their work provides a starting point for understanding Johnson which, in turn, allows for a fuller appreciation of his relationship with the Kennedys.[5]

The first substantial attempt to analyze Johnson was Doris Kearns's *Lyndon Johnson and the American Dream* (1976). Similar to Eric Goldman's earlier book, Kearns's work drew upon personal observations and her insights as a trained scholar. As a student of government at Harvard, she had worked in the Johnson administration as a White House Fellow during the spring of 1967. Assigned to the Labor Department, her contact with the president increased after he withdrew from the presidential campaign in March 1968. He took Kearns into his confidence and expressed a desire to "teach" her. "I want to do everything I can," he explained, "to make the young people of America, especially you Harvards, understand what this political system is all about."[6]

Kearns proceeded to work closely with Johnson. As his administration came to a close, he pleaded with her to return to Texas with him to help write his memoirs. "Those memoirs are the last chance I've got with the history books, and I've got to do it right." He made extravagant promises to entice her away from Harvard. He offered her a position at the University of Texas, a chance to engage in social work, and material rewards. On his last day in office, Kearns finally agreed to work with him part-time. Johnson was elated. "Now you take care of yourself up at Harvard," he said. "Don't let them get at you, for God's sake, don't let their hatred for Lyndon Johnson poison your feelings about me."[7]

For the next four years Kearns took temporary breaks from teaching to spend time with Johnson at his ranch, where she helped write the first volume of what was intended to be a three-part memoir. Their relationship grew more intimate after he began experiencing chest pains in the spring of 1970. Confiding to Kearns his "instinct" that he was dying, he began to discuss his childhood in disturbing detail. He told Kearns that she reminded him of his mother, Rebekah, who had died in 1958. Talking to Kearns, he explained, he felt that he was somehow communicating with Rebekah. His subsequent discussions of his childhood revealed an unhappy and anxiety-ridden boy. These recollections, in turn, became the foundation for Kearns's psychological biography. Attempting to relate his adult behavior to his earlier experiences, Kearns brought cohesion to Johnson's world-view. She moved past the constraints of traditional biography and sought to identify past patterns of behavior based on psychoanalytic generalizations. She then related these consistencies to his adult actions and emotions.[8]

According to Kearns, Johnson's ambitions and actions were grounded in his childhood need for approval. Although he felt close to his mother, Rebekah's love for her son was conditional. She tried to force "enlightenment" on him by abruptly withdrawing affection when he did not meet her standards of intellectual or cultural accomplishment. When he quit violin lessons as a small boy, Johnson remembered that "she walked around the house pretending I was dead." Upset that he did not want to go to college, she ignored him for weeks, refusing to speak to or even look at him. "We'd been such close companions," he recalled, "and, boom, she'd abandoned me."[9]

Meanwhile, the conditions for his father's approval directly conflicted with Rebekah's expectations. In order to gain Sam's acceptance, Lyndon had to behave in manly fashion. Sam often humiliated his son by calling him a coward when he failed to meet standards of manliness. He created tests of courage and masculinity for Lyndon, insisting, for example, that he hunt and kill an animal. Johnson's attempt to please his father created internal stress; once, after shooting a rabbit, he became sick. Throughout his early adolescence Johnson remained inordinately concerned about his father's approval.[10]

So, according to Kearns, Johnson faced a double bind: in order to win the love and approval of one parent, he had to oppose the other. The dilemma condemned him to perpetual rejection. Kearns theorized that Johnson pursued political power in order to attain humanitarian objectives, thereby fulfilling *both* parents' expectations. His quest for power was attributed to Lyndon's father, who had served several terms in the Texas legislature and saw politics as a "manly" pursuit. Johnson's desire to use power for benevolent reform was derived from Rebekah's cultural and humanitarian convictions. Johnson's power to do "good works" would thus win for him the approval he was denied at home. Kearns might have added that Johnson's insecurities were relieved by the pursuit of power for humanitarian purposes—a goal that could free him from self-absorption and emotionally resolve the clash between his parents' expectations.[11]

Kearns's interpretations were sharply criticized when they appeared. Robert Divine, an historian who reviewed most of the Johnson literature, dismissed her analysis as "too pat." "In one fell psychological swoop," he wrote, "she accounts for all the contradictions in his political career." Divine did not mention that Kearns's reliance on psychoanalytical theories, especially those of Sigmund Freud and Erik Erikson, may have constrained her analysis. She never went beyond these rather traditional theorists to consider more current concepts, especially Kleinian investigations of narcissistic insecurity. In essence she chose theories that conveniently fit her thesis and ignored others that might have been more appropriate. Moreover, her emphasis on psychological explanations minimized the social and cultural forces that molded Johnson. His later hostility toward the Eastern intellectual community, for example, was hardly unique among residents of small Southern communities.[12]

Apart from problems of method, there were more serious, fundamental problems with Kearns's psychoanalytic interpretation. Important material was derived from interviews with Johnson, a pattern which developed during her stays at the Johnson ranch. She would awake early in the morning and sit in a chair in her bedroom. Before sunrise the former president would enter her bedroom and curl himself beneath the blankets on her bed. He would then speak into the darkness about his deepest fears and regrets. Because there were no recordings of the sessions, one must place faith in Kearns's notes written later in the day. Moreover, Johnson used these occasions to gain Kearns's sympathy, lying when necessary to do so. His explanation for the loss of a college love and his description of a teenage trip to California, for example, were fabricated. Her characterization of Sam was based on Lyndon's scornful recollections. (Although Sam demanded manliness, he was not anti-intellectual. He had studied diligently to be certified to teach in Texas, taught school for three years in his young adulthood, and dreamed of becoming a lawyer.) By accepting Johnson's recollections at face value, Kearns artificially heightened the contrast between his parents. Faulty interpretations also occurred as a result of flawed research. Contending that Johnson's Great Society was motivated by a strong desire to help less fortunate segments of society, Kearns cited as evidence a collection of editorials which he wrote as editor of his college newspaper. They promoted hard work and charity. Robert Caro, however, discovered that many of Lyndon's editorials were ghost-written and were intended to curry favor with faculty and administrators.[13]

Johnson's distortion of facts and his cultivation of Kearns led some reviewers to suspect that she had been manipulated. All his life, Garry Wills argued, Johnson had surrounded himself with protégés whom he sought to impress. Like his conversations with Bobby Baker or Bill Moyers, Johnson's discussions with Kearns were designed to gain him attention. He was fully aware that Kearns was taking notes about their conversations; sometimes he insisted that she do so. He presented himself as a sensitive intellectual who felt entrapped by the Vietnam War. While Wills acknowledged a probable element of truth to Johnson's recollections, he correctly noted that "Vast areas of the Johnson psyche are missing from this book—the shrewd and bluffing masculine side, obscene and voracious and game playing—because he did not think that it would 'play' in Cambridge." Johnson, Wills concluded, worked diligently to gain Kearns's sympathy and sought to exploit her Harvard connections in order to shape the assessment of an important and potentially hostile segment of historians.[14]

Although flawed, at the time it appeared *Lyndon Johnson and the American Dream* provided the most extensive published observations to date about Johnson's private side. The reminiscences that Kearns had collected were no small accomplishment. Although Johnson was manipulative, it does not automatically stand to reason that everything he told Kearns was a lie. On several occasions his self-portrait was less self-serving than one would expect if he intended to use Kearns solely to manage history. Kearns noted Erik Erikson's contention that it is not only important how a person speaks of his past but *when* he speaks it. Did Johnson, sensing his approaching death, come to terms with himself and his life's regrets? Or was he the consummate politician until the very end? As in almost every facet of his life, Johnson's sincerity remains in question.[15]

Robert Caro's *The Years of Lyndon Johnson: The Path to Power* (1983) also examined extensively the roots of Johnson's character. The 882-page book was the first volume of Caro's anticipated four-part biography of Johnson. For seven years Caro diligently explored Johnson's early political career. He not only relied on materials in the Johnson Library but, more notably, obtained unique interviews with people closely associated with Johnson, including boyhood friends, neighbors, college classmates, and Washington colleagues. Thus armed, Caro was able to navigate around several of the self-serving fabrications that Johnson had earlier given to biographers.[16]

In Caro's portrait of the Johnson family history and the social and cultural aspects of the Texas hill country, Rebekah was an unhappy and frustrated woman. The daughter of a lawyer, a state legislator, and a lay preacher, she was raised in a life of leisure, wealth, and refinement. But her world crumbled when her father lost money in a disastrous financial venture and died shortly thereafter. Before he died he had introduced her to a fellow legislator, Sam Johnson. Although remarkably different in upbringing and manner, Sam and Rebekah found a common bond through their high principles and idealism. But their marriage condemned Rebekah to a life of hard work, affording few outlets for her cultural and intellectual endeavors. Sam, meanwhile, was an incompetent farmer and suffered repeated economic hardships. An ardent advocate of populism and a man of high integrity, he refused bribes from Texas lobbyists. His ethics distinguished him from his contemporaries but burdened the family economically. The couple lived in a world of principles and poverty. According to Caro, these were the two facets their son rejected.[17]

Caro concurred with Kearns on Johnson's childhood need for attention. As a young boy he was determined to be noticed. He frequently ran away from home, often hiding outside the house so that he could hear his mother's frantic cries as she searched for him. His attention-seeking behavior also manifested itself through his incessant lying. At school he made himself the center of attention by dressing differently from other students, by being first in line for games, or by writing his name in giant letters on the blackboard. According to Caro, it was Johnson's determination to "*be* somebody" that became his central motivation in life.[18]

After Sam made a particularly bad investment in cotton when Lyndon was a teenager, the son came to view his parents as losers and entered a period of rebellion. He scorned his father and exaggerated the inadequacies of his mother. Escaping from his family's poverty, he journeyed to California where he worked as a law clerk. He entertained dreams of becoming a lawyer but soon realized it would be more difficult than he had thought. Johnson returned to the hill country a year later, appearing more serious and determined. After incessant prodding from his parents and a humiliating fight with a local boy, he decided to go to college. His decision to attend Texas State Teachers College at San Marcos, however, was not intended to satisfy his parents. He went to college to dominate. He developed skills in flattery and sycophancy. He bragged about his intellectual abilities, black-mailed a popular girl, borrowed money he never repaid, gained control of student employment, and rigged student government elections. "The methods Lyndon Johnson used to attain power on Capitol Hill," Caro wrote, "were the same ones he had used on College Hill."[19]

Caro's depiction was clearly derogatory. Johnson's ambition was "so fierce, so consuming that no consideration of morality or ethics, no cost to himself—or to anyone else—could stand before it." His genius was "for discerning a path to power, an utter ruthlessness in destroying obstacles in that path and seemingly bottomless capacity for deceit, deception, and betrayal in moving along it." Unlike his parents, Johnson was "unencumbered by philosophy or ideology." Instead he was characterized "by an utter refusal to be backed into firm defense of any position or any principle." His viciousness compelled him not only to defeat his opponents but to destroy them. He was determined to "bend others to his will."[20]

Caro's analysis called into doubt several of Kearns's psychoanalytic assumptions. It was not Rebekah's rejection of Lyndon that inspired him to produce "good works." For Caro, Johnson was motivated to "better" society only when his own interest coincided with the interests of his constituents or financial backers. Caro also disputed Kearns's conclusion that Johnson attached himself to strong political personalities in order to replace his weak father. Ignoring explicit psychoanalytic interpretations, Caro argued that Johnson's sycophant tendencies were intended only to selfishly advance his political ambitions.[21]

Caro amassed a wealth of unique information, thoroughly disproved numerous myths about Johnson's past, and convincingly underscored the dark side of Johnson's personality. But his reductionist interpretation is a major problem with his book. That a web of social, cultural, and familial factors can consistently inspire only a ruthless lust for power seems too pat. Reading Caro, one must believe that the first fifteen years of Johnson's life did little to foster in him *any* sense of concern for the downtrodden who surrounded him. Occasionally Caro depicts Johnson's compassion for farmers in his district and for the poor Mexican children he taught at Cotulla. But, in general, Johnson is an ogre. The day-to-day witnessing of broken loved ones in his family and community would seem to have instilled greater long-term compassion than Caro is willing to acknowledge. The reader is further asked to believe that adroit politicians such as Sam Rayburn, who adhered to high moral standards and was sincerely interested in the advancement of social welfare, were utterly hoodwinked by Johnson's façade. Johnson's sincerity was indeed suspect, but expedient and benevolent motives rarely separate out clearly in the human psyche, and his self-interest in itself does not preclude elements of benevolent reform.

Caro's one-dimensional view of Johnson has come under considerable criticism, especially after the publication of his second volume, *Means of Ascent* (1990), which centers on Johnson's notoriously corrupt campaign for the Senate in 1948 against Coke Stevenson. While Caro's portrayal of Johnson in *Path to Power* has some shades of gray in its character depictions, *Means of Ascent* removes all remnants of Johnson's positive qualities. "Bright and dark" threads ran through Johnson's life, Caro notes, but during the period from 1941 through 1948 "Johnson was all but totally consumed by his need for power, and by his efforts to obtain it." The 1948 primary, therefore, was transformed into a morality play—good versus evil, Stevenson versus Johnson. Critics and former aides alike have lambasted Caro for "beating Lyndon Johnson over the head" and removing *all* of his subject's subtleties, ambiguities, and complexities.[22]

In neither volume does Caro account for Johnson's character. What made Johnson so selfish and ambitious? Instead of placing Johnson's personality or behavior within a psychological framework, Caro periodically touches on a wide range of explanations: the cultural and social conditions of the hill country, the parental conflicts between Sam and Rebekah, and the rapid change in economic life-styles are all held partly accountable. Occasionally Caro quotes relatives and friends who argued that Johnson's convictions were "born in him." Such folklore may offer as fruitful an explanation for Johnson's adult behavior as psychoanalytic assumptions. But by avoiding the "traps" of a specific analytical framework, Caro thinly plants a number of explanations for Johnson's obsession with power without being held strictly accountable for any one of them.[23]

Although Caro shuns psychoanalytical explanations, he implicitly concurs with many facets of Kearns's interpretation. Both authors depict Johnson as suffering from a severe lack of self-esteem. They agree that his distorted world-view was the result of familial disruptions and tensions within the community. In both works his adult behavior is tied to an inferiority complex developed in childhood; Johnson had a deficient sense of self that prompted him to absorb those around him in order to acquire temporary esteem. For Kearns, Johnson compensated for his poor sense of self through the accumulation of power and achievement. He wanted power in order to produce benevolent reform. For Caro, Johnson wanted power for power's sake. Caro sees little of the empathy and sincerity that Kearns had sensed in her subject. But the full relevance of this data to a precise analytical framework can be found neither in Kearns nor Caro, but in a third interpretation.[24]

Writing in the *Psychohistory Review*, Hyman Muslin, a psychoanalyst, and Thomas Jobe, a physician and professor of the history of psychiatry, sought to apply the self-psychology theories of Heinz Kohut to the personality of Lyndon Johnson. During the early 1970s Kohut expanded on early object-relations theory, particularly the work of Melanie Klein. He introduced a concept to psychoanalytical thought called the "selfobject." According to Kohut, when a significant other, usually the mother, fails to convey to an infant that he is good, the infant fails to move from the world of I/I of all young infants to an I/Thou world where he feels so secure in himself that he can permit an other (Thou) to exist. Kohut's psychological dialogue is between images within the child and real outside people. In order to relate to other people as "selfobjects," an individual experiences them in a way that promotes a sense of emotional stability by reinforcing his pre-existing image of himself. We never outgrow the need for "selfobjects," i.e., other people, to reinforce our own inner sense of adequacy. During times of stress, for example, an individual looks to others to provide reassurance and relief from feelings of anxiety. Thus Kohut shifted the study of self-functioning from internal motivations to the external world of people and things internalized into the psyche.[25]

Drawing on Kohut, Muslin and Jobe analyzed the development of Johnson's personality by focusing on his personal relationships during his childhood, adolescence, and college years. They confined themselves to "empathic data-gathering"; they were primarily concerned with Johnson's expressed feelings about these periods in his life. Searching for continuity, the authors then sought to "capture the experience" of Johnson as he developed and functioned in the political arena. They called their article "The Tragic Self of Lyndon Johnson and the Dilemma of Leadership."[26]

According to Muslin and Jobe, Rebekah's attempt to fulfill her dreams through her son permanently impaired his sense of self—his internal, subjective state based on the sum total of his experiences. Rebekah failed Lyndon in his need for adequate mirroring. Like all children, he needed to be noticed, understood, and respected by his mother. Instead Rebekah projected her own plans, expectations, and fears onto her son. Johnson therefore never became an independent self because his identity or state was contingent on his mother's personal predicaments. Striving to please his mother, he saw himself as responsible for her emotional comfort. He lacked the framework within which he could vent his emotions independent of his mother's feelings. He failed to move from the I/I world to I/Thou; others could not exist independent of himself.[27]

Since Lyndon's sense of self-worth was so dependent on his mother, he displayed panicky fears of abandonment when she no longer devoted the attention to him that he wanted. His attention-seeking behavior was interpreted by Muslin and Jobe as signs of uncertainty and confusion as he demanded recognition of his selfhood; he sought to alleviate stress through behavior designed to attract his mother's attention. When that proved unsuccessful, he tried to compensate for his poor self-image by turning his attention to men whom he might emulate. When he was five years old he frequently visited his grandfather, who provided "the perfect escape from all my problems at home." His grandfather's unqualified love and affection, however, were abruptly denied when Sam and Rebekah moved off their farm to Johnson City, several miles away.[28]

After Lyndon's grandfather died, he remembered becoming closer to his father. He adopted Sam's crude and colorful style of speech. He emulated his father's walk, dress, and various aspects of his behavior, such as his friendliness and rowdiness. He was fascinated by his father's tales of the state legislature and enjoyed accompanying him on his campaigns. His feelings changed, however, after Sam made a disastrous investment in cotton. Feeling rejected by the conditions that his mother placed on love, and no longer able to idolize his father, Lyndon became "a rebel with a cause, the cause of being against what both mother and father valued."[29]

Muslin and Jobe contended that, by the end of his teenage years, Johnson had developed into his characteristic self. The withdrawal of his mother and the failings of his father ensured a lifetime search for a mirror who would assure him of his own worth. "It is important," the authors wrote, "to grasp this central aspect of Johnson's self—the unremitting drive to protect his self from any scintilla of inferiority. At any cost to *anyone*, his self had, from childhood, to be protected" against feelings of inadequacy. He forever "demonstrated the incessant striving of the unfed infant and youngster." He would consistently view people in terms of himself and what they could do for him. At college he exhibited a style that would guide him throughout his political career; he would make "unrestrained efforts to attach himself to whomever he identified as the purveyor of worth, power, or monies." Throughout his life he was in "an urgent state of self-need, striving to the end to extract nurturance from his surroundings that would finally ensure him relief from his chronic emptiness, agitation, and fear of rebuff."[30]

The authors accept at face value two questionable assumptions about Johnson's past which were fundamental in the evolution of his "tragic sense of self": Rebekah withdrew her affection from Lyndon, and Lyndon came to scorn his father. Admitting to inadequate documentation, Muslin and Jobe base their first contention on three observations: Rebekah bore four more children; she was sick after giving birth to each child; and her son's behavior was symptomatic of a deprived child. Do these observations add up to a withdrawal of motherly affection? In itself the presence of four more children in the Johnson household does not imply that Rebekah rejected her oldest and most cherished child. Although she was sick after giving birth, her illnesses were relatively short, probably not long enough to affect Lyndon severely. And although Lyndon clearly "acted out," it does not necessarily follow that Rebekah was the source of his behavior. Mothers are crucial in determining a child's behavior, but Lyndon's frequent attempts to "run away" may have been a child's search for adventure in the boredom of the hill country. His grandiose manner, meanwhile, was hardly a trait unique to a young man reared in a land known for its tall tales. Cultural reasons may well be behind the behavior that Muslin and Jobe assume was motivated solely by psychological factors.[31]

Regarding Johnson's scorn for Sam, Muslin and Jobe are selective in their evidence. They do not account for Lyndon's eagerness to seek Sam's advice when pursuing his career. In 1937, for example, Johnson confronted an extremely difficult decision about entering a special election for the United States Congress. Young and relatively unknown, he faced formidable opponents. On the eve of his decision he drove home fifty miles in bad weather to ask his father's opinion. His father later campaigned on his behalf and continued to serve as a consultant. Sam was not quite the "fallen idol" that Muslin and Jobe portray.[32]

An additional flaw in Muslin's and Jobe's analysis centers on their unsuspecting regard for Johnson's empathic expressions. Although they acknowledge that Johnson was an expert manipulator of "selfobjects," they neglect fully to consider this trait when mining from the biographies his feelings about his childhood. The vast majority of their data is derived from the writings of Kearns and Caro; they compensate neither for Johnson's manipulativeness with Kearns nor for Caro's reductionist interpretation.[33]

Finally, Muslin's and Jobe's exclusive reliance on Kohutian theory seems constraining. The authors acknowledge the boundaries of their investigation; they use Johnson as a case study to apply Kohut's "selfobject" theory to a historical figure. Nevertheless, they neglect a number of interpretations that could define Johnson's personality in less disparaging terms. For example, while Johnson may have pursued power in order to restore self-esteem damaged in childhood, one might argue that this was a healthy response to a personal crisis. Feeling bad about himself, he asserted himself in such a way as to regain control of his environment and repair his self-image. Furthermore, he was not unique among politicians in his desire for power. Presidents of such markedly different personality types as Franklin Roosevelt, John Kennedy, and Ronald Reagan have all pursued power. It is unfair, therefore, to point to Johnson's insecurity as the exclusive cause of his desire for power.

One might also argue that, rather than a lack of self-esteem, Johnson may have suffered from an idealized self-image. He was neurotic, but his underlying motivation was not so much a search for power as a search for glory. Johnson always craved the attention of crowds and felt energized by public approval. His excessive need to be loved would not have followed only from a desire for power. He may have needed constant reassurance from others that he was the image he believed himself to be. Thus he became hypersensitive to criticism because it forced him to confront his self-critical tendencies.[34]

The observations of Muslin and Jobe tend to overwork and overinterpret data within a narrow theoretical framework. They theorize about Johnson's entire life on the bases of a handful of questionable events derived from hearsay and from a subject well known for his manipulative statements. To be sure, Muslin and Jobe preface their analysis by warning that theory serves only as a "guide" for interpreting a person's life. Keeping in mind the flaws in their data and the fact that Kohutian theory is scarcely a final truth, one should weigh their analysis with caution and skepticism.[35]

These interpretations—of Kearns, Caro, and Muslin and Jobe—are flawed partly because they use tainted data and partly because they fail to consider the spectrum of forces that influenced Johnson's behavior. One cannot evaluate Johnson's response to the Kennedys by relying on any one theory or generalized point of view. It is much too simplistic to conclude, as Kearns does, that Johnson was motivated solely by his childhood insecurities, or, as Caro does, by his desire to "be somebody." Few, if any, people can be reduced to such uncomplicated formulas. Lyndon Johnson, like all people, was a complicated personality, consisting of many separate layers that overlapped and often interacted with one another. His insecurity, obsession with power, and search for an adequate self-image became salient at different times, depending upon the situation.

While the weaknesses of these interpretations make them less than perfect, they nevertheless provide a starting point for measuring Johnson's relationship with the Kennedys. As we examine Johnson's behavior, elements of each interpretation come to the fore. His quest for power was fundamental to his decision to become John Kennedy's vice president, and his lack of power in the New Frontier generated internal stress and depression. Fearful that he would be abandoned and removed from the 1964 ticket, he mirrored the Kennedy style and altered his manner and appearance, hoping for greater acceptance. Coming to power upon the violent death of his mentor, he felt like an unworthy usurper and therefore absorbed many of John Kennedy's paraphernalia—his surviving relatives, his staff, his agenda, his image—hoping to gain the public's vicarious trust and affection. As president he grew increasingly anxious of being displaced by Robert Kennedy, the man who better embodied the elements of the "mystique" and who reminded the public of Johnson's illegitimacy. At issue was not what the Kennedys did to Johnson, but why he responded to them the way he did. Many contemporaries were politically displaced by the success of the Kennedys. Only one, however, seemed pushed to self-destruction.

II

FROM SENATE TO WHITE HOUSE

Lyndon Johnson was only nine years older than John Kennedy, yet he belonged to a different time and world. He was big, boisterous, intimidating, and expressive. He grew up in a land of dirt roads, bare feet, outhouses, and oil lamps, and was raised in a household that straddled poverty and relative comfort. While pursuing a degree from a small state teachers' college, he worked as a schoolteacher in poor and middle-class sections of southwest Texas. He longed to escape a land for which he held embarrassed affection, yearning for power and recognition through national politics. Kennedy, on the other hand, was gaunt, urbane, reflective, and cerebral. He was raised in an urban environment of wealth and status and was drawn to the stylishness and aura of the Cambridge elite. He attended private schools as a child, traveled the world as a teenager, graduated from Harvard, and published his first book, *Why England Slept,* at the age of twenty-three. Antithetical in upbringing, manner, and temperament, Kennedy and Johnson eventually formed a political partnership which seemed intrinsically strained.[1]

Lyndon Johnson loved politics, and he pursued his career with fierce determination. In college he worked diligently to learn how the system worked, manipulating students, organizations, administrators, and faculty members. Shortly after graduation he became a secretary to Democratic Representative Richard M. Kleberg of Texas and soon emerged as one of the most influential secretaries in Washington. By 1933, at age twenty-four, he was elected speaker of the Little Congress, an organization composed of congressional secretaries which he eventually transformed into a source of personal power. Two years later he joined the New Deal, utilizing valuable contacts to become director of the National Youth Administration in Texas. He served in that capacity until 1937, when at the age of twenty-eight he won a special election for a seat in the House of Representatives, a position to which he was re-elected for six successive terms. As chairman of a special Naval Affairs subcommittee, he investigated waste in naval war, a task that won him a Silver Star when he traveled to the South Pacific for a firsthand view of the war.[2]

For John Kennedy, a political career was more his father's ambition than his own. In college he had withdrawn from campus politics after losing an election in his freshman class. But Joseph Kennedy, Sr., was intent upon vicariously fulfilling his own political ambitions through his sons. He had been instrumental in the publication and promotion of John's first book, knowing it would win his son considerable respect among Boston's educated elite. John gained further national attention during World War II when the *New Yorker* published John Hersey's account of his PT-109 heroics in 1944. His father generated wider distribution of the story by arranging for *Reader's Digest* to publish a condensed version of it. After the war John Kennedy was aimless. He flirted with a journalism career and covered the charter conference of the United Nations in San Francisco for the International News Service. At his father's urging he ran for Congress in the spring of 1946, beginning the political career that Joseph had envisioned for his oldest son before he was killed in the war. John received 42 percent of the vote in a crowded Democratic primary and went on to win the general election through an energetic campaign and the aid of his father's money and influence. He was re-elected twice to the House and gained a reputation among his colleagues for being aloof and independent.[3]

Advancing to the Senate, both Johnson and Kennedy eyed the presidency, but each relied on a different political style in promoting his career. Johnson built his reputation through the accumulation of power and a noted record of achievement. His temperament was suited to life in the Senate. Elected in 1948 under notoriously fraudulent circumstances, he developed skills as a power broker and quickly worked his way up the Senate ranks. He was named Democratic Whip in 1951 and Minority Leader in 1953. When the Democratic party won a majority in the Senate in 1955, he became the youngest Majority Leader in that body's history. During his Senate career he served on prestigious committees, including Armed Services, Interstate and Foreign Commerce, and Finance and Appropriations.[4]

Kennedy devoted less attention to traditional avenues of power and instead advanced his presidential ambitions through media strategies designed to exploit his charismatic personality. Elected to the Senate in 1952 in a surprising upset of incumbent Henry Cabot Lodge, he showed little patience or inclination for the daily grind of legislation. His years in the Senate, like his years in the House, were marked by few serious distinctions or covert power plays. De-emphasizing cloakroom politics, he concentrated on self-promotion to achieve national recognition. He sought high-exposure committee seats, serving on the Government Operations, Labor and Public Welfare, Foreign Relations, and Joint Economic committees. He cultivated friendly relations with journalists, developed his television skills, and wrote a 1956 Pulitzer prize–winning book, *Profiles in Courage*. His marriage to Jacqueline Bouvier, as well as the birth of his first child, received extensive coverage in the nation's tabloids, especially *Life* magazine. His national appeal was firmly established during the 1956 Democratic convention where Kennedy narrated a party film, *The Pursuit of Happiness,* nominated Adlai Stevenson, and withdrew his vice-presidential nomination through a gracious speech. By 1959 his national reputation rested more on his celebrity than his political accomplishments.[5]

While Kennedy advanced his career through image management, Johnson maneuvered more traditional mechanisms of power. Known for his willingness to compromise, he avoided protracted debate and used his personal persuasive skills to advance a record of achievement in the Senate. His most remarkable performances came in 1957 and 1960 when he persuaded Southern senators not to filibuster pending civil rights acts. He was subsequently credited with helping to pass the first civil rights legislation since Reconstruction. The passage of these bills not only transformed him from a regional politician into a national statesman but illustrated his leverage as Majority Leader. In that position he coopted colleagues by controlling the allotment of office space, the scheduling of legislation, and the appointments of committee delegations. He exercised leadership in a manner that enhanced his importance by making others, especially freshman senators, obligated to him.[6]

Despite their identical ambitions and conflicting styles, Johnson claimed that his relationship with Kennedy had always been one of mutual "admiration, fondness, and respect." Before the 1956 Democratic convention they often exchanged personal and political courtesies. After Kennedy underwent serious back surgery in the fall of 1954, Johnson called Kennedy's father to inquire about John's condition and the rumors that he was dying from a concealed illness. Joseph assured Johnson that his son was not terminally ill and would return to the Senate. Not wishing to disturb the ailing senator, Johnson instructed Joseph to "Tell him for me how much we all love him." The Kennedy patriarch told Johnson that his son had been "very touched when he got your letter," and he characterized John as "one boy" with "real affection for you."[7]

Like most young senators at the time, John Kennedy depended on Johnson for his Senate stature. In December 1954 he informed Johnson of his desire to fill any vacancy on the Senate Foreign Relations, Appropriations, Finance, or Armed Services committees in place of his current, less distinguished assignments. Johnson replied that the decision-making process was "always tough" but promised to present his qualifications "forcefully." "It has been many years," he wrote, "since I have enjoyed working with anyone as much as I have with you." Days later, however, Kennedy was informed that his requested appointments had been denied because he lacked seniority. In rejecting Kennedy, Johnson tried to make the physically ailing senator feel appreciated. He had been receiving updates on Kennedy's health and awaited his return: "We certainly do miss you, Jack." Although the Senate was running smoothly, "it would go even better if I had my strong right arm, Jack Kennedy, on tap."[8]

After Johnson suffered a serious heart attack in the summer of 1955, Kennedy sent a get-well telegram to the newly elected Majority Leader. Noting the extensive press coverage of Johnson's illness, Kennedy thought he "must be happy to know of the impact you have made made [sic] throughout the world in such a relatively short time." Kennedy promised to pray for Johnson and believed that the illness "should never have happened to such a nice guy." Two months later Johnson thanked Kennedy for his concern; he would "deeply treasure" his letter. Noting that he was nearing full recovery, he expressed regret that it had been a long time since he had had the chance to "visit my good friend Jack Kennedy." "Now that I am up and about," he wrote, "I want you to know how much I appreciate [your letter] and how very much I appreciate your friendship." On his return to Washington, "one of the first things that I want to do is to have a good visit with you."[9]

John Kennedy persisted in finding ways to help Johnson and to advance his own interests in the process. As in the past, his father sometimes intervened on his behalf. With the Democratic convention just nine months away, Joseph Kennedy made a curious telephone call to Johnson in October 1955, urging him to run for president and offering John's help. The purpose of the call is speculative. Appreciating Johnson's power in the Senate and his capacity to advance or hinder the careers of his colleagues, Joseph may have made the offer out of political courtesy and concern for the long-term interest of his son. He may have also been laying the groundwork for a Johnson-Kennedy or Kennedy-Johnson ticket for 1956 or 1960. Regardless, Johnson thanked Joseph for the offer but claimed disinterest in the office.

John Kennedy, meanwhile, continued his pursuit of more high-profile committee seats. In January 1956 his staff privately drew up a list of arguments for better assignments, alleging unfairness and neglect. After another vacancy occurred on the Foreign Relations Committee that spring, Kennedy again wrote to Johnson, reminding him of their recent conversations and the fact that "with one or two exceptions, no other Democratic Senator has such limited committee assignments." Johnson rejected the request, much to the growing frustration of Kennedy's aides. "Lyndon Johnson has finally come through, making up for his failure to appoint you to the Foreign Relations and Finance Committees," Kennedy's legislative assistant wrote him. "He has recommended that you be appointed to the Boston National Historic Sites Commission!"[10]

The political relationship between Johnson and Kennedy remained outwardly cordial during most of the 1950s. Kennedy generally cooperated with Johnson by voting with the Majority Leader for measures such as the United States Information Agency bill, against the McClellan Labor bill, and in favor of rejecting an Eisenhower cabinet appointment. At the close of the summer session of Congress in 1956, Johnson expressed appreciation to Kennedy for his loyalty. "You have done a great deal for me," he wrote, noting in particular his gratitude for Kennedy's gesture to save him from a politically uncomfortable situation. Johnson, Kennedy, and another senator had been responsible for the decision not to hold hearings on the extension of minimum-wage legislation to retailers. "But when that decision was communicated to the labor unions," Johnson wrote, "Jack Kennedy told them that it was his decision alone. That was a graceful gesture by a good man and good Senator."[11]

Johnson reciprocated Kennedy's generosity a few weeks later at the 1956 convention. In Chicago Johnson emerged as a favorite-son candidate, gaining control of the Texas delegation. When Stevenson opened the vice-presidential selection to the delegates, the choice was narrowed to Tennessee Senator Estes Kefauver or Kennedy. Detesting Kefauver, Johnson announced on the second ballot that "Texas proudly casts its vote for the fighting sailor who wears the scars of battle." Kennedy did not win the nomination, but the ensuing media attention gave him considerable recognition.[12]

After the events of the convention, Johnson developed a new appreciation and respect for Kennedy's public appeal. In August he wrote Kennedy to congratulate him on his newfound popularity. He characterized his support of Kennedy's vice-presidential bid as "one of the proudest moments of my life" because it gave him an opportunity to express his "high regard" for him. With self-referential overtones, Johnson praised Kennedy, asserting, "I can never go wrong backing Jack Kennedy. You justified my confidence by the way you conducted yourself at Chicago. . . ." His letter to Joseph Kennedy following the convention expressed similar praise. Johnson was "proud" of John as well as the Texas delegation and the Southern delegates for supporting the bid. The occasion was a turning point in Kennedy's stature, he claimed, for it "lighted the brightest lamp of hope" for the Democrats—alluding, perhaps, to the 1960 presidential campaign. In a handwritten note, John thanked Johnson for his help at the convention. The occasion allowed him to "appreciate and remember [his] friends." He invited Johnson to call on him "anytime."[13]

After the 1956 convention Johnson invited Kennedy to visit his ranch and was again impressed with the young senator's reception in Texas. On election eve Kennedy appeared on television to make a final plea for Stevenson. In a letter to the senator, Johnson recalled his recent visit, praised his television appearance as a "swell job," and credited him for making a "wonderful impression." "You had dignity and you were forthright in your presentations," he wrote. Reflecting on Kennedy's trip to Texas, Johnson noted that he had made "a hit with our folks down here and you won . . . many friends. . . . People still talk to us and write us about their favorable impression of you. . . ." One person on whom the eloquent and intellectual senator made a positive impact was Johnson's mother, Rebekah. After her death in September 1958 Kennedy sent his condolences and reminded Johnson of having met her two years earlier. Johnson thanked Kennedy: "Your telegram was heart-warming because it recalled to my mind one of my fondest memories of my mother—the meeting in San Antonio when she was so pleased and proud to meet you."[14]

Johnson became almost paternal toward Kennedy after the 1956 election. In December he invited him to speak at a Law Day gathering at the University of Texas, scribbling on the letter of invitation, "Think this is a very good one for you." When Kennedy declined the invitation, citing his busy senatorial schedule, Johnson expressed his understanding but hoped that during the upcoming year he could find the time again to visit Texas "where you are very popular and very well liked." In January 1957 Kennedy finally won his long-awaited seat on the Senate Foreign Relations Committee—an important milestone toward enhancing his image as a foreign-policy expert. On this occasion he was forced to compete for the position against Kefauver, who had four years' more seniority. Johnson was determined to deny Kefauver the seat and convinced a third senator with the same seniority to apply. With two senators of equal seniority vying for the same position, he declared a draw in the Steering Committee and gave the position to Kennedy. Syndicated columnist Doris Fleeson speculated that the appointment was "the opening gun of an effort to put across a Johnson-Kennedy ticket at the Democratic National Convention in 1960." Others reasoned that, under Johnson's rule of leadership, Kennedy was due to assume a more prestigious position. Whatever Johnson's motives, Kennedy was appreciative, sending him a two-page summary of fifteen favorable newspaper editorials. "I hope these will be of aid and comfort to you," he wrote. Johnson thanked him for the feedback and complimented Kennedy by noting the wisdom of his own decision: "To me, the most significant thing is that practically all of them agree with my estimation that Jack Kennedy is a very able and very patriotic United States Senator."[15]

Between the two men there were occasional moments of tension. Five months after his appointment to the Foreign Relations Committee, Kennedy spoke before the Women's Press Club. After quoting the political philosophies of Henry Clay and George Norris, he noted that senators "must fight for measures which are almost certain to lose." Shortly thereafter, Johnson's aide, George Reedy, requested from Kennedy a transcript of the address. Reedy's interest signaled to Kennedy that his remarks may have inadvertently offended Johnson. Apologetically, he wrote Johnson to remind him of his admiration: "I think you know that I have praised your leadership, in both the written and spoken word, in every part of the country and to every group of whatever philosophy. . . ." Kennedy emphasized that he spoke only in "general terms, and without referring even impliedly to you." He offered press clippings as proof that his remarks were not directed at the Majority Leader and noted that he had always admired Johnson's judgment in pursuing legislation.[16]

The tone of Johnson's return letter was patronizing. He was "fully aware" that no criticism was intended: "I know you much too well to think that there is any meanness or littleness in your soul." He explained that he merely wanted a copy of the text because the press was often misleading and others had informed him of the speech. He closed by reminding Kennedy of the benefits of cooperation: "You never have to set the record straight for me, just carry on the way you have been, and you will always find that Lyndon Johnson is your friend." The letter was followed by a telephone conversation the next day.[17]

Throughout 1957 their relationship grew increasingly comfortable. Kennedy's support for the 1957 Civil Rights Act won him special recognition from Johnson. Kennedy had attempted to strike a balance in the bill's specific provisions, reaffirming his independent political nature but angering both Northern liberals and Southern conservatives in the process. "If they want to look for that courage they talk about," Johnson commented, "they ought to look [at Kennedy]." In the summer of 1957 Kennedy accepted

Johnson's invitation to speak before the Texas State Teachers Association but then noted the likelihood that he would have to decline because of his wife's pregnancy. He apologized and offered to speak on other occasions. Johnson again invited Kennedy to the ranch sometime in the near future. The day after his daughter Caroline was born by cesarian section, Kennedy traveled to Dallas in November during a tour of the Southwest and spoke at the Teachers meeting.[18]

In the summer of 1958, as presidential politics gained increasing attention, Kennedy sought to advance a substantive record in preparation for his re-election to the Senate and the 1960 Democratic convention. He suffered several legislative defeats, however, which diminished his stature in the Senate. Johnson, who also eyed the 1960 nomination, refused to use his pull to help Kennedy garner enough votes to increase unemployment compensation. Nor was Kennedy successful in securing an amendment that would have allowed President Eisenhower to give aid to small communist countries if it would hinder "Sino-Soviet domination." Also that summer, the Kennedy-Ives Labor Reform Bill came under partisan attack from Republicans anxious to make the bill appear weak and ineffective. It was subsequently stalled in the House Labor Committee. Johnson sent his condolences to Kennedy. "Even though the measure did not become law," he wrote, Kennedy's efforts had helped in the passage of an alternative labor bill that was "fair, honorable, constructive." "Any man can be a good leader," Johnson added, "when he has good friends like Jack Kennedy." Kennedy sent Johnson two speeches in which he claimed that his bill had become a political issue manufactured by the Republicans to use against the Democrats in the upcoming election. "Jack Kennedy is a man of good sense and the American people are people of good sense," Johnson replied. "They aren't going to buy any goldbricks."[19]

That fall, Johnson and Kennedy remained on amiable terms. Johnson congratulated Kennedy on his landslide re-election to the Senate and sought his advice on a forthcoming meeting with the newly elected president of Mexico: "I know I will gain strength from your counsel which comes from experience and intimacy with these problems." Kennedy was self-deprecating, noting his certainty that "your own knowledge and ability are far more effective than any suggestion I could make." He praised Johnson for "doing a superb job in your post election activities" and requested a position on either the Joint Committee on Atomic Energy or the Joint Economic Committee. Johnson assured Kennedy that the Steering Committee "will give most sympathetic consideration to your request." Kennedy was subsequently appointed to the Joint Economic Committee.[20]

On the surface, Johnson had a congenial working relationship with

Kennedy. Like most letters exchanged between public officials, theirs were cautious, diplomatic, and overly generous. Mindful of the hierarchy of power, Kennedy paid proper homage to Johnson, once requesting an autographed photograph from Johnson after sending him a signed copy of *Profiles in Courage*. Kennedy's inscription was direct and laudatory: "To the greatest majority leader in the Senate's history." Aware of Johnson's extreme sensitivities, he later recalled that writing a birthday greeting to him was like "drafting a state document." Young and inexperienced, he was vulnerable to the Majority Leader's authority. "I spent years of my life," John Kennedy once lamented, "when I could not get consideration for a bill until I went around and begged Lyndon Johnson to let it go ahead."[21]

Johnson, too, was careful to cultivate Kennedy, instructing aides to scan his Pulitzer prize–winning book and to write a complimentary letter. As he had done with other colleagues, he was mindful of special occasions, such as birthdays, and sent Kennedy appropriate congratulatory messages. Aware of Kennedy's rising political stock, Johnson was outwardly courteous, helping to shape the career of the man who "lighted the brightest lamp of hope" for 1960. But the partnership that Johnson was beginning to form with Kennedy in the late 1950s was different from the alliances he had initiated in the past. First, Kennedy was of a political mold to which Johnson was unaccustomed. Traditionally, the people with whom Johnson aligned himself were great achievers such as Franklin Roosevelt, Speaker of the House Sam Rayburn, and Senator Richard Russell. Kennedy did not meet Johnson's usual standards of success. He possessed neither skills as a power broker nor significant legislative achievements which would warrant Johnson's high estimation. Second, unlike his past partnerships, Johnson was Kennedy's superior. With careful cultivation he could use this rising political star to further his own ambitions. His flowery praise and his efforts on Kennedy's behalf, therefore, were likely intended to draw the young senator closer for political purposes, not only helping the Majority Leader to advance Senate legislation but prompting speculation of a Johnson-Kennedy dream ticket in 1960.[22]

The political relationship that Johnson formed with Kennedy was emotionally difficult. At a personal level Johnson was deeply jealous of Kennedy's glamour, wealth, and "playboy" life-style, viewing him, according to his aide Harry McPherson, as "the enviably attractive nephew who sings an Irish ballad for the company, and then winsomely disappears before the table-clearing and dishwashing begin." He was also apprehensive about Kennedy's noted reputation for war heroism. Although Johnson received the Silver Star during World War II, the medal was bestowed under questionable circumstances, and he had achieved nothing approximating the notoriety that

John Kennedy had received for his PT-109 heroics. "Johnson always had the feeling that Jack was doing these incredibly brave things on that wonderful torpedo boat," one aide recalled, "while all he did was sit in Melbourne, Australia." Likewise, Johnson, who often exaggerated his own reputation as a "lady's man," was intrigued by Kennedy's promiscuity. Shortly after he was elected vice president, he summoned Bobby Baker to him in the Senate chamber, asking, "Is ol' Jack gettin' much pussy?" "His eyes sparkled," Baker recalled, "as I related the latest Kennedy tale, though he kept his face as carefully composed as if we might be discussing the arms race with Russia."[23]

The envy Johnson felt toward Kennedy often turned into resentment as he denied that Kennedy possessed the qualities that he secretly admired. In retirement, for example, Johnson remembered Kennedy as "weak and pallid," "a scrawny man with a bad back, a weak and indecisive politician, a nice man, a gentle man, but not a man's man." Such insults may have been based on his own sense of inadequacy stemming from his childhood, for Kennedy possessed the paradoxical qualities that Sam and Rebekah Johnson desired. He was a war hero who had saved the lives of his crew when his PT boat was cut in two by a Japanese destroyer. Yet he was also the intellectual who had won the Pulitzer prize in 1957. He could play touch football in the afternoon and attend the opera at night without sacrificing his manliness.[24]

Johnson's letters to Kennedy were indeed generous in their praise, but they also conveyed subtle insecurities which forewarned of tension in their relationship. His repeated references to Kennedy's popular appeal, for example, suggested that he admired his traits for the wrong reasons. He did not value his eloquence, charm, and elocution because they made Kennedy worthy as a person. Rather, he admired those qualities because they helped Kennedy to win approval and affection. Consistent with his own poor self-image, Johnson viewed Kennedy as a reflection on himself, someone whose popularity and appeal he found threatening or advantageous to his own goals. The self-referential language of his letters suggested, too, that he linked the junior senator's actions to his own fortunes. His success was an opportunity for Johnson to bestow or withhold approval. Even Kennedy's ability to impress Rebekah was turned into "one of my fondest memories." Such self-involvement signaled potential dangers. If John Kennedy could be a source of pride, he also had the capacity to provoke self-doubt.

Rivals

The 1960 campaign accentuated the contrast between Johnson's and Kennedy's approaches to national politics. By the late 1950s Johnson's political style had become outmoded. Decades of reform within the party structure had de-emphasized the role of party regulars. Since the New Deal, civil service reform had limited federal patronage and diffused party power on the state level. The delegate selection process had shifted from congressmen and senators to governors and local leaders. Senators running for president had to rely on state politicians for delegate support. By 1960 the nomination process depended on a long, active campaign courting delegates and appearing before state conventions, local organizations, and Democratic dinners.[25]

Immediately after the 1956 election Kennedy began working aggressively for the 1960 nomination. He had lost his bid for the vice presidency in part because he had lost the support of local and state leaders. Within three and a half years he fulfilled speaking engagements in every state, appeared on dozens of national television programs, and fine-tuned his campaign themes and style. He also wrote for or was featured in several dozen prestigious magazines, and he synthesized a collection of his addresses and writings into a book. Through mailings, telephone calls, Christmas cards, and personal visits, Kennedy courted not only national Democratic leaders but state, county, and city officials who might be named delegates or have influence in choosing future delegates. As the convention neared, *Time* characterized him as "the most politically glamorous candidate, the people's choice."[26]

Like Kennedy, Johnson desired above all to be president. But unlike Kennedy he refused to campaign openly for the presidency until one week before the convention. His reluctance stemmed largely from his chronic insecurity toward elections. Throughout his career he perceived campaigns as tests of affection and worth, an anxiety complicated by his misfortune of having suffered through several close elections. He was first elected to the House of Representatives with only 27 percent of the vote. He narrowly lost his first bid for the Senate in 1941. And in 1948 he won his Senate seat by a margin of eighty-seven votes. Recalling his landslide victory in 1964, he noted that it was the first time he ever felt truly loved.[27]

Johnson measured his self-esteem by ballots. He interspersed periods of active and energetic campaigning with episodes of retreat and depression. A friend recalled that "in almost every campaign he ever ran, he got sick in the middle of it, almost a psychological thing. He tried some way to get out of it." Even in 1964, when he enjoyed enormous popularity, he wanted to withdraw just days before the convention. Predictably, before the 1960 primary season, Johnson expressed doubt. "I don't want to get a bug in my mouth that I can't swallow," he remarked. "I don't have the disposition, the training or the temperament for the presidency." He cited his "poor" health as impeding his capacity to hold higher office, though doctors informed him that he had recovered sufficiently from his 1955 heart attack. Bobby Baker sensed that Johnson was paralyzed by a "deep fear of defeat." James Rowe, Johnson's long-time political adviser, speculated about Johnson's thinking process: "This is impossible, and why get my hopes up? I'm not going to try. If I don't try, I won't fail."[28]

Kennedy may have rekindled in Johnson negative feelings about an earlier campaign. Johnson had lost his first bid for a Senate seat in 1941 when he was beaten by an expert at media manipulation, W. Lee "Pappy" O'Daniel. O'Daniel was a popular Texas governor who had been a radio personality during the late 1930s, captivating Texans with his warm, friendly, and relaxed voice. Exploiting his celebrity status, O'Daniel entered politics and won the governorship. In 1941 he announced his candidacy for the Senate; Johnson was soon hospitalized with "nervous exhaustion." During the campaign, O'Daniel drew enormous crowds, running on the theme of throwing the "professional politicians" out of Austin. Emerging from his illness, Johnson launched an energetic fight, only to lose by several thousand votes. Like O'Daniel, Kennedy was a political celebrity who portrayed himself as an alternative to the "professional politician."[29]

In 1960 Johnson faced practical obstacles which compounded his existing fears. If he had launched a more aggressive campaign, he contended, his Southern heritage would have made his nomination impossible. No Southerner had been nominated or elected president since the Civil War. His refusal to enter Northern primaries, however, merely heightened the perception of him as a regional candidate, untested and unknown in the national arena. His support of gas and oil interests, meanwhile, emphasized his sectional tag by generating concern that he was a lackey of wealthy Texas lobbyists. Johnson was also considered an anomaly. "He's competent, efficient and informed," a Massachusetts politician told the *Wall Street Journal*, "but no glamor boy. He can't match Kennedy or even Adlai Stevenson. People don't like 'politicians'—and Johnson is an acknowledged expert." In short, his authority in the Senate did not translate into popular appeal among most voters. One week before the convention, *Time* regarded him as "little known to the public."[30]

Still, Johnson possessed considerable assets which would have made him a serious contender had he decided to step forward. His support in the South was solid, and Northern conservatives found him appealing as well. He was also gaining increased publicity, evidenced by regular cover stories in

34

leading magazines about his legislative duties and power. His impressive experience with the nation's finances, foreign relations, and armed forces, as well as his position as Majority Leader, made him, according to the *Journal*, "one of the two or three most powerful men in the country and certainly the most powerful in his party."[31]

While each man monitored the other's strengths and weaknesses in 1959, Johnson and Kennedy remained on relatively amiable terms. Johnson sent Kennedy frequent letters, thanking him for placing his speech in the *Congressional Record*, for his hospitality during a trip to Boston that spring, and for his help during the summer session. He invited Kennedy to visit him in Texas, and Kennedy, in return, was mindful to send Johnson a congratulatory telegram on his twenty-fifth wedding anniversary. Their relationship was somewhat more antagonistic on the Senate floor. That spring the news media suspected Johnson of mismanaging Kennedy's labor reform bill. Some Kennedy supporters commented that Johnson's initials, LBJ, stood for "Let's Block Jack." When Johnson and Kennedy attended a Democratic dinner in Pennsylvania, reports circulated that the Texan was testing Northern political waters in preparation for the upcoming campaign. The two men began to exchange public quips. Introducing Johnson at a dinner in Boston, Kennedy noted, "Some people refer to Senator Johnson as the next President of the United States, but I see no reason why he should take a demotion." "I promise my backing to Jack Kennedy for any office," Johnson replied with a dramatic pause,"—to which he is nominated by the Democratic Party."[32]

Greater strain was evident by the fall of 1959 when Johnson began more actively to pursue the nomination. His friend and confidant Sam Rayburn announced the formation of an "unofficial" Johnson for President committee in October 1959. Johnson embarked on a campaign swing through Arizona, Missouri, Kansas, and Iowa. As Kennedy gained momentum, Johnson supporters countered by calling for a leader "with a touch of gray in his hair." A "Lyndon B. Johnson for President Newsletter" was widely circulated, contending that an "LBJ Movement Is Booming Across Nation." His possible candidacy was allegedly generating wide-range support from labor unions, Democratic organizations, Republican groups, and newspapers.[33]

In dealing with Johnson's political forays, Kennedy tried to keep the tone of their relationship on a positive level. When the press reported that a Kennedy aide had insulted Johnson, he immediately sought to placate the Majority Leader, writing that he was trying to find out who, if anyone, was responsible for the "disparaging" comment. "I have, as you know, a warm admiration and a personal affection for you and I am extremely anxious that nothing mar our fine relationship." Kennedy wanted to avoid such incidents in the future and sent a memorandum to his staff detailing the ground rules for their public comments about potential candidates. In response, Johnson called Kennedy's message to his staff "a fine memorandum." Agreeing to the ground rules, he promised to pass them on to his own staff. "Certainly, I don't want anything to hurt our warm friendship and mutual respect."[34]

After Kennedy officially announced his candidacy in January 1960, Johnson continued publicly to deny any intention to run for president. His aides were growing increasingly anxious. John Connally, one of Johnson's chief campaign advisers, thanked Kennedy for sending them a copy of his declaration but reminded him that "we are doing everything possible to persuade our own Senator Lyndon B. Johnson to make an effort for the nomination." Indeed, friends implored Johnson to enter the race, fearing that Kennedy's Catholicism would guarantee the election to Nixon. Johnson was so adamantly opposed that many allies deserted him for more active candidates.[35]

Reporting on Johnson's effort, Rowland Evans and Robert Novak assessed it as "the least coordinated, worst managed pre-convention campaign in history." Johnson made few practical moves to gain the nomination; he believed that the people would ultimately be drawn to his talent and experience. He depicted himself as the responsible statesman; while others were "running around the country making noises," he remained in Washington, faithful to his duties. At the same time he worked to discredit Kennedy by characterizing him as an absentee senator. He purposely forced roll-call votes and quorum calls to emphasize Kennedy's absence. Clinging to false hope, he insisted until a few weeks before the convention that Kennedy's Catholicism would deny him the nomination.[36]

At issue was Johnson's unwillingness to accept new political trends. Aides contended that he was simply ignorant of national politics. Believing that his popularity and authority over the Senate could be used as leverage, he never systematically cultivated relations with state officials outside of Texas. His effort to depict Kennedy as an absentee senator was futile, generating little concern among voters who were unfamiliar with quorum calls. Kennedy himself was perplexed by his opponent's inattentiveness to delegate support and believed Johnson was surprised by the changing conditions. It seems unlikely, however, that Johnson's inactivity can be blamed entirely on his supposed naiveté. It would be highly uncharacteristic for someone so politically astute to have so seriously misjudged the political environment. In light of the constant prodding of aides, he must have known that his wheeler-dealer style had become a liability in an age of media politics and the courtship of local leaders. Aware of Kennedy's impressive public appearances, he must also have known that he was no match for the junior senator's popular appeal.[37]

Unwilling to participate in the new political process, Johnson resorted to a clumsy attempt to broker the convention. Five weeks before it was to begin, he decided that Congress could not complete its legislative agenda before the upcoming convention. With the cooperation of his mentor, Sam Rayburn, they recessed Congress seeking to use impending legislation as political blackmail to gain support from his colleagues. The maneuver, however, was transparent. *Time* reported that the action was "generally read as a last-minute start of a stop-Kennedy movement." Most Democrats resented the "power-play" and stiffened their resolve for Kennedy.[38]

Powerless to halt Kennedy's momentum, Johnson became angry with the front-runner. Discussing the junior senator with colleagues, he constantly referred to him as "young Jack" or "the boy." On one occasion he and Rayburn visited President Dwight Eisenhower at the White House and ridiculed Kennedy as a young, wealthy upstart unfit for the Senate and certainly lacking in the qualities necessary for the presidency. Indeed, Johnson told Eisenhower, Kennedy was "a dangerous man." He sometimes became brutal in his criticism. When Peter Lisagor of the *Chicago Daily News* once mentioned Kennedy to him, Johnson vented his "enmity and hostility." He referred to Kennedy as a "little scrawny fellow with rickets" and other diseases. "Have you ever seen his ankles?" Johnson asked. Making a small circle with his fingers he noted, "They're about so round." Hugh Sidey recalled that Johnson was "vicious" and "quite violent at times" in his attacks. He complained of Kennedy's wealth and his absenteeism in the Senate. He also cited Kennedy's ingratitude. Johnson credited himself with guiding Kennedy's career, giving him the best committee assignments when his "daddy" had called him up and begged on behalf of his "little boy." He alleged that "old Joe Kennedy" would run the presidency if his son were elected. Consistent with his mixed feelings, however, Johnson would suddenly praise Kennedy, noting with awe his rising popularity in the polls.[39]

Johnson's maliciousness culminated during the Democratic convention. After months of procrastination he declared his candidacy on July 5, just eight days before the balloting in Los Angeles. Although his two-thousand-word statement never mentioned Kennedy by name, it was laced with innuendo. Johnson alluded to Kennedy's youth and inexperience as disqualifying him for the presidency, especially in light of Cold War responsibilites. Calling for an open convention, he implied that Kennedy had been "elbowing through 179 million Americans—pushing aside other Senators and Governors and Congressmen—to shout 'Look at me, and nobody else!' " Johnson merely wanted the delegates "to look long, to look hard, and to look wisely to find the right man."

Questioned by reporters, Johnson maintained that his own sense of duty as

Majority Leader did not permit him to campaign actively. He alluded to Kennedy having missed "hundreds of votes" in the Senate since January. "This I could not do. . . . Some one has to tend the store." "Jack was out kissing babies while I was passing bills," Johnson later said within earshot of reporters. His voice, *Time* observed, had an "edge of bitterness in it, betraying his sense of grievance, his not-so-secret dislike for 'young Jack.' " "I think you're rewarded for what you do, what you produce," he continued, "and not for kissing babies. I'll believe this until I'm proven wrong."[40]

Candidates

Despite the boldness of Johnson's declaration, he entered the 1960 campaign with typical ambivalence. According to Reedy, part of Johnson "really wanted to go to the convention and get it over with." Another part, however, was determined to make a fight of it. He rejected Baker's assessment that his late-hour effort was doomed. "Jack Kennedy and other senators can go gallivantin' around the country kissin' asses and shakin' hands when they want to," he barked. "But if I'd done it, the Senate business wouldn't have gotten done and the press would have crucified me for running out on my job." He continued to believe that Kennedy would not win the nomination despite his primary victories. "He's winnin' those beauty contests," he told Baker, "but when it gets down to the nut-cuttin' he won't have the old bulls with him."[41]

Unorganized and rushed, Johnson hoped to win the nomination by undercutting Kennedy's front-runner status and convincing Adlai Stevenson to declare his candidacy. Stevenson's popularity among liberal delegates would sap strength from the Kennedy forces, preventing him from winning on the first ballot. Stevenson's reputation as a "two-time loser" would then stall his own efforts. Johnson reasoned that both Kennedy's and Stevenson's support would disintegrate, and the delegates would turn to the man of experience as a compromise candidate.[42]

In the weeks leading to the convention, Johnson engaged in extensive Kennedy-bashing. He criticized the junior senator for suggesting that the United States apologize to the Soviet Union for the U-2 incident, in which a U.S. spy plane had been downed. He reminded the public that Kennedy's Catholicism would hurt the party's chances in November. Meanwhile, his campaign workers leveled serious charges. Shortly before Johnson announced his candidacy, former President Harry Truman had made an issue of Kennedy's youth and inexperience and called on the candidate to withdraw from the race. In response, Kennedy arranged for a news conference. He argued that "strength and health and vigor" were a prerequisite for the presidency, especially when one recalled the frequent occurrence of heart attacks in the White House. Watching the televised news conference, Johnson believed, correctly, that Kennedy had alluded to his own history of heart problems.[43]

Shortly after Kennedy's rebuttal, the director of Citizens for Johnson, John Connally, circulated rumors that Kennedy was secretly suffering from Addison's disease, an adrenal deficiency which is often fatal if not controlled. India Edwards, the former vice chairperson of the Democratic National Committee and co-chairperson of Citizens for Johnson, added to the controversy. "Doctors have told me," she told reporters, "that [Kennedy] would not be alive were it not for cortisone." Clark Clifford recalled that the entire Kennedy family was "outraged by the charge" and became "embittered" toward Johnson. Robert Kennedy worked quickly to counter the accusation. He issued medical documents to reporters from a 1958 physical examination indicating that his brother's "adrenal glands do function." Johnson was forced to retreat on the issue. Asked by reporters about the accusation, he replied that Kennedy's active campaign traveling clearly indicated that "he doesn't have any health problem."[44]

The degree to which Johnson directed the attacks on Kennedy's health is not known. Reedy denied that the accusation originated with Johnson, despite his history of undermining opponents through personal attacks. A member of the Kennedy staff recalled tracing the rumors to the Johnson camp but not to Johnson himself. Those who have written about the 1960 campaign have generally agreed that he was probably not directly responsible for initiating the charge. But he likely played a role in spreading the Addison's disease rumors.[45]

Six years earlier, Johnson had expressed a personal interest in Kennedy's health. Following Kennedy's near fatal back surgery in late 1954, he called Joseph Kennedy to inquire about rumors that the senator was critically ill. Curiously, Johnson kept a three-page transcript of their conversation, although he assured Joseph that their conversation was in "the greatest confidence." The rumor, Johnson explained, was that Joseph had told columnist and friend Arthur Krock that his son had "a situation like Senator Taft's," referring to Robert Taft's secret and fatal bout with cancer. Joseph expressed alarm and emphatically denied that his son was seriously ill: "He has neither of the things he is supposed to have—he hasn't cancer; he hasn't Parkinson's disease." Likely alluding to the back surgery, Joseph noted, "He did have a very close call, but that thing is corrected. . . ." The father never elaborated about the nature of the "thing," nor did Johnson ask. Joseph admitted talking to Krock but contended that he never gave any indication that his son was "that kind of sick."[46]

Perhaps Johnson's conversation suggests little more than a curiosity about Kennedy's health. Nevertheless, it indicated that he had cause and opportunity to believe that Kennedy's long-term health may have been at risk. Johnson was known to collect personal information about Senate colleagues to gain political advantage. He was likely well aware of Kennedy's various brushes with death. Kennedy had twice received last rites following operations on his back and once remarked to columnist Joseph Alsop that he suffered from an adrenal condition which might cut short his life. And Alsop was friendly with Johnson. Johnson's comments to reporters about "that skinny little fellow with all those diseases" cast further suspicion on his complicity. His more cynical detractors could note that the doctor who treated Kennedy for his adrenal deficiency found his office ransacked during the 1960 campaign. Furthermore, after Kennedy's assassination, the Johnson White House kept for its files updated press disclosures confirming the late president's bout with Addison's disease.[47]

Regardless of Johnson's possible involvement, raising the health issue underscored the desperation of his campaign. The rumor was one of several ploys designed to stop Kennedy. Republican Senator Hugh Scott, a Johnson ally from Pennsylvania, wrote an open letter to the delegates accusing Kennedy of being an "absentee Senator." Johnson insulted Kennedy when speaking before delegates. "This young fellow I appointed to a foreign relations committee claims he knows more about foreign affairs than I do," he noted. "You know, there are some people who will throw crutches at their doctors and get smarter than their daddy." The Johnson team tried to convince delegates that Kennedy's first-ballot nomination was not settled. Meanwhile, they issued inflated numbers for Johnson's own delegate support and claimed that a national surge for him was under way. Shortly before the first ballot, Johnson reminded the public of Joseph Kennedy's controversial past as American Ambassador to Great Britain in the 1930s. "I wasn't any Chamberlain-umbrella policy man," he remarked. "I never thought Hitler was right."[48]

Robert Kennedy was particularly upset by Johnson's tactics. "I've seen Bobby mad," Kenneth O'Donnell recalled, "but never as mad as the day he heard what Johnson said about his father." During the convention, Bobby Baker had breakfast with Robert and offhandedly mentioned that he thought the innuendo about Johnson's health was unfair. Kennedy turned red with anger. "You've got your nerve," he replied. "Lyndon Johnson has compared my father to the Nazis and John Connally and India Edwards lied in saying my brother is dying of Addison's disease. You Johnson people are running a stinking damned campaign, and you're gonna get yours when the time comes!"[49]

Continuing his attacks, Johnson found one last opportunity to block Kennedy's nomination. Although the Kennedy camp operated with great efficiency, it made a mistake on which Johnson sought to capitalize. Someone had sent a telegram to the delegations of each state requesting an opportunity for Kennedy to speak before that state's delegation. Inadvertently, one such telegram was sent to the Texas delegation. In his return telegram to Kennedy, Johnson quickly granted his request and further suggested that the two candidates meet before a joint session of delegates from Massachusetts and Texas for an informal debate. According to Evans and Novak, Johnson believed that Kennedy could not withstand a direct confrontation. He prided himself on being an expert debater, having taught debate in high school and engaged in public debates. Kennedy refused Johnson's request. In a second memorandum, Johnson persisted: "May I earnestly, Jack, urge you to reconsider your refusal and permit your delegation to join with ours for this important discussion of issues." Kennedy had little choice but to accept, sending a telegram noting that he would meet with Johnson before the Texas delegation but would not request the presence of the Massachusetts delegates. The two candidates would then "proceed in anyway you and the delegates deem advisable."[50]

Johnson moved forward, revitalized at the thought of debating Kennedy. "Once again he was a candidate for the presidency with a chance," noted Philip Graham, publisher of the *Washington Post*, "even an unlikely one." He arranged for television cameras and reporters to occupy the Biltmore Hotel's ballroom. In his hotel room he worked on his debate strategy. Listening to Johnson, Graham was concerned that he "seemed a bit harsh and personal." Past debates had been fearful experiences for Johnson, and he would usually try to insult his opponents. Believing that Johnson was overworked, Graham advised that the tone for the debate should be more profound and convinced him to get some sleep beforehand.[51]

During their "debate" that afternoon, Johnson characterized Kennedy as a man of "high intellect" and "unusually high character," as well as "a dedicated and devoted public citizen." But for the greater part of fifteen minutes he tried to diminish his opponent. Using broad physical gestures, he noted that, unlike "some Senators," he himself had answered all fifty quorum calls during the lengthy debate over the civil rights bill that year. The crowd erupted in cheers. He emphasized his own superior experience and voting record, reminding the delegates of his many years in Congress. He attacked Kennedy's voting record on price-support farm policy and natural resources. In short, his comments before the delegates were representative of his campaign strategy: he sarcastically demeaned Kennedy while presenting himself as the voice of responsibility and accomplishment.[52]

Visually, Johnson's arguments were obscured by a speaking style ill-suited for the "cool" medium of television. Playing to the immediate audience and not to the cameras, he used flamboyant gestures that distracted viewers from the content of his comments. Waving his arms, flapping his hands, pointing his finger, thrusting his head, pausing excessively, and lowering and raising his voice level, he appeared more like a preacher than a president. He had campaigned in similar fashion for the Senate in 1941. Audiences then had found it excessively domineering and arrogant. Television audiences in 1960 were likely to react in a similar way.[53]

While Johnson "preached," Kennedy listened and smiled. When he rose to speak before the delegates, some reporters noticed his legs shaking and a trace of nervous perspiration on his upper lip. In tone, however, he was composed. Regarding his absenteeism, Kennedy remarked that because Johnson had not been specific in his accusation, he assumed he was referring to "some of the other candidates." His feigned naiveté brought laughter from the audience. He praised Johnson's "wonderful record" on answering Senate quorum calls and defused his differences with him on issues. After speaking for only three minutes, he left his audience laughing: "I leave here full of admiration for Senator Johnson, full of affection for him, strongly in support of him for Majority Leader and confident that in that position we'll be able to work together." Seated behind Kennedy, Johnson tilted his head backward, smiled broadly, stood up, and vigorously shook hands with the man who had defeated his final effort.[54]

Kennedy's generous comments made Johnson's attack appear mean-spirited. Journalists were impressed by his ability to use his wit and grace to deflate his opponent. Johnson aides conceded that Kennedy did "a tremendous job." "My God," John Roche reflected, "Jack made mincemeat of him."[55]

The "debate" reinforced Johnson's anxiety about media politics: voting records and experience could be secondary to style and image. The political methods that had once won him power and boosted his self-esteem proved limited by 1960. Kennedy transcended Johnson's strengths, and he did so with the tools of elocution that Rebekah had sought to instill in her son. "It was the goddamnedest thing," Johnson recalled:

Here was a young whippersnapper, malaria-ridden, and yellah, sickly, sickly. He never said a word of importance in the Senate and never did a thing. But somehow with his books and his Pulitzer Prizes he managed to create the image of himself as a shining intellectual, a youthful leader who would change the face of the country.

Johnson acknowledged that Kennedy had a sense of humor, "looked awfully good on the goddamn television screen," and played a fair political fight, "but his growing hold on the American people was simply a mystery to me." Harry McPherson recalled that the defeat offered Johnson a poignant lesson. He was beaten by "the kid whom he had liked and whose grace I thought he envied, who knew so much less than he about getting things done in Washington, and so much more about the search for delegates and the building of an image."[56]

Recalling the 1960 convention in later years, Johnson felt he had been beaten "overwhelmingly and humiliatingly." His halfhearted campaign produced halfhearted support. While he found solace in the knowledge that he had failed only because he never really tried, he nevertheless failed. In the end, the young charismatic candidate had bested the older political professional. As Johnson watched the balloting on television from his hotel room, he appeared outwardly relaxed. Surrounded by reporters, he joked and played the amiable host. When Kennedy secured the nomination, Johnson did not acknowledge the rejection he must have felt. "Quite the contrary," an aide recalled, "he seemed . . . possibly relieved when it was all over with."[57]

Partners

The circumstances surrounding the formation of the Kennedy-Johnson ticket are difficult to grasp. "I don't think anybody will ever really know how this all really came about," John Kennedy once confessed. "The whole story will never be known. And it's just as well that it won't be." Embarrassed by the circumstances, Robert Kennedy recalled that he and his brother "promised each other that we'd never tell what happened. . . ." Although each camp had its own version of events, all agree that the selection process was farcical. In the end, John Kennedy reluctantly joined in an alliance with a bruised and dejected partner. The clumsiness of the decision had serious long-term consequences; its details are vital in understanding Johnson's polarized feelings toward John and Robert Kennedy.[58]

John Kennedy's decision to select Johnson as his running mate was not as astonishing as some suggested at the time. In the Senate, Kennedy had respected Johnson's political sophistication and strength of personality. "Lyndon would make the ablest president of any of us running," Kennedy told a reporter in 1960, "but he can't be elected." Members of his staff shared this assessment. Before the convention, Theodore Sorensen and his assistant, Myer Feldman, prepared for Kennedy a list of potential vice-presidential candidates. Johnson headed their list "as far and away the outstanding candidate"; his political stature made him a logical choice. During the first day of the convention, when Philip Graham and Joseph Alsop advised Kennedy to select Johnson, he was so receptive that both men suspected he would politely reject their advice.[59]

Although Kennedy and some members of his staff were disposed to select Johnson, they assumed that the Majority Leader would reject the offer. Few believed he would sacrifice his powerful congressional position for the anonymity of the vice presidency. When Ben Bradlee asked Kennedy before the convention about the possibility of nominating Johnson, Kennedy was blunt: "He'll never take it." Nevertheless, he believed that Johnson should be given the right to refuse. His congressional power, his sensitivity to slights, and his representation of an important electoral state made him an important ally whom Kennedy could not afford to alienate. What Kennedy did not appreciate, however, was Johnson's own political predicament and his propensity to link his career to those who might eventually open power to him.[60]

The people closest to Johnson recalled that after his defeat for the presidential nomination, his future seemed bleak. His authority in the Senate would be diminished regardless of who won the election. With Kennedy as president, the role of the Majority Leader would be less significant than it had been during a passive Republican administration. As leader of the Democratic party, Kennedy, not Johnson, would get credit for passage of legislation. Should Nixon be elected president, Johnson did not believe he could develop the congenial relationship he had enjoyed with Eisenhower. The vice president's reputation as a loner, as well as his distrust of rival institutions, would make working with him difficult.[61]

Throughout Johnson's life, no matter which institution he was a part of, people in power served as a means to further his own ambitions. College faculty members, Richard Kleberg, or more prominent political figures such as Roosevelt, Rayburn, or Russell, were subject to Johnson's constant adulation and flattery. By emulating their personal traits and political style, he hoped to make each mentor accommodating to his purposes. Through them he would derive approval and establish his own realm of leadership. Asked at the convention why he had accepted the vice presidency, Johnson was blunt: "Power is where power goes." The vice presidency was a stepping-stone to the ultimate prize that might be won either by the unfortunate death of the president or through his eventual election as the rightful heir. Indeed, while there is no documentary evidence to the point, Johnson may have accepted a spot on the ticket anticipating Kennedy's death in office from Addison's disease. This possibility assumes a degree of legitimacy in light of his conversation with Joseph Kennedy in 1954, his frequent references to Kennedy's sickly physical appearance, and his likely involvement in spreading the Addison's disease rumors at the convention. Moreover, Johnson may have thought that Kennedy would be as disengaged from the presidency as he had been in Congress. In many ways, Kennedy's political life-style had been similar to that of Johnson's old boss, Kleberg. In Congress both men were extremely wealthy, uninterested in legislative duties, and attentive to Washington's social life. And Johnson had exerted unprecedented authority as Kleberg's congressional secretary.[62]

Shortly after Kennedy was nominated on July 13, Johnson was informed by Rayburn and Connally that he might be offered the vice presidency. Expressing disbelief, he went to bed after sending Kennedy a congratulatory telegram and offering his help during the upcoming campaign. Kennedy's return telegram thanked Johnson for his "generous and heartwarming message," and added, "I would like to come see you today." At about 8:30 a.m., Kennedy called Johnson and arranged to meet in Johnson's hotel room at 10:30. Johnson and a small group of aides remained uncertain about Kennedy's intentions.[63]

The Johnson camp's version of what followed was different from the Kennedys'. According to Walter Jenkins, Johnson's long-time aide, Kennedy offered the vice presidency, and Johnson more or less declined. He wanted a few hours to discuss his decision with his wife, Lady Bird, and Sam Rayburn. According to Robert Kennedy, however, his brother returned to their hotel suite convinced that Johnson had accepted. "You just wouldn't believe it," John remarked. "He wants it." Robert expressed shock, "Oh, my God!" "I didn't offer the Vice Presidency to him," John later recalled. Taking his hand from his pocket and extending his open palm, he explained, "I just held it out like this, and he grabbed at it."[64]

Following Kennedy's conversation with Johnson, each side assessed the benefits and drawbacks of the proposed ticket. Robert Kennedy was adamantly opposed. He was not only concerned about the reaction of liberals and labor leaders, he was bitter about the vicious tone of Johnson's brief campaign. Pierre Salinger and Kenneth O'Donnell were also against the nomination. Further opposition came from labor leaders, who reminded Kennedy that Johnson had backed the controversial Landrum-Griffin Labor Bill of 1959. Walter Reuther, president of the United Automobile Workers, went so far as to warn Kennedy of a floor fight to prevent the nomination.[65]

While Kennedy initiated damage control, the Johnson camp weighed their end of the decision. Although initially opposed to the offer, Rayburn grew fearful that, without Johnson on the ticket, Nixon might win in the fall. Texas would be an important swing state. Arranging a meeting with

Kennedy, he tried to clarify the offer. Kennedy told Rayburn that Johnson would have a valuable role in his administration. He agreed with Rayburn's assessment that, with Johnson on the ticket, there was a greater likelihood of defeating Nixon. Rayburn then said he would support the ticket on the condition "that you go on the radio or television and tell the people you came to us and asked for this thing." Typical of the ambivalence surrounding his selection of Johnson, Kennedy agreed, and Rayburn subsequently advised Johnson to accept.[66]

Just as Johnson resolved to accept the nomination, John and Robert Kennedy began to have doubts. "We spent the rest of the day," Robert recalled, "alternating between thinking it was good and thinking it wasn't good . . . and how could he get out of it." John was ambivalent. According to Robert, he thought Johnson "would be so mean as Majority Leader that it was much better having him as Vice President, where you could control him. . . ." But John also "thought it would be unpleasant with [Johnson], to be associated with him." He wanted to remove Johnson but not at the expense of irreparably damaging their relationship. The Kennedy brothers finally agreed to bluff Johnson with warnings of mounting opposition and courteously give him a chance to decline. Actually, the opposition was manageable and weighed little on John's decision. "The President just had this uneasy feeling about him," Robert recalled. John instructed Robert that, if he chose, he could try to persuade Johnson to refuse. He and his brother were unsure what Johnson's response would be, but John had nevertheless decided "to get rid of him." Operating on his brother's instructions, Robert arranged to see Johnson. "Obviously, with the close relationship between my brother and me," he recalled, "I wasn't going down to see if he would withdraw just as a lark on my own."[67]

Arriving at Johnson's hotel suite, Robert talked with Rayburn, informing him of the growing opposition and the difficulty that the nomination would face. Rayburn fully understood Robert's real intentions; he was asking Johnson to withdraw while pretending not to be acting for his brother. After Robert left, Rayburn expressed outrage at the Kennedys. Johnson, meanwhile, began packing to go home. Robert returned to Johnson's suite a second time. On this occasion he met directly with Johnson and offered him the chairmanship of the Democratic National Committee, from which he could launch a future presidential bid.[68]

Johnson was visibly shaken. "[H]e is one of the greatest sad-looking people in the world," Robert recalled. "You know, he can turn that on. I thought he'd burst into tears. I don't know whether it was just an act or anything. But he just shook, and tears came into his eyes. . . ." At his moment of rejection, however, he stood firm. "I want to be Vice President," he told Robert. "If I am Jack's choice, I'll fight for it." Wanting to avoid a rift, Robert acquiesced. Meanwhile, Philip Graham called John Kennedy and was told that Robert was "out of touch and doesn't know what's been happening." Johnson spoke with the presidential nominee, seeking reassurance. "Do you really want me?" he asked. "Well, if you really want me, I'll do it." John then read him a press statement announcing his vice-presidential choice.[69]

Less than twelve hours after losing the presidential nomination, Johnson agreed to abandon Congress in order to serve as "young Jack's" running mate. For a man who placed great value on the estimations of others, the situation was especially demeaning and stressful. Graham noticed that Johnson was "considerably on edge," "in a state of high nerves," and "seemed about to jump out of his skin." Even after Kennedy had assured him of his final decision, he continued to feel hurt. As he stood before the door to his hotel room, ready to read his statement of acceptance to the press, he remarked, "I was just going to read this on TV when Bobby came in, and now I don't know what I ought to do." On television Johnson performed well, but his depression and anger soon returned. He condemned the "little shitass" Robert Kennedy for causing all his difficulties.[70]

Questions surrounding the decision haunted Johnson forever. Was the vice presidency sincerely offered? Did Robert attempt to "dump" him? If so, was he acting on his brother's behalf? Four months after John Kennedy's death, a newspaper column written by an old Kennedy friend, Charles Bartlett, claimed that Kennedy had made the offer under the assumption that Johnson would refuse. In response to Bartlett's article, Joseph Alsop wrote to the new president to assure that he could "testify without hesitation" that the offer was sincere. Johnson thanked Alsop for his two-page account of the events: "I find your version of what happened more in keeping with what I know the truth to be. You're a good friend, and a perceptive one. . . ."[71]

After Graham died in the summer of 1963, his account of the convention (noting the ambiguousness of Kennedy's offer) was reprinted verbatim in Theodore White's *The Making of the President 1964*. Katharine Graham, his widow, recalled that Johnson was "furious" at her for allowing its publication. Constructing his own version of events, Johnson ordered an aide to research Texas Governor Price Daniel's alleged conversation with John Kennedy about the decision-making process. According to Daniel, it was *Kennedy* who had arranged to talk with Rayburn and worked to convince the Speaker to support a Kennedy-Johnson ticket. It was a scenario that Robert considered inconceivable.[72]

In his six-hundred-page memoir published in 1971, Johnson devoted only two pages to the 1960 convention. He depicted himself as a reluctant candidate but firmly in control. Drawing from Daniel's scenario, he claimed Kennedy had *asked* to talk to Rayburn rather than the reverse. The implication was that Kennedy was so determined to nominate Johnson that he initiated a meeting in order to convince Rayburn. Robert's attempt to "dump" him from the ticket, meanwhile, was only subtly implied. After being told of the mounting opposition, Johnson wrote glibly, "I told Bobby that I appreciated *his* concern, but that *his* information did not greatly surprise me" [emphasis added]. He failed to mention that Robert tried to remove him from the ticket in exchange for control of the party's national committee. Nor did he acknowledge that John invited him onto the ticket despite his personal attacks on the candidate and his family. The only acknowledged tension occurred when Rayburn asked Robert, "Who speaks for the Kennedys?" Johnson assured the reader that Robert had deferred to his brother.[73]

In part, Johnson's distorted account reflected the illegitimacy he felt after assuming the presidency. If the public believed that Kennedy did not genuinely want him as his vice president, then Johnson would be viewed as a usurper and his presidency would be spurious. Unable to accept this harsh conclusion, he constructed evidence to make clear that his predecessor viewed him as a desirable vice president. Only then could Johnson convince himself, after Kennedy's death, that he was a legitimate president. In the process he came to perceive the two brothers in distinctly opposite terms. Toward John he felt a measure of affection, believing they had entered into a sincere alliance. But Robert evoked feelings of rejection. For the next eight years Johnson remained wary, convinced that the younger brother was determined to undermine him politically.

If Johnson seemed delusional or overly sensitive, his reaction was understandable. The convention had turned his world upside-down. The most powerful Democrat in Washington had been reduced to a ceremonial attendant. He was the consummate politician, but Kennedy possessed something he lacked, something that had won the junior senator the party's approval. "[T]here was something in John Kennedy himself," Johnson recalled, "some sort of dignity that people just liked when they saw it, for without this his incredible rise to power simply makes no sense at all." Visiting Hyannis Port shortly after the convention, Johnson pondered the reasons why he had been rejected in favor of a man with so little experience. "Tell me," he asked a friend, "just what is it that people like so much in Jack Kennedy?"[74]

The question spoke of emotional and political insecurities that would gnaw at Johnson for the next three years. Reporters Evans and Novak believed that it "betrayed a sense of unfulfillment in Johnson." Despite all his past success, "he felt the pain and anguish of not being loved. What Johnson was asking in that innocent question . . . was really this: why do they love Jack, but not me?" The question also suggested a desire to assimilate John Kennedy's attributes—to link himself to a new mentor in order to strengthen himself for the future. If he could deduce why the public had greater affection for John than himself, then he could remodel himself to suit new political demands, just as he done in the past. The qualities that John Kennedy embodied, however, were sorely lacking in Johnson. Youth, charm, grace, sardonic wit, Ivy League background, a handsome appearance—these were characteristics strange to him. Indeed, they were qualitics that Rebekah had yearned for in her son but which he was never able to give her. Joining the New Frontier, Johnson was heading into personally troublesome territory.[75]

C H A P T E R

III

THE LOST
FRONTIERSMAN:
KENNEDY'S
VICE PRESIDENT

The political partnership formed between John Kennedy and Lyndon Johnson did not foster an immediate spirit of unity. Shortly after Johnson's nomination, Kennedy forgot to invite his running mate to an important meeting during which the new Democratic party chairperson was selected. "I think I'll go back to Texas," the vice-presidential nominee remarked to his aides, "make a couple of speeches and the hell with it." Meanwhile, Robert Kennedy remained embittered. Word had reached him that Johnson had made disparaging comments to reporters about John Kennedy during the weeks before the convention. Robert implored journalist Peter Lisagor to relate the information. "I knew he hated Jack," Kennedy responded, "but I didn't think he hated him that much."[1]

Johnson generally felt detached from the heart of the campaign, sensing he had little to offer the Kennedy team which was praised for its expert knowledge of regional and state politics. A national campaign was a new and intimidating experience for him, and he was reluctant to confront large, potentially unfriendly crowds in regions of the country that were unfamiliar to him. "I'm not going to let the liberals cut me up and embarrass Jack Kennedy," he explained. "And they will, just because I'm a Texan and a

Southerner." His attitude was sometimes so fussy that aides referred to him as "a Mongol emperor."[2]

Ultimately, however, Johnson proved to be an active and enthusiastic running mate. He traveled to major urban centers throughout the nation, insuring that, despite his regional differences with the Democratic nominee, the Kennedy-Johnson ticket was united. Particularly impressive and important was his appearance at a "unity meeting" of Southern Democratic governors in Nashville. At a rally there he spoke to an enthusiastic crowd of more than eight thousand, pledging his support for the party's civil rights plank and defusing the controversy surrounding Kennedy's Catholicism. "Wherever I may go," he promised, "I will never speak as a Southerner to Southerners or as a Protestant to Protestants or as a white to whites. I will speak only as an American to Americans." Kennedy, he declared, "wears no man's collar—but he wears the collar of all the people." Positive press reports of the Nashville trip prompted Kennedy to send a congratulatory telegram: "You got us off to a great start." Making a whistle-stop tour of the South on the "LBJ Special," Johnson continued to turn his Protestant, Southern heritage into an asset for the ticket. When he appeared with Kennedy at the Alamo, he challenged anti-Catholic protesters by heralding the sacrifices of the Kennedy family during World War II. "And then that little ole Massachusetts boy took his little ole torpedo boat and rammed into the side of a Japanese cruiser," he reminded his audience, "and there wasn't nobody around askin' what religion he was." Subsequent references to the PT-109 incident and to Joseph Kennedy, Jr.'s death during the war not only deflated the religious issue but genuinely moved John.[3]

Typically, Johnson interspersed periods of active campaigning with episodes of depression. He was hurt by Republican senators who referred to Kennedy as "the Majority Leader's Leader." He was upset by John's reluctance to appear in public with him. "Nixon and Lodge are always making joint appearances," he told one aide. "When am I going to appear with Jack?" After rumors circulated that he and Kennedy were not on friendly terms, a major, nationally televised "reunion" was staged in New York City. The Kennedy slights and Republican jabs, however, took an emotional toll. Johnson's drinking increased, and on one occasion he "startled" several Republican senators by criticizing Kennedy's poor legislative skills and crediting himself for Kennedy's success in the Senate.[4]

During the campaign's last week, Johnson returned to Texas to make one final push. The support of his conservative constituency was in serious jeopardy due to accusations that he had "sold out" to the Northern, liberal wing of the party. Determined not to embarrass himself in the eyes of the nation or John Kennedy, Johnson turned the criticism to his advantage.

Appearing at the Adolphus Hotel in Dallas, he was met by a hostile crowd. He could have avoided a confrontation, but he chose to walk straight through the gathering. Aware that television cameras and reporters were present, he sensed that the visual images and stories to follow would generate a backlash of sympathy and support. He and Lady Bird waded through the protesters and were jostled. When they arrived next in Houston, some people in the crowd held signs of support. "We Apologize," one sign read. "We Love You."[5]

On election night Kennedy carried Texas by a mere 46,233 votes. The ticket also carried Louisiana and the Carolinas, states crucial to Kennedy's narrow margin of victory. Had he not won those four states, the electoral college would have been evenly split. He would then have needed the unlikely support of unpledged electors from Mississippi and Alabama. According to Arthur Schlesinger, Kennedy had entered into the partnership with his running mate aware not only that Johnson was "temperamental, edgy and deeply sensitive" but that he was pivotal to their victory. The new vice president might be politically indispensable in 1964.[6]

Margaret Mayer, a journalist for the *Dallas Times-Herald,* was with Johnson the night he became vice president and recalled never having seen "a more unhappy man." "There was no jubilation," she noted. "Lyndon looked as if he'd lost his last friend on earth." Johnson was now on the periphery of power. His relationship with his newest mentor had been thus far strained. Indirectly Johnson had opened power to Kennedy, but he himself was now an outsider. The apprenticeship would not be easy. "It was clear to me," Mayer observed, "and a lot of other people that even then he didn't want to be vice president."[7]

The Outcast

Johnson's precise feelings and role during the Kennedy administration are difficult to determine. The Johnson Library has yet fully to release documents pertaining to his vice presidency, compelling researchers to depend on less reliable secondary evidence. Accepting these limitations, however, an examination of Johnson's vice presidency reveals consistencies which point to a troubled figure. For a man whose political energy was fueled by power and recognition, Lyndon Johnson was ill-suited to the anonymity of the office. Throughout his career he had thrived on activity, exerting power, twisting arms, bluffing, compromising, and always demanding of himself and his staff inordinate hours of work. With his power now depleted and his achievements few, he was emotionally vulnerable.

Johnson's anxiety was evident even before he assumed office when he initiated several actions intended to maintain his Senate power. Although Senator Mike Mansfield had been chosen as the new Majority Leader, Johnson managed to retain his plush office in the Senate Building. The territorial concession by Mansfield allowed Johnson valuable access to his former colleagues for conversation and persuasion. He also convinced Mansfield to keep Bobby Baker as secretary to the Majority Leader, giving the vice president a conduit to his former colleagues. He soon became enthusiastic about a scheme that would allow him to exert further influence in Congress. Kennedy, he argued, had been "an indifferent senator." "All those Bostons and Harvards," he explained to Baker, "don't know anymore about Capitol Hill than an old maid does about fuckin'." Johnson therefore planned not only to attend all future meetings of the Senate Democratic Caucus but to preside over that body. "It's gonna be just the way it was!" he exclaimed.[8]

Privately, Baker was "astonished and horrified" by both the proposition and Johnson's "excessively manic" behavior. Senate tradition would not permit such an intrusion of the executive branch into its inner confines of authority. Moreover, many senators had resented Johnson's domination of the Senate and were anxious to be rid of him. But Baker felt it was useless to try to dissuade Johnson from his plan. On January 3, 1961, Mansfield and Johnson met together with the Senate Democratic Caucus. At Johnson's urging, Mansfield proposed that the rules be altered to allow the vice president to become chairperson of the Democratic Conference. Sensing a direct threat to the separation of powers, the senators strongly opposed the proposal and rebuked their former leader. "Those bastards sandbagged me," Johnson told Baker. "They plotted to humiliate me, all those goddamn redhots and troublemakers."[9]

Soon Johnson was unsuccessful in yet another attempt to expand his powers. After the inauguration one of his aides composed an executive order designed to give the new vice president significant authority within the administration. The order informed all departments and agencies that he was to have "general supervision" over a number of issues. Reports, information, and policy plans routinely sent to the president would also be delivered to the vice president. Arthur Schlesinger recalled that Kennedy was "astonished" at the proposal's presumptuousness. Some White House staff members compared it with William Seward's famous letter to Abraham Lincoln in which the Secretary of State suggested that he be bestowed with presidential powers. Like Lincoln, Kennedy gracefully ignored the request, and Johnson never again raised the issue.[10]

In general, Kennedy was ambivalent about making Johnson an active member of the New Frontier. Early in the administration, political scientist Richard Neustadt, an informal Kennedy adviser, wrote to Johnson's assistant, Bill Moyers, that the newly elected team was intent on "breaking new ground in the evolution of the Vice Presidency." Kennedy initially tried to give Johnson significant tasks and keep him informed of important issues and events. Johnson was appointed to the chairmanships of the President's Commission on Equal Employment Opportunity and the National Aeronautics and Space Council. He was also invited to staff and cabinet meetings as well as to press conference briefings. His most valuable role was serving as a roving ambassador. Following Johnson's visit to Dakar, for example, a State Department official informed Kennedy, "[The] Vice President's outgoing personality, warmth and sincerity, as well as his faithful attendance at all functions [during a] rigorous program, created [a] most favorable impression and made many friends for [the] U.S."[11]

Beyond surface appearances, however, Kennedy did not utilize Johnson's talents to their fullest potential. Letters and memoranda at the Kennedy Library show few references to Johnson. He remained, for all intents and purposes, a minor player. The president's inattentiveness was sometimes reflected by his aides. Lee White, the administration's liaison on Capitol Hill, admitted that on several occasions he "clean forgot" to inform Johnson of upcoming meetings pertaining to civil rights legislation. During other meetings the vice president failed to receive copies of documents because White had forgotten he would be attending. Staff members sometimes neglected to inform him of schedule changes. In pursuing legislation, the president relied on his own personnel, like Lawrence O'Brien, to whom he felt more comfortable giving orders. Kennedy may have lacked complete trust in Johnson. Some administration officials feared he might reassert his old Senate power in order to embarrass Kennedy in his relations with Congress. Meanwhile, concerned aides of the vice president attempted to involve him more actively in the administration. Liz Carpenter, Lady Bird's secretary, called Charles Bartlett, a journalist and friend of the Kennedys, and asked him to talk to the president about his failure to question the vice president during cabinet and National Security Council meetings. When Bartlett raised the matter, the president felt guilty for not engaging him, but he did not alter his treatment of Johnson.[12]

The working relationship between Kennedy and Johnson was further strained by disagreements over approaches to issues. Kennedy was particularly unimpressed with Johnson's involvement in civil rights matters. As chairperson of the Equal Employment Opportunity Commission, Johnson wanted representatives of large corporations to serve as committee members in an effort to find voluntary solutions to discrimination in the labor sector.

Attorney General Robert Kennedy, however, wanted to enforce existing laws. According to Robert, his brother believed that Johnson was using the commission as "a public relations gimmick." "That man can't run this committee," John confided to Robert. "Can you think of anything more deplorable than him trying to run the United States? That's why he can't ever be President of the United States."[13]

Yet Kennedy gave conflicting signals, wanting Johnson to show greater initiative within the administration. "I know he's unhappy in the vice-presidency," the President told Baker. "It's a horseshit job, the worst fucking job I can imagine." He acknowledged that there was little for him to do, but he was particularly disturbed by Johnson's lack of contributions and cautiousness during meetings. Kennedy appreciated that Johnson intended his silence as loyalty, but the president genuinely wanted his input and thought he would "feel better" if he spoke his mind. In short, he wanted Baker to tell Johnson "how much I truly appreciate him as vice-president. Convey to him I know he's got a tough role and that I'm sympathetic."[14]

Socially, Kennedy was similarly ambivalent in his treatment of Johnson. The president was often careful to include Johnson in White House functions and made it a point to mention him during remarks before gathered groups. Johnson's birthdays presented occasions for Kennedy to express his appreciation. "I must say that the reports of your activity in Lebanon and Teheran show absolutely no sign of old age," Kennedy wired to Johnson when he was in the Middle East. "Please don't wear out your staff of junior New Frontiersmen." On other occasions President Kennedy could be insensitive. Before intimate White House parties, the Chief of White House Protocol, Angier Biddle Duke, was forced to call Kennedy aides to remind them to invite Johnson. "Nobody was terribly interested in him," he recalled. On one occasion, Johnson complained to Kennedy's secretary, Evelyn Lincoln, that his name was not on the guest list for a White House dinner. "Tell him that you have checked," Kennedy instructed Lincoln, "and you found there was no mistake." Kennedy essentially admitted that Johnson was a peripheral concern when he asked Duke to devote special attention to pleasing the vice president and Lady Bird. "I want you to watch over them," he instructed, "and see that they're not ignored. . . . Because I'm going to forget. My staff is going to forget. We're all going to forget. We've got too much to do around here. . . ."[15]

Kennedy staff members more blatantly insulted Johnson. Behind his back, some referred to him as "Uncle Cornpone." Of particular amusement were his social *faux pas:* At an unveiling at the National Gallery, Johnson wore white tie and tails when everyone else wore black tie; he bellowed a Texas holler inside the Taj Mahal to test its echo; West German Chancellor Konrad

Adenauer was pitied for having to spend a weekend at Johnson's Texas ranch. Kennedy's social secretaries made cautious plans to exclude the Johnsons from the official photograph during state dinners because the couple detracted from the aura of the other heads of state. "I think there was some contempt on their part," Johnson confidant Harry McPherson recalled. "Contempt because he was a Southern 'pol,' not a swinger, nobody that you would invite to get thrown in the Hickory Hill swimming pool or to go to a fashionable party in New York."[16]

By 1963 John Kennedy had grown tired of placating Johnson. According to Robert, John became "rather irritated" because Johnson opposed various pieces of legislation or foreign policy decisions "but did not come up with alternative solutions." Fatigued by his frequent complaints, Kennedy would stage conversations to make Johnson feel as if his grievances were being addressed. "I don't know what to do with Lyndon," he told columnist Arthur Krock. "I've got to keep him happy somehow. My big job is to keep Lyndon happy." By 1963, Robert Kennedy recalled, the president and Johnson had reached "a difficult time in the relationship. . . ." He privately referred to Johnson as "Landslide," a disparaging reference to his narrow margin of victory in the 1948 Senate election. In May, Ben Bradlee noted in his diary that "LBJ's simple presence seems to bug [Kennedy]. It's not very noble to watch, and yet there it is." The night before his death, the president complained to Jacqueline that his vice president was "incapable of telling the truth."[17]

In general, Kennedy's response to Johnson was often contradictory. He claimed that he wanted Johnson's active participation in meetings but he also acknowledged that the vice president was easily forgettable. He was disturbed that Johnson offered criticism without suggesting alternatives but expressed sympathy for the inherent limitations of Johnson's office. Given the intensity of Johnson's insecurity, the task of soothing Johnson's concerns may have been beyond Kennedy's capabilities.

Regardless of John Kennedy's treatment of him, Lyndon Johnson can also be faulted for his detachment from the administration. As vice president, Johnson was largely disinterested in Senate affairs, showing little inclination actively to pursue Kennedy's domestic agenda. In the past he had been reluctant to become heavily involved in policy debates if he could not lead the discussion. As a novice congressman he often appeared bored during meetings. Years went by when he was not even listed in the House record. In the White House he grew similarly despondent. "I got the sense of an increasingly frustrated and gloomy man," Schlesinger recalled, "so his presence became almost spectral by 1963." During meetings with legislative leaders or Kennedy aides, he would offer advice when it was solicited, but even then he seemed disinterested. Kennedy himself took notice. One month before his death, he confided to Bradlee: "The steam really went out of Lyndon, didn't it, when they wouldn't let him into the party caucus?" Although Johnson ventured overseas on eleven occasions and traveled throughout the country on the president's behalf, he had to be heavily prodded and stroked by Kennedy.[18]

Aware of his minimal role within the administration, Johnson sometimes deluded himself about the nature of his involvement. He contended that his reticence during meetings was actually an act of loyalty, for Kennedy staff members were looking for an excuse to disparage him. "You don't know how they treat me over there," he explained to Bobby Baker. "Oh sure, Jack Kennedy's as thoughtful and considerate of me at those meetings as he can be. But I know his snot-nosed brother's after my ass, and all those high-falutin's Harvards, and if I give 'em enough rope they'll hang me with it." He feared that the aides would leak to the press that he was "a damned traitor" if he spoke out against administration policy. On other occasions Johnson exaggerated his participation. Once, Kennedy told reporters that the vice president had been part of every major decision in the administration except the Bay of Pigs invasion, attempting to save him from the embarrassment of being associated with the fiasco. Johnson, however, became "strangely upset" by Kennedy's remark and worked to convince journalists that he *had* been involved in the flawed decision.[19]

Consistent with his erratic mood swings, Johnson could sometimes become enthusiastic about his authentic role in the administration. He insisted on his own that, as head of the Space Council, he participate in a parade in New York City honoring the astronauts. Once, Theodore Sorensen called him asking for advice in securing the passage of a civil rights bill. Johnson was verbose, and his transcribed observations totaled twenty-seven pages. He occasionally enjoyed his trips overseas. As in his early Texas barnstorming days, large crowds and public attention energized him. His most satisfying trip came in August 1961 when Kennedy sent him to West Berlin as an important symbol of America's determination to maintain the city's freedom. "Lyndon loved it," reporter Jack Bell recalled. "This was the first real thing that Kennedy had given him, really the first big show."[20]

Johnson tried to fit in socially as well. Although he felt snubbed during White House social functions and never could understand "all the fuss and excitement" about Kennedy's cultural impact on Washington, he sought to involve himself in the social activities of the capital, buying an expensive mansion in which Liz Carpenter arranged elaborate parties. Johnson also changed his eating habits as well as those of his staff to reflect the tastes of the New Frontiersmen. He insisted that his aides eat salads garnished with only three shrimp, as Robert McNamara ate his, and, having read that the president enjoyed eating soup, he stocked the vice-presidential plane with canned soups despite his general distaste for the product.[21]

Johnson was unhappy in his role, but he demonstrated remarkable restraint. Like his apprenticeships in the past, his relationship with Kennedy was marked by loyalty and subservience. "I do not know of any reporter," Tom Wicker recalled, "who got a 'leak' from Johnson that damaged or denigrated the President." In public he was careful to show deference by walking several steps behind Kennedy. When a small public controversy erupted over a speech that Johnson gave at the United Nations, he was quick to send a message to Kennedy. "I'm sincere," he told Duke. "I would like to be part of his team and to play on the team. If he thinks I'm out playing for myself, carving out areas of foreign policy, it's not so. How can I get through to him?"[22]

Even in private, Johnson was similarly loyal. Jack Valenti recalled that a guest at the Johnson Ranch once became "vitriolic" about President Kennedy. Johnson "damn near ordered him out of the house" and forbade any negative statements about the president in his presence. Sometimes his frustrations could not be fully concealed. But his criticisms were reserved for those within his inner circle and were neither public nor directed personally against the president.[23]

In his surviving letters to Kennedy, Johnson expressed affection and adulation. After Kennedy sent him a birthday message, Johnson replied in a letter than he had been "feeling sorry for myself" until he received the message. "That was the best thing that happened all day." "I am constantly amazed, amid all you have to do," he wrote on another occasion, "that you never overlook the extra kindness." For Christmas in 1961 Kennedy gave him a copy of his ghost-written book *To Turn the Tide* and a cigarette box. Johnson's handwritten thank-you letter called the gifts "cherished treasures" which he promised to pass down to his daughters and grandchildren. Reflecting on his "long, long thoughts" about the past year, he noted that it was "one of peaks and depths for us." "Never was I prouder," he recalled, "than the day last January 20 when I sat on the platform and heard my President rally his countrymen 'to begin now.'" He expressed empathy for Kennedy in the "lonely battle" of maintaining global peace but assured him, "you are not alone in it." "We have friends here and around the world who have thrilled to your leadership," he wrote, and he praised the effectiveness of his courageous actions. He closed with a ringing proclamation of loyalty. "Where you lead—I will follow." The letter prompted a Kennedy staff member to inquire whether Johnson's name should now be included on a guest list for an upcoming luncheon. In general, however, Kennedy was uncomfortable with Johnson's reverential tone.[24]

Unaware of Kennedy's discomfort, Johnson persisted in conveying his devotion, sometimes communicating through a third party. When Kennedy faced a difficult civil rights matter in Mississippi, Johnson had Secretary of State Dean Rusk convey a message to the president through Kennedy's appointments secretary, Ralph Dungan. Johnson appreciated John and Robert Kennedy's efforts to seek his advice on the matter and "felt that he had been treated better than any other Vice President and knew it." He was therefore "distressed" by press reports suggesting that he was dissatisfied with the president's handling of the situation. "Obviously," wrote Dungan, "the Vice President was using the Secretary in order to get a message to you."[25]

There was, however, a sad desperation in Johnson's desire to win the president's approval. During photograph sessions with the National Security Council, the Chief of White House Protocol noticed that Johnson "would always hang in the back as if he was unwanted." Duke would call for the vice president to come forward, which in turn prompted the president to look about and ask, "Where's Lyndon? Where's Lyndon?" "Johnson liked that," Duke recalled, "and he'd come up front."[26]

Although friendly toward Kennedy, Johnson never felt emotionally close to him. According to Baker, he wanted desperately to relax with the president late at night over a few drinks and talk politics, but he was never invited to share such intimate moments. He was also unable to broach emotionally sensitive topics. When Eunice Kennedy held a benefit to raise funds for mental retardation, the occasion was particularly poignant because John Kennedy's sister, Rosemary, was mentally handicapped. Reaching out, Johnson wrote that the event served as "a reminder of many personal pangs of family sorrow." He praised the Kennedy family for having "translated its sorrow into making life better for a great many retarded children." The discussion of such a personal issue, however, disturbed him. A note at the bottom read, "Liz [Carpenter] says that Mr. Johnson 'felt funny' about doing this and has decided to have Mrs. Johnson write the letter and send it over her signature."[27]

Reflecting upon his vice presidency, Johnson remembered that he "detested every minute of it." The vacuous nature of the office and its ceremonial trivialities paralyzed him. "[Y]ou sit there like a bump on a log," he recalled, "trying not to get in the way." Kennedy was keenly aware of the source of Johnson's unhappiness. "Lyndon's an activist if ever one was born," he noted privately, "and he's simply a miserable son-of-a-bitch in that office." Johnson was so distressed that he spoke of withdrawing from the ticket in time to return to the Senate in 1964, or perhaps to publish a newspaper. "You don't really have any idea," he explained to Bobby Baker, "how unhappy I am now."[28]

Outwardly, Johnson's depression was acute. He spent night hours lying in bed, staring at the ceiling. Despite his heart condition, he gained weight and drank heavily. He tried playing golf, but he lacked enthusiasm. He once dreamed of being confined to a few yards of space in the Executive Office Building far from the White House's West Wing. As he worked his way through a stack of mail, he saw from his window people hurrying home from work. "I started to get up from my chair," Johnson told Doris Kearns, "but I couldn't move. I looked down at my legs and saw they were manacled to the chair with a heavy chain. I tried to break the chain, but I couldn't. I tried again and failed again. Once more and I gave up; I reached for a second stack of mail. I placed it directly in front of me, and got back to work."[29]

Whether Johnson's dreams were real or embellished to capture Kearns's sympathy is impossible to determine. It is significant, nonetheless, that he referred to his vice presidency as he had his teenage years at home. Both situations were marked by feelings of powerlessness and entrapment. And from both environments he removed himself. As a teenager he went to California. As vice president he withdrew into himself. "It was a nightmare," recalled George Reedy, referring to Johnson's waking hours, "—a time in which he wallowed in self-pity, emotional binges, and suspicion to the point of paranoia."[30]

Johnson and Kennedy staffers recalled that the relationship between the two men was outwardly amiable and considerate. John Kennedy's weariness with Johnson remained relatively well concealed and was not carried into the political arena. Kennedy was sometimes curious what others thought of Johnson's presidential potential for 1968. But he reacted adversely to suggestions that he be removed from the 1964 ticket. Boasting of his own youth and high approval ratings, he had good reason to believe that he would be re-elected in 1964 and complete eight years in office. Political decisions for 1968 could wait. Meanwhile, his personal discomfort about Johnson was reserved for a select group of aides and friends, leaving the vice president to believe that their partnership was healthy and intact. For his part, Johnson forever maintained that "Jack Kennedy always treated me fairly and considerately." Approaching the relationship with his own set of contradictions, he felt neglected and useless as vice president, yet he consistently praised Kennedy for his kind and generous treatment toward him.[31]

Except for his political value in attracting Southern votes in the next election, Johnson was largely irrelevant to the aims of the New Frontier. By the spring of 1963 he seemed lost in its glamour, youth, and excitement. *Time* devoted a special article to "What Happened to LBJ," taunting him for his loss of stature. Coming out of seclusion, Johnson gave a special television interview during which he defended his role in the administration. He blamed reporters for raising the question about his obscure role in the Kennedy administration and thought it was "cruel and inhuman" for them to do so. He denied he was unhappy and asserted that he had a challenging job. Kennedy and his staff kept him briefed, he participated in policy discussions, and his advice was "considered." "From a personal standpoint," he concluded, "I am very happy. I have everything a man could want. I have a fine relationship with the people with whom I work. I have a lovely family. I enjoy my work. I left my desk after 9 o'clock last night."[32]

The Nemesis

Nowhere did Johnson's depression and frustration express themselves more completely than in his relationship with Robert Kennedy. "He didn't blame [his misery] on Jack," Reedy recalled, "he blamed it on Bobby." During the 1960 convention he had divided "Kennedy" into two distinct entities—the "good" John and the "bad" Bobby. Ignoring evidence to the contrary, he chose to believe that John had sincerely wanted him on the ticket whereas Robert had acted independently to remove him. By "splitting" the Kennedy brothers, Johnson made the Kennedy force less powerful and more manageable. He focused his frustrations away from the president, to whom he needed to show loyalty, and projected them onto a surrogate. Robert became a convenient scapegoat, allowing Johnson to relieve his internal stress with minimal risk to his career.[33]

Johnson's disdain for Robert Kennedy was mutual. During an oral history interview conducted in 1964, Robert characterized Johnson as "mean, bitter, vicious—an animal in many ways." His hostility toward the vice president was painfully obvious throughout the Kennedy administration. Observing the conflicts between the two men over civil rights issues, for example, Lee White, a legislative liaison, sensed that Robert was "tougher with Johnson than he needed to be or should have been." His "brusqueness or abruptness or roughness" was particularly disturbing to "a sensitive soul like Johnson." Making light of Kennedy's animosity, aides reportedly gave him a voodoo doll made in Johnson's likeness in the fall of 1963. Two years later, after the birth of one of Robert's sons, his sister, Eunice, mockingly suggested that he name the child Lyndon Kennedy.[34]

61

Aware of Robert's animosity toward him, Johnson grew uncomfortable with the attorney general's working relationship with the president. "Every time they have a conference," he explained to an aide, "don't kid anybody about who is the top adviser. It isn't McNamara, the chiefs of staff, or anybody else like that. Bobby is first in, last out. And Bobby is the boy he listens to." In October 1963, during a conversation with three reporters from the *New York Post,* Johnson likened Robert's and John's relationship to that of the Diem brothers in South Vietnam. Journalist James Wechsler was startled by the comparison between two presidents with "a very strong brother." "The inescapable overtone," he recalled, "was that . . . Bobby Kennedy was running things, and in view of the Vietnam analogy . . . [it] seemed to be an extremely bitter thrust." Believing that Robert had undue influence and disliked him, Johnson was convinced that the "runt" determined to complete the task he had initiated in Los Angeles, replacing him as the heir presumptive to the Kennedy legacy. Johnson's loyalty and service to John would be rebuked by the ambitions of the "flesh and blood" successor.[35]

Johnson's concern about Robert was so prevalent, and his behavior so peculiar, that those closest to him thought he was "paranoid." He was convinced that Robert not only poisoned the president's opinions against him but also the judgments of reporters; together they were engineering his removal from the 1964 ticket. According to Reedy, this possibility became "an obsession with [Johnson]—a conviction that peopled the world with agents of the President's brother all seeking to do him in." When the Justice Department investigated the business transactions of Texas oilman Billy Sol Estes, Johnson sought to conceal his nebulous relationship with the man. By doing so, he increased suspicions of wrongdoing. "His reasoning was simple," Reedy recalled. "The whole thing existed as a Bobby Kennedy plot and to talk about it to the press was to help Bobby Kennedy." Johnson fervently resisted world tours, suspecting that Robert was conspiring with the press to set him up for political embarrassment. When the president sent his sister, Jean Kennedy Smith, and her husband, Steve, as Johnson's traveling companions, Johnson suspected the brother-in-law was a "spy" for Robert.[36]

Johnson's suspicions culminated in the summer of 1963 when his former protégé, Bobby Baker, was investigated by the attorney general for influence peddling. Johnson believed that Robert was leaking information to the press about the case. Soon it was learned that while in Congress Johnson had accepted a "hi-fi" stereo set from one of Baker's associates, and the same man had been compelled to buy advertisements on Johnson's television and radio stations in Austin. As other, more serious allegations against Baker surfaced, the former secretary to the Majority Leader sensed that Johnson was "petrified that he'd be dragged down." Johnson subsequently distanced himself from Baker and deluded himself into believing that he hardly knew him. He further imagined that Robert Kennedy conducted secret daily press briefings on the scandal. Reedy was prompted to launch a personal investigation, but when he informed Johnson that he found no evidence of any covert briefings, Johnson simply dismissed him as "naive." He then sought to prove the existence of collusion by attempting to trap reporters into confessing. Talking to them about unrelated matters, he would suddenly confront them with his "knowledge" of the briefings. The ploy, Reedy recalled, led some reporters to speculate "as to his mental stability."[37]

The Kennedy brothers denied to friends and private interviewers that they sought to use the Baker scandal against Johnson. The idea was illogical. Despite their misgivings about Johnson, they were hardly anxious for a public scandal within the executive branch that would call into question the president's judgment. Indeed, John Kennedy told Ben Bradlee that the idea of replacing Johnson was "preposterous on the face of it. We've got to carry Texas in '64, and maybe Georgia." There would have been virtually no way for Kennedy to remove the vice president without embarrassing himself or alienating large factions of the Democratic party. Moreover, the president was scarcely anxious to dissolve the ticket that had attracted the Southern votes crucial to his 1960 victory.[38]

Nevertheless, Johnson's concern for his political future was not entirely unjustified. He was increasingly subject to rumors surrounding his sordid past. Each one was potentially devastating even if proven false. In June 1961, for example, Henry Marshall, a Department of Agriculture official, was found murdered in a remote section of Johnson's ranch while investigating Estes's financial dealings. A year later, Bradlee mentioned to Kennedy that *Newsweek* was investigating the crime and suspected that the murder was tied to a romantic affair. The president was "all ears" and "urged" Bradlee to talk with the attorney general. The Baker scandal, meanwhile, gained enormous media attention by the fall of 1963. One month before his death, Kennedy speculated about the various investigative findings surrounding the case. The president was well briefed but confident that Johnson had not been "on the take since he was elected." He was less sure, however, if he had been involved in illegal dealings while in the Senate.[39]

Given the precarious nature of Johnson's beginnings with the Kennedy team, his sense of isolation as vice president, John's growing impatience, and Robert's blatant hostility, the innuendo and gossip did little to persuade Johnson that his future was safe. Although Kennedy was well aware of Johnson's sensitivities and insecurities, he never directly assured him that his place within the New Frontier was secure. By the fall of 1963 Johnson reportedly believed that the Kennedy family inner circle had held a secret meeting and decided to drop him from the 1964 ticket. Allegedly, Jacqueline Kennedy was the only dissenting vote.[40]

Trying to preserve his dignity and political future, Johnson sought reconciliation with the person whom he thought might save him from his misery. One night in 1962, after a White House dance, Lyndon Johnson and Robert Kennedy scrambled eggs together in an upstairs kitchen of the executive mansion. "Bobby, you do not like me," Johnson noted candidly. "Your brother likes me. Your sister-in-law likes me. Your Daddy likes me. But *you don't like me*. Now why? Why don't you like me?" According to witnesses, Johnson incessantly badgered Robert with the question, insisting on an answer. Robert never responded, leaving him to guess that their differences were rooted in the events of the 1960 convention. "I know why you don't like me," Johnson surmised. "You think I attacked your father. But I never said that. That report was false . . . I never did attack your father and I wouldn't and I always liked you and admired you. But you're angry with me and you've always been upset with me."[41]

Unable to solicit Robert's acceptance, and perhaps sensing that his rejection reflected John's disappointment with his vice president, Johnson remained isolated from the administration. His "splitting" of John and Robert was near completion. He firmly believed that he and John had formed a lasting partnership, and he reminded reporters and the public that the "last thing President Kennedy said to me" in Dallas was his desire to keep the winning ticket together. "President Kennedy worked so hard at making a place for me, always saying nice things, gave me dignity and standing," he told Helen Thomas in late 1968. "But in the back room they were quoting Bobby, saying I was going to be taken off the ticket." Robert forever remained "the little son-of-a-bitch." Indeed, Johnson was convinced that he wiretapped his telephone during the Kennedy administration and into his own presidency. After November 22, 1963, the "good" Kennedy was gone, and Johnson continued to "go forward together" with his spirit. But the surviving "bad" Kennedy would also claim rights to his brother's memory.[42]

CHAPTER

IV

THE CARETAKER: PRESIDENT JOHNSON AND THE KENNEDY FAMILY

Upon the assassination of John Kennedy on November 22, 1963, Lyndon Johnson became the thirty-sixth president of the United States. Although he had achieved his lifelong ambition, he assumed office not through electoral victory but through the murder of his predecessor, a popular president whose glamour, wit, and style had captivated millions of Americans. Following in the footsteps of a martyred president, he correctly anticipated that much of the public would view him as an interloper. "I took the oath," he told Doris Kearns:

I became President. But for millions of Americans I was still illegitimate, a naked man with no presidential covering, a pretender to the throne, an illegal usurper. And then there was Texas, my home, the home of both the murder and the murder of the murderer. And then there were the bigots and the dividers and the Eastern intellectuals, who were waiting to knock me down before I could even begin to stand up. The whole thing was almost unbearable.[1]

Few experiences evoked Johnson's anxiety more than the deaths of his political mentors. When Franklin Roosevelt died, William S. White found Johnson standing in the corridor of the Capitol building with "tears in his eyes," a "shaking jaw," and "a white cigarette holder" in his hand. "He

65

was just like a daddy to me always," he told the reporter. Sam Rayburn's death in 1961 was also a moving experience, especially occurring in the midst of his unhappy tenure as vice president. "Every death was hard on him," one friend noted. "He was more sober. Death hurts him. . . ."[2]

Older than "Jack," Johnson did not share the son-father relationship with him that he had with Roosevelt and Rayburn. Nor was their relationship as lengthy or as intense. Nevertheless, Kennedy had given him access to power, and their relationship, as far as Johnson was concerned, had grown courteous and respectful. So Kennedy's death prompted customary depression. What's more, Johnson had been traveling just two cars behind the president when he was murdered. As vice president he was among the first to be informed of Kennedy's death. "The greatest shock that I can recall," he noted, "was one of the men saying, 'He's gone.' "[3]

Returning to Washington, Johnson was solemn. Undersecretary of State George Ball met the new president at Andrews Air Force Base and perceived him as "near a state of shock." "He moved erratically," Ball wrote, "and I saw twitches in his face." That evening at his Washington home, when a local television station aired a retrospective of Kennedy's life, Johnson covered his eyes. "Turn it off," he said. "It's all too fresh. I can't watch it." Although he was surrounded by friends, he felt alone. Raising a glass of orange juice to a portrait of Rayburn, he seemed at a loss: "Oh, Mister Sam, I wish you were here now. How I need you." He insisted that his entourage stay at his home that night. Horace Busby recalled sitting in the president's bedroom as he tried to fall asleep. Each time that he thought Johnson had finally drifted off to sleep, Busby started to leave the room. But the president would awaken and summon him back.[4]

Johnson's sadness and fears may have been tinged with guilt. In retrospect he claimed that as vice president he had always been highly conscious of Kennedy's mortality. "Every time I came into John Kennedy's presence," he recalled, "I felt like a god damn raven hovering over his shoulder." He was disturbed by rumors that soon surfaced that he had conspired in the murder. Circumstantial evidence made him suspicious to those who searched for a larger explanation for Kennedy's death: Johnson's unsavory political past; his well-known yearning for power; the widespread gossip that he might be dropped from the 1964 ticket; the disrespect he showed for Kennedy at the 1960 convention; and the location of the murder.[5]

Although Johnson was emotionally burdened, aides and scholars have judged the transition period to be his finest hour. Years of pent-up political energy seemed released by his sudden acquisition of power. He worked immediately with Kennedy's cabinet and advisers to assess foreign and domestic policy matters. In the days surrounding the funeral he conferred with major heads of state. Working sixteen-hour days he reviewed the budget and plotted his strategy to break through the congressional stalemate that had burdened Kennedy's legislative initiatives. By August 1964 his accomplishments included passage of the tax reform bill, a reduced budget, a civil rights bill, the wheat-cotton bill, the wilderness bill, a $375 million bill to improve the nation's mass-transit system, and, finally, Johnson's own $948 million anti-poverty package. Perhaps most important, he projected an image of able leadership which was heralded by the press for conveying stability. Appearing frequently on television during his first months in office, Johnson seemed humble but confident.[6]

After guiding the nation through the transition, Johnson reflected on his actions. "We were like a bunch of cattle caught in the swamp . . . ," he told Kearns. "I knew what had to be done. There is but one way to get the cattle out of the swamp. And that is for the man on the horse to take the lead, to assume command, to provide direction. In the period of confusion after the assassination, I was that man." He refused to be overwhelmed by emotion. He consciously worked to convey control, aware of public scrutiny and the apprehension that some people felt about him. "Any hesitation or wavering, any false step, any sign of self-doubt, could have been disastrous," he wrote. "The nation was in a state of shock and grief. The times cried out for leadership."[7]

The leadership that Johnson offered, however, was linked to the past and tied to Kennedy's incomplete presidency. As an accidental president, Johnson needed to respond to the public's failed expectations and to be mindful of his surrogate role. If he intended to win the Democratic nomination and remain in power, if he wanted to win the public's trust and lessen his image of illegitimacy, his actions and attitudes needed to appear congruous with the perceived intentions of the martyred president. Trying to move the nation forward and secure his own position, he often reached backwards, embracing the image and substance of his predecessor.

A significant part of Johnson's effort to woo public support involved the cultivation of the two most tangible remnants of the past, John Kennedy's brother and his widow. Should they express dissatisfaction with his presidency, Robert and Jacqueline Kennedy had the potential to jeopardize Johnson's leadership and his future ambitions. From the very beginning the new president sensed there would be "real problems" in dealing with surviving Kennedys. In the interest of continuity he sought reconciliation. "[W]hat can I do, I do not want to get into a fight with the family," he told a cabinet member. "The aura of Kennedy is important to us all."[8]

The Widow

Few people reflected John Kennedy's charismatic aura more conspicuously than his widow, Jacqueline. Her beauty, eloquence, and extravagant taste made her the perfect counterpart to her husband's "princely" image. After the assassination she displayed remarkable courage and strength during four days of public mourning. As a popular First Lady and a surviving link to the martyred president, she was a powerful symbol of the past and fundamental to Johnson's image of continuity. Johnson was drawn to her both politically and emotionally. With her qualities of femininity, beauty, wealth, intelligence, and culture, she often evoked his sentimentality and softer qualities.[9]

During his vice presidency Johnson had seemed genuinely fond of Jacqueline. Like many people in Washington, he was impressed with her charm and poise and shared satisfaction in her success. "You continue to get good press," he wrote after a public appearance in 1962, "and I'm always glad to be there to see it happen!" He sent with his letter some press clippings and a pun noting that her speech before the Rural Electrification Administration had "electrified" America. Once, Johnson received a piece of mail addressed, "The Vice-President & Mrs. Kennedy." The error amused him, and he kept the envelope in order to humor others. No matter how minor the chore, the vice president went out of his way to assist the First Lady. During her renovation of the White House, she asked him to help retrieve a chandelier that had been a part of the original mansion. One of them hung in the vice president's office in the Capitol building. Johnson cheerfully returned it to the White House.[10]

Johnson's demeanor toward women was in marked contrast to his behavior toward men. In the company of women he was gracious, warm, vulnerable, and charming. So Kennedy women in general were more attracted to him than Kennedy men. During his vice presidency, for example, Johnson developed a close relationship with President Kennedy's younger sister Jean, traveling with her during his trip to India in 1962. They exchanged numerous casual letters in which she referred to herself as "Baby Sister," and Johnson responded in kind. President Kennedy's wife, sisters, and sisters-in-law "were fairly sympathetic with Johnson for a long time," Harry McPherson recalled. "[W]omen *qua* women find him an attractive man. And I think that sustained him with the Kennedy women for some time."[11]

Like many women, Jacqueline found Johnson charming and recalled being impressed with his "expansive personality." At White House parties she made it a point to dance with him and recalled that he was "very gallant, courtly." The day after her husband's funeral she wrote him a

68

hcartfclt letter which fondly recalled their relationship. "[M]ost of all, Mr. President," she wrote, "thank you for the way you have always treated me . . . before, when Jack was alive, and now as President." She remembered the lack of "strain" in the relationships between the presidential and vice-presidential families. She complimented him for his political courage in accepting the vice presidency and for serving as "Jack's right arm." "But more than that," she affectionately wrote, "we were friends, all four of us. All you did for me as a friend and the happy times we had." "You give so much happiness," Johnson responded in a handwritten letter, "you deserve more. We think of you—pray for you and grieve with you. Would say more but you would have to read it and I fear want to answer it—don't."[12]

The qualities associated with Jacqueline Kennedy were similar to those of important women in Johnson's life, especially his own mother, Rebekah, when she was young. Throughout his adult life he seemed to have an affinity for women who were intelligent, cultured, and wealthy. His affections, however, were seldom reciprocated. In high school and in college he was spurned by wealthy women because their parents disapproved of Lyndon's impoverished background. After college he dated Claudia Taylor, the daughter of a successful businessman. Proposing to her on their first date, he married her a short time later. Wealthy, cultured, a graduate of the University of Texas, Lady Bird was typical of the women in Johnson's life.[13]

Some biographers have accused Johnson of courting women of wealth and status in order to further his own political ends. There was, however, one important exception. During the late 1930s and early 1940s, after his marriage to Lady Bird, Johnson had an intense romantic affair with Alice Glass. A young, attractive woman, she was the common-law wife of Charles Marsh, a wealthy but considerably older man who was instrumental to Johnson's career. Johnson's affair with Glass involved enormous political risk, prompting one friend to conclude that it demonstrated Johnson's capacity to love selflessly, to place another person above his own self-interest. Jacqueline Kennedy bore a remarkable resemblance to Glass. They were both wealthy, elegant, intelligent, witty, and independent. They also shared many of the same interests—horseback riding, fox hunting, art, fashion, and architectural design. Both women were also strikingly beautiful. Both were of similar age when they entered Johnson's life. Both were attracted to men of wealth and power. Jacqueline seemed to inspire an element of selflessness in Johnson as well.[14]

Years after the assassination, Johnson remained moved by the widow. "It was a tragic thing to observe Mrs. Kennedy," he recalled. "Here was this delicate, beautiful lady, always elegant, always fastidious, always the fashion plate," now soiled with her husband's blood. As president he did much to comfort her. Aboard Air Force One, Jacqueline had accidentally referred to him as "Lyndon" and quickly apologized, promising not to make the error in protocol again. "Honey," Johnson replied, "I hope you'll call me that for the rest of your life." He rejected Secret Service advice that he immediately occupy the White House, noting it would be "presumptuous" of him to do so. He sent word to Jacqueline that she should take all the time she desired in leaving the White House. He did not move into the presidential mansion until two weeks later.[15]

Although Johnson, like many Americans, had previously been awed by Jacqueline's public image, it was her courage during the crisis that most impressed him. "I have never seen anyone so brave," he noted on the night of the assassination. Four months later he was asked during a television interview to discuss the most memorable event of the Kennedy assassination. He recalled Jacqueline's "greatness, her gallantry, her graciousness, her courage, and it will always be a vivid memory, and I will always appreciate the strength that came to me from knowing her. . . ." According to Pierre Salinger, after the assassination Johnson often became "highly emotional" when reflecting on her generosity during his vice presidency. "She always made me feel at home," he told his press secretary.[16]

Emotionally partial toward the former First Lady, Johnson worked with her to build a lasting tribute to her husband's memory. She had a "terrible fear then that [John Kennedy would] be forgotten," she acknowledged, and asked the new president's help in renaming Cape Canaveral and the space center in Florida in his honor. Johnson met her request immediately, calling the governor of Florida within the hour and arranging for Cape Canaveral to be renamed Cape Kennedy. In late November 1963 he wrote to "Jackie," sending her a copy of the executive order establishing the Kennedy Space Center. "It is clear that once again you have hit with unerring taste on the right thing to do," he wrote, signing his letter, "Love, Lyndon."[17]

On the same day she asked for the renaming of Cape Canaveral, Jacqueline also requested that Johnson approve the Pennsylvania Avenue Renovation Commission which had been initiated by President Kennedy. Her long-time concern for the historic preservation of the White House was also met, and her frequent thank-you notes expressed appreciation for Johnson's help in fostering her husband's memory. "It is so important to me that we build the finest memorial," she wrote, after his donation to the Kennedy Library, "so no one will ever forget him—and I shall always remember that you have helped the cause closest to my heart."[18]

Some fifteen years later, Jacqueline still appreciated Johnson's kindness and generosity. She recalled that Lyndon and Lady Bird "were wonderful to me." "Lyndon Johnson was extraordinary," she remarked. "He did everything he could to be magnanimous, to be kind. It must have been very difficult for him." She was especially touched by his allowing her so much time to leave the White House, much more time, she felt, than was socially acceptable—"a great courtesy to a woman in distress." "The man had incredible warmth . . . ," she concluded. "I was really touched by the generosity of spirit . . . I always felt that about him."[19]

The affection between Jacqueline Kennedy and Johnson was, however, mixed with opportunism on both sides. According to journalist Charles Bartlett, Jacqueline's relationship with Johnson entailed a degree of political gamesmanship. In the weeks after her husband's death she initiated various efforts to ensure that the public would fondly remember the Kennedy presidency. Johnson was part of that process. She told Bartlett that she had "always liked Johnson" and felt he was "very generous." But she also acknowledged that her brother-in-law Robert encouraged her "to put on my widow's weeds and go down to his office and ask for tremendous things . . . and he has come through on everything."[20]

Johnson's response to Jacqueline suggested more than political self-interest. Some actions were highly personal. Jacqueline was touched that he would call her "quite a lot in the beginning." At Christmas his daughter delivered presents for John Jr. and Caroline Kennedy, and he remembered their birthdays with presents and cards. When Jacqueline moved to her own Georgetown home in early February, he attended a housewarming party. "The President came to that," Jacqueline recalled, "completely by surprise. He just went out of his way to do everything like that."[21]

It is difficult, however, to determine where Johnson's compassion for Jacqueline ended and his own self-interest began. He had little choice but to respond to her requests, for he would have appeared callous had he refused her. Furthermore, he had a clear interest in constructing the Kennedy myth. By elevating John Kennedy's memory, he contributed to an emotional environment that, if properly tapped, could inspire public support for pending legislation which awaited passage by Congress.[22]

Johnson's sympathy for Jacqueline never prevented him from understanding her value in smoothing his transition to power. Immediately after the assassination he was intent on identifying himself with her. Aboard Air Force One in Dallas, discussions about camera angles and lenses made the late president's aides fearful that Jacqueline would be a party to the swearing-in ceremony. She was similarly taken aback when she saw fresh clothes laid out for her in the cabin of the plane. Johnson insisted upon waiting for Jacqueline before taking the oath of office. "I want her here," he explained to Judge Sarah Hughes. He grew visibly impatient with her delay but, in the end, obtained a prized photograph. One of the most powerful images of that fateful day was the somber president with his hand on the Bible, flanked by his wife and Jacqueline.[23]

Johnson's political intentions for Jacqueline became increasingly apparent during the transition year. Several weeks after the assassination, he raised with Salinger the possibility of naming her ambassador to France or Mexico. In February the *Washington Post* reported that she was being considered as a Special Adviser on the Arts. Also in February Johnson made his first public appearance with the widow since the funeral. After signing John Kennedy's prized tax reform bill, he went to her Georgetown home, presenting her with the ceremonial pens.[24]

The 1964 campaign provided further opportunities to link himself with Jacqueline. In late September a Johnson aide noted the "tremendous advantages" of using her during the campaign's "final stages": "Mrs. Kennedy's support and expression of her knowledge of the faith and confidence that JFK held for Mr. Johnson can be our homerun ball even if the going doesn't get rough." The suggestion was passed on to Johnson, but Jacqueline was never approached. Two weeks later the president made a surprise but well-publicized visit to her Manhattan apartment. The occasion won him an above-the-fold, front-page photograph in the *New York Times* of himself and Jacqueline smiling outside her apartment building. They did not meet again for two and a half years.[25]

In general, Johnson had difficulty persuading Jacqueline to link herself publicly to his presidency. He invited her to every state dinner at the White House, but she refused. She also declined an invitation to attend a ceremony that dedicated a White House garden in her name. Returning to those familiar surroundings, she explained, would be too painful, but her absence nevertheless fueled press reports that she was distancing herself from the new president. Jacqueline believed that "the press did blow it up an awful lot" but that Johnson understood her reasons. She conceded, however, that she appeared inconsiderate. "I wouldn't blame [the Johnsons] at all," she noted, "if they thought sometimes, 'Listen, couldn't the girl just....'" Indeed, there were occasions when it appeared that she deliberately intended to undercut Johnson. On election day she abstained from voting, later explaining that it was too emotional for her not to be able to vote for her husband. She was aware that her action generated adverse publicity and "hurt" Johnson.[26]

Jacqueline genuinely liked Johnson and was grateful for his generous treatment, but emotional and political boundaries prevented her from returning affection to a man who had replaced her husband as president and who stood in the way of her brother-in-law's future ambitions. Salinger recalled that Johnson was sometimes "bitter" about his inability to woo Jacqueline.

"He couldn't understand, after all his kindnesses to her, why she wouldn't come down." Throughout his life he had expected personal and public gifts to be reciprocated through gratitude and affection. Observed Doris Kearns, who herself was the recipient of Johnson's favors: "It was as if the exchange somehow created a magic bond that linked the recipient to the giver, a bond compounded, in Johnson's mind, of dependence, interest, even love. . . ."[27]

Johnson perceived Jacqueline's behavior as a statement against himself. His generosity was expected to produce dividends, and her rejection re-affirmed his image as an interloper. He nevertheless continued to reach out. During the Christmas following his landslide victory in 1964, he wrote to her: "Time goes by too swiftly, my dear Jackie. But the day never goes by without some tremor of a memory or some edge of a feeling that reminds me of all that you and I went through together." Two weeks later she declined his personal invitation to attend his inauguration, breaking a long-standing tradition where wives of former presidents were in attendance. In later years Johnson continued to grant her generous favors while receiving little in return. Had she been a man, Johnson's personal bitterness and political resentment would likely have manifested itself more actively.[28]

The Brother

After John Kennedy's death, Robert became the head of the family and a recipient of much displaced affection. "You have inherited the leadership as spokesman for the Kennedy family and the Kennedy team," Dean Markham, an old and close football friend from Harvard, wrote Robert a week after the assassination. "It is not a mantle that can be set aside or passed on to another." Robert keenly understood that the initial effectiveness of the Johnson presidency was in part contingent on his approval. "We're impor-tant to Johnson," he told Richard Goodwin. "I'm the most important because my name happens to be Kennedy." He also knew that the sem-blance of unity was going to be difficult. Since the 1960 Democratic convention, the tension between Johnson and him had been relentless and personal. "They were very unalike, anyway," Clark Clifford recalled. "I doubt under the best of circumstances they would have developed much of a friendship." "[T]heir temperaments," Jacqueline Kennedy noted, "were different."[29]

John Kennedy's death altered the context of their rivalry; *President* Johnson was no longer vulnerable to the attorney general's authority. The man who once felt mistreated and threatened by Robert now had significant control over his abuser. But Johnson's authority over Kennedy was limited.

Robert possessed formidable assets that were important, if not indispensable, to the president's ambitions in 1964. Johnson's only attempt to run for national office had ended in humiliation, and Robert had been vital in organizing his brother's victory. Furthermore, Johnson could not afford to alienate the Kennedy faction of the party. If he fired Robert or pressured him to resign, the Kennedy forces might regroup before the August convention and challenge the nomination. Johnson therefore considered it essential that he and Robert at least appear to be on amiable terms.

John Kennedy's death generated no sudden feelings of affection between the two rivals. "He skipped the grades where you learn the rules of life," Johnson remarked. "He never liked me, and that's nothing compared to what I think of him." Robert, meanwhile, viewed Johnson as a usurper and was irritated by the sight of him as president. When he met Air Force One at Andrews Air Force Base after its return from Dallas, he was determined that Johnson would not exploit the occasion. He swiftly boarded the plane, shuffled past the new president without acknowledging him, and proceeded to the cargo section. He and Jacqueline Kennedy then quickly departed from the back of the plane with the casket, preventing Johnson from appearing before television cameras with the widow.[30]

Tensions increased the next day. Several Kennedy cabinet officials advised Johnson that, for the appearance of order and control, he should move into the Oval Office as soon as possible. Johnson was uncomfortable with the suggestion. He spent the first night working out of the vice president's office in the Executive Office Building. Acting as the chief liaison with the Kennedys, national security adviser McGeorge Bundy discussed with Kennedy the symbolic necessity for Johnson to occupy the White House offices. Robert became annoyed but agreed that Monday morning would be an appropriate time. Bundy wrote the president a memorandum detailing the arrangements, but Johnson never saw it.[31]

On Saturday morning Johnson walked into the Oval Office and, according to Kennedy, informed the secretary that she was to "clear your things out of your office by [9:30] so my girls can come in." The incident, according to Robert, was one of "four or five matters" during Johnson's first week in office "which made me bitterer, unhappy at least, with Lyndon Johnson." Consequently, Kennedy was reluctant to attend Johnson's first cabinet meeting scheduled for the Saturday morning after the assassination. "I was rather fed up with him," he recalled, prompting Bundy to again intercede on Johnson's behalf.[32]

Kennedy arrived at the meeting late. According to Agriculture Secretary Orville Freeman, his "countenance was cold and scornful." When he entered, several cabinet officials stood up, but Johnson remained seated. The attorney general's presence immediately shifted attention away from the president, and, as the meeting progressed, an unacknowledged strain became apparent. Kennedy grew bitter over pledges of support to Johnson. "What he wanted," Kennedy recalled, "is declarations of loyalty, fidelity from all of us." Johnson, meanwhile, was convinced that Robert was intentionally late in order to destroy the meeting's mood. "There was real bitterness in Lyndon's voice on this one," wrote one official.[33]

During the next few days Johnson and Kennedy continued to bicker. Johnson wanted to make a plea for unity through a nationally televised address before Congress on Tuesday. John Kennedy's burial was set for Monday. Robert disapproved. "I thought we should just wait one day," he recalled, "—at least one day after the funeral." Bundy argued on Johnson's behalf, much to Robert's irritation. "Why do you ask me about it?" he snapped at Bundy. Johnson delivered the address on Wednesday.[34]

Johnson pursued a variety of strategies to win Robert's favor. In late November he tried to explain the incidents aboard Air Force One and to clarify his move into the Oval Office. "People around you are saying things about me," Johnson told him. "You can't let your people talk about me and I won't talk about you and I need you more [than your brother did]." Robert gave the president little encouragement, prompting him to rely on Kennedy's aides as a conduit. Kennedy heard from them that Johnson "thought I hated him, and what he could do to get me to like him, and why did I dislike him . . . and whether he should have me over for a drink or have some conversation with me." The president later sent a message through Arthur Schlesinger: "[I]n effect, that President Johnson loves you, wants to be friends with you, that the door at the White House is always open to you." "Your brother would have been very proud of the strength you have shown," Johnson wrote Kennedy on New Year's Day. "As the New Year begins, I resolve to do my best to fulfill his trust in me. I will need your counsel and support."[35]

Kennedy remained with the administration due less to Johnson's pleas than his own political sagacity. Markham had warned that, if he resigned, his decision could "boomerang": "Public sentiment will be on his side, and the feeling will be that he tried to cooperate and work with you, but you didn't want to." Kennedy might have resigned in such a fashion as to gain public understanding. He could have cited overwhelming grief and his inability to transfer loyalties. Instead he remained despite his displeasure, viewing himself as a link between his brother's legacy and Johnson's policies. The emotional difficulty of the task, however, heightened ill feelings. It was, Robert recalled, a "difficult time between the two of us." Johnson was "able to eat people up," and a working relationship with him remained "difficult unless you want to 'kiss his behind' all the time." He was particularly irked by perceived slights to his dead brother and contended that the new president was not properly attributing his legislative achievements to John's earlier efforts.[36]

Johnson's aides were keenly aware of Kennedy's restlessness. Eric Goldman observed that Kennedy "walked through the White House halls, his manner nervous, staring straight ahead, so indrawn he sometimes neglected to say hello to men he knew well." His emotional strain was punctuated by angry outbursts. Disturbed by newspaper reports about his unhappy relationship with Johnson, he verbally accosted Jack Valenti: "I don't appreciate the leaks coming from the White House and from you. I suggest you cut it out." Valenti was "stunned" by the accusation.[37]

Johnson's patience with Kennedy was limited. Once, Kennedy complained that his brother would have handled a particular situation differently. "President Kennedy is no longer President," Johnson tersely reminded him. He further alienated Robert through an imprudent conversation with Pierre Salinger. Discussing Texas folklore, he noted the myth that cross-eyed people in general were punished by God for being bad. Elaborating on the notion of "divine retribution," he then expounded that John Kennedy may have been murdered in connection with his involvement in the Trujillo and Diem assassinations. Salinger relayed the conversation to Kennedy. According to Schlesinger, the remark "made the gulf [between Johnson and Kennedy] ultimately impassable...."[38]

Throughout the winter and spring of 1964 Johnson was successful in maintaining a public semblance of a united front. But his callous slip-ups showed that the task of deferring to Robert was personally troublesome. The "aura of Kennedy" was important to Johnson, but it could not compensate for his deep-seated hostility toward the man who had tried to dump him from the 1960 presidential ticket. In aligning himself with the "heir apparent," Johnson did more than merely place himself in a personal bind. Politically he was in the process of creating a dilemma which he would find increasingly difficult to remedy. By linking himself to Robert and thus paying homage to John Kennedy's memory, Johnson inadvertently contributed to a legacy that would ultimately serve Robert's interests more than his own. Lyndon Johnson was slowly becoming wedged between two Kennedys—one a reminder of an illusory past, the other promising the fulfillment of a mythical future.

The "Bobby Problem"

The 1964 election offered Johnson a chance to establish independence from the "aura of Kennedy." "To achieve greatness," Stewart Alsop wrote in January 1964, "Johnson must first achieve election in his own right." If he could be elected without the aid of the Kennedys, his power would hinge less on the memories of his predecessor and more on his own distinct leadership. As the August Democratic convention neared, Robert Kennedy's future role in the administration became the subject of considerable speculation. Those who hoped for a Kennedy restoration looked toward Johnson to choose the attorney general as his running mate. Johnson's aides knew it would never happen. "I don't want to get elected because of the Kennedys," the president explained privately. "I want to get elected on my own. That's a perfectly normal feeling, isn't it?" Normal or not, his desire for legitimacy created a problem. He needed to move forward toward independence without alienating those who yearned to restore the past.[39]

Johnson's dilemma was in part contingent on Robert Kennedy. Did he expect to be offered the vice presidency? Would he accept it? If he were not asked, would he try to prevent Johnson's nomination? Kennedy was becoming increasingly restless. In January he told reporters that he was committed to the administration only until the November election. In March he announced that he would resign before the next inauguration. Stories soon circulated about the formation of a "government-in-exile" composed of former New Frontiersmen. Its purpose was to complain about the unfairness of an abbreviated Kennedy presidency and to plan for remedying the situation. Stories of an impending challenge from Robert Kennedy contributed to Johnson's "razor-edge sensitivity" about the family. "To him, they were ever present and ever active," Eric Goldman recalled, "pestering everything he tried to do."[40]

Although Johnson had pleaded with Kennedy to remain with the administration, he clearly did not wish Robert to exert real authority. The president did not see or speak with him during the entire month of December 1963. Kennedy rarely attended cabinet meetings, and Johnson seldom solicited his advice. Upon Kennedy's return from the Far East in January, for example, the president gave him only a cursory greeting. Robert withdrew further, believing correctly that Johnson was interested only in his symbolic value.[41]

Johnson, meanwhile, was preoccupied by speculation about Kennedy's political intentions. "Every day, as soon as I opened the papers or turned on the television, there was something about Bobby Kennedy," he recalled. "There was some person or group talking about what a great Vice President he'd make." Some aides thought he was obsessed by the issue, so much so they labeled it the "Bobby Problem." Several Kennedy holdovers encouraged his fears by keeping Robert's plans ambiguous. "The pulling and tugging of the Kennedy partisans," Valenti recalled, "the tiptoeing around the subject that was the staff ballet in the West Wing, the grim, unsettling political climate it was creating, all these pushed and shoved against the daily schedule."[42]

Interested in a spot on the ticket, Kennedy put pressure on Johnson. In February Paul Corbin, a party leader from Buffalo, New York, and a Democratic National Committee staffer, created a well-organized write-in campaign for Kennedy's vice-presidential nomination. The effort was intended to force Johnson's hand by demonstrating popular support for a Johnson-Kennedy ticket during the New Hampshire primary. Whether Corbin acted independently of Kennedy was speculative. At the time, however, many reporters were convinced that Corbin was following Kennedy's direction. Kennedy mildly disavowed Corbin's actions, but it came too late to halt campaign momentum and was not taken seriously by his close associates. "He's much closer now [to actively seeking the vice presidency]," *Newsweek* quoted one Kennedy confidant.[43]

During an interview with the three major networks, Johnson denied being upset with Corbin's activities and considered Kennedy's renunciation "a good one." "I take his word," Johnson said, "that he has done nothing to encourage those efforts, and all of this stuff that you read about is newspaper talk." Privately, however, Johnson was irate. Meeting with Kennedy, he demanded that Corbin leave New Hampshire and resign from the DNC. Kennedy pleaded innocence and assured him of Corbin's upright intentions. "He was loyal to President Kennedy," Robert argued. "He'll be loyal to you." "I know who he's loyal to," Johnson replied. "Get him out of there." Kennedy recalled being taken aback by Johnson's response. It was "a bitter, mean conversation. The meanest tone that I heard anybody take.... I said ... I don't want to have that kind of conversation with you." After the meeting Johnson called Kennedy, informing him that Corbin had been fired from the DNC. "I'll tell you one thing," Kennedy responded to an aide, "this relationship can't last much longer."[44]

The Corbin episode was one of several incidents in which Kennedy was suspected of "floating trial balloons" about his political future. During the month before the convention, Ben Bradlee, the Washington bureau chief for *Newsweek* and a close friend of the late president, spent sixteen hours one day with Robert while he traveled around the country. His subsequent article on July 6 was a virtual advertisement for a Johnson-Kennedy ticket. Bradlee prefaced his interview by noting politically influential people who "argue that the so-called Kennedy cult is part of the new American fabric and electorate," and that Robert was not only qualified for the vice presidency but a logical choice. Kennedy, meanwhile, implied that Johnson had somehow mismanaged his brother's legacy. "I don't want any of that to die," he

told Bradlee. "People are still looking for all that idealism." He acknowledged that he had become a "symbol" of the past and was looking for some
way to "keep all that alive." Kennedy speculated about the advantage to the
party of his presence on the ticket, convincing Bradlee that he was seeking
some means to "satisfy his deep—almost religious—desire" to fulfill the
Kennedy legacy. "Kennedy himself obviously wants the [vice presidency],"
Bradlee concluded, "but not without reservations and not to the exclusion of
other jobs."[45]

Kennedy's activity during the remainder of July generated still more
speculation. During his four-day visit to Poland he was greeted by large,
emotional crowds, receiving wide coverage in the press and reminding the
American people of the late president's popular visits to Europe. In West
Berlin he repeated the famous "Ich bin ein Berliner" declaration that John
had made in 1963. "I am not a candidate for the Vice Presidency," he told
students at Warsaw University, "but if you were in America and could vote
for me, I would be." Kenneth O'Donnell later boasted that Kennedy's
European tour "added to Johnson's anxieties and deepened his suspicions of
Bobby's intentions."[46]

White House aides monitored Kennedy's efforts. After Marguerite Higgins
published a piece noting Horace Busby's opinions on the vice-presidential
nomination, Busby wrote Walter Jenkins to assure that he had not talked to
Higgins and advised that others avoid her. Busby characterized her as "a
No. 1 Bobby fan" who "seemingly has some sources close to us." In late
July a memorandum of unknown origin was sent to Johnson detailing
Kennedy's recent visit to Chicago. Its author had it on good authority that
Mayor Richard Daley favored Kennedy for vice president but would not
push the matter if Johnson did not want him. Johnson was warned that
because of Daley's close personal relationship with Kennedy, they were
likely to be sharing information.[47]

Of special interest to Johnson was Robert's scheduled appearance at the
Atlanta convention. A film tribute to John Kennedy and a speech by Robert
were planned for the first day of the convention, before the nomination of
the vice president. According to Clark Clifford, Johnson was "afraid" that
Robert "might very well stampede the convention and end up being . . . the
vice presidential nominee." The White House therefore gave orders to
Wolper Productions that no pictures of Robert should appear in the film. The
final edited version contained only two obscure images of Robert. Johnson
then met with the convention's arrangements committee and convinced its
members to reschedule the tribute. The film and Robert's tribute were
moved to the end of the convention, the day *after* the vice presidential

nominee would be chosen. Officially the White House explained that Johnson did not wish to begin the convention on such a dark note.[48]

Johnson also tried to alter the vice presidential selection process. In mid-April Senator Scott Lucas of Illinois convinced all nine county Democratic chairmen from his downstate congressional districts to sign a pledge giving Johnson a "free choice" in picking his vice-presidential running mate. Lucas was acting with the knowledge of Johnson's political associate and friend Cliff Carter, who informed the president of the effort. When Carter sent the pledge to other delegates in New Jersey, however, they balked, arguing that a blank check would demean the entire convention process. The ploy was subsequently abandoned.[49]

Johnson discussed with his aides a number of alternative nominees who would satisfy the Kennedy faction of the party without blatantly overshadowing his presidency. He considered nominating a Catholic intellectual for the ticket, such as Minnesota Senator Eugene McCarthy. Kennedy's brother-in-law Sargent Shriver, who was Catholic and currently the director of the War on Poverty, was also discussed. "But in another way," Bill Moyers recalled, "Shriver was not acceptable, and that was *because* he was a member of the family. The message that filtered through from the family was that if you are going to take a Kennedy, it's got to be a *real* Kennedy, which Shriver isn't." Moreover, the choice of Shriver was too obvious a ploy to appease the Kennedys. Johnson would have been making the public concession he was trying to avoid.[50]

By late July Johnson sensed that he was losing control of events when, among other things, Nancy Dickerson filed an alarming story. Dickerson reported for NBC radio a meeting of Kennedy personnel at Hyannis Port and cited "rumors" that Robert and Jacqueline Kennedy had discussed plans to attend the Democratic convention; they anticipated an outpouring of emotion which, they felt, could be harnessed on Robert's behalf to secure the vice presidency. Jacqueline's desire to "help" her brother-in-law upset Johnson. After the broadcast, Lady Bird's press secretary, Liz Carpenter, called Dickerson to obtain a transcript of her report. Upon reading it, Johnson allegedly remarked, "If Nancy says such a thing on the air, then Jackie and Bobby really are behind the build-up."[51]

Marguerite Higgins was one of several journalists who reported that Dickerson's information was responsible for prompting Johnson to make a public statement about Kennedy's vice-presidential chances. In a memorandum to Johnson, Busby heightened the conspiratorial nature of events by alleging that Higgins had been "sold" the story by the Kennedy faction. He had heard through another reporter that she was "the victim of someone trying to foster an image of bad blood between the Johnsons and Mrs.

Kennedy." Busby informed Johnson that "obviously it was in the interest of the Kennedys to cultivate her and they have done so."[52]

In reality, Dickerson's story merely hastened Johnson's decision. Johnson already had numerous objections to nominating Kennedy. Reminiscent of his criticism of John Kennedy four years earlier, he told his aides that a man who might be president should have "a little gray in his hair." Robert neither understood the mechanisms of Congress nor appreciated that the United States was "a big place, with lots of different kinds of people and different thoughts and interests, who are not brought together by playing the game of royal family." A Harris poll revealed that 33 percent of the Southern Democrats would bolt the ticket if Kennedy were chosen. Once the Republicans nominated Barry Goldwater in July, his extremism virtually assured Johnson a victory in November. "Look't here," he told his brother Sam. "I don't need that little runt to win. I can take anybody I damn please."[53]

The real motive behind Johnson's decision was not lost on those involved. Valenti knew that Johnson removed Robert to escape the "looming shadow of the Kennedys" which threatened to "engulf him and probably strangle him." Even Kennedy knew that Johnson's decision rested more on who he was than on whom he would alienate. "Actually," he told *Newsweek,* "I should think I'd be the last man in the world he would want [as vice president] ... because my name is Kennedy, because he wants a Johnson Administration with no Kennedys in it, because we travel different paths...." "I think he's hysterical," Robert added privately, "about how he's going to try to avoid having me."[54]

In later years, after retiring from politics, Johnson discussed with Kearns the decision to "dump" Kennedy. He described powerful feelings that had haunted him at the time but that he never dared to confess publicly. "Somehow it just didn't seem fair," he said:

I'd given three years of loyal service to Jack Kennedy. During all that time I'd willingly stayed in the background; I knew that it was *his* Presidency, not mine. If I disagreed with him, I did it in private, not in public. And then Kennedy was killed and I became the custodian of his will. I became President. But none of this seemed to register with Bobby Kennedy, who acted like *he* was the custodian of the Kennedy dream, some kind of rightful heir to the throne. It just didn't seem fair. I'd waited for my turn. Bobby should've waited for his. But he and the Kennedy people wanted it now. A tidal wave of letters and memos about how great a Vice President Bobby would be swept over me. But no matter what, I simply couldn't let it happen. With Bobby on the ticket, I'd never know if I could be elected on my own.[55]

Johnson's recollection was revealing. There was some hint of political revenge; he was going to do to Robert in 1964 what Robert wanted to do to him at the 1960 convention. More important, he revealed a paradox that plagued his thinking for the next four years. On the one hand, he had to legitimize his power "no matter what." Otherwise he would never know if he was truly worthy without Kennedy. Yet he was binding himself to the past through John by reaffirming his rights to the Kennedy legacy. As the "custodian of [John Kennedy's] will," Johnson implied that he, not Robert, was the dream-keeper and the "rightful heir to the throne."

Determined to put an end to the mounting rumors, Johnson arranged for a "summit" between himself and Kennedy at the White House on July 29. Kennedy met with O'Brien before seeing the president and was fully aware of the meeting's purpose. "He wanted the vice-presidential nomination," O'Brien recalled, "but we both realized there wasn't much chance that he'd get Johnson's support. Johnson didn't need him, and he didn't want him." Johnson, however, was reluctant to break completely with the past.[56]

Before the meeting Clark Clifford prepared for the president a memorandum detailing five points Johnson wanted conveyed to Kennedy about his role in the upcoming campaign. Titled "The President's Campaign Objectives," it sought to mask Johnson's animosity with carefully worded flattery and compensation. The first point noted the president's desire to "win a victory as clear and sweeping as possible, in vindication of the Administration of President Kennedy and President Johnson." Johnson acknowledged that he wanted to justify his own achievements. But a victory was also "the most important service he can give to the memory of the man who put him on the ticket. Everything the President does will be done in the light of this overreaching purpose."

The second point noted that the Democratic party had many people well qualified to serve as vice president, but it was necessary to choose someone in sharp contrast to William Miller, the Republican party's vice-presidential nominee. The third point noted that, though Kennedy was qualified, Goldwater's nomination and the need to appeal to the South eliminated him as a potential nominee. Johnson wanted Kennedy's help nonetheless. Three reasons were offered:

a. Only his help can sustain the full effectiveness of the original Kennedy/Johnson partnership.
b. The Attorney General's support will be decisive with very large numbers of American Catholics, and with the younger people of all faiths too.
c. The Attorney General has an unequaled talent for the management of a campaign.

The fourth point of the memorandum stated that the "best possible means" of achieving these goals was for Kennedy "to be the campaign chairman, and the President would like to draft him for this service." The final point noted that, after the election, Johnson would like Kennedy to "accept a most senior post in the new Administration." Cloaking his rejection of Robert in terms of political expediency and pragmatism, Johnson implied that Kennedy's presence on the 1964 ticket might hinder the achievement of his brother's goals.[57]

In anticipation of the "summit," Johnson had a written text prepared which he then read to Kennedy. There were discrepancies between the information contained in Clifford's memorandum and Johnson's three-and-a-half-page statement. Like the memorandum, the text outlined the political conditions leading to his decision and underscored his reasons for eliminating Kennedy. After much consideration, he had concluded that it was "inadvisable" for Kennedy to be his running mate. The "decisive factor" was Goldwater's nomination and its regional implications. The statement reiterated Johnson's responsibility to the Kennedy legacy: "I have an obligation to lead the Democratic Party to victory in this election and to carry out the program started by President Kennedy and continued by me. I must use the best judgment I have . . . in making decisions of this kind."

Unlike Clifford's memorandum, the prepared statement was vague about Robert's future role in the administration. He was told that he had a "promising future" and reminded that his distinguished name was "associated with the highest ideals in American public service." Johnson hoped that Robert, after the election, would accept "important governmental assignments and missions," or replace Adlai Stevenson as United States Ambassador to the United Nations. Kennedy was also asked obliquely to "help" during the campaign. The text concluded by noting that their mutual honesty about the matter "constitutes the basis upon which you and I can build a lasting relationship that would prove valuable to both of us and to our country."[58]

Johnson had intended his three-and-a-half-page text to be the "official" record of his meeting. Mindful of the occasion's historical implications, he sent a copy to Valenti with a note reading, "Give these to Vicky. They're very important for my memoirs." The differences between the memorandum and subsequent text were subtle but important. Absent from the text was Johnson's request that Kennedy manage his campaign. The offer of "a most senior post in the new Administration" was also missing. Johnson's proposal of the UN ambassadorship was bogus, since the job was generally perfunctory and would have served to distance him from his rival. Sometime between the preparation of the memorandum and the writing of the text, Johnson had become unwilling officially to acknowledge his need for Kennedy.[59]

Kennedy's own account of the meeting depicted Johnson as more conciliatory and deferential. He noted that after Johnson read his statement, they
engaged in a forty-minute conversation. Johnson made compromises and
promises absent from his written statement. According to Kennedy, Johnson
claimed that he "thought that I had high qualifications to be President; that
he wanted to work toward that end." After flattering Kennedy, he assured
him that "if I wished to go around the country and speak he would never be
jealous of me. . . ." Further, he urged Kennedy to continue serving as
attorney general or to assume another post in the administration if he
desired. He lauded Kennedy's staff in the Justice Department and expressed
admiration for the remaining New Frontiersmen. "He said he really could
not count on his own people," Robert recalled. Johnson then asked him to
run his campaign. Kennedy rejected the offer, arguing that he was "reluctant" to serve as both attorney general and as campaign manager. The
remainder of the conversation centered on Johnson's continued efforts to
distance himself from the Bobby Baker scandal which was gaining increasing attention that summer.[60]

Johnson wanted Kennedy's help, but he did not want anyone to know
it. Consequently, he sought to mislead others about the content of
their conversation. After his meeting with Kennedy he lied to Kenneth
O'Donnell, claiming that Robert had asked *him* for the job as campaign
manager. It took greater effort to fool the public. On Johnson's advice,
McGeorge Bundy spoke with Kennedy and suggested that Kennedy leak to
the press that he was pulling out of the race for the vice presidency.
Kennedy angrily opposed the idea, arguing that it would be presumptuous of
him to withdraw his candidacy when he had never declared it. Robert's aides
condemned Bundy as "a Machiavellian turncoat." After Johnson consulted
with his eldest and most experienced aides, Clark Clifford, Abraham Fortas,
and James Rowe, he devised a strategy intended to obscure the fact that the
president had arranged the meeting specifically to remove Kennedy from
contention.[61]

Speaking to reporters on July 30, Johnson said it was "inadvisable" for
cabinet-level officials or those who frequently participated in cabinet meetings to be considered as vice-presidential nominees; their important duties
should not be distracted by politics. The decision eliminated not only the
attorney general but also such less likely candidates as Robert McNamara,
Adlai Stevenson, Dean Rusk, Sargent Shriver, and Orville Freeman. Years
later, Johnson continued to insist that Kennedy was a victim of political
circumstance. Kearns, who was instrumental in preparing his memoirs,
noted that he persisted in reversing the order of events. According to

Johnson, he had first decided to remove the entire cabinet from contention and then summoned Kennedy to explain his reasoning.[62]

Johnson's aides were divided about the effectiveness of the smokescreen. The news media were not fooled. The *New York Times* noted that Johnson and Kennedy had "never been on close terms" and cited party leaders who felt that the decision showed that Johnson wanted to win on his own, "with no hint of having relied upon the Kennedy name to put him into office." *Newsweek* described Johnson's maneuver as a "coldly calculated decision." "It was still a Johnson-Kennedy party until yesterday," one aide told the magazine. "You even had some Kennedy people going along on the basis that if anything happened to Johnson, they'd have a Kennedy as President. Now Johnson has cleared the air."[63]

The public posturing may have appeared contrived, but Johnson was relieved of Kennedy. "Now that damn albatross is off my neck," Johnson told an aide. Goldman recalled that he acted like a man who had "exorcised his devil." His delight became reckless. The day after his announcement, he gloated during a White House lunch with Ed Folliard of the *Washington Post*, Tom Wicker of the *New York Times*, and Douglas Kiker of the *New York Herald-Tribune*. Recounting the "summit," Johnson said he watched Kennedy "like a hawk watching chickens." As he told him that he would not be the nominee, Robert's "face changed, and he started to swallow. He looked sick. His Adam's apple bounded up and down like a yo-yo." Johnson mimicked Kennedy's "funny voice" and re-enacted Kennedy's gulp "like a fat fish."[64]

Johnson's insulting account soon circulated around Washington. Angered by the breach of confidence, Kennedy confronted Johnson, who denied having spoken with *anyone* about their meeting. Kennedy was incredulous, and Johnson vainly promised to check his calendar. "He tells so many lies," Kennedy remarked about a week later, "that he convinces himself after a while he's telling the truth. He just doesn't recognize truth from falsehood." Johnson's lie suggested that the Kennedy albatross had been lightened, not removed.[65]

The Convention

Consistent with Johnson's chronic insecurities, no degree of precaution was adequate in his struggle to deny Robert Kennedy the vice-presidential nomination. Aware of the unpredictability of conventions, he soon worried that his personal elimination of Kennedy did not necessarily guarantee that the delegates would not nominate him against the president's wishes. So

Johnson worked to cement the decision by further orchestrating people and events.[66]

Two Kennedy holdovers, Lawrence O'Brien and Kenneth O'Donnell, had been instrumental in John Kennedy's political campaigns since 1952. Johnson had convinced them to remain with his administration, hoping to use their connections with big-city political leaders during the fall campaign. At the same time he worried that they might engineer Robert's nomination for the vice presidency. Consequently, during the convention Johnson literally isolated the two aides, placing them in a remote motel on the outskirts of Atlantic City. He also used the Federal Bureau of Investigation to monitor Kennedy's activities. Since coming into office Johnson had developed an amiable relationship with FBI Director J. Edgar Hoover, who sent the new president "material" on Robert and replaced an FBI liaison close to the Kennedys with Cartha DeLoach, an old friend of Johnson's. Several weeks before the convention Johnson ordered DeLoach and a team of thirty FBI officials to Atlantic City, ostensibly to collect information about possible civil disruptions. According to William Sullivan, a former director of the FBI, their actual purpose was to gather data useful to the president, "particularly in bottling up Robert Kennedy." DeLoach instructed agents not to disclose the existence of the FBI team to the Secret Service or the attorney general. They eventually sent to the White House forty-four pages of information acquired through the use of informants, wiretaps, and the infiltration of political groups. The amount of material specifically pertaining to Kennedy is unknown.[67]

Also of concern in terms of circumventing Robert Kennedy was the timing of the release of the Warren Commission Report. After the murder of Lee Harvey Oswald, Johnson had issued an executive order creating a special commission headed by Chief Justice Earl Warren to investigate the assassination of John Kennedy. He hoped that the report would quiet rumors that Kennedy had been the victim of a conspiracy. One far-flung theory speculated that Johnson had the president killed in order to prevent the investigation of Bobby Baker. Johnson wanted the commission to issue its report before the Democratic convention. As long as the public entertained the remote possibility that he had somehow engineered the assassination, Robert stood to benefit. McGeorge Bundy met with the commission's chief counsel, who agreed to issue the report about two weeks before the convention. Bundy did not want it published too close to the convention because it would be "bad for President Kennedy's memory, bad for the administration, and confusing to the country." It soon became clear, however, that the commission could not finish its report by the first week in

86

August and thus meet Johnson's needs. He decided to delay its publication until September 24, one month after the convention.[68]

Relatively confident that Robert could not ambush the convention, Johnson next worried that the attorney general's mere appearance there might overshadow his own presence and triumph. On the one hand, Johnson wanted to exploit the emotional power that his relationship with John Kennedy had accorded him. But he also wanted the convention to be a celebration of himself. He therefore undertook the delicate task of paying homage to the Kennedy past while building his own distinct image. He specified that two forty-foot portraits of himself flank the convention platform. He planned for delegates to sing renditions of "Hello Lyndon" to the tune of "Hello Dolly." Initially he insisted that the White House approve all convention speeches. The White House then sought ways to minimize John Kennedy's "presence" without appearing callous. In the weeks preceding the convention, for example, Douglass Cater, a special assistant to the president, expressed alarm that Johnson might be upstaged by the film tribute to President Kennedy. He had previewed the film and considered it "well done" but was disturbed by its closing "tear-jerker" music from the Broadway show *Camelot*. Cater acknowledged that the song was "highly schmaltzy" but nonetheless predicted "the delegates will be left weeping." He had "mixed feelings about its propriety at a convention." "It would be less dramatic but probably less risky to show that film sequence without the music," Cater wrote. "I have a vague unrest about engaging in such an emotional bender just before the Johnson acceptance speech."[69]

To remedy the situation, Cater suggested that Johnson himself consider giving the tribute to John Kennedy. An alternative solution would be to insert a filmed tribute by the president at the end of the Kennedy film and "make it known that you are viewing the proceedings from your convention suite." The possibility of having Johnson himself pay tribute to Kennedy alarmed other aides. "If the President appears for the memorial before accepting the nomination," James Rowe warned, "it will make his speech 'one hell of an anti-climax.'" Later it was decided that Robert Kennedy would give the tribute to his brother. But the potential impact of his appearance demanded caution. The White House resisted pressure from the television networks that they reschedule the event earlier in the week when audience interest would be highest.[70]

Johnson and his staff made additional scheduling adjustments to prevent the tribute from overshadowing the acceptance speech. A lull was created between the Kennedy tribute and Johnson's speech in order to allow the delegates ample opportunity to regain their composure. Plans were arranged so that Robert would speak on behalf of his late brother and introduce the film tribute. Next there would be memorial tributes to Eleanor Roosevelt and Sam Rayburn, followed by Hubert Humphrey's acceptance speech for the vice-presidential nomination. The elapsed time between the Kennedy tribute and Johnson's speech was approximately an hour and a half.[71]

Despite safeguards against Robert Kennedy's nomination, despite efforts to minimize John Kennedy's shadow, and despite enjoying enormous popularity, Johnson remained pessimistic. In a manner similar to his earlier campaign behavior, he threatened to quit rather than face a strong challenger. "If they try to push Bobby Kennedy down my throat for Vice President," he warned, "I'll tell them to nominate him for the *presidency* and leave me out of it." Just days before the convention he told aides that he was going to withdraw his nomination. "Nobody, he said, really wanted him," George Reedy recalled. "The heart and soul of the Democratic Party was with Bobby Kennedy." There was "something terribly convincing" about Johnson's concerns. Reedy pleaded with Johnson to reconsider, raising the threat of a Goldwater victory. "[H]e said that was preferable to four years of internecine warfare between himself and Bobby Kennedy."[72]

Those who best knew Johnson understood what was at the heart of his depression. By rejecting the convention before it could reject him, Johnson sought to protect his self-esteem. "He wasn't just playing games with his intimates," his long-time friend Abraham Fortas recalled. "He was playing games with himself, too." Fortas speculated about Johnson's thought process: "This is not the right thing to do. Maybe I won't do it after all. Maybe something will happen; the convention won't really want me, and even if they do want me, I shouldn't have it, shouldn't do it." Lady Bird Johnson, who had often witnessed her husband's erratic moods, wrote a reassuring letter:

Beloved—
You are as brave a man as Harry Truman—or FDR—or Lincoln. You can go on to find some peace, some achievement amidst all the pain. You have been strong, patient, determined beyond any words of mine to express. I honor you for it. So does most of the country.

To step out now would be *wrong* for your country, and I can see nothing but a lonely wasteland for your future. Your friends would be frozen in embarrassed silence and your enemies jeering.

I am not afraid of *Time* or lies or losing money or defeat.

In the final analysis I can't carry any of the burdens you talked of—so I know it's only *your* choice. But I know you are as brave as any of the thirty-five [previous presidents].

I love you always.
                                                                                      Bird

Lady Bird suspected that her husband was reluctant to run for the presidency because "he knew how hard it was going to be and that it was going to get worse." She could not "describe his feelings and why," but she sensed he was worried "how some of those lowering clouds that were on the horizon might rise up to storm proportions."[73]

Johnson went on to capture the Democratic nomination. Hubert Humphrey was nominated as his vice president, partially appeasing Kennedy supporters. Until the last day of the convention, John Kennedy's "presence" was generally underplayed. A portrait of the late president hung above the podium, along with Truman's and Roosevelt's, and a banner proclaiming "Let Us Continue." Occasionally a speaker in the hall would recall John Kennedy, bringing a roar of approval from the delegates. Outside the convention hall, however, a wellspring of emotion seemed anxious to erupt. Kennedy souvenirs saturated the commercial districts. Memorabilia from the Kennedy Library were displayed on the boardwalk, and a bronze bust of the late president with a flame in front of it was on exhibit in Kennedy Plaza, across the boardwalk from the entrance to the convention hall. All week long, when Robert and Jacqueline Kennedy entered and exited hotels in Atlantic City, they attracted huge and enthusiastic crowds.[74]

The tone of the convention shifted markedly on the night of the Kennedy tribute. Although the attorney general was scheduled to give a two-minute introduction to the film, he was greeted by a sixteen-minute ovation. The meaning of the applause was "for each individual to assess or deduce on his own," Chet Huntley reported for NBC. "And questions arise as [to whether] the ovation is on behalf of the Attorney General himself . . . a living symbol of the late President. . . . Did the convention want him as vice-president?" Regardless, the reception surprised reporters and television audiences alike.[75]

Throughout the ovation Robert smiled and looked teary-eyed. Attired in a familiar black suit and tie which he had worn almost continuously since the assassination, he spoke humbly and tentatively. His speech had been carefully crafted and edited by numerous Kennedy personnel and friendly journalists. On the advice of Theodore Sorensen, he had memorized the speech and now spoke informally and quietly into the microphone. His first mention of John Kennedy brought expected cheers from the delegates. He recalled his brother's dedication to help the mentally ill, the aged, and various minorities. The Cuban missile crisis and Test Ban Treaty were cited as part of John's foreign policy legacy. The Democratic party and the people were praised as the source of his brother's strength. The undertone of the speech made clear that Robert would do his best to fulfill John's dreams. Meanwhile, the delegates should transfer their commitment and energy to

Johnson and Humphrey. Unknown to the audience, Robert had twice deleted from his final text the assertion that "President Kennedy would feel his life was worthwhile . . . if the same effort and support that was given to him is given to President Johnson and Senator Humphrey. . . ." Instead he inserted a quote from *Romeo and Juliet* given to him by Jacqueline.

[W]hen he shall die,
Take him and cut him out in little stars,
And he will make the face of heaven so fine
That all the world will be in love with night,
And pay no worship to the garish sun.

Criticism emerged over the implication of the quote; John Kennedy's presence in the heavens would always be more brilliant than the common appearance of the "garish" Johnson. Kennedy's defenders claimed that it was not intended to disparage Johnson. Only his hypersensitivity, they argued, would allow for such a negative interpretation.[76]

Following Robert's speech, delegates were shown the twenty-minute Kennedy film, *A Thousand Days*. It contained intimate images of John Kennedy plucking a flower and playing with his son. The soundtrack of Richard Burton singing *Camelot* over pictures of Kennedy brought thousands of delegates to tears. The event caused some people to acknowledge Johnson's astuteness in rescheduling it after the vice president was selected.[77]

Johnson did not attend the memorial tribute. Nor did he watch the film. According to his diary entry, he took a nap. Was he afraid to face the emotion of the moment? Aides contended that he simply did not wish to intrude on the occasion. Standing in for her husband, Lady Bird watched the film from the presidential box with Robert and Ethel Kennedy. Johnson came to the box after the film, inspiring the crowd to sing another rendition of "Hello Lyndon." Robert and his wife tried moving toward the rear of the box. Johnson motioned them forward where they sat uncomfortably together in the front row. Sitting restlessly, Johnson watched the succeeding ceremonies and prepared for his acceptance speech—an address upstaged by John Kennedy's memory.[78]

Johnson's speech had been crafted to balance homage to John Kennedy with his own identity. Aides had suggested that he mention his predecessor and possibly quote the late president. One suggested that he emphasize a "highly desirable" theme of sacrifice that underscored Kennedy's inaugural address. So Johnson called for the nation to "rededicate ourselves to keeping burning the golden torch of promise which John Fitzgerald Kennedy set aflame." Invoking Kennedy's name six times, he asked the nation not to rest "until we have written into law of the land all the suggestions that made up the John Fitzgerald Kennedy program. And then let us continue to supplement that program with the kinds of laws that he would have us write." As he strained to assert his independence, he found himself looking backwards.[79]

V

MANAGING THE WHITE HOUSE: JOHNSON AND THE NEW FRONTIERSMEN

Lyndon Johnson's appeal to the Kennedy family extended beyond blood relations. It also included the White House staff. One of his first priorities upon assuming office was to convince the most prominent Kennedy aides to remain with the Johnson administration. The effectiveness of the transition depended in part on their willingness to work for him. Johnson's decision was controversial and unpopular among some of his long-time advisers, who questioned whether the New Frontiersmen could effectively transfer their loyalties. The Kennedy team had been exceedingly loyal to the late president. Indeed, twenty-two years after the assassination, McGeorge Bundy contended that "no one in the twentieth century aroused more loyalty and devotion" than John Kennedy. Their capacity to work for Johnson, a man so different in background and temperament, was naturally limited.[1]

John Kennedy's aides were important symbolically in Johnson's effort to convey continuity. Members of the cabinet and the White House staff reflected the late president's Ivy League, Northeastern style, representing the "new generation" of postwar Americans to whom the "torch" had been passed. While working for Kennedy, aides such as Robert McNamara, McGeorge Bundy, Theodore Sorensen, and Pierre Salinger had emerged as well-known public figures in their own right. In part, Johnson asked them to remain in order to reassure the public. "I simply couldn't let the country think that I was all alone," he explained to Doris Kearns. He sought to unite those forces that had garnered Kennedy strength and prestige: the "Irish Mafia," the Harvard professors, the cabinet, and White House technicians. "I needed that White House staff," he recalled. "Without them I would have lost my link to John Kennedy, and without that I would have had absolutely no chance of gaining the support of the media or the Easterners or the intellectuals. And without that support I would have had absolutely no chance of governing the country."[2]

Lacking complete confidence in his own personnel, Johnson respected the talent and intellect of the Kennedy team. While he quietly developed his own team of advisers, he relied on the experience of aides who were familiar with Kennedy's agencies, departments, and programs. He was also constrained politically. Unlike Harry Truman, who replaced many of Roosevelt's staff during his first six months in office, Johnson did not have three years in which to assert his independence. With the Democratic convention only nine months away (and having never been tested independently before the national electorate), any attempt to dismiss the Kennedy team or to encourage a mass exodus might split the Democratic party and hamper his chances of being nominated.[3]

Johnson's willingness to defer to the Kennedy staff suggested the seriousness with which he regarded the situation. Harry McPherson praised his ability to "bite the bullet . . . to do the tough thing; to swallow his own sensitivities, his own pride . . . and to risk a lot for the sake of larger goals." Before the first cabinet meeting he wanted to avoid any sign of overassertiveness. "Suddenly *they* were outsiders," he recalled, "just as I had been for almost three years, outsiders on the inside." The meeting was attended by all the members of Kennedy's cabinet, including Robert Kennedy, and by John Kennedy's Special Counsel, Theodore Sorensen, and his press secretary, Pierre Salinger. Johnson's prepared remarks emphasized the gravity of the occasion. He noted that he, like President Kennedy, had confidence in them, and he reminded them of his availability to them and the need for honesty. "The death of a GREAT leader like President Kennedy magnifies the anxiety of the nation," read his prepared notes. "With your help, the transition from President to President will go forward with dispatch. . . . I want you all to stay on. I need you."[4]

During the next few weeks Johnson used numerous tactics in order to win their favor. One by one, he told each staff member that he needed his help. He was careful not to imply that he was even remotely enthusiastic about or comfortable with his rise to power. He assured them that he would bring into his administration only four or five of his own people—and, he added, they were not of the same caliber as the Kennedy men. Adopting a self-deprecating stance, he asked them for patience because he could not absorb information as quickly as his predecessor. He instructed his own staff to move cautiously in seeking better office space. During the first few months in office he made the Kennedy staff active participants in decisions. "I had inherited neither their loyalty nor their enthusiasm," he wrote. "Those I would have to earn. . . . I had to prove myself."[5]

The response of the Kennedy aides toward Johnson was mixed. Historian and special assistant Arthur Schlesinger noted on the day after the assassination that Kennedy aides were divided between the "loyalists" and the "realists." "The loyalists," he explained, "were those who were there because of their association with Kennedy and who had other things to do, as I did. The realists were those who loved Kennedy but loved power, the opportunity to do things, more." Schlesinger's definition was rather arbitrary. Sometimes the distinctions between "loyalist" and "realist" were blurred. Lawrence O'Brien, for example, had worked exclusively for John Kennedy since 1952 and had considerable affection for the late president. But his continuation with the Johnson administration made him a "realist" by Schlesinger's definition. Nevertheless, in a highly generalized fashion the "realist-loyalist" split distinguished the staff's reaction to Johnson. Some Kennedy aides felt tormented by their personal devotion to John Kennedy, making it difficult, if not impossible, to work for Johnson. Other aides redefined their attachment and tried to achieve John Kennedy's goals through his successor.[6]

"Loyalists"

Throughout his life, whether at Choate or Harvard, in the navy or in Congress, John Kennedy had a unique gift for attracting loyal and devoted followers. Famous for his charm, he was exceptionally skilled at the art of making friends and using them for his purposes. The fidelity that Kennedy inspired was never stronger than among the "loyalists." Members of this group of Kennedy devotees were distinguished by three general traits. First, they were drawn to John Kennedy personally. "Those who had come to labor for the New Frontier," Richard Goodwin acknowledged, "were not linked by common, crusading ideals . . . but by John Kennedy—personality, will, and magnetic radiance of power. . . ." After the assassination, Goodwin noted, "That bond was now gone." Second, most "loyalists" were members of the White House staff rather than cabinet officials or heads of agencies and councils. Finally, their official duties consisted largely of presenting John Kennedy to the public. They were his wordsmiths and tacticians, responsible for promoting the president's popular image. Their personal attraction to him resulted in their dedication to him as a public figure.[7]

The "loyalists" found it difficult, if not impossible, to be at ease working with Johnson. The tension was immediate. Due to their extreme sensitivity to the events in Dallas, many "loyalists" exaggerated Johnson's supposed boorish behavior. Some Kennedy aides questioned why Johnson was so intent upon taking the oath of office immediately in Dallas. Others were offended by his supposed rude treatment of Jacqueline during the return flight. One aide told Robert Kennedy that Johnson's behavior aboard Air Force One had been "obscene." Actually, Johnson showed patience and compassion toward Jacqueline and Kennedy aides during the days after the assassination. Lawrence O'Brien, who admitted he was offended by Johnson's indiscretions, recognized his generosity. Nor was Johnson's "obscene" behavior reflected in the letters of surviving members of the Kennedy family, which thanked him for his "solicitude" and for his "efforts to make lighter the burden of grief."[8]

The emotional and political dynamics between Johnson and the "loyalists" varied with each individual. Arthur Schlesinger's relationship with John Kennedy had been brief but devoted. During the 1950s he was a founding member of the Americans for Democratic Action and an active supporter of the Stevenson campaigns. He was drawn away from the Stevenson camp in 1959 when Kennedy solicited his support in an effort to gain influence with the intellectual communities. Kennedy became receptive to the historian's projections that the 1960s would witness a resurgence in social awareness and activism. His campaign rhetoric subsequently emphasized the challenges of the 1960s and the need for strong Democratic leadership. The New Frontier, a term which Schlesinger helped to coin, promised to "get the country moving again."[9]

After Kennedy's election, Schlesinger accepted an ambiguous appointment as special assistant to the president. "I went to Washington not because I enjoyed working for the government, but because I wanted to work for President Kennedy," he explained in 1966. "My usefulness was really a personal relationship with President Kennedy." Joining the Kennedy administration at the age of forty-four, he had the unique opportunity to serve as the president's "resident intellectual," ambassador to the liberals, and adviser. Although on the periphery of power, he believed he developed a close, working relationship with Kennedy.[10]

Theodore Sorensen first joined John Kennedy's senatorial staff in 1953 as a researcher and speechwriter. A young, progressive lawyer from Nebraska, he did much to shape Kennedy's liberal attitudes in the Senate. Among his more controversial but valuable contributions to Kennedy's reputation was his role as a ghost-writer. He was instrumental, for example, in writing *Profiles in Courage,* a book for which Kennedy accepted the Pulitzer prize. Sorensen eventually became known as the president's "alter ego." Indeed, his commitment was so complete that he affected a Boston accent and assumed the gestures and mannerisms of the president. He was so shaken by Kennedy's death that years later he remained disoriented.[11]

John Kennedy's press secretary, Pierre Salinger, was a third major "loyalist" whose personal devotion to the Kennedys was transformed into a professional relationship. Salinger was a former popular reporter for the *San Francisco Chronicle* and a staff member of the Stevenson campaigns. Working for *Collier's* magazine in 1956, he was in the midst of writing a major story on the Teamsters Union when the magazine folded. The next year Robert Kennedy rescued him from his job as an assistant news editor for *House and Home* magazine. At the time Robert was an investigator for the Senate Rackets Committee, of which Senator John Kennedy was a member, and he was impressed with Salinger's writings on the Teamsters. Salinger joined the Kennedy staff during the 1960 campaign and later accepted a position in the New Frontier as press secretary.[12]

Kenneth O'Donnell's relationship with the Kennedys dated to his days at Harvard. O'Donnell was a star quarterback for the school's football team and was befriended by his teammate Robert Kennedy. He worked for John Kennedy during his senatorial campaigns, and, like Salinger, he was employed by Robert as an aide for McClellan's Rackets Committee. Perceived by reporters as mysterious and private, O'Donnell served as the president's appointment secretary. Nicknamed the "Iceman," he was known for his hard-nosed manner. Johnson aides were particularly struck by his desire to protect the Kennedys.[13]

In general, the "loyalists" were important image managers. Schlesinger bolstered Kennedy's intellectual image and gave him a winning theme. Sorensen polished his rhetoric. Salinger acted as a buffer between Kennedy and the press. O'Donnell promoted and protected him politically. In life they provided John Kennedy with words, slogans, and symbols, serving as conduits between him and the public. They continued that role after his death.

Schlesinger was especially distraught after the assassination. Speaking with Robert McNamara the next morning, he suggested that, except for cabinet officials, "the whole crowd of us should clear out." He also discussed with McNamara and others the possibility of denying Johnson the nomination in 1964. Later he met with several academicians who had worked for the Kennedy administration, reiterating his despair and intentions. If Johnson was aware of Schlesinger's underhanded actions, he did not convey his displeasure. On the Tuesday after the assassination, the new president rejected Schlesinger's resignation and, as he had done with other members of the Kennedy staff, mockingly threatened to have him arrested if he sought to act on it. The two men had never been close. Johnson was uncomfortable with Schlesinger's background as a Harvard-educated, Eastern intellectual. But it was precisely these qualities that he appreciated as conveying continuity. "He is," Horace Busby wrote in January 1964, "necessarily, bellweather [sic] among many liberals and intellectuals with his fate indicating White House attitude toward relations with the broader intellectual community." Johnson pleaded with Schlesinger to remain, and reluctantly he agreed.[14]

Sorensen also found it difficult to work with Johnson. His major contribution during his three months with the administration was his help in writing the president's early addresses, yet he remained emotionally on edge throughout this time. While driving to the Capitol for Johnson's State of the Union Address, Valenti asked him if he could look at the speech Sorensen had written. Sorensen literally smothered the draft, refusing to allow Valenti to hold or see it. "He was resentful of the President's men," Valenti recalled, "the President's personal staff involving themselves in the [prose he had written]."[15]

Salinger's tenure was similarly strained despite having been on "entirely friendly terms" with Johnson during the Kennedy presidency. Johnson had a high regard for Salinger, believing him largely responsible for Kennedy's successful press relations. Indeed, during the 1960 campaign he told Salinger that he could use him as an image-maker. On the morning after the assassination Johnson contacted Salinger. "I need you more than [Kennedy] ever did." During the next four months, however, Salinger felt estranged from the White House and was overwhelmed by memories of Kennedy. He drank excessively at night and seemed anxious to protect the dead president's reputation during the day. He once distributed a memorandum to the White House staff restricting reporters' access to information about the late president. "There is no objection to releasing any public statements concerning President Kennedy," Salinger warned, "but I do NOT want any background statements, off record statements, background press conferences, etc. released to ANYONE without my permission."[16]

By the spring of 1964 Schlesinger, Sorensen, and Salinger had each resigned from the administration, departing with considerable grace. In late January 1964 Schlesinger wrote Bill Moyers announcing his intention to resign "in the most helpful possible way." Among his reasons for leaving was "an urgent feeling of obligation" to write a book on President Kennedy. Johnson's public letter in response accepted his resignation "with much regret." The façade quality of the departure was implicit in the historian's subsequent letter to Moyers. "I think I sensed your hand in the President's reply to my letter of resignation," he wrote, "and I want to say how grateful I am."[17]

Shortly after the State of the Union Address, Sorensen also announced his resignation, stating his plan to write a book about Kennedy as "a subconscious way of doing the last thing I can for Jack Kennedy or his memory." Johnson accepted the departure "reluctantly and regretfully." He added that "the memory of John F. Kennedy will be made richer by your book." The two men made clear that there were no personal or policy differences between them. Nevertheless, the press sensed that Sorensen's departure represented a definitive shift away from the Kennedy era.[18]

In mid-March 1964 Salinger resigned, ostensibly to campaign for the California Senate. Impressed with Salinger's image-management skills, Johnson had drawn heavily on his advice, depending upon him much more than Kennedy had. But several disagreements arose that infringed upon Salinger's authority and compounded his already depressed state. Breaking protocol, he did not formally consult with Johnson about his decision to leave, informing him only hours before announcing his resignation to reporters. Johnson's public response had the familiar refrain of regret and reluctance. He denied during a press conference that he was upset by the manner in which Salinger left, and he disputed the notion that the resignation was another sign that the Kennedy aides were "anxious" to leave.[19]

The next departure of a major Kennedy "loyalist" did not occur until after the November election. During the Kennedy administration Johnson's relationship with O'Donnell had been strained. The aide was vehemently opposed to Johnson's vice-presidential nomination, and after the election he continued to harbor animosity. O'Donnell worked for Johnson for more than a year, but much of his time was spent at Democratic National Committee headquarters where he helped Johnson bridge relations with big-city Democratic leaders in the North and with other Kennedy forces. Once elected, Johnson no longer needed O'Donnell. When the aide offered his resignation in January 1965, Johnson was indifferent. "Well, it's all right with me," he told him, "and when you leave, take [Dave] Powers with you. He's never worked for anybody around here except you and the Kennedys anyway."[20]

During the transition year, lesser-known "loyalists" also departed. Like many White House staffs, Kennedy's had included numerous "cronies." David Powers had worked for John Kennedy's earliest campaigns and was hired largely to entertain the president with his Irish wit and storytelling abilities. He resigned with O'Donnell to accept a position at the Kennedy Library. Theodore Reardon had been friends with the Kennedys since the 1930s and held a nominal role as a White House administrative assistant for cabinet affairs. He went into private business in February 1964.[21]

Among the "loyalists" were two aides who contributed significantly to the substance of the Johnson presidency, Myer Feldman and Richard Goodwin. Feldman had been closely associated with Sorensen during the 1950s and was actively involved in Kennedy's 1960 campaign. After the election he accepted a position as deputy special counsel to the president, serving as Sorensen's liaison with various departments. Impressed with Feldman's work during the 1960 campaign, Johnson was advised that he was "too valuable and too experienced not to be involved in the [1964] campaign in a responsible position." After Johnson's inauguration, Feldman, along with O'Donnell and Powers, resigned.[22]

At age twenty-nine, Goodwin had been the youngest member of President Kennedy's staff. He served as a speechwriter but was also active in civil rights and foreign aid matters. Unpopular with certain Kennedy aides, Goodwin was exiled to an administrative position in the Peace Corps. Johnson had admired his talents and, after the assassination, hired him as a speechwriter and policy-maker. He soon became a leading architect of the Great Society's domestic programs, but, according to Valenti, his friendship with Robert Kennedy prompted Johnson to believe that he "might at some time turn on him." Leaving the administration in September 1965, he became an outspoken critic of the Vietnam War and remained close friends with the Kennedys. In 1968 he served as a speechwriter for Eugene McCarthy, but after Robert Kennedy entered the presidential race, he switched to Kennedy.[23]

The "loyalists" did not leave the administration solely out of selfish considerations. Although they were talented in substantive areas, especially regarding domestic policy, Johnson's own skills in formulating and passing legislation made them expendable. "I'm a little better at that than you," he reminded Goodwin. Kennedy aides were themselves well aware of their limited role in this area. "[F]rom Johnson's viewpoint," Schlesinger recalled, "there is no reason why people who were so personally involved with Kennedy . . . should have been kept." Although Johnson often boasted that he never asked any Kennedy staff member to leave, he sent strong signals indicating that some aides would not be missed. From the first day of his presidency he drew increasingly on his own "loyalists." Kennedy aides looked for their chance to leave, and Johnson let them go. He wanted independence while falsely assuring the public that he was not rejecting the Kennedy legacy. Six months after becoming president he struggled to convince Tom Wicker that, despite the resignations of a half-dozen Kennedy aides, he had retained Kennedy's staff organization. Except for the press office, he argued, the branches were headed by "Kennedy men."[24]

Although Johnson did not label the divisions among the Kennedy staffers as Schlesinger had, he sensed a "loyalist" resistance and believed "it complicated my task." Some Kennedy men were bitter and vicious toward Johnson. "To the most passionate of these," McPherson recalled, "Johnson was simply a usurper." While McPherson could understand their "heartache," he thought their behavior was contrary to John Kennedy's high regard for Johnson's skills. The departing aides turned contemptuous toward fellow Kennedy staff members who remained with Johnson, calling them "turncoats" and "traitors." "I knew that some of them hated my guts for staying with Lyndon Johnson," O'Brien recalled. Schlesinger dismissed their behavior as harmless but conceded that it was suspicious: "[Johnson] could hardly be blamed for resentment and mistrust."[25]

Between 1965 and 1966 Schlesinger, Sorensen, and Salinger each published separate accounts of the Kennedy years. Their popular and flattering books served as an early trilogy in John Kennedy's elevation to myth. Schlesinger's *A Thousand Days* and Sorensen's *Kennedy* were two of the ten best-selling books published in 1965. Salinger went on to run for the Senate, winning the Democratic primary with the help of a last-minute public appearance with Jacqueline Kennedy. During the campaign he mimicked Kennedy's hand gestures, speech pattern, and at times even his Boston accent. After losing the general election he published a popular and affectionate account of his years with John Kennedy. Other Kennedy personnel, such as O'Donnell, Powers, Evelyn Lincoln, Maud Shaw, and Paul Fay, wrote glowing accounts of the Kennedy years. "[W]e became a part of the problem," McGeorge Bundy acknowledged, "in our elegiac mood as supporting actors. . . . We were a part of what became a conventional idealization of a deeply human Presidency. In our prosaic way we too helped color reality with legend."[26]

Johnson's inability to maintain close links with the "loyalists" had long-term implications. He alienated those who were most closely identified with the Kennedy years and who later popularized a myth that shadowed his presidency. Perhaps of more immediate importance, he lost aides exceptionally skilled at public relations—Kennedy's speechwriters, press agents, and promoters. Achieving a working relationship with them would have been difficult. Indeed, their existing contempt for Johnson, their depressed emotional state, and Johnson's domineering personality may have made a working relationship impossible. But if Kennedy aides had been willing to adjust their skills to Johnson's personality, and if Johnson had been more receptive to outside advice, his public image might not have suffered as much as it did. As it was, he never developed an effective public relations team and had to contend with unfavorable comparisons with a glorified past.[27]

"Realists"

Johnson's relationship with the Kennedy "realists" differed markedly from his involvement with the "loyalists." The "realists" generally included members of Kennedy's cabinet and heads of executive agencies and departments. Their backgrounds and participation in the Johnson administration suggested that, though they had considerable affection for John Kennedy, they had an overriding commitment to government service.

Lawrence O'Brien was closer to Kennedy than most "realists." The son of an Irish immigrant, he was raised in a politically active family in Springfield, Massachusetts. As a teenager in the 1930s he followed in his father's footsteps and involved himself in local Democratic affairs. Early in his career he developed innovative campaign strategies based on the premise that a greater number of registered voters would benefit Democratic candidates. After World War II he tested his theories, managing two congressional races for his friend Foster Furcolo. Furcolo narrowly lost the first election in 1946 but easily won two years later. O'Brien served as Furcolo's administrative assistant until 1950 when they had an unexplained falling-out. He returned to Massachusetts disgusted with the political process. A year later, however, he agreed to help Congressman John Kennedy in his bid for the Senate.[28]

Beginning in 1952 O'Brien played a vital role in organizing Kennedy's campaigns and became a popular member of the so-called "Irish Mafia." During the Kennedy administration he served as the president's special assistant and congressional liaison. Like Kennedy, O'Brien was hard working but cautious in dealing with Congress. Although they won few real victories, he and Kennedy laid the groundwork for important legislation. The limited accomplishments did not taint his feelings for Kennedy. "My twelve years with him," he recalled, "were a golden age. I never expect to know anything like them again."[29]

Other "realists" were less attached to Kennedy than O'Brien but were similarly dedicated bureaucrats. McGeorge Bundy graduated first in his class at Yale in 1940 and became a Junior Fellow at Harvard. After serving in the army during World War II, he helped War Secretary Henry Stimson write his autobiography and assisted in implementing the Marshall Plan.

Republican in background, he later became a political analyst for the Council on Foreign Relations and taught at Harvard. He disliked Richard Nixon and joined an intellectual committee in support of John Kennedy's candidacy in 1960. Kennedy, meanwhile, was impressed with Bundy's intelligence, and, upon his election, appointed him Special Assistant for National Security Affairs. Bundy never developed a close personal relationship with President Kennedy. "I followed the man, not the coffin," he recalled. "The transition was easier for me. I hadn't given a year of my life campaigning for him."[30]

Like Bundy, Robert McNamara had a brief, professional relationship with John Kennedy. He graduated with honors from the University of California at Berkeley in 1937 and from the Harvard Business School in 1939. After teaching at Harvard he served with the army air corps during World War II, where he developed the logistical system for mass bombing raids on Germany and Japan. After the war he moved up the ranks of the financially troubled Ford Motor Company. Relying on strict cost-effective methods, he was part of a team known as "the whiz kids," helping to revitalize the company. In November 1960 the company reached for the first time outside the family and named McNamara president. One month later Kennedy named him Secretary of Defense. Similar in temperament and background, Kennedy and McNamara shared a close professional relationship, prompting the secretary to recall his tenure in affectionate terms.[31]

Joining the holdovers of the New Frontier's foreign policy–makers was John Kennedy's much maligned Secretary of State, Dean Rusk. Rusk's early background resembled Johnson's. Just six months younger than Johnson, he was born into poverty in Georgia. Working his way through college, he graduated from Davidson College near Charlotte, studied at Oxford on a Rhodes scholarship, and became a member of the faculty at Mills College in California. During World War II he worked under General George Marshall, who convinced him to join the State Department as assistant chief of the Division of International Security Affairs. During the early 1950s he was appointed Assistant Secretary of State for Far Eastern Affairs and helped formulate American policy toward Korea and China. In 1952 he resigned from the State Department to become president of the Rockefeller Foundation. Seeking an unobtrusive foreign policy adviser, Kennedy appointed Rusk Secretary of State. Although Kennedy liked Rusk personally, he grew frustrated with the State Department's cautious approach to global problems and Rusk's ambivalent decision-making style. The president tended to circumvent the State Department's cumbersome bureaucracy, turning to the National Security Council and Central Intelligence Agency. He intended to replace Rusk after the 1964 elections.[32]

The "survival" rate of the "realists" during the Johnson administration was determined less by their relationship with the Kennedys than by the success of their own efforts. Those involved in domestic affairs had greater longevity than those who guided foreign policy. Johnson and the domestic "realists" shared a deep commitment to social reform, allowing for an agreeable working relationship. Unlike his foreign policies, his domestic efforts were far more successful—and success tended to breed congeniality.

O'Brien was the first Kennedy staff member whom Johnson asked to remain with his administration. Returning from Dallas aboard Air Force One, Johnson told O'Brien that, though he was free to leave, he would have a "blank check" in terms of pursuing John Kennedy's domestic program if he stayed. During the next few days the new president appealed to O'Brien's sentiments, reminding him that by passing Kennedy's program he would be best serving the late president's legacy. The strategy worked. "I decided there was no better tribute I could make to President Kennedy's memory," O'Brien recalled, "than to stay and continue to work on his legislative program."[33]

As the administration's liaison to Congress, O'Brien gained considerable power and prestige. After modest review, Johnson generally accepted his advice. Together they achieved passage of landmark legislation, including the Civil Rights Act and the anti-poverty bill. Although suspicious of O'Brien's affection for the Kennedys, Johnson allowed him to direct the 1964 campaign. Afterwards he implored O'Brien to remain during the upcoming legislative sessions. "We can wrap up the New Frontier program now, Larry," he promised. "We can pass it all now." Although O'Brien had planned to return to private life, he wanted to complete the Kennedy agenda. He was moved by Johnson's enthusiasm and skill in passing social legislation. He also felt an emotional commitment to the late president. After accepting the prestigious cabinet position of postmaster general in August 1965, he continued to guide Johnson's legislative programs. He left the administration on friendly terms after Johnson decided not to seek reelection in March 1968. Retaining his affection for the Kennedys, he joined Robert Kennedy's presidential campaign.[34]

Other domestic "realists" played important roles in creating the Great Society, Johnson's elaborate domestic program which sought reform in such areas as education, civil rights, and poverty. Walter Heller, chairman of the Council of Economic Advisers, had a friendly relationship with Johnson when he was vice president and worked well with the new president during the transition year. Heller left the administration in November 1964 after working with Johnson to secure passage of the 1964 Revenue Act and initiating the War on Poverty. He remained an unofficial adviser while teaching economics at the University of Minnesota. Director of the Budget Kermit Gordon also made the transition, as did Labor Secretary Willard Wirtz, Agriculture Secretary Orville Freeman, and Interior Secretary Stewart Udall, all of whom remained at their posts for the duration of the Johnson administration. Even those legislative liaisons who were close to Kennedy, such as Lee White, Henry Hall Wilson, and Mike Manatos, successfully made the transition.[35]

Kennedy "realists" involved in foreign policy, however, were ultimately less fortunate. Johnson had had nominal foreign policy experience. Unlike his predecessor, he felt greater satisfaction in dealing with domestic affairs in which he could effectively use his skills of persuasion and one-on-one negotiation. In the Senate he had accepted Cold War assumptions, and during his vice presidency he had had no significant role in foreign policy matters other than symbolic trips abroad. Consequently, once he assumed office, he depended on those advisers who not only understood John Kennedy's intentions but had guided the nation through a series of crises from Berlin to Cuba.

Like the domestic "realists," the foreign policy "realists" were committed to Johnson less by personality factors than by substantive goals. Bundy, McNamara, and Undersecretary of State George Ball met Johnson at Andrews Air Force Base upon his return from Dallas. The new president wasted little time in soliciting their support. "You're the men I trust the most," he noted. "You must stay with me. I'll need you. President Kennedy gathered about him extraordinary people I could never have reached for. You're the ablest men I've ever seen." He emphasized that he wanted them to remain not only because of their link to Kennedy but because of their talent.[36]

According to Jack Valenti, Johnson was very attracted to Bundy's credentials—"the New England artisan, Yale-educated, Harvard-trained, with a tough intellect and that casual, almost negligent confidence that seems to be part of the bloodline." Referring to him as "my intellectual" and "indispensable," Johnson appreciated both his foreign policy expertise and his symbolic value. He dispatched Bundy to debate academic critics of the Vietnam War and relied on him for highly publicized fact-finding and troubleshooting missions. Bundy's real authority vastly increased throughout 1964 as Johnson's key adviser in the escalating conflict in Southeast Asia.[37]

After the assassination McNamara was unsure whether he could or should remain with the administration. His prior relationship with the vice president was "more guarded than warm," and he doubted he could relate to a man so different from Kennedy in manner and style. He nonetheless decided to remain out of a sense of duty to overhaul the military structure and a belief that he would have a freer hand under Johnson than he had had under Kennedy. Johnson, meanwhile, was elated with McNamara's promptness, diligence, preparedness, and his wide range of knowledge apart from defense. He also liked McNamara's ability to work in harmony with Rusk. "They know everything there is to know about their departments because they've been there a long time," Johnson said. "I needed them." Years later, in his memoirs, he characterized McNamara as a "source of great strength to me."[38]

Of all the Kennedy "realists," Johnson had the easiest working relationship with Dean Rusk. During his vice presidency Johnson had appreciated Rusk's respectful treatment of him. The secretary had regularly briefed him on foreign policy matters and actively sought his advice. Rusk's Southern background and mild temperament appealed to Johnson, as did his intelligence and credentials. The two men also shared a similar history in the Kennedy administration. Both had been ostracized, and, in contrast to Kennedy's operational style, they believed that America's foreign policy benefited from structure rather than shortcuts. Their compatibility was evidenced by Rusk's longevity. Unlike McNamara and Bundy, he served for the duration of the Johnson administration.[39]

The most important decisions in which the foreign policy "realists" participated during the transition year concerned Vietnam. During the Kennedy administration, United States military involvement in Southeast Asia had increased markedly. By November 1963 Kennedy had committed sixteen thousand American "advisers" to the war. Although his ultimate designs in Vietnam remain cloudy, his actual intentions were less relevant than the way Johnson construed them. As in almost all areas of his fledgling administration, Johnson wanted to maintain the image of continuity.

Johnson's first cabinet meeting was crucial in establishing his initial Vietnam policy. Among those present were McNamara, Rusk, and Bundy, each highly conscious about the new realities of power. Johnson was now president. They looked to him, trying to gauge his response when the topic of Southeast Asia was broached. Because Johnson sought to respond to the Vietnam conflict in a manner consistent with his predecessor's wishes, he looked to the "realists," trying not to overstep his bounds of authority. The result was that both he and the "realists" stifled open debate, assuming that the other's silence indicated agreement with Kennedy's existing policy. "During those months," George Reedy recalled, "it would have been entirely possible for [Johnson] to interpret the Kennedy staffers as believing that JFK would have *pressed* the war in Vietnam and for Kennedy staffers to interpret LBJ as *wanting* to press the war in Vietnam."[40]

Superficial analysis might suggest that Johnson escalated the war based on what he assumed to be Kennedy's belligerent intentions, and what he thought was the "realists'" concurrence. Certainly Johnson's deference to the "realists" was consistent with his awe of their experience and credentials. But miscommunication alone did not prompt Johnson's decision. His Cold War assumptions, North Vietnam's aggression, military assurances, and his personal fear of appearing weak all contributed to the myriad of forces leading to escalation. Still, his desire for continuity was germane to his decisions. Even when the war took on an entirely new path, he sought consistency. According to Horace Busby, after the Gulf of Tonkin incident in August 1964 the President was "afraid that something he might do would cause the Kennedy presidency to be lost and we would lose a lot of momentum."[41]

If Johnson had been inclined to de-escalate the war, he could have allied himself with one "realist" who had consistently opposed military solutions in Vietnam. Undersecretary of State George Ball had a familiar background for a "realist"—graduating with a law degree from Northwestern University and serving as a bombing strategist during World War II. Like some "realists," Ball was capable of having a warm, friendly relationship with John Kennedy. He appreciated and admired Johnson's skills and developed a good working relationship with him as well. Although willing to listen to Ball's criticism of the war, Johnson did not change course. His refusal spoke of his selectivity in deciding which "realists'" advice he would follow, pursuing the opinions of those aides who agreed with his inclinations. Ball resigned in September 1966, convinced he could no longer "significantly influence policy."[42]

As the war situation degenerated, Johnson became increasingly frustrated with those "realists" who had been closest to the Kennedys. By 1967 McNamara began to express doubts about the war and suffered guilt over the casualties incurred. Johnson, however, interpreted his secretary's change of heart as a result of his affection for the Kennedys. Rather than face the realities of McNamara's objections to the war, he conjured up the notion that Robert Kennedy was poisoning his staff's thinking and encouraging dissent. Seeking to insulate himself from pessimistic assessments, Johnson gradually diminished McNamara's access. In November 1967 McNamara left the Defense Department to direct the World Bank.[43]

Johnson was similarly suspicious that McGeorge Bundy was somehow under the influence of Robert Kennedy. The national security adviser sought from the start to assure the president of his commitment to the administration. In early December 1963 he sent a memorandum to the president clarifying a column by Charles Bartlett suggesting that he and others might soon resign. "I told [Bartlett]," Bundy wrote, "that he, of all people, ought not to be talking as if President Kennedy's best appointments were likely to desert President Kennedy's successor." In the spring of 1964 Bundy wrote in an article for *Foreign Affairs,* "Loyalty to President Kennedy and loyalty to President Johnson are not merely naturally compatible, but logically necessary as part of a larger loyalty to their common purpose." Despite such efforts, he never felt he was able to gain Johnson's trust. Johnson became increasingly abusive toward Bundy, and Bundy was convinced that he would not achieve his desired appointment as Secretary of State. He resigned in the spring of 1966 to become president of the Ford Foundation.[44]

The departure of McNamara, Bundy, and Ball suggested that a "realist's" capacity to "survive" in the Johnson administration was determined by two factors, sometimes related and sometimes separate: their commitment to the war and their relationship with the Kennedys. A "realist" such as Rusk, who was remote from the Kennedys and committed to the war, stood the greatest chance of surviving. A "realist" attracted to the Kennedys but committed to the war could still survive, but once his opinion of the war wavered, Johnson was likely to interpret the shift in terms of loyalty.

Johnson's relationship with the Kennedy staff was doomed by circumstances and personality conflicts. Had his vice presidency been more agreeable, had his anxieties been less urgent, and had his achievements been sustained, he might have dealt effectively with the ambivalent feelings of the Kennedy aides. Consistent with his insecurities, he had always considered loyalty essential for a "successful" working relationship with his personnel. While most presidents wanted committed aides, Johnson wanted them to "kiss my ass in Macy's window at high noon and tell me it smells like roses." Any hint of displaced affection, any sign of disagreement over policy was suspect, prompting an exaggerated counterreaction. Believing that aides could not be attracted to the Kennedys without diluting their commitment to himself, he imposed standards that made a naturally difficult situation impossible.[45]

Six months after assuming office, Johnson expressed appreciation to those aides who had remained. During a ceremony on the eve of what would have been John Kennedy's forty-seventh birthday, he reaffirmed their common commitment to substantive achievements. He thanked the assembled cabinet and National Security Council for their "courage and comfort and strength." He credited them for their devotion to Kennedy and for taking up the late president's cause despite their grief. He reminded them that they were the ones truly committed, noting the higher purpose of serving the nation rather than the man. "[John Kennedy] would have been satisfied," he concluded, "to see so many of you assembled here this morning."[46]

Concentrating more on the substance of his presidency than its image,

Johnson was able to produce remarkable achievements, but he created long-term complications in terms of his struggle with the Kennedy "mystique." In later years, as the Vietnam War unraveled his presidency, the "loyalists" alleged that, had John Kennedy lived, he would not have pursued a policy of escalation. In response, Johnson insisted correctly that he had always acted on the advice of Kennedy aides. He quoted his predecessor and utilized surviving "realists" to set the public record straight. But his arguments were no match for his predecessor's devotees, who seemed to dedicate themselves full time to exalting the Kennedy past. Defeated on two fronts, Lyndon Johnson lost those Kennedy aides who were skilled at manipulating public opinion while he retained those whose advice led to a policy disaster.

VI

"LET US CONTINUE": JOHNSON'S LEGISLATIVE RECORD AND THE KENNEDY SHADOW

Speaking before the nation and a joint session of Congress on November 27, 1963, Lyndon Johnson embraced John Kennedy's domestic agenda. Citing the slain president's achievements in space exploration, the Peace Corps, employment, the aged, mental illness, "and above all the dream of equal rights for all Americans," Johnson proposed that "the ideas and the ideals which he so nobly represented must and will be translated into effective action." His two major policy concerns that evening were civil rights and tax reform. Invoking his predecessor's name seven times, he declared that the country should "highly resolve that John Fitzgerald Kennedy did not live—or die—in vain." Expanding upon Kennedy's inaugural pledge to "Let us begin," Johnson asked, "Let us continue." The phrase, Jack Valenti recalled, "committed Johnson in ways that nobody really imagined. . . . Then he began to endorse all the Kennedy legacy."[1]

Johnson's reasons for adopting Kennedy's cause were varied. In hindsight he contended that Kennedy's policies were in keeping with his own ideology. "If you looked at my record, you would know that I am a Roosevelt New Dealer," he told Budget Director Walter Heller. "As a matter of fact, to tell the truth, John F. Kennedy was a little too conservative to suit my taste."

As a former state director of the National Youth Administration and as a congressman active in obtaining New Deal benefits for his district, Johnson had been an ardent New Dealer during the 1930s and early 1940s. But his emotional commitment to social reform often seemed contingent more on the political climate than on moral imperatives.[2]

In terms of his immediate concerns, Johnson's appropriation of Kennedy's legislation was intended to serve his ambitions. In preparation for the address to Congress, a White House aide noted Johnson's need to develop "a forceful image immediately." One "problem" with his professed liberalism centered on his sincerity: he "must be liberal, but not so obvious that it begins to look forced." By moving Kennedy's pending legislation, he could quickly build a record for the upcoming campaign. In particular, the civil rights and tax reform bills offered him an opportunity to establish credentials among liberals who had opposed his nomination for vice president. Achieving passage of this legislation was a task perfectly suited to his skills. Relying on his unmatched legislative experience and drawing on public sympathy for the martyred president, he could maneuver Congress out of its deadlock. "Whether Johnson will be able to maintain the memory of Kennedy's death as a goad to further legislation," Meg Greenfield reported in early December, "is the question hanging over the Congress now."[3]

Beneath surface motives, aides sensed in Johnson an emotional commitment to Kennedy. According to his long-time friend Abraham Fortas, the new president saw himself as a "surrogate for President Kennedy." Although his dedication to Kennedy's policies was "facilitated" by a basic agreement with him on social issues, Johnson felt a great sense of duty and obligation to the past. "I loved Jack Kennedy, just like you," he explained to Richard Goodwin, "but he never really understood the Congress. I do. And I'm going to pass all those bills you cared about."[4]

By pursuing his predecessor's agenda, Johnson furthered his own political ambitions in a manner that comforted the nation. "In the best sense," Walter Rostow recalled, "Johnson was opportunistic . . . [for having] channeled the powerful waves of popular feeling in the wake" of the Kennedy assassination. In doing so, however, he ran the risk of conveying the image of a caretaker rather than a leader. Aware of this drawback, Johnson formulated his own legislative legacy, not only because activism was consistent with his nature but because the creation of his own policies could help him emerge from the Kennedy shadow. Thus he embarked on a twofold strategy that at once drew him nearer to and away from the Kennedy "mystique."[5]

Civil Rights

Despite Johnson's pronounced dedication to Kennedy's civil rights bill, his past record left many liberal members of the Democratic party skeptical. During the first twenty years of his career Johnson had opposed every civil rights measure that had come before him. In 1940 he voted against an anti-lynching bill. In 1942, 1943, and 1945 he opposed anti-poll-tax bills. In 1946 he voted against an anti-discrimination amendment to a federal school-lunch program. Two years later he attacked President Harry Truman's civil rights plank at the Democratic convention as "a farce and a sham—an effort to set up a police state in the guise of liberty. . . ." In 1950 he voted no on a proposal that outlawed segregation in the armed services.[6]

Johnson's record should not suggest that he did not empathize with minorities. One researcher who studied his years as state director of the National Youth Administration was convinced that he was not racist, though "the practical situation tempered his private attitudes." Others have argued that, during his Senate years, Johnson grew to appreciate racial equality as a legitimate concern of the federal government and sometimes took a courageous stand. In 1954, for example, he was one of only three Southern senators who refused to sign a Southern manifesto supporting segregation. Many of his closest aides were convinced that he had compassion for blacks. Their accounts of Johnson are replete with anecdotes reflecting his private attempts to eradicate racial injustice. Nevertheless, some correctly questioned his motives in supporting the Kennedy bill.[7]

Three pragmatic considerations had moved Johnson to oppose past civil rights measures. First, the bills which he had opposed could not have passed. Not since 1875 had Congress passed a civil rights bill. Second, Johnson had been concerned about his personal political future. Trying to court the Senate leadership, he had cooperated with the conservative coalition which prevented broad expansion of the New Deal in areas of health care, labor unions, and civil rights. Third, as a senator representing the entire state of Texas after 1948, his constituency had been more conservative than his 10th congressional district. Seeking to appease his financial backers and pursuing the majority white vote, Johnson had opposed any federal intervention in the Southern states and thus had helped preserve the racial status quo.[8]

By 1957 public attitudes toward civil rights had shifted, and Johnson had adjusted accordingly. Northern white voters had begun exerting pressure on Washington for social justice. Several matters intensified their attention: the Supreme Court decision in 1954 in the case of *Brown v. the Board of*

Education of Topeka, Kansas; the subsequent failure of Southern states to desegregate their schools; and the passive resistance movement led by Martin Luther King, Jr. In response to political pressure the Eisenhower administration submitted a civil rights bill to Congress in 1956. Its most controversial provision granted the Justice Department the right forcibly to intervene when civil rights were violated in areas such as housing, employment, and especially education.[9]

As Senate Majority Leader, Johnson allowed pragmatism to guide his response. A significant portion of the black vote was beginning to drift away from the Democratic party in favor of promises offered by Republicans. Johnson feared that if the Democratic-controlled Senate failed to pass a Republican civil rights bill, black support of the party might further decline. Moreover, his failure to support civil rights might brand him as a sectional politician and "unpresidential." "I knew that if I failed to produce on this one," he told Doris Kearns, "my leadership would be broken into a hundred pieces; everything I had built up over the years would be completely undone." Through a process of bargaining and compromise, Johnson gained a consensus between Northern moderates and Southern conservatives. The end result was a moderate bill, without the forced-intervention provision but moderate enough for the South and strong enough, even without forced intervention, for the North.[10]

From 1961 through 1962 President Kennedy was reluctant to sponsor civil rights legislation, sensing neither adequate support in the Senate nor popular demand. The administration instead quietly pursued equality through the Justice Department and government agencies. But this tactic failed to appease the growing demands of civil rights leaders. By 1963 blacks were increasingly vocal and well organized in the South. National media attention devoted to sit-ins, boycotts, and marches elicited increased sympathy among Northern whites. By the time riots erupted in Birmingham, Alabama, Kennedy felt compelled to respond more substantively than he had in the past.[11]

After much delay and reluctance, Kennedy submitted a civil rights bill to Congress in the summer of 1963. Its primary provision was to prohibit discrimination in places of public accommodation—a purpose repugnant to many white Southerners. Johnson had been largely excluded from the planning sessions for the bill. Speaking with Theodore Sorensen on June 3, he opposed submitting the legislation and criticized the Kennedy team for not being adequately prepared to deal with Congress. "I don't know who drafted it; I've never seen it," he noted. "Hell, if the Vice President doesn't know what's in it how do you expect the others to know what's in it? I got it from the *New York Times*." Johnson was sensitive to the timing of the legislation and believed that its proposal then would hurt later efforts. He advised the president first to consult with black leaders to assure them of his good intentions. He further suggested that Kennedy go to a Southern city, look its leaders "in the eye," and argue "the moral issue and the Christian issue." When the bill was sent to the House, Johnson was convinced that its provisions would have to be compromised. By the time of the assassination, the bill had gotten through the House Judiciary Committee but was stalled in the Rules Committee. Kennedy seemed reluctant to press the matter, lacking confidence that he could secure enough votes for its passage in the Senate.[12]

After November 22, Johnson's constituency had again changed, and again he adjusted. "Those Harvards think that a politician from Texas doesn't care about Negroes," he told Goodwin. "In the Senate I did the best I could. But I had to be careful. I couldn't get too far ahead of my voters. Now I represent the whole country, and I have the power." Johnson was determined to use the bill to enhance his reputation among liberal Democrats. As he had done in 1957, he viewed the bill in personal terms. "I knew that if I didn't get out in front on this issue, they would get me," he told Kearns.

They'd throw up my background against me, they'd use it to prove that I was incapable of bringing unity to the land I loved so much. . . . I couldn't let that happen. I had to produce a civil rights bill that was even stronger than the one they'd have gotten if Kennedy had lived. Without this, I'd be dead before I could even begin.[13]

Johnson worked diligently to strengthen the Kennedy bill and to secure its passage. At press conferences he pledged to make "no deal" with Congress. Indeed, he expanded the bill to include the same forced-intervention provision that he had bargained away during the debate over the 1957 bill. He conferred with various civil rights groups, invoking Kennedy's name to assure them of his sympathy. During his State of the Union Address in January 1964 he reasserted the need to fulfill Kennedy's legislative agenda "not because of our sorrow or sympathy, but because they are right." Speaking at a dedication of the John F. Kennedy Education, Civic, and Cultural Center, he heightened the legislative stakes by implying that bigotry had killed Kennedy. He consulted Robert Kennedy and assured him that the bill was in keeping with his brother's intentions. (Kennedy suspected that Johnson was merely trying "to pacify me" or spread responsibility if passage failed.) On January 31 he sent to the House the new and expanded 1964 Civil Rights Act. Less than two weeks later it passed.[14]

The Senate was more difficult to manage. Johnson bargained with selected senators, spending hours calling them, or their wives, and using flattery and appeals to their morality. He called on civil rights leaders to exert pressure on the Southern and conservative senators. Understanding that it was vital to obtain Republican support in order to compensate for the entrenched Southern bloc, Johnson cultivated Senator Everett Dirksen of Illinois, offering a Corps of Engineers project for his state in return for the two-thirds vote required for cloture, thus limiting debate and the potential for a filibuster. Johnson directly challenged his former mentor Richard Russell, warning that, despite his behavior in the past, he would not compromise on this bill. A Southern senator told the Washington director of the National Association for the Advancement of Colored People that Johnson "had put so much pressure on everybody that there wasn't any doubt that the bill was going through." After much maneuvering and debate, but no compromise, the Senate passed the bill on July 2, seventy-three to twenty-seven. "We could have beaten Kennedy on civil rights," Richard Russell told Orville Freeman, "but we can't Lyndon."[15]

Johnson was careful about publicizing his victory, downplaying his role in order to avoid a white Southern backlash. Although he often praised Dirksen's help, insiders knew who was responsible. Johnson signed the 1964 Civil Rights Act into law on national television on the same day it was ratified by the Senate. He reminded viewers that the law had been "proposed more than one year ago by our late and beloved President John F. Kennedy." During the signing ceremony on July 2, Robert Kennedy was present but was given no prominent position. Although Johnson had promised to obtain his approval on passing the legislation, the attorney general had played no serious role. Indeed, he seemed to begrudge the president his victory, contending that John more rightly deserved credit for passing the bill than Johnson. Although Robert acknowledged that he and his brother had anticipated difficulty in managing the Senate, he believed that John, too, would have won Dirksen's favor. Dirksen liked John "a great deal," Robert argued, "and much, much, much more than he liked Lyndon Johnson." Indeed, according to Robert, Dirksen may ultimately have cooperated with Johnson out of respect for John's memory.[16]

As Johnson handed out ceremonial pens after signing the bill, he seemed to ignore Robert Kennedy, who stood in the background, staring at the floor. At one point Roy Reuther grabbed him, pulling him to the front. "Mr. President," Reuther remarked, "I know you have reserved a pen for your Attorney General." Johnson gave Kennedy a handful of pens. The scene reflected more than Johnson's animosity toward Robert; it illustrated his desire to distance himself from the past. Johnson may have been willing publicly to downplay his own role, but he did not want the Kennedys to gain credit for a bill he had worked so hard to pass. Although he had originally advanced the 1964 Civil Rights Bill as the dutiful executor of John Kennedy's legacy, his success separated him from his predecessor. In the area of civil rights Lyndon Johnson was the achiever, a point made emphatically clear in 1965 and 1968 when he passed two more civil rights bills, marking the most impressive accomplishments of his presidency and moving far beyond the expectations of the New Frontier.[17]

Try as he might, however, Johnson could not escape the Kennedy shadow. President Kennedy's reputation among blacks had improved markedly since the summer of 1963 when he had declared his moral commitment to civil rights and met with organizers of the March on Washington. A Harris poll of blacks ranked him behind only Martin Luther King and the NAACP in having most advanced the cause of equal rights. After his death, blacks developed a profound affection for the late president. National surveys showed that 49 percent of blacks, compared with 30 percent of the general public, felt they were more upset by the assassination than "most people." In early 1964 black writers began describing Kennedy as the second Lincoln. He was later immortalized as a liberator of blacks in a popular song, "Abraham, Martin, and John."[18]

The emotional bond that blacks felt toward President Kennedy reinforced Robert's assumption that, had he lived, the civil rights bill would have been passed. Indeed, as the movement became more frenzied during the mid-1960s, some people argued that if Kennedy were still president, blacks would not have felt the disenchantment that pushed them to violence. Although the premise was questionable, it fixed John Kennedy's image as a moral leader of the movement and underscored Lyndon Johnson's role as a mere political operator.

The War on Poverty

Johnson, his staff, and the Kennedy holdovers understood the need to build a legislative legacy independent of the past. Less than twenty-four hours after the assassination, an internal memorandum warned the new president that he "must support Kennedy['s] program but still emerge as Lyndon Johnson." Discussing with Walter Heller pertinent matters surrounding the transition, Johnson was informed that Kennedy had been in the preliminary stages of developing an "assault on poverty" program. The late president, however, had set it aside until after the 1964 election so as to maintain cordial relations with Southern conservatives. Johnson seized the idea, telling Heller to "move full-speed ahead. . . . That's my kind of program. It will help people."[19]

In the following months, aides offered various suggestions to encourage Johnson in his pursuit of legislative autonomy. Richard Goodwin, a former

115

Kennedy aide who had been vital to the 1960 campaign, implored him to formulate his own legislation before the next election. He argued that, though the New Frontier was politically moderate, Kennedy had retained liberal support because of his "background, origins, [and] expressed convictions." Kennedy's problem was convincing conservatives that he was not too radical. Johnson, however, had to prove his liberalism, not only by passing pending legislation but by creating "a program more sweeping and bold than before." Goodwin targeted blue-collar workers who "must get the feeling that here is someone who cares about them," but he acknowledged the difficulty of developing a precise program. Johnson lacked the advantage of coming into office with a collection of campaign ideas, projects, and advisers. Nor could he expect the established agencies to develop new ideas; they were too defensive about the change in power. Goodwin therefore recommended a "working group" consisting mainly of people outside of government who would prepare "an expansive domestic program" by January 1965.[20]

Johnson agreed with Goodwin's assessment. "We've got to use the Kennedy programs as a springboard to take on the Congress," he told the aide, "summon the states to new heights, create a Johnson program, different in tone, fighting and aggressive." Aware of the fragile nature of mandates, he could not wait until January 1965. He planned to compromise and make concessions to Congress during the transition year. "I have to get elected," he noted, "and I don't want to scare people off. Next year we'll do even more, and the year after, until we have all the programs."[21]

Out of these memoranda and conversations arose Johnson's War on Poverty, dramatically declared during his State of the Union Address in January 1964. What had originally been a mere legislative consideration within the previous administration was about to become the cornerstone of the Great Society. The program generated enthusiasm among the Johnson staff. Aides urged him to appear on television in order to "review *your* program." "Up to this point," Jack Valenti wrote, "you have been carrying on Kennedy's programs—NOW, it's your show."[22]

Johnson's reasons for addressing poverty, rather than other social issues, were complex. Some aides believed he was morally committed to helping the downtrodden. Johnson often spoke of his empathy for the poor, claiming to have acted "from experience, the experience of a boy who knew what it was like to go hungry, the experience of a boy who saw sickness and disease day after day." But his political instincts were also correct. He exploited an opportunity to address a broad range of issues which had been given short shrift since the New Deal. He thus created a program which comprised the most extensive domestic legislation since the 1930s.[23]

In trying to emerge from the Kennedy shadow, however, Johnson had chosen an ambiguous issue. The Office of Employment Opportunity Act, the foundation of the War on Poverty, included a number of consolidated programs which were either developed by Kennedy men within the Johnson administration or reflected items on Kennedy's long-term agenda in areas such as education, employment, housing, food stamps, and area redevelopment. The Kennedy organization was able to cast aspersions on Johnson and claim the poverty issue for its own. "What does he know about people who've got no jobs or are undereducated?" Robert Kennedy remarked. "He's got no feeling for people who are hungry. It's up to us." Robert found John's last cabinet notes on which the late president had written "poverty" several times and circled the words. He had them framed and hung in his Justice Department office. The Kennedy staff claimed publicly that the eradication of poverty was their fallen leader's last request.[24]

There was some truth to the charge that Johnson was constructing his own legacy based on his predecessor's ill-defined groundwork. But there was less validity to the notion that John Kennedy was planning an anti-poverty program on the scale that Johnson envisioned. During the summer and fall of 1963 Heller had been lobbying for a poverty program, but Kennedy gave the issue low priority, neither sensing a strong mandate from the people nor wishing to offend Southern committee chairpersons in Congress who were hostile toward social welfare programs. His interest was heightened late in his administration when a *New York Times* article cited the poor conditions of Kentucky miners. Heller, along with other New Frontiersmen, subsequently developed a small-scale program which involved neighborhood-based organizations. The community action program was intended to serve as a local planning board for each community and to coordinate new federal anti-poverty programs. Heller, however, failed to broach the idea with the president before his death.[25]

Informed of the community action plans, Johnson was ambivalent. On the one hand, he was attracted to its Kennedy origins. "If *they* thought it up," Horace Busby recalled, "that was it." On the other hand, he was uncomfortable with its small scale. Although the proposal offered a careful, systematic approach which would avoid waste, its impact would not be immediate enough to be felt before the fall election. The Labor Department was also against the proposal, preferring large-scale employment programs which would add directly to the poor's income. Johnson opted for a large, well-publicized program which would offer concrete results quickly enough to win public opinion.[26]

In order to create a legislative legacy on a grand scale, Johnson needed money. A second priority that he had declared in his November 27 address to Congress was passage of Kennedy's tax reform bill. During the summer of 1963 the House of Representatives had passed the bill. By the time of the assassination, however, it had stalled in the Senate Finance Committee. Everything that Johnson wanted to do in terms of his own social programs was contingent upon its passage. "Unless he got the tax cut," Valenti recalled, "they weren't sure they could keep the economy moving upward in this ascending spiral."[27]

Kennedy had submitted to Congress an $11 billion tax cut. The delay in its passage was due to the discrepancy between Kennedy's proposed federal budget of $102.2 billion and an estimated revenue of only $93.1 billion. The Finance Committee was reluctant to address a tax reduction bill in light of a potential $9 billion deficit. In December 1963 Johnson met with economic advisers to devise a solution. He maintained that he would not be able to secure the Senate's vote unless he could bring the budget under $100 billion. He had talked with Senator Harry Byrd, chairman of the Finance Committee, and was told of the need to make a money-saving gesture. The new president was also aware that Kennedy's popular support had been damaged by an image of fiscal irresponsibility: "I knew we had to turn that feeling around."[28]

Pressuring Congress, Johnson reasserted his demand for passage of the tax cut during his State of the Union Address on January 8. He announced that the budget had been successfully pared to $97.9 billion. Warning that delaying enactment would hurt consumption, investment, and employment, he echoed Kennedy's campaign pledge "to keep this country moving." His budgeting gesture, rhetoric, and personal persuasion moved the Tax Revenue Act out of the Finance Committee. The Senate passed it in February. "So at that moment," Valenti recalled, "it was really as he said, 'Let us continue.'" Again, appearing before a television audience, Johnson signed into law the largest tax reduction in history and reinvoked the name of "our late, beloved President John F. Kennedy." He then drove to Jacqueline Kennedy's Georgetown home where he publicly presented her with the ceremonial pens.[29]

Meanwhile, Johnson advanced the Office of Employment Opportunity Act. On February 1 he named Sargent Shriver, the late president's brother-in-law, as director of the OEO. The selection of Shriver was shrewd, giving the impression of continuity while driving a wedge within the Kennedy camp. Robert Kennedy had been interested in commanding the War on Poverty, but Johnson would not give such a high-profile position to a political rival. Shriver, meanwhile, was director of the Peace Corps and friendly with one of Johnson's closest aides, Bill Moyers. He had shown his loyalty by informing Johnson of Robert's various complaints against the president after the assassination. (In the months and years ahead, Shriver further irritated "blood" Kennedys by lobbying on his own behalf for the vice presidency in 1964 and claiming the Kennedy mantle when he ran for president in 1972.) Shriver concurred that the War on Poverty needed to be waged on a grand scale with quick victories; the community action programs would "never fly." Johnson relinquished the planning strategy to Shriver, who devised a comprehensive legislative package, including job training, work relief, remedial and adult education, rural assistance, small loans, and a domestic version of the Peace Corps.[30]

In securing passage of the OEO bill, Johnson drew on his years of experience with Congress. He lobbied senators and congressmen, appealing to their own interests and moral obligations. Appeasing hostile Southern conservatives, he persuaded Philip Landrum, a Democratic congressman from Georgia, to floor-manage the bill instead of black Congressman Adam Clayton Powell of Harlem. As chairperson of the Education and Labor Committees, Powell had been the expected floor manager. Johnson also assured Southern conservatives that Adam Yarmolinsky would not be placed in an anticipated position with the OEO. Yarmolinsky was an official with the Defense Department, which was urging desegregation of Southern military bases. The OEO bill passed in Congress on August 20, one week before the Democratic convention. Johnson's skill in managing its passage, while simultaneously advancing the civil rights and tax bills, impressed Kennedy staff members unaccustomed to such aggressiveness. "I never saw anybody work with Congress like that," Lawrence O'Brien commented. "The man's a genius."[31]

By the spring of 1964 Johnson's activism had won him respect from the public and press. "No problem seemed too big to tackle, no audience too small to regale, no hand too remote to shake," *Newsweek* reported. "And everywhere, everything he touched turned to political gold." A Harris survey on the eve of the Democratic convention showed the public overwhelmingly impressed with Johnson's accomplishments. In contrast to John Kennedy, he was rated thirty-three points higher in "getting congress to act," twenty-eight points higher in "controlling spending," eighteen points higher in "keeping the economy healthy," and eleven points higher in "handling race problems." Moreover, 75 percent of the voters approved of his record. In the fall the Survey Research Center of the University of Michigan concluded that Johnson's two most positive attributes in terms of voter appeal were his experience and his achievements.[32]

Johnson's legislative success, however, did not translate into love for Johnson the person. "One clear pattern," *Newsweek* reported in the spring, "even Mr. Johnson's supporters are less taken with him personally than they are impressed by his record of getting things done." Unlike the appeal of Eisenhower and Kennedy, Johnson's "impact on the electorate is dominated by voters' reaction to what he has done as opposed to what he is or seems to be." At his best he was described as a "hard-working President, bright and clever, a friendly, warm, earthy person." At his worst he was "too much of a wheeler-dealer politician, too corny in style, who tends at times to be evasive."[33]

Johnson's leadership style contrasted markedly to John Kennedy's, bringing with it an undertone of disappointment. Kennedy had avoided the "dirty work" of Congress in favor of lofty expressions of purpose and goals. Johnson exploited and manipulated the system. Each legislative victory heightened his reputation as a political operator who got things done through shrewd bargaining and arm-twisting. Critics charged that he was motivated more by self-interest than by benevolence. "What else has he got?" a New England Democrat remarked upon passage of the OEO bill. "Not any other thing. Everything else is New Frontier and JFK. He wants to go before the voters with a major bill of his own and this is it." Johnson's opportunism diminished him in comparison with his predecessor, who, Kennedy "loyalists" contended, had been intrinsically moved by the hardships of poverty. In sum, Johnson displaced idealism with a less attractive mode of realism. The change vaguely insulted Kennedy's memory and made segments of the public uncomfortable.[34]

Aware of this stigma, some members of the press came to Johnson's defense. "LBJ isn't JFK?" *New Republic* asked. "So what? He's impulsive, emotional, sentimental, sensitive, bumptious, corny, prolix, able and Texan. He's also on the right side of some fine things, and is pushing them with skilled and ferocious energy." James Reston reminded readers that politics was, by its nature, unsavory. Johnson may have been less charismatic than Kennedy, but he wrestled successfully with the realities of politics. "The lovers of style are not too happy with the new Administration," he concluded, "but the lovers of substance are not complaining."[35]

During the fall campaign Johnson proceeded as planned to appeal to Kennedy liberals by promoting himself as the executor of his predecessor's will. "I tried to pick up where President Kennedy had left off," he told one audience. "I tried to carry forward a program for all of you that he had dreamed for you." He called for future programs which "must meet the standards of President Kennedy." He claimed that he had made a promise to both God and his family that he would forever "carry on for him and for you, in his program, in your program." Once, he suggested that Barry Goldwater might threaten Kennedy's dream. The message was repeated in fourteen states. In Massachusetts he added a personal touch, referring to

Kennedy as "my beloved benefactor and friend." He had come back to Boston, he explained, because "I never wanted [John Kennedy's friends and constituents] to have the slightest doubt about me." Sometimes he quantified his commitment, noting that he had inherited fifty-one bills that John Kennedy had pending in Congress. Each bill, he boasted, had been passed through the Senate since he became president.[36]

After the election Johnson continued to identify his own achievements with Kennedy, hoping to inspire even more legislation. Speaking to an audience of young adults at a dedication of a Job Corps center in the spring of 1965, he imagined two presidents who were watching approvingly from Heaven. One was Lincoln. The other was "the man who originally conceived of the poverty program and who dreamed of it, but was not spared to see his dreams come true." "How much I know he must enjoy this very moment," Johnson told them. "President Kennedy is watching all of you. He would be mighty proud of you." Later that year he spoke for the late president when trying to move Senate leaders to further legislative action. After recalling that he had been "called upon to pick up the torch," he wanted "on his behalf—watching us from Heaven—to thank every member here for your help in carrying on some of the things he was leading us toward. . . . I know he thanks you."[37]

By drawing on Kennedy's rhetoric and plans, citing his heavenly approval, and exalting the past, Johnson hoped to win the confidence of Kennedy's supporters. But in doing so, he repositioned himself into Kennedy's shadow. He heightened John Kennedy's reputation as a man of inspiration and idealism while reinforcing his own image as a mere politician trying desperately to gain vicarious affection. The dilemma was painfully revealed during a visit he made to a poor Appalachian family while president. He had spoken to the mother and father about how he was making efforts on their behalf. He had been pleased by their conversation and had promised them he would continue to work for a better future. "But then as I walked toward the door," he recalled, "I noticed two pictures on the shabby wall. One was Jesus Christ on the cross; the other was John Kennedy. I felt as if I'd been slapped in the face."[38]

For the remainder of his presidency Johnson resented his predecessor receiving credit for the War on Poverty, despite having promoted the notion himself. Once, he sought confirmation that he, not Kennedy, was its true creator. "I want to see what John Kennedy has said about a war on poverty in any of his speeches," Johnson instructed his aides. "Get all the quotes— ask [researcher Fred] Panzer to do it. Anything he said on a programmed war on poverty." Within days, Panzer informed him that Kennedy spoke only of "individual efforts"; he "rarely spoke in terms of a unified, comprehensive campaign to strike" at poverty. There were no references to "anti-poverty," "war on poverty," or "economic opportunity" in the presidential papers. Panzer contrasted Kennedy's lack of references to Johnson's numerous comments. Johnson's frustration, however, became generalized as he tried to prove he was somehow "better" than his predecessor. He was asked in a memorandum if the 1964 year-end analysis of the Democratic party should be "the 1-year Johnson record" or "the 4-year Kennedy record." Johnson picked the former. In the summer of 1966 he wanted a summary of his achievements during his first thousand days in office. The time frame paralleled the duration of the Kennedy administration. Aides warned against making the data public, but Johnson persisted until his last weeks in office in seeking box-score comparisons.[39]

The competitiveness underscored Johnson's frustration with Kennedy's legacy. Privately he turned hostile, demeaning Kennedy's style as ineffective. "Kennedy," he remarked, "couldn't get the Ten Commandments past Congress." He bragged that he passed the legislation that the "Harvards" could not. "They say Jack Kennedy had style," he noted during a meeting with senators, "but I'm the one who's got the bills passed." His comments illustrated his fundamental misunderstanding of the changing nature of politics. He had tried to surpass Kennedy in terms of substance when presidential success was becoming, increasingly, a matter determined by image. Substantive comparisons might prove him superior by his own criteria, but in the new political era accelerated by Kennedy, achievements perhaps mattered less than style.[40]

CHAPTER

VII

PROJECTING THE JOHNSON IMAGE

While the public appreciated Lyndon Johnson's policies, it became clear that his vast achievements were obscured by an unpopular political style. Aware of the growing importance of image, White House aides devoted considerable attention to remodeling the president during the transition year of 1964. Some wanted to highlight his regionalism and expansive personality in an effort to let "Johnson be Johnson." Others were entrapped by past standards and borrowed from the image-management techniques of earlier presidents, most notably Franklin Roosevelt. In order to exploit immediate sentiments, however, aides sought to imbue Johnson with John Kennedy's attributes.

Within the first few weeks of the administration, Johnson's image problems were addressed by his aide Horace Busby, a former reporter who had served as press secretary to Senator Johnson since 1948 and as a consultant and speechwriter while he was vice president. In mid-January 1964 he brought to the president's attention a survey by *Public Opinion Index for Industry*. As an interest holder in a lucrative Washington newsletter, *The American Businessman*, Busby was impressed with *Index*, a publication intended for the same audience. It offered regular national opinion samplings conducted by the Opinion Research Corporation of Princeton, New Jersey, and had recently published comparative surveys contrasting the popular images of John Kennedy and Lyndon Johnson. One poll was conducted a few days before the Kennedy assassination, another about a month later.[1]

Busby sent Johnson a six-page summary of the polls plus a three-and-a-half-page "Comment and Analysis" which he qualified as "my purely

123

personal interpretation." He began by recalling Kennedy's declining popularity during his last fourteen months in office. The late president's strong
posturing on such issues as civil rights, taxes, and medical care accounted,
in part, for the shift in his approval ratings. But he did not win the expected
support that firm stances on these issues had traditionally brought: "This
would suggest some need to evaluate the success—or lack of it—of the
Kennedy Administration people in communicating outside Washington the
favorable image generally communicated in Washington itself." Busby then
cited a disturbing aspect of the poll: data indicating that Johnson, during the
November poll, was "an unknown quantity to a majority of Americans."
"Where 24% of the public felt they knew 'a great deal' about President
Kennedy," he reported, "only 5% had the same feeling toward President
Johnson." Since the assassination, poll results would likely show that
Johnson's personality was better known. But Busby cautioned that "this
does not erase the fact that the void of being 'an unknown quantity' still
remains to be filled." The upcoming election necessitated immediate actions
in image management, for the White House had to take the initiative before
Johnson's opponents fixed a negative perception of him.

In developing an effective image-management strategy, Busby thought
that the differences in the ratings between Johnson and Kennedy "may
provide clues to 'strong' and 'weak' points." According to the November
poll, Johnson's image as vice president was "generally on the plus side."
His most "favorable" quality was a "warm and friendly personality," which
35 percent of the people believed he possessed, while his most "unfavorable" quality was that he appeared "too much of a politician." Although
Kennedy was rated nineteen points higher than Johnson on the measure of a
"warm and friendly personality," this discrepancy was considered a strength
compared with measures of other qualities. Kennedy, for example, was rated
twenty-eight percentage points higher than Johnson in terms of "speaking
his own mind." And there was a 23 percent difference in public perception
of each man "being serious and thoughtful." "The principal plus of the
Johnson image until November 22 was personality," Busby concluded.
"This is a key strength to be exploited."

Busby recommended that Johnson balance his "political" image with his
"warm and friendly personality." He warned, however, that it "must be
exploited with care. Too much effusion—e.g. folksiness, etc.—only brings
to the fore [Johnson's] highest rated unfavorable quality: that of being too
much of a politician." Concluding that "personality is the main force of
identification between the public and the Presidency," he urged Johnson to
"convey a stable, steady, somewhat remote and reflective personal image so
that the people can individually feel close to the President. . . ." Kennedy, as

well as Eisenhower and Franklin Roosevelt, "profited enormously in terms of public affection" because they were perceived as "above run-of-the-mill politicians." "A concerted program should be developed and implemented in the very near future to create the seedbed for this type of image to flourish about President Johnson." Other presidents had won "public affection" by masking their "political" temperaments. Johnson had to project an image that disguised what he was—an astute bargainer, a brilliant manipulator of the political system.

Although Busby had drawn from the success of several role models, the most valued lessons came from Kennedy. The late president had been "fartherest" above Johnson in four personality categories: (1) "speaking his own mind," (2) "having strong convictions," (3) "being progressive and forward looking," and (4) "being serious and thoughtful." The four categories had traditionally been "weak points" for Johnson while they were vital to the public's affection for Kennedy. Johnson therefore needed to concentrate "deliberately in image activities on communicating these points." Busby credited Johnson for thus far developing his "progressive" image: "The other categories, however, require more subtle handling and more concentrated effort than the situation has permitted until now." He concluded his analysis by comparing the president's image with Goldwater's and Rockefeller's. While pleased that Johnson's personal image was strong, he advised that his positive traits "be carefully exploited, cultivated and added to by deliberate image activities."[2]

Busby's analysis reflected an ambivalence that burdened the administration. On the one hand, he sought to depart from Kennedy's image by deliberately promoting Johnson's "folksy" attributes. Presumably this entailed an emphasis on his Western heritage as well as an effort to identify him with the general population rather than East Coast urbanites. On the other hand, Busby advised Johnson to emulate characteristics reminiscent of Kennedy, especially thoughtfulness. Johnson's conflict with the Kennedy "mystique" was not confined to himself and was not simply a manifestation of his own insecurities. It was reflected in his "manager's" mind. Moreover, the president was becoming entrapped by past images, forced to appear as something he was not and pursuing standards that would prove difficult to achieve.

The Media Environment

Johnson was disposed to accept Busby's advice. Throughout his career he had been mindful of public perceptions and had altered his appearance, media strategies, and expressed convictions accordingly. As a young congressman he had mimicked President Franklin Roosevelt, smoking cigarettes through a holder and practicing his mannerisms in front of the mirror. In the Senate, Johnson had emulated many of Richard Russell's characteristics, displaying a mild, unassuming temperament and downplaying his usual flamboyancy. As vice president he had also adjusted his style to suit the New Frontier. "Johnson always lived in the shadow of Kennedy," aide Robert Kintner recalled. He altered his appearance and manners to appear more "Eastern." He dressed stylishly, trying to match Kennedy's notoriety as a trend-setter. Impressed with Kennedy's reputation as a "ladies' man," he employed physically attractive secretaries. He became concerned about etiquette and wanted a refined young man to be with him in order to handle small talk at social occasions. "The problem with his mimicry," George Reedy recalled, "was that he extended it beyond all bounds. He had an idea that he could become a great man by imitating great men and this led to some odd moments."[3]

Appreciating the importance of image, President Johnson enlarged the functions of the White House press office. He hired four different press secretaries in five years, in part trying to find someone to "sell" him with the same expertise with which Kennedy had been marketed. At one point he expanded his image-management team by hiring Robert Kintner, a former president of the National Broadcasting Company and a long-time friend of the Kennedys. He instructed his staff to watch his television appearances and forward critiques to him. A steady stream of recommendations on how best to portray the president circulated among the White House staff. Reflecting on the administration, Harry McPherson noted, "I was surprised and a little bit chagrined at how much of it has to do with P. R. . . . . We just spent a hell of a lot of time in that."[4]

Attracted to innovative media techniques and privately drawn to Kennedy's style, Johnson was receptive to suggestions that he emulate selected aspects of Kennedy's public image. But his ability to convey continuity was hindered by his personal style. His approach to people and politics was the opposite of Kennedy's and incompatible with emerging social trends. During the 1950s, popular works such as David Riesman's *The Lonely Crowd* and William H. Whyte's *The Organization Man* had identified pervasive social types who epitomized mass conformity and consumer values. Riesman was critical of "other-directed" personalities, those who changed their behavior out of an exceptional sensitivity to the actions and wishes of others. The desire to be liked by others provided a chief source of direction. In politics Riesman referred to "other-directed" personalities as "inside dopesters," those who lacked political emotionalism and brought a consumer orientation to politics. Whyte, meanwhile, defined the "organization man" as one who saw the group as the source of creativity. In politics he was more involved in the process than in the end results.[5]

Although Riesman and Whyte focused their studies on corporate leaders, they recorded a shift in mass culture which in turn was reflected in political leadership. By their definitions, Johnson embodied certain qualities of the "other-directed organization man." To be sure, he was a complex individual who defied simplistic definitions. His political efforts were seldom undertaken for the good of the organization. More often he sought to advance himself at the expense of the very institutions of which he was a part. Yet his surface image appeared consistent with the conformist characteristics identified by Riesman and Whyte.

During the 1960s such writers as Norman Mailer, Tom Wicker, and John William Ward credited John Kennedy with rebuking the "plastic" world from which the Riesman-Whyte character type was drawn. His youth, idealism, detachment, competitiveness, energy, and intellect distinguished him from his contemporaries. He was praised for bringing a fresh, innovative manner to politics which re-defined leadership and sought to bypass the cumbersome bureaucratic process. Kennedy was "the Holden Caulfield of American politics," Wicker wrote in 1965. "To idealistic young people, to skeptical intellectuals, to Americans weary of the materialism and mass culture of their society, he struck all the right notes."[6]

Michael Maccoby's 1976 analysis of postwar corporate and political scenes delineated a new personality type that emerged during the early 1960s. Believing that the "other-directed organization man" fit the 1950s better than the 1960s, Maccoby discovered a character type whose traits allowed him to advance above the status quo. The "gamesman" enjoyed challenges, risks, fresh approaches, and shortcuts. He was competitive, innovative, and rebelled against bureaucracy. He also delivered by turning a profit for the corporation or a victory for a political party. "[I]t was Kennedy," Maccoby charged, "who most embodied the new competitive, adventurous spirit and became the model for the corporate gamesman."[7]

Although effective in passing legislation, Johnson's "style" was a throwback to personality traits against which Kennedy had revolted. Maccoby described Johnson as an old-style "jungle-fighter," one who "behaviorally acted out in [his] ruthless suppression of opponents and castrating domination of subordinates by [his] force. . . ." Whereas Kennedy was a cosmopolitan figure, Johnson was a "cornball" and a "slob." He read few books, had little interest in art and ideas, and preferred barbecues to opera. Manipulating political power was virtually the only thing that interested him. Whether he was in the House of Representatives or the Senate, he worked his way up the political "corporate ladder" by "wheeling and dealing." The era of the "gamesman" was ill suited for "the Antichrist of New Politics." What the public wanted was cool detachment. What they got was a man passionately involved with the system. Johnson was Willie Loman to Kennedy's Caulfield.[8]

In addition to contending with changing popular images, Johnson was burdened by an incompatible media environment. Since he first came to Washington in the early 1930s, the social composition of reporters had undergone important changes. Independent polls conducted in 1936 and 1962 showed later Washington correspondents to be better educated, increasingly liberal, and predominantly from northeastern areas of the country. Moreover, definitions of journalism were changing. According to Wicker, professional journalism during the first twenty years of the postwar period stressed "objectivity." The reporter's primary role was to preserve the official record. Although Wicker offered no empirical evidence, he sensed that print journalism's attempt to compete with television in the 1960s generated an increasing number of "subjective" pieces. Unable to match television's "objective" eye, reporters complemented the nightly news programs by inserting analysis, background, and commentary into their stories. The result was a reporting style that became more adversarial during the Johnson years.[9]

Johnson did not perceive these precise changes in journalism, but he did suspect that the social and cultural background of the news media worked against him. He was convinced that "the metropolitan press of the Eastern seaboard" limited his appeal as a national political figure. He was hurt by the wave of "derisive articles about my style, my clothes, my manner, my accent, and my family. . . ." The news media's disdain for the South represented "an automatic reflex, unconscious or deliberate, on the part of opinion molders of the North and East in the press and television."[10]

To some degree Johnson was correct in his assessment. "A special excitement went out of Washington when John Kennedy died," Ben Bagdikian reported in the winter of 1964. "I don't hate Johnson," a noted reporter told Harry McPherson. "I just hate the fact that all the grace and wit has gone from what the American President says." Johnson's insecurities, however, prompted him to exaggerate the pervasiveness of this attitude. He characterized all reporters as members of the "Eastern press" and believed they were infatuated with the Kennedy style. Wicker, who was raised in South Carolina, noted, "Even I was considered pro-Kennedy, although I was not favorable toward Kennedy." "Johnson was paranoid about the press," *Newsweek*'s Charles Roberts recalled. "He not only feared that JFK and his charisma would be a hard act to follow, but he felt from the beginning that the White House press was prejudiced against him." According to Roberts, Washington reporters regularly received complaints from Johnson and his staff that "the White House press was so pro-Kennedy that it was anti-Johnson." "I assured him that this was not the case," he recalled. "But in his five years in office he was never disabused of that notion that Washington correspondents were effete, elitist, pseudo-intellectuals who never gave him a fair shake."[11]

Johnson's media environment was further complicated by the television presidency he had inherited. During the previous twenty years television had inundated American society. In 1945 there had been eight thousand television sets in the United States. By 1960 the number had increased to some fifty million. Television's prestige was heightened by its coverage of political conventions and congressional hearings during the 1950s. Appreciating its potential, Kennedy developed a variety of formats to exploit the medium, becoming the first television president. From 1960 through 1963 he appeared on television through four debates, seventy press conferences and interviews, a half-dozen White House–sponsored documentaries, and nine "video chats."[12]

Johnson's physical appearance, background, and temperament were poorly suited to the new television era. Although literature on communication theory is extensive and contradictory, there is general agreement on the qualities necessary for an effective television image. As a predominantly visual medium, television creates an intimate but fleeting form of communication which places new demands on political leaders. An attractive physical appearance, a "cool," sincere presence, a willingness to use theatrical devices, and an ability to convey messages succinctly were paramount to Kennedy's success. His press conferences "cast him as the keen young executive of the computer generation," Tom Wicker noted, "a pace-setter for a generation that believed in living well, looking sharp and knowing all the answers."[13]

Johnson was less capable of exploiting television's opportunities. His mannerisms were too overbearing, his accent too strong, his appearance too homely. His years of political stumping prepared him inadequately for such a "cool" medium. Although his performances before small gatherings were excellent, "when he went before television, something happened," Jack Valenti recalled. "He took on a presidential air, he fused a kind of new Johnson which wasn't the real Johnson. He became stiff and foreboding." Johnson appreciated television's importance but was repelled by its theatrical demands. He refused to practice his media skills and found the process demeaning and artificial. Rejecting an offer by CBS to film his staff, he explained to Reedy that "you have much more work than you can handle and these men are workers not actors." On another occasion Valenti had convinced Johnson to consult with a Hollywood producer. After the press reported the arrangements, Johnson became "infuriated" and canceled future meetings. He never devoted the necessary attention to developing and refining his television skills.[14]

Johnson's general mistrust of television was complicated by Kennedy's legacy of successful performances. Johnson was especially uncomfortable with press conferences. During the weeks after the assassination, Pierre Salinger suggested that the president experiment initially with a variety of informal press conference settings. Moyers agreed that Johnson should avoid television press conferences "at least for a while." He disparaged them as "little more than a circus at which a few reporters could ham it up." The Kennedy shadow underscored Johnson's resistance. According to Valenti, he "felt that the Kennedy phantom which ran down every corridor in the White House . . . would come alive like Banquo's ghost at every one of these press conferences and [reporters] would compare him unfavorably with Kennedy."[15]

Initially Johnson met with small groups of journalists in the Oval Office. The change was well received by reporters. Soon, however, the networks and press urged him to appear on television. Wicker reported in February 1964 that, according to aides, the "primary reason" he had not held a televised press conference was his fear of direct comparisons with Kennedy. His first televised press conference came four months into his presidency, after which he was sent encouraging reviews. "[I]f today's appearance is any indication," read a report from ABC network radio, "the President need have no fear [of being compared with Kennedy]." His performance was proof that Johnson "can handle the big ones."[16]

Johnson's frustration in competing against Kennedy prompted ambivalence about image management in general. "All that talk about my lack of charisma was a lot of crap," he told Doris Kearns. "There is no such thing as charisma. It's just a creation of the press and the pollsters." Such comments seemed intended to reassure himself that his image was beyond his control. His denial, however, sometimes shifted toward competitiveness. Shortly after the assassination he criticized aides for "not getting my picture on the front page the way you did Kennedy's." During a 1964 campaign appearance he brought reporters to the restraining fences that held back a crowd. "You all say I've got no charisma," he allegedly told them, "—that crowds don't respond to me like they did to Kennedy. You fellows stay right here beside me and I'll show you that you're wrong."[17]

Kennedy's popularity, despite substantive shortcomings, convinced Johnson that media managers were responsible for the late president's "success."

But he exaggerated their abilities. After Pierre Salinger resigned, for example, Johnson demanded that his new press secretary, George Reedy, mold his image as Salinger had shaped Kennedy's. He wanted to arrange press conferences in such a fashion that every question would be known in advance. It was a "demand," Reedy believed, "that was apocalyptic in its sheer loneliness." When Reedy told Johnson of the impossibility of "planting" every question, the president kept insisting that Salinger had done so for Kennedy. Reedy finally came to understand what had caused Johnson to misunderstand the process. Because Kennedy had been provided a list of anticipated questions and had been so adept at conducting press conferences, Johnson assumed that Salinger had prearranged the questions with reporters.[18]

It is tempting to exaggerate the length of Kennedy's shadow, as Johnson himself often did. He could not have been expected to appreciate larger trends at work. The shifting popular images, the changing nature of journalism, and television's theatrical subtleties were complex and interrelated. So Johnson directed his frustrations onto his predecessor. Kennedy had exploited new media conditions so effectively that he came to symbolize the standards which Johnson both pursued and resented. Johnson's last press secretary, George Christian, lamented that, since Kennedy, all presidents have measured themselves against his image and "fret about not being as adept at capturing the public's imagination." Johnson and his successors have "tried to create an artificial atmosphere that's not really reflective of their own character or ability." Wicker similarly sensed that "Johnson always remained highly conscious of the Kennedy competition." Although aides refused to discuss the "mystique's" impact for the record, they privately acknowledged its haunting presence. John Kennedy was more a representative of an era than he was a pioneer. Perceiving him as the latter, Johnson adjusted his image, less to adapt to changing trends than to match Kennedy—and this compounded his inability to project an effective image.[19]

The Johnson Image

Given his flamboyant nature and his propensity to make himself the center of attention, it was inevitable that Johnson would brand his unique personality onto the news media and public. Images of rocking chairs, sailboats, and elegant balls were quickly replaced by barbecues, beagles, and horseback riding. Magazine articles described him as a mixture of Judge Roy Bean, Paul Bunyan, and John Wayne. His behavior after the assassination was heralded for conveying the necessary strength, confidence, and calm. His legislative accomplishments communicated shrewdness and power. Reporters and voters were drawn to his "common man" image. "The most difficult thing we have to cope with," one Republican remarked, "is the image of Johnson as just one of the folks."[20]

By early April, Busby sent Johnson a fourteen-page memorandum expressing tentative satisfaction with the development of his image. Once concerned that Johnson was an "unknown quantity," he noted that the "impact upon public awareness" since March "is phenomenal." But he cautioned that "of itself impact is not image." Johnson faced a number of persistent problems, including his Senate image as a tactician lacking in goals. He was subject to charges of "regionalism, parochialism, cloakroomism, non-intellectualism" which would affect the public's perception of him as a national leader.

Ironically, Busby found that the public perception of Johnson as a man *not* concerned with image endeared him to the "average man"; it gave him a rare sense of appearing apolitical. Both Eisenhower and Kennedy had benefited from appearing aloof and indifferent to politics. But because of Johnson's well-known political nature and experience, his "common man" image was susceptible to Republican attacks that it was "shallow and superficial." To strengthen his populist image, Busby recommended that he expand his appeal to a broad range of people and, learning from his predecessors, issue a call to action "against specific obstacles, opposition, and opponents." A lack of immediate threats or common danger made it "desirable not to minimize the importance of style in the prepared activities under White House auspices." Kennedy's image had suffered because he appeared preoccupied with the East. Johnson therefore should "establish [a] genuine rapport with the vast middle majority of America—particularly beyond the Eastern seaboard."[21]

Others also sought to broaden Johnson's populist image. In January Valenti urged the president to initiate a television program called "Letters from the People." Johnson would sit before television cameras and respond to selected White House mail allowing the public to "identify with the President in a warm, human way." Valenti did not think the program would be "too folksy." "On the contrary it is in keeping with your style, your manner. . . ." He further recommended a television address explaining his State of the Union message. It would "expose you as a sensible, tough, compassionate, and down-to-earth leader. . . ." In March columnist James Reston privately recommended a media strategy intended to permit Johnson's "genuine personality" to come through. The president should visit selected poverty areas on weekends, allowing the news media to cover his conversations with workers and lower-income people. He should then follow his visits with a "warm, very human type" televised address. Reston suggested that the program be called *Weekend with the President* and be produced every two months. It would "play to your great skill and warmth in informal dealings with people."[22]

One area in which Johnson excelled was stumping before large audiences. In earlier campaigns for Congress or in overseas travels as vice president, he was enthusiastic about meeting throngs of "common folk." "Oh Boy!" Johnson once exclaimed to an aide after hearing the roar of approval. "Listen to that! It even beats screwing." Reedy remembered that after Johnson engaged crowds, shaking hands with thousands of people, he admired the scratches on his hands and talked about them in loving terms; there was "something post-orgasmic about the scene." That spring he embarked on a series of tours across the Northeast and through the poverty pockets of the Appalachian region. Attempting to secure passage of his anti-poverty legislation, he toured small towns, donned his Texas hat, and thickened his accent to appeal to the "common man." "Few have managed to brand their personality on the presidency so quickly and so indelibly," *Time* reported. "Corny as a johnny-cake, folksy as a country fiddler, persuasive as a television pitchman, he is also both efficient and effective."[23]

Memories of John Kennedy, however, sometimes cast Johnson's traits in a negative light. In late December 1963 he invited West Germany's Chancellor Ludwig Erhard to his ranch in Texas, where the itinerary included a Western-style barbecue. Lady Bird Johnson feared that the event might contrast poorly to the Kennedys' more stately occasions. Seeking reassurance, she asked Tom Wicker, "What do you think people out East will think about it?" Her concern was justified. A Kennedy holdover publicly disparaged the reception: "I didn't know whether to laugh or cry." Major magazines analyzed the change in style, usually to Johnson's detriment. A popular refrain heard in Washington that spring typified the reaction. "From Kennedy to Johnson—from culture to corn."[24]

Defending Johnson, his friends and aides argued that he was gearing his culture for the people, not to elitists. Others recalled correctly that Kennedy used to fall asleep during cultural events. "He's Lyndon Johnson," an aide remarked, "he's got to be Lyndon Johnson, and he's going to continue to be Lyndon Johnson. He's not going to try to be something that some newspapermen seem to want him to be." But the real Lyndon Johnson brought with him additional image problems. In April he invited reporters to his Texas ranch and gave them a guided tour of his property. Riding his Lincoln Continental, he drove over eighty-five miles an hour, covering his speedometer with his hat and narrowly avoiding a head-on collision. It was later reported that he also had a cup of beer "within easy sipping distance." Two weeks later Johnson continued his indiscriminate behavior when he raised two pet beagles by their ears on the White House lawn. The photograph was widely circulated and inspired a wave of derisive political cartoons, editorials, and letters to the editor.[25]

Sensitive to the "bias" of the "Kennedy press," aides felt that cultural prejudices prompted undue attention to the incidents. Picking up a beagle by the ears was common practice among hunters who insisted upon a rugged regimen for their dogs. And driving across the range with a beer in hand represented an acceptable Texas life-style. Johnson believed that the reporters, as guests of the ranch, had violated the rules of hospitality in reporting the incident, and that they would not have done so had they been covering Kennedy.[26]

At issue was a sense of unfairness. Both Kennedy and Johnson had strong regional accents. But the former's was considered cultured and intellectual while the latter's was regarded as "ignorant." Both men swam nude in the White House pool; Kennedy appeared dashing while Johnson seemed uncouth. Kennedy was often every bit as "crude" as Johnson, preferring a James Bond movie to Shakespeare. But people saw what they expected to see. In an age when the most popular television show was *The Beverly Hillbillies,* Johnson's "outlandish" behavior confirmed expectations. Like the television character Jed Clampett, he seemed suddenly thrust into a situation for which he lacked the proper refinement. Each idiosyncrasy was proof of his "backwardness."[27]

In an effort to offset Johnson's "crudities" and to convey some degree of continuity in terms of image, staff members sought to blend his image with Kennedy's. Beneath the highly publicized barbecues and hootnannies, they suggested, there resided in the White House a "closet" Kennedy. The degree to which aides deliberately sought to model Johnson after Kennedy is difficult to discern. Johnson's aides were intelligent and perceptive people who recognized the limitations of image management and the sheer impossibility of trying to remodel their president after a man so different in manner and appearance. Their effort to reconstruct Johnson likely reflected their absorption of the cultural trends that emerged in the early 1960s—the same trends that had influenced Johnson. Like Johnson, they looked to Kennedy as a role model, for he possessed those characteristics that not only separated him from the political crowd but garnered great public affection.

Among the images that aides sought to imbue in Johnson was that of an intellectual. Although he lacked a prestigious academic background, Johnson possessed a superior intellect. His political skills during one-on-one confrontations were unequaled. His ability to maneuver legislation, study and formulate policies, and cultivate support were, by all accounts, remarkable. Aides with elite educations agreed that he was vastly intelligent. Johnson's problem therefore was not one of intelligence but of image. As sociologist Milton Gordon elaborated in 1964, intellectuals, as a social group, were popularly perceived as people with creative minds. They were "people for whom ideas, concepts, literature, music, painting, the dance have intrinsic meaning—are part of the social-psychological atmosphere which one breathes." Occupationally they were often employed as college professors, researchers, journalists, and artists. Their intelligence was conveyed less by their deeds than by their pursuit of "existential" excellence through words, ideals, and philosophy. John Kennedy had been a representative figure of this intellectual subculture. He was a Harvard graduate and Pulitzer prize–winning author who, as president, surrounded himself with aides of similar Ivy League backgrounds. During his administration he entertained poets, novelists, and musicians in an attempt to promote artistic excellence. He emphasized detachment, idealism, and elegant education. Later an adviser reminded Robert Kennedy that he, too, was part of "the nebulous new 'existential politics' which are emerging in our more affluent, better educated, aculturized [sic] society."[28]

At a surface level, Johnson's intelligence was no match for the Kennedy image. His expansive behavior, Southern accent, and "corny" demeanor appeared inferior by contrast. Measurements of intellect based upon academic standards had always intimidated him. "The men of ideas think little of me," he once told Kearns, "they despise me." At college he frequently exaggerated his Intelligence Quotient scores and lied about the number of A grades he received. As president he was uncomfortable in the presence of academics. "He victimized himself," Busby recalled, "by frequently bemoaning the fact that he had men with prestigious educations around him—Ivy Leaguers and Rhodes scholars—and he only had an education from Southwest Texas State Teachers College in San Marcos."[29]

Johnson tried to compensate for his feelings of inadequacy by demeaning those with "superior" educations. Intellectuals, he said, were out of touch with the reality of politics. They were "overbred smart alecks who live in Georgetown and think in Harvard." When speaking to them he exaggerated his Texas "twang" as if to remind them of the irony of his superior position. He sometimes tried to humiliate them by conducting lengthy discussions in a bathroom, defecating in their presence.[30]

Although aides did not try to pass Johnson off as an academician, they did try to create an environment that suggested similarities to the previous administration. In late January Busby thought that the current political lull made it "the best of times for creative and inventive image-broadening activities." It was tactically important to maintain the initiative through "unexpected and imaginative" actions which projected "more personality" and reflected "a greater breadth of interest and concern." He suggested that Johnson portray himself as above the political fray by associating with the academic and cultural communities, which he characterized as "*an important segment still withholding judgment.*" He did not believe that a "frontal assault" would be beneficial. "*But the time is ripe for a varied, subtle exploitation of Presidential acquaintances and friendships . . .*" [emphasis Busby's].

Busby recommended that Johnson court artists and intellectuals like conductor Erich Leinsdorf and writer John Steinbeck. He should also maintain close links to Kennedy's special assistant, Arthur Schlesinger, by sending him to Europe to deliver favorable lectures. His role would send strong signals to intellectuals and liberals about the new president's attitude toward them. Busby further recommended that Princeton historian Eric Goldman be appointed to the White House; his presence would cultivate "a broader segment of the academic community many of whom, outside the East, are somewhat Anti-Schlesinger."

Busby suggested other ways to woo the artistic community, including a White House Conference on the Arts. Johnson's support of the space industry during his vice presidency had alienated members of the social sciences. Therefore he needed to conduct a White House conference on social sciences that would be "fully acceptable" to "liberal intellectuals." He should also court "a full range of religious leadership," including the Mormon Church from whom Kennedy "won unusual applause" during his visit to Salt Lake City. The president and Lady Bird might be photographed reading books in order to dispel the "widespread false impression that [the] President is not a 'reader.' "[31]

Johnson acted upon some of Busby's suggestions. During the 1950s Steinbeck had been closely identified with liberal Democrats such as Adlai Stevenson. Although he did not initially approve of John Kennedy, an invitation to the 1961 inauguration was the beginning of a warm relationship. Kennedy's expressed concern for the arts and literacy won Steinbeck's approval. In the fall of 1963 Kennedy sent the writer on a good-will tour of eastern Europe. After the assassination Steinbeck wrote Johnson a letter of support and was invited to the White House to report on his trip. Although the novelist had been unfamiliar with Johnson, his wife had known Lady Bird when they attended school together at the University of Texas. Following Busby's January memorandum, Steinbeck and his wife were frequently invited to the White House, sometimes as overnight guests. He and Johnson found an immediate rapport, aided in part by their similar suspicion of academic intellectuals. Throughout the next year Johnson frequently contacted Steinbeck and sought his advice. In mid-July he announced that the Medal of Freedom had been conferred on him. In October Steinbeck and thirty-three other Nobel prize recipients announced their support for Johnson's election.[32]

Johnson also renewed an old relationship with conductor Erich Leinsdorf, who was appointed a trustee for the Kennedy Center for the Performing Arts. Although he was unsuccessful in retaining Arthur Schlesinger, Eric Goldman was appointed to the administration in early February 1964. In December 1963 Johnson had summoned Goldman, telling him of his desire to use intellectuals in his administration. "Was he seriously interested in the 'best minds,'" Goldman wrote, "or was this merely a move he felt politically wise in view of President Kennedy's appeal to the intellectual community?" Busby's memorandum suggested the latter. Upon Goldman's appointment, an aide told *Newsweek* that the addition of "a Princeton man will dilute the Harvard influence and perhaps change our image a little."[33]

During the year the news media devoted attention to Johnson's favorite painters and the art work currently displayed in the White House. The president signed the Kennedy Arts Center Bill in January. The Johnsons frequently visited art exhibits and museums around the country and hosted a variety of cultural events. Johnson's reading habits were also addressed. McGeorge Bundy informed the president that he had talked with a reporter "in an effort to knock down the notion that you don't read and study." The *New York Times* reported that, though Johnson had little time for reading books, he was more attentive than Kennedy when reviewing briefing papers.[34]

During the early months of the administration, aides staged media events designed to demonstrate the depth of Johnson's knowledge. In April Busby was concerned that press conferences were not producing interpretive pieces and suggested that Johnson follow Kennedy's lead by holding "backgrounders." This involved an informal discussion with reporters under the condition that they neither attribute comments directly to the president nor use direct quotes. It allowed the president to discuss various ideas without being held accountable for them. It also provided Johnson with an opportunity to give "outlines of philosophy and direction." There was a need to state "philosophically and reflectively" the "direction of the country." Position papers would be coordinated with public statements, White House reports, and studies to provide "greater thoughtfulness and long-term perspective." All these efforts, Busby concluded, would "help strengthen the image of variety and breadth of White House interests."[35]

Busby also sought to win for Johnson the approval of intellectual groups associated with Kennedy. In April the White House hosted a group of historians, whom Busby deemed "the real opinion molders." Noting that the president lacked prior contact with the "greatly distinguished group," Busby asserted that their "contemporary judgment means most in determining the adjectives applied to any President or Presidency: 'great,' etc." He therefore recommended that Johnson "be expansive, ebullient with them." Afterwards Busby characterized the meeting as a "very gracious success": "Even James McGregor [sic] Burns, Kennedy's biographer, asked for two folders of matches to take home to his sons." Johnson had impressed the intellectuals as a "strong Executive," something Kennedy had not done. "[I]t is a ripe time to make friends—and penetrations with them."[36]

Other suggestions encouraged Johnson to match Kennedy's image as both a family man and intellectual. Goldman proposed "a Presidential family hour on TV to mark our national holidays." The first program could be entitled, "July 4th with the President" and would consist of the president talking with four or five well-known intellectuals such as Barbara Ward or Arnold Toynbee. Johnson would moderate a discussion on the philosophical meaning of the occasion, allowing him to demonstrate his "interest in the nation's distinguished writers and thinkers" and project his "lesser known aspects." Johnson rejected the suggestion.[37]

On two occasions in 1964 the administration sought outside advice on White House efforts to alter Johnson's public image. Reporter Robert Spivack recommended that Johnson give a commencement address at City College in New York. Because it was considered a "poor man's school," a speech there would "emphasize your interest in those who have to work for an education and can't go to Yale, Princeton, etc." He also suggested "A speech at the ground-breaking of the Kennedy Library at Harvard. Here you would talk to the rich, the well-born and the intellectuals." Bill Moyers informed Johnson of a conversation he had had with Brandeis professor John Roche. Roche noted that many intellectuals were disappointed with Kennedy's reluctance to address moral issues; many compared Johnson favorably in this regard. He recommended informal gatherings with the academic community. Two years later Roche was appointed a full-time special assistant.[38]

Between March and August 1964 Johnson accepted a number of honorary degrees and spoke at commencement ceremonies at various colleges, as did Lady Bird Johnson. Johnson did not speak at the groundbreaking ceremony at the Kennedy Library, but he did appear at a fund-raiser for the library which was attended by many academic friends of the Kennedy family. Earlier that spring he spoke at a dedication of the John F. Kennedy Educational, Civic, and Cultural Center on Long Island. He also originated and announced the establishment of a program that named 121 outstanding high school students "Presidential Scholars." His attempt to woo the intellectuals did not end after the November election. In December 1964 Douglass Cater, a former editor for the *Reporter,* urged Johnson to expand upon a Kennedy technique used to court academics by inviting artists and intellectuals to the inauguration: "It contributed a great deal to the new spirit of culture in the nation's capital." The administration subsequently invited fifty American artists and writers.[39]

The task of trying to win favor with the intellectual community must have been straining for Johnson. Outwardly he understood the political necessity of conveying respect. Inwardly he remained hostile and bitter. On one occasion he revealed his mixed feelings simultaneously. Driving around his ranch with Jack Valenti and Tom Wicker of the *New York Times* in the spring of 1964, Johnson spotted a glass bottle lying in the road. Stopping his car, he ordered his Ivy League–educated aide to retrieve it. As Valenti humiliated himself by scrambling along the road, Johnson felt compelled to praise those qualities for which he held contempt. "He's a Harvard man," he told Wicker. "He's got more Harvard Degrees than Mac Bundy."[40]

In addition to presenting a more "thoughtful" exterior, Johnson emulated other aspects of the Kennedy image. Among the personal traits popularly associated with the late president were youth, athletic prowess, family values, and a reputation as a trend-setter. Kennedy had been famous for touch football games, sailing at Hyannis Port, establishing the President's Program on Physical Fitness, and honoring athletic heroes at the White House. His image as a family man was promoted by numerous photographic essays in the nation's tabloids. He was also well known for being fashionable, setting standards for hair and dress styles.[41]

Implicit in the recommendations by Johnson's image managers was that he borrow many of the "personality" images associated with Kennedy. "*A good, strong, happy family image,*" Busby suggested in January 1964, "*is the best counterattack on political smears: i.e. to offset any image of you as 'one of the boys in the back room'* " [emphasis Busby's]. He suggested a variety of what we now know as photo-opportunities, including a photograph of the president and First Lady "strolling *alone,* hand in hand, in White House gardens." It would "convey [the] President in repose, as antidote to press and public worries over President's non-relaxation." Johnson should also be photographed bowling with one of his daughters. The image would demonstrate the "graceful, in-motion Presidential form," show the president's concern for his health, create a "favorable image" among the nation's bowlers, and "convey [a] wholesome and welcome teenage image for either or both daughters, as well as father-daughter closeness." He further suggested that Johnson be photographed wearing a hat. Pierre

Salinger would inform the press that the president "thinks every man ought to have and wear a cap." The image "would serve as a style-setting story with much friendly, good-feeling publicity." Furthermore it would be a "very effective counter to present Eastern over-emphasis on the ten-and-five gallon hats."[42]

Many of the images to which Busby alluded were emulated by Johnson during his first year in office. The president was not photographed bowling, but a number of illustrations and articles reflecting his recreational interest in sports were published. They included photographs of him playing golf, riding horseback, and boating. The White House was visited by tennis and track stars, baseball players, and Olympic athletes. The president's visits to baseball games and horse racing events were widely publicized. Photographs and stories about his relationship with his daughters were published in *Life, Look,* and *U.S. News and World Report.* In February Johnson approved the hat industry's plan for an "LBJ" hat, a modified version of a Western cowboy hat that was later described as a "hit." In March *Business Week* praised Johnson's innovative influence on the garment industry. He was often photographed wearing business hats and golf caps. In August the Fashion Foundation of America named him as the best-dressed man in public life.[43]

Was Johnson's image management designed to mimic Kennedy, or did his efforts merely reflect established trends? Clearly he was following a well-established tradition by former presidents who marketed their personalities in order to generate public support. Theodore Roosevelt was a master innovator, using his flamboyancy and publicizing family members in order to enhance his appeal. Athletes had visited the White House since the Coolidge administration, and golf was a sport associated more with Eisenhower than with Kennedy. Moreover, Kennedy had an aversion to hats. Nonetheless, the suggestions that Johnson emphasize more personal facets of his character were consistent with Busby's advice that he learn from Kennedy's image. At the very least, the White House expanded on an image process which Kennedy had greatly accelerated, and aides sought to identify Johnson with contemporary trends.

Other situations were explicitly intended to portray Johnson in a "Kennedyesque" fashion. In July 1964, for example, Busby sought to depict Johnson photographically in a youthful, intellectual setting reminiscent of the Kennedy era. Scheduling a meeting between the president and American Field Service students, he reminded Johnson that Kennedy had conducted a similar meeting in 1963, resulting in "much publicity of a mob scene, et al." A similar scene of enthusiastic young adults surrounding the president would be inappropriate due to recent urban race riots. "At the same time," he wrote, "I wouldn't want a notably less demonstrative showing vis-a-vis the Kennedy image." Busby therefore suggested that "reasonable prudence be exercised . . . to avoid excesses—but do give photographers some shots of you among the young people."[44]

The Johnson administration also made a deliberate effort to imitate Kennedy as a trend-setter. In the summer of 1965 a men's fashion magazine, GQ, contacted the White House, requesting that it feature President Johnson on the cover of its March 1966 issue. A magazine executive noted that the National Convention for Menswear Retailers of America would meet in Dallas that spring. He suggested that "the only logical and fitting choice [for the cover] was President Johnson—to be shown in the Western casual dress he usually wears during weekends at the LBJ ranch." The publication sent with its request a back issue depicting Kennedy on the March 1962 issue: "The appearance of President Johnson on our cover would naturally be of great significance to us, as well as to the entire men's apparel industry."[45]

Johnson and his aides responded favorably. Moyers informed the president that the editors wanted to portray him as "a fashion setter" by showing him wearing ranch clothing. He noted the success of the Texas hats and cited a precedent: "Attached is a cover they did of President Kennedy. This resulted in much publicity for him because of the impact it had on the industry. It set the trend for the two-button suit. Presumably, the appearance of the President would create similar publicity." Moyers could think of no reason why Johnson should not pose for the cover and ensured that the final photographs would be cleared by the White House. Johnson agreed, and photo sessions were arranged that fall and winter. In March Johnson was pictured on GQ's cover. Rather than wearing Texas apparel, however, he was photographed standing on the front porch of his ranch house wearing a dark, two-button suit similar to the one worn by Kennedy.[46]

The effort at matching Johnson with elements of Kennedy's image revealed a fundamental misunderstanding of image projection. Photographing Johnson in an Ivy League suit on his ranch was contrived and comical. The suggestion for photographs of him in "graceful, in-motion Presidential form" were clearly outside his bounds. Johnson was extremely clumsy and nonathletic. Measuring close to six feet, four inches tall and weighing over 225 pounds, he was ill-advised to depict himself in a manner of which few his stature were capable. Indeed, one attempt to illustrate the president's leisure activities proved embarrassing. When Johnson was pictured in Life during the summer of 1964 while boating on Granite Shoals Lake in Texas, one reader wrote to the editors, "After seeing the picture of President Johnson in a bathing suit, I feel he should be advised to see Rudi Gernreich [a swimsuit designer]. Mr. Gernreich surely could design a better one . . . preferably one that wasn't topless."[47]

On a cosmetic level, Johnson competed against a figure who conveyed similar images with less effort and more skill. One professional photographer characterized Kennedy as "the most manipulative model" he had ever met. When Kennedy was photographed without his shirt, his body was that of a natural athlete. He was careful to stage or censor photographs in order to depict himself as healthy and vigorous. When photographed sailing at Hyannis Port, he instructed his aides to pull in their stomachs and once prevented a picture from being released because it showed "the Fitzgerald breasts." Kennedy was weight conscious, often adjusting television lights and the angle of his head in order to mask an emerging double-chin. Such self-awareness convinced Johnson's press secretary, George Christian, that Kennedy had a "natural ability" in understanding how to "sell himself."[48]

Johnson had little inclination for such concerns. He overate, frequently drank alcohol, sometimes smoked cigarettes, and had little patience for athletic recreation. Although he was often vain about his appearance, he also had an "earthy" quality that dismayed his aides. He thought nothing of lifting his shirt in front of photographers to display the scar from his gall bladder operation. Such insensitivity, along with an unflattering appearance, hindered his ability to compete against Kennedy and underscored the differences between them.

"Getting Right" with Kennedy

As the fall campaign neared in 1964, Johnson's desire to identify himself with the Kennedy image intensified and entailed new strategies. Historically, presidential candidates had often aligned themselves with political icons of the past. Thomas Jefferson, Andrew Jackson, Abraham Lincoln, and the Roosevelts were invoked by numerous political parties and organizations in an effort to attract support for their cause. So, too, did Johnson try to "get right" with Kennedy. He helped memorialize the late president, incessantly invoked his name, and adjusted his rhetorical style so as to resurrect memories of his predecessor. Moreover, he reopened relations with Robert Kennedy, the living reminder of a mythic past.[49]

Since the days immediately following the assassination, Johnson had been highly conscious of events and symbols surrounding the memorialization of the slain president. By participating in the mythification process, Johnson linked himself to a formidable legacy and augmented his appeal for the fall campaign. Republican challenger Barry Goldwater would be running not

142

only against Johnson. He would be running against John Kennedy's heir. With this in mind, Johnson appeared at public functions as a surrogate for the late president. At the Joseph P. Kennedy, Jr., Foundation Awards Dinner in February, he gave a magnanimous speech before members of the Kennedy family. He made an unexpected appearance at a dinner honoring the Kennedy Library sponsors and conducted a memorial ceremony on the eve of what would have been John Kennedy's forty-sixth birthday. After presenting a tribute that nearly moved Robert Kennedy to tears, the president and First Lady visited Kennedy's grave for the second time since the funeral.[50]

Johnson's obligation to Kennedy's memory was carefully weighed. Reedy, for example, opposed making November 22 "National Unity Day." He considered the proposal "insulting" to Kennedy and believed that memorials "should be based upon what he did—not on the fact that he died." He also noted that the idea was, "to a certain degree, an indictment of all of those who opposed him while he was alive." "On the whole," he concluded, "I think it would be better if this proposal never saw the light of day." Aides were concerned about drawing too much attention to the past. Busby did not think it was "appropriate" to dedicate the foreword to a book by the Atomic Energy Commission to President Kennedy. The September publishing date coincided with the fall campaign when "such emphasis is backward-looking." But he did not wish publicly to broach the issue.[51]

Johnson eventually resented the myth to which he contributed. He "grinned appreciatively" when former President Harry Truman criticized the excessive honoring of Kennedy, hoping it would not involve renaming "every pup and kitten." He became hostile toward symbols of the Kennedy era, once refusing to appoint a "Kennedy man" to the General Services Administration in part because of his tie clip. "Every time I see that elongated son of a bitch with his PT-109 tie pin, flashing it in my face," he remarked, "I almost go through the roof."[52]

Although shadowed and frustrated by the emerging Kennedy myth, Johnson appreciated its political value. Columnists accurately predicted that he would use his identity with Kennedy as "a sword and buckler" against his opponents during the election year. By the spring he was already exploiting the myth before partisan audiences, intimating to party regulars that he was the rightful heir. During the first major fund-raiser for the Democratic party, he recalled "the valiant man who should have been here tonight." The perseverance of the government, he noted, proved "the righteousness of the cause he led and the cause that you support," and he promised to fulfill his predecessor's goals. Speaking before the Democratic National Committee just days before the convention, he reiterated his commitment to Kennedy's program.[53]

As the fall campaign began, Johnson persistently invoked Kennedy's name and at times mimicked his rhetorical style. Before his first post-convention speech at Cadillac Square in Detroit, for example, aides were disturbed that the prepared text lacked a sense of "personal leadership" that Kennedy had conveyed there in 1960. The speech was revamped according-ly, promising to "get the country moving again" and pledging "that if all Americans will stand united we will keep moving." The address also contained inverted sentences reminiscent of Kennedy's rhetoric: "Either we will move to meet these changes, or they will overwhelm us"; "Reality rarely matches dreams, but only dreams give nobility to purpose."[54]

Shortly after the Cadillac Square speech, Theodore Sorensen, who had been John Kennedy's chief speechwriter, sent a private memorandum urging Johnson to adopt another Kennedy speaking strategy. He expressed a widespread concern that Johnson might face "white backlash" as a result of his civil rights efforts. If Goldwater attacked Johnson in that area, Sorensen recommended that he participate in a format similar to Kennedy's Houston Ministers' speech in 1960 and "address a slightly hostile Northern white group." Although Johnson rejected Sorensen's advice, his early speeches were so reminiscent of Kennedy's that they provoked internal criticism. In mid-September W. J. Jorden, a former *New York Times* reporter working for the State Department, complained that the "distinctive Johnson style of presentation" was absent from his speeches. Johnson needed to be more himself and to convey his effective "highly individualistic manner." "Too often, there is a Kennedy or pseudo-Kennedy tone in prepared remarks." This was particularly evident when he quoted famous political figures from the past. On such occasions "it is not Lyndon Johnson that is talking." Jorden thought the president was giving "an erroneous picture" of himself and his leadership style. Cater forwarded Jorden's critique to the president.[55]

By the last week in September a more "authentic" Johnson emerged. During a campaign swing through New England he was greeted by large and enthusiastic crowds. "The result for Johnson was intoxicating," Evans and Novak observed. "Millions welcomed him in John Kennedy's home ground and the caution of the previous month evaporated." It was in New England that Johnson allegedly took reporter Frank Cormier to a restraining fence, proudly boasting that he had as much charisma as Kennedy. He stood atop his limousine and spoke through a bullhorn to the throngs of people who surrounded him. His more authentic characteristics of a "country preacher" emerged. As in his old stumping days in the Texas hill country, he came alive with passion and energy.[56]

The reception temporarily bolstered Johnson's lagging confidence. The idolatry surrounding Kennedy had prompted mixed emotions in the president. On the one hand, he feared he would not be as well received in 1964 as Kennedy had been in 1960. On the other hand, he yearned to win a landslide victory which would put his predecessor's slim margin of victory in 1960 to shame. Unfortunately, when Busby sent Johnson a progress report, it was evident that, though he would likely win in a landslide, he still lacked the personal affection that was accorded the late president. A September 25 Gallup poll rated Johnson highest on qualities of being "Well-qualified," "Experienced," and "Intelligent." He was rated lowest on the character traits that his image-management techniques had sought to improve: "Attractive Personality" and "Intellectual." Voters had not warmed to Johnson personally, but they nevertheless respected his performance. Wanting Johnson to project more of his personal characteristics, Busby reminded him that "Kennedy succeeded on [the] force of personality much more than orthodox issues." Johnson's personality would not pale in comparison. "[Your weakness] is not on eloquence, et al:" he wrote, "what the country wants from this President is himself—plain-spoken, practical, etc, not eloquence or style." Johnson soon drifted into melancholy, contending that the enthusiasm of the crowds was inspired more by negative feelings toward Goldwater than positive feelings toward himself.[57]

Johnson distanced himself from the Kennedy image in September, but he did not break with it completely. From late September until the November 3 election he referred to Kennedy in approximately seventy separate speeches. When Johnson mentioned Kennedy he usually struck a reverent tone and recalled courageous foreign policy decisions. During the campaign Goldwater had made imprecise comments about the use of nuclear weapons and heightened his reputation as a reckless reactionary. As part of a broad strategy to portray his challenger as irresponsible, Johnson drew on Kennedy's memory to remind voters of the need for rational behavior during a nuclear age. One innovative television commercial, for example, consisted of five minutes of nuclear explosions, ending with John Kennedy's voice-over announcing that a nuclear test-ban treaty had been successfully concluded. His predecessor's efforts on behalf of the treaty, Johnson noted, should prompt everyone to "go home tonight and thank the good Lord that John Fitzgerald Kennedy gave us the leadership that made that treaty possible." Such tributes did more than elevate Kennedy's stature; they reinforced Johnson's role as the "keeper of the flame"—and the proper successor.[58]

Johnson's most frequent invocation pertained to Kennedy's actions during the Cuban missile crisis. The crisis had been promoted as a supreme foreign policy victory, a classic example of "cool" control in a nuclear age. On September 9 Goldwater made the mistake of questioning that image. During a speech in Seattle he charged that the late president had deliberately manipulated the crisis in order to generate "maximum domestic political impact" for the upcoming congressional elections. The next day Richard Scammon, director of the Bureau of the Census, informed Cater that Goldwater's "attack" "could easily become one of the two or three most important single developments in the whole campaign. There are numberless Americans, in both parties and in none, who will deeply resent this assault upon the late President." Scammon hoped that aides were devising a counterattack. Clark Clifford also implored Johnson to take advantage of a "unique opportunity to answer Goldwater in the shameful attack. . . ." Johnson, Clifford argued, had a higher obligation to refute Goldwater—"a responsibility which you owe, on behalf of the American people, to the memory of President Kennedy." He sent a two-and-a-half-page statement which he suggested be read during an upcoming press conference; it called Goldwater's statement a "shameful, despicable charge against a great American who cannot answer back." Relaying the material to the president, Busby noted a staff consensus that he treat the issue as a "personally disreputable attack upon President Kennedy."[59]

Patiently waiting for the correct opportunity, Johnson first challenged Goldwater by exalting Kennedy for having "halted the Communist aggression," and he paralleled his predecessor's firmness in Cuba with his own actions in the Tonkin Gulf the previous August. He then repeatedly claimed that he participated in thirty-seven White House meetings surrounding the crisis and expressed pride in Kennedy's handling of the situation. He characterized the late president as "the coolest man at that table," an appraisal that he repeated nearly twenty times before the election. Actually, Johnson's participation had been nominal. He was at the first meeting but then traveled to Hawaii in order to maintain a semblance of normality. "He wasn't there at all when the decisions were being made," Robert Kennedy recalled.[60]

Johnson did not let the facts preclude an effective campaign ploy. He persistently recalled having observed John Kennedy's "caution," "the steel in his spine," and his "wisdom" and "care." Khrushchev and Kennedy had "knives" at each other's "ribs" or "stomachs." Each night when Johnson went to bed, he thought he had seen his wife and children for the last time. He confessed his own private doubts about Kennedy, "a man much younger than I was, and I thought much less experienced than I was. . . ." But in each version Kennedy emerged as "the coolest man in town," and Johnson reminded the audience of his own involvement.[61]

Johnson had waited one month after Goldwater's charge before specifically answering his opponent, timing the rebuttal to coincide with the second anniversary of the crisis. "It adds no luster to a man's statesmanship," he noted, "and it is no tribute to a man's character, to refuse to give John Fitzgerald Kennedy the credit that he is justly entitled to when he is not here to claim it for himself." In Boston he lamented that he was saddened by those who questioned Kennedy's motives: "I don't want to even discuss it because I just think they must not know what they do." With less than a week remaining in the campaign he condemned "some voices" who claimed that Kennedy "framed it all up." He expressed hope that after the election "one unthinkable charge will be removed from the political record—that what happened two years ago today, some said, was an election trick—by a martyred President—who is not now here tonight to defend himself."[62]

In addition to identifying himself with Kennedy through rhetorical references, Johnson used other campaign devices as well. Few symbols of the Kennedy era seemed more powerful than the late president's grave. It evoked memories of the assassination and became an important shrine for seven million devotees who visited the memorial during the first year after the assassination. Although it was a macabre reminder of the past, it allowed Johnson to show his respects in a personal and emotional fashion that no Republican could duplicate.[63]

In October Busby suggested a photo-opportunity in which Johnson would visit the Tomb of the Unknowns as well as Kennedy's grave. He characterized the visits as "appropriate" and "logical." "Goldwater will be on night TV with personal attack," he noted. "News clips of the President in a dignified, solemn role would be effective contrast." Johnson did not pay his respects at Kennedy's grave that fall. But he did participate in a publicity event that recalled the assassination: he was pictured sitting in the limousine in which Kennedy was murdered. The 1961 black Lincoln Continental had been rebuilt and made "bullet proof" during the summer of 1964. In October Johnson first rode in the car during a parade in Washington, D.C. The parallels between his use of the car and the assassination seemed almost intentional. Nearly a year before, Kennedy had been seated in the same automobile, on the same side of the seat, during a noontime parade in a motorcade which traveled through the downtown of a Southern city. The connotations drew considerable press attention and produced an awkward image. A photograph of Johnson was widely distributed, showing him sitting uncomfortably beside the smiling and seemingly oblivious foreign dignitary. A White House spokesperson assured reporters that the car was 90 percent rebuilt.[64]

Clearly, someone as politically astute as Johnson was aware of the event's symbolic importance. It seems doubtful that the "armored" car was used solely for his physical protection. He had seldom demonstrated concern for his safety during the campaign. His deliberateness in using the car for symbolic purposes was plainly evident when the White House later announced that Johnson planned to travel to Dallas, where he would ride the same car during a motorcade that virtually duplicated Kennedy's fateful route. Indeed, John Connally intended to ride with Johnson, and together they would pass beneath the Texas School Book Depository. The White House canceled the planned visit after rumors of assassination plots against Johnson surfaced and major events in the Soviet Union and China necessitated abrupt changes in campaign scheduling.[65]

Johnson's effort to link his image to John Kennedy that fall extended to repairing relations with Robert. Since the convention they had been distant political partners. One week before the August convention Kennedy announced his pending resignation as attorney general in order to run for the Senate in New York. Johnson was reportedly "miffed at Bobby for not discussing the New York picture with him," but Kennedy's public letter of resignation credited Johnson with continuing his brother's legacy. Republican leaders were hopeful that Robert's well-known displeasure with Johnson would divide an otherwise united party. In mid-September there was considerable concern that a "Kennedy backlash" was developing. Stewart Alsop reported an "undercurrent of resentment against President Johnson among some key Democrats" who viewed him as a usurper.[66]

In mid-October Johnson traveled to New York to campaign on Kennedy's behalf for the Senate. He recalled that "first and foremost" he wanted Kennedy to win; his presence in the Senate would be more helpful to the administration than the Republican incumbent Kenneth Keating's. Johnson also noted "another important reason" for his decision to appear with Robert—"the loyalty I felt to the memory of his brother." Left unspoken were the advantages of being seen with the Kennedys. Johnson wanted to use Robert in order to link himself to the "mystique." Robert, meanwhile, sought Johnson's support in order to gain the confidence of party regulars who disparaged him as a "carpetbagger." He had been losing ground in recent polls and was anxious to exploit Johnson's popularity. Kennedy's campaign manager constructed new posters: "Get on the Johnson-Humphrey-Kennedy Team." Campaign buttons were printed proclaiming, "Johnson Wants Kennedy."[67]

The two candidates appeared together before large crowds in New York City, Rochester, and Buffalo. Kennedy spoke in glowing terms about Johnson, praising his contributions to the Kennedy administration and calling him "already one of the greatest Presidents in the United States." "I treasure those statements," Johnson replied in Rochester. "I consider them among my most prized possessions. I know of no one who is in a better position to know my relationship and my work with our late, beloved President than you, and you make me feel very humble and very proud and very obligated. . . ." Johnson's speeches heralded the former attorney general, urging New Yorkers to elect him to ensure that "we win President Kennedy's programs and my program." "[Y]ou don't very often find a person that has an understanding and the ability and the heart, the compassion, that Bob Kennedy has," Johnson commented.[68]

While exchanging political courtesies, Johnson and Robert engaged in petty taunts. On September 5 the *New York Times* reported that Robert was ineligible to vote in New York and had decided against returning to Massachusetts to cast his vote on election day. "Mr. Kennedy," the *Times* noted, "will thus miss his chance to vote for President Johnson." When Johnson traveled to New York he called off a videotape session in which he planned to endorse Kennedy's senatorial campaign. A Johnson aide explained that the president had a hoarse voice.[69]

On election day Johnson sent a telegram to Kennedy, expressing his hope that New Yorkers would elect "a young Senator who will be in step with the nation's needs and provide the imagination and progressive action your fine record as Attorney General so clearly illustrates." That evening the president carried New York state by two million votes. Kennedy won by 600,000 votes. The president had the satisfaction of knowing that his coattails had opened power to a Kennedy. That night he watched the returns on television and carefully observed Kennedy's victory speech. In thanking those who had helped in his campaign, he did not mention the president. Johnson gave no outward sign of being offended, but there was a tinge of pain. "I felt a vacancy," Valenti recalled, "[but] the president's demeanor masked whatever anger or disappointment he may have felt." The two men were, by then, well known for their mutual hostility, but both were adroit politicians who appreciated their circumstances and the need to appear cordial in public. As each embarked on his own independent path, their relationship would be severely complicated by competing ambitions.[70]

Despite extensive efforts at image management, Johnson failed to alter his image substantially in 1964. Consistent with earlier polls, fall surveys indicated that the American people liked the Johnson presidency, but they disliked Johnson. A study conducted by the Survey Research Center of the University of Michigan indicated that his most detrimental quality continued to be his appearance as "too much a 'politician.' " Voters thought he lacked integrity and ethical standards. In terms of his positive qualities, Johnson benefited significantly from his identification with the Kennedy legacy. His two most attractive attributes were his experience and his record. Ranking third in terms of voter appeal was his willingness to continue Kennedy's policies. Stewart Alsop's own informal survey showed similar preferences, concluding that Kennedy's memory was perhaps Johnson's second greatest asset. "A lot of people who loved Kennedy," he predicted, "are going to vote for his successor as a sort of memorial tribute."[71]

Giving his own victory speech in Austin on November 3, Johnson drew on the memory of John Kennedy one last time in the campaign while subtly asserting his independence. He thanked his supporters and recalled his long career, then noted, "A very different part of history is heavy on my mind tonight." He wanted to "complete here tonight a journey that was cut short 11 months and 11 days ago." On the day Kennedy was killed the late president had carried a speech which he intended to deliver in Austin that night. "He would have said then," Johnson noted, "and so I am going to say it for him now." He then read two paragraphs from Kennedy's never-delivered speech, pledging to keep the country moving and united. As he had done throughout the campaign and his first year in office, he sought strength from his predecessor, but he was troubled by the process. "And now we look ahead," he concluded. "For those who look backward to the past will surely lose their future."[72]

CHAPTER

VIII

EMERGING FROM
THE KENNEDY
SHADOW

On election day, November 3, 1964, Lyndon Johnson achieved the mandate he had sought since assuming the presidency. Winning 62 percent of the vote, he defeated Barry Goldwater by then the largest plurality in American history, and his coattails gave the Democrats significant majorities in both houses of Congress. The victory gave Johnson considerable satisfaction and outer confidence. Having won the election in his own right, he had attained a measure of independence from the Kennedy past. Determined to achieve a lasting legacy, he embarked upon the creation of the Great Society, the massive legislative program intended to eliminate poverty and racial injustice. At the same time he quietly escalated America's involvement in Vietnam, trying to postpone painful choices between "guns and butter." His many achievements and failures during this period resulted from a myriad of forces, raising issues beyond the scope of this book. In terms of the Kennedy "mystique," however, an important transformation occurred. Johnson's focus shifted away from John Kennedy and toward Robert; the forces that once strengthened him now intimidated him.

Speaking with Doris Kearns after leaving the White House, Johnson described the problems that beleaguered him in 1965. He had struck out on his own, he recalled, departing from the Kennedy past, especially in terms of the Vietnam War. For that he suffered personal criticism. Why, he asked

151

himself, did the liberals condemn his Vietnam policies? He offered a litany of reasons: "Because I wasn't John F. Kennedy. Because I wasn't friends with all their friends. Because I was keeping the throne from Bobby Kennedy. Because the Great Society was accomplishing more than the New Frontier." He felt "sabotaged" by a handful of unnamed intellectuals in the news media who manipulated public opinion against the war. "Then Bobby began taking it up as his cause and with Martin Luther King on his payroll he went around stirring up the Negroes and telling them that if they came out into the streets they'd get more." Seemingly undone by some diabolical conspiracy, Johnson maintained that communists controlled the news media, manipulated liberal members of Congress, and poisoned the opinions of his own staff.[1]

Kearns contended that Johnson's sense of persecution was more than bitter retrospection rooted in a failed presidency. It indicated psychological instability. To support her assessment she cited two aides—Richard Goodwin and Bill Moyers—as having heard diatribes similar to those she had heard. According to her sources, Johnson allegedly experienced abrupt mood changes during the spring and summer of 1965. During conversations with his staff his voice became intermittently passionate and soft. He would laugh inappropriately and deliver screeds filled with ludicrous accusations and derogatory name-calling, seeking to blame others for the criticism he suffered.[2]

Richard Goodwin was a former Kennedy staff member who remained at the White House until September 1965. Twenty-four years after leaving the Johnson administration, in a memoir, he elaborated on the president's psychological dysfunction. Johnson's "always large eccentricities," he charged, "had taken a huge leap into unreason." He and Moyers had frequent conversations about the president's emotional state and once considered the possibility of calling publicly for a psychiatric investigation. Both aides consulted confidentially with psychiatrists; Goodwin's considered Johnson a "textbook case of paranoid disintegration."[3]

At issue was whether Johnson's "ravings" were chronic or merely a temporary release of stress. Goodwin avoided a definitive assessment, concluding that Johnson "experienced certain episodes of what I believe to have been paranoid behavior." He qualified that his judgment was based upon a layman's understanding of psychology and "purely on my observations of his conduct." His discomfort in flatly assessing Johnson's psychological state suggests that even he was not entirely convinced. Moreover, if Goodwin seriously believed that the president was "paranoid" and that his instability might have grave global consequences, why did he confide his suspicions only to Moyers and a psychiatrist friend? Goodwin suspected that his reluctance publicly to discuss his suspicions was the result of "a very large mistake of judgment [about Johnson's emotional state] or of timidity." Considering his disdain for Johnson, the former seemed plausible.[4]

Moyers, meanwhile, has refused to discuss his former colleague's allegations, leaving only Goodwin and Kearns to have publicly contended that the president was "paranoid." Their eventual marriage casts some doubt on the independence of their appraisals. Goodwin has faced harsh criticism from former Johnson aides who worked closely with the president during this period. Secretary of State Dean Rusk characterized his assessment as "nonsense." Others dismissed Johnson's irrational comments as his way of "screaming at the universe." The outbursts, according to Horace Busby, were "a way not of being unbalanced but of achieving balance." Jack Valenti responded that Goodwin could not square Johnson's "berserk" behavior with his concurrent display of "disciplined, thoughtful, persistent, intellectually irresistible Presidential powers of persuasion."[5]

While the debate continues, Johnson's hysterical comments cannot be entirely discounted. The fact that he achieved marked legislative success does not in itself mean that he was mentally stable. Moyers's reticence on the matter might be construed as silent agreement. And while Johnson's sense of persecution may have been expressed as a temporary release of anxiety, his complaints were consistent with larger patterns of behavior. Traditionally he had protected his self-esteem by overestimating the forces against him. And since becoming a national candidate in 1960 he had constantly worried that the Eastern, pro-Kennedy press and intellectuals intended to undermine him politically. Having been elected in his own right, he was solely responsible for the success or failure of his presidency. This pressure, combined with his innate insecurities, may have triggered exaggerated fears.

While the precise nature of Johnson's fear remains open to question, there is little doubt that his growing anxiety toward critics as well as toward some members of his own staff prompted disconcerting behavior. In this context Robert Kennedy played a pivotal role; he was the common thread that bound Johnson's "enemies"—the quintessential Eastern, elitist, intellectual liberal, the "darling" of the news media and friendly with others in Washington who possessed similar qualities. As the "heir apparent," he symbolized hope to those who yearned for the restoration of the Kennedy presidency. Thus Johnson viewed him as the leader of his opponents, "the guiding spirit," Goodwin recalled, "of some immense conspiracy designed to discredit and, ultimately, to overthrow the Johnson Presidency."[6]

From a practical standpoint, Kennedy was not in a position seriously to challenge Johnson. "Why does he keep worrying about me?" he asked

Goodwin. "I don't like him, but there's nothing I can do to him. Hell, he's the President, and I'm only a junior Senator." Kennedy was not altogether popular with his Senate colleagues, and his stature in Congress was low. Like his brother John, he rejected traditional avenues of congressional power and did little to gain influence with Senate leaders during his tenure. Furthermore, a large segment of the public was highly skeptical of him. Gallup polls indicated that approximately the same percentage of people who favored Robert because he was a Kennedy disapproved of him because they thought he capitalized unfairly on his name. Only 38 percent thought he was as capable as John when he was in the Senate.[7]

Johnson and his staff, however, had reason to be wary. Although less "loved" than John, Robert was still the "heir presumptive" and remained, according to *Newsweek,* a "haunting reminder of the past—and a rich lode of speculation for the future." He was willing to capitalize politically on his brother's memory, and his celebrity status was worrisome in an age when "success" seemed increasingly measured by style as much as by substance. Moreover, Kennedy's disdain for Johnson, combined with his enormous ambitions, made him a particularly threatening rival. As early as May 1965 the White House suspected his presidential ambitions when Johnson received a business card announcing the formation of "Robert F. Kennedy For President Clubs."[8]

The administration's precise suspicion toward Kennedy was registered in a memorandum from Harry McPherson to the president in June 1965. McPherson was a close friend of Johnson who was working in the State Department when he outlined Kennedy's strengths and weaknesses. Concerned about Johnson's "obsession" with the senator, McPherson assessed his long-term plans. He predicted that Kennedy would use the Senate as "a platform in his search for power" and cultivate those factions partial to the previous administration, including liberal senators, journalists, foundation executives, intellectuals, and the like. "Most of these people mistrusted him in the past," he wrote Johnson, "believing him (rightly) to be a man of narrow sensibilities and totalitarian instincts." But through a liberal voting record, Kennedy would endear himself to those who scorn the "self-seeking blowhards" of the Senate and who would come to view him as "a voice of reason and enlightenment."

McPherson added, "His brother did all this, of course"; John Kennedy was also a member of the Senate but never part of its inner power structure. McPherson was certain, however, that Robert's effort to court liberals was more strained: "Bobby, as I say, has little of the attractiveness of Jack among the intellectuals in the newspapers and universities. But he will try to develop it in the course of 'pure' voting and adventurous speeches. And we know the intellectuals are as easy a lay as can be found." While conceding that "Bobby is an absolutist" and has "little tolerance for those who cross him," McPherson warned that the intellectual segments "can still *use him* to get across radical ideas."[9]

Scholars, aides, and political observers have debated this disparaging view of Kennedy. Valid or not, Johnson and his aides believed it. Acting upon these assumptions, they underestimated Kennedy's handicaps while exaggerating his advantages. Johnson was still disciplined enough not to allow his hostility and fear of Robert to diminish his respect for the "mystique." He deferred to its power and, during critical periods, appropriated the legacy for his own purposes. But his energy and attention shifted increasingly from John to Robert. When he conversed with reporters, in his own mind he was meeting with the Kennedy press. When he met with intellectuals, he faced those whom he believed wished to replace him with Robert. And when he dealt with Robert directly, he was convinced that the junior senator was plotting to dethrone him.[10]

Defying the JFK Image

During the week surrounding the first anniversary of the Kennedy assassination, Johnson showed signs of wanting to distance himself from his predecessor's memory. Always courteous in public, he accepted a sculpted bust of John Kennedy for temporary display in the cabinet room and spoke graciously of the late president during its unveiling. That same day he issued "A Rededication" proclamation, pledging to uphold Kennedy's ideals. Three days later his two daughters were among the earliest visitors to the late president's grave, where each left a yellow rose. On behalf of the Johnsons, Major General Chester Clifton, a friend of the Kennedys, placed a huge wreath at the memorial. And on December 2 Johnson paid further tribute during the groundbreaking ceremony for the John F. Kennedy Center for the Performing Arts.[11]

Johnson's sense of obligation, however, was limited. He refused elaborate recognition of the first anniversary, rejecting Valenti's suggestion that he present a five-minute television tribute. He avoided appearances with the Kennedy family, declining Robert's personal invitation to attend a memorial mass. Physically removing himself from the occasion, he traveled to his Texas ranch where he entertained his old friend Governor John Connally, who had been wounded in Dallas one year earlier. Later they attended an interfaith memorial mass in Austin. Throughout the week Johnson carefully considered his activities. Valenti warned that it would be "ill-received" if the president went hunting on the day of the anniversary. "I submit the backlash from this could be severe," Valenti wrote. Johnson agreed.[12]

As his inauguration approached, Johnson continued to assert his independence from the past. Like the 1964 Democratic convention, the January festivities were intended to celebrate Lyndon Johnson, not John Kennedy. Memorabilia in the president's honor inundated Washington's commercial atmosphere, featuring his likeness on medals, bracelets, plates, plaques, and ashtrays. For the first time the inaugural parade was headed by the Texas contingent rather than that of the District of Columbia. The text of the inaugural program focused on the future. "All that has happened in our historic past," its first line read, "is but a prelude to The Great Society." No photographs of John Kennedy were included in the program, and he received only a passing reference in its forty pages of text. "[T]he Johnson Administration," the program asserted, "was successor to the unfinished Kennedy Administration, both vindicating the aims of one and moving forward with the additional purposes of the other." In preparation for the ceremonies, Johnson decided that, unlike Kennedy's inaugural, no top hats or claw-hammer coats would be worn. Nor would there be white tie and tails at the subsequent ball. During the parade he stood in the reviewing stand with his pet beagle.[13]

The deviation from the Kennedy image was not easily achieved. When planning the festivities, the White House sought to maintain some continuity. Jacqueline Kennedy was personally invited by Johnson to attend the swearing-in ceremony, and he maintained the Kennedy practice of inviting leading intellectuals. Meanwhile, aides sought ways with which to celebrate the president without offending Kennedy's memory. In early December Horace Busby suggested that the theme for the inauguration be the 175th anniversary of the presidency. It would "eliminate adverse comments or unwelcome pressure for associating the late President Kennedy with your Inauguration." A celebration of the anniversary would allow photographs of Kennedy in programs and social functions to blend in with other images of ex-presidents, thus preventing Kennedy from receiving "special treatment."[14]

As if to bid farewell to the past, the newly elected president visited John Kennedy's grave the day before January's State of the Union Address. The next day Johnson, who just one year earlier had promised to "let us continue," did not mention Kennedy in his speech. Nor did he mention his predecessor in his Inaugural Address two weeks later. The Kennedys, meanwhile, maintained a low profile. Jacqueline remained in seclusion in her New York apartment. Robert and Edward sat on the inaugural platform, but neither paid his respects to Johnson. Afterwards Robert stopped at his brother's grave where he knelt in silence before reporters and photographers.[15]

After the inauguration Johnson did not entirely abandon his link with the past. During the year he identified himself with his predecessor for many of the reasons that he had done so in the past—a sense of obligation, political self-interest, genuine fondness, and a desire to demonstrate continuity. He mentioned Kennedy during speeches before foreign delegations, commencement audiences, and partisan gatherings. Seeking to gain support for a variety of legislation pertaining to health care for the aged, education, and space exploration, he recalled John Kennedy's earlier commitments and sometimes shared credit with him when acts were passed. On occasion he reminded legislators that John Kennedy was watching them from heaven in an attempt to pressure them to extend funding for the War on Poverty. Announcing the appointments of former New Frontiersmen, he noted that, like John Kennedy, he had similar faith in the appointees' abilities. At a Democratic party gathering he quoted from "the man whose great steps I follow." Johnson cited Kennedy's definition of courage: "A man does what he must—in spite of personal consequences. . . ." "I want you to know," Johnson added, "that it is that spirit which guides me in all that I do." He also remained sensitive to publications questioning whether John Kennedy sincerely wanted him as vice president.[16]

Despite these frequent exaltations of his predecessor, Johnson's own acts of independence, combined with the passage of time, made John Kennedy's "presence" less formidable. The president vigorously pursued his legislative agenda, securing the passage of the Voting Rights Act, establishing the Department of Housing and Urban Development, and signing a $4 billion Public Works Appropriation Act and a $320 million Highway Beautification Act. He took pride in bills that separated the Great Society from the New Frontier, publicizing them with elaborate signing ceremonies. Meanwhile, he began obliquely to denigrate the Kennedy presidency. During an interview with William Leuchtenburg in September 1965 he insulted Kennedy's cabinet, reminded the historian of Kennedy's failure to censure Senator Joseph McCarthy in the 1950s, and charged that "no man knew less about Congress than John Kennedy." Leuchtenburg was "startled" by Johnson's increasing "animus against JFK."[17]

Johnson's substantive distinctions extended to his image-management strategies as he actively projected his Western image and resisted Kennedy's media techniques. Following a December staff meeting in which Johnson's image was discussed, Busby re-evaluated the White House's media techniques and prepared a summary for the president. Disapproving the news media's focus on Johnson's personality, he recommended "sophisticated adjustments in our own thinking and approach." The election resolved many of the questions raised by the media about Johnson's ability to get elected in his own right. "The new interest of all media," Busby observed, "—and the public as well—attaches not to the man but to what he stands for: i.e., ideas, interests, actions, friends, associates. For all of us, this is a profound change." Writing on behalf of other White House staff members, he called for "a wrenching change in our attitude toward, approach to and relations with the media world."

Busby faulted himself and other aides for miscalculating the president's image during the past year. When addressing the "news media or intellectual community or 'Kennedy people,' " they had "grown accustomed to thinking and talking in terms of the man, rather than ideas, agenda, actions of the future." "[T]his frame of reference must change." The news media and the public had become more concerned with Johnson's policies and thinking. "Unfortunately, we aren't geared to this from past practice." He warned that reporters would return to personality-oriented topics unless the staff "are able to talk about programs rather than personnel, problems or similar non-substantive material." Johnson needed to learn from his predecessor:

For a Corollary, the Kennedy "image" was—for the President personally—a foam atop a heady brew of intellectual ferment, in Washington and out. If the people around him had been hesitant, reluctant or simply ill-equipped to talk about plans for the future, the now-existing Kennedy image would never have risen to the top. President Kennedy was the beneficiary of the accessibility and self-confidence of his associates, intimate or peripheral. But, by contrast, the edginess, evasiveness and simple "in the dark" ignorance of persons in this Administration works against any successful image program.

Busby recommended that Johnson allow his own people greater access to the media and that the staff emphasize the substance of the administration: "So long as our thrust focuses on the 'man,' the negative [reporting] will continue—on the 'man'—and will prove irritating. Conversely, stories about programs of the Great Society will generally portray the President favorably. . . ."[18]

Busby never sent his memorandum to the president, and his advice that aides concentrate on substance rather than on "the man" was crossed out. He concluded by promising specific suggestions in the future, but there was no record of a follow-up memorandum. Various explanations may account for his apparent reluctance. First, the recommendations placed him in a contradictory light. Having once argued that "personality is the main force of identification between the public and the President," he now criticized that focus and wanted to promote policies and programs. Second, the recommendation that staff have greater access to the press was contrary to the president's fear of leaks and his desire to maintain tight control of the information flow. More important, however, in terms of the Kennedy "mystique" Busby's memorandum underscored a general dilemma within the administration. Aides wanted to be innovative by promoting policies rather than personality. They were willing to distance Johnson from Kennedy's attributes. But the strategy of allowing staff members greater access to the news media was derived from the Kennedy era. Aides sought to move away from Kennedy's image but found themselves drawn to his media strategies. They were inspired by the very past from which they wanted to disassociate the president.

This sense of entrapment reached deep into the thinking of the White House staff as advisers sought to appropriate John Kennedy's media techniques in order to improve Johnson's image. In late December 1964 and early 1965 they recommended repeatedly that he conduct televised press conferences from the State Department auditorium twice a month. "While the large televised conference should not become a compulsory institution (as it became during Kennedy's time)," Douglass Cater noted, "it does have advantages that are not possible with the impromptu press conference." The suggested location and frequency were identical to Kennedy's press conferences. Hoping to improve the technical aspects of the news conferences, the administration hired a lighting expert from the ABC television network who had worked for the late president. Jack Valenti advised Johnson to give reporters greater forewarning of press conferences, noting the lengthy advance notice that Kennedy had given them.[19]

Johnson was not persuaded to alter the format of his press conferences. Publicly he dismissed the Kennedy-style conferences as "a kind of prearranged show where some reporters get to stand up and be on TV." He conducted as many press conferences as Kennedy had, but they were less extravagant and awkwardly arranged. Kennedy's conferences were held in an ornate theater, with proper lighting, before several hundred reporters. They were also conducted in the late afternoon to ensure a large television audience. Of Johnson's eleven press conferences in 1965, eight were held well before 4 p.m. Their locations varied and included a small White House theater, the Rose Garden, the East Room, and the Johnson Ranch. Several were held on the weekend when audiences were nominal.[20]

Undaunted, aides persisted in recommending that Johnson employ other formats developed by John Kennedy, such as "A Conversation with the President," a televised discussion between the president and three network correspondents. Johnson had successfully duplicated this format in March 1964 but had since resisted appearing on another program. After the election, aides implored him to initiate a second appearance, citing the approval of network executives. The program would reveal him to be "warm, engaging and down-to-earth" while the extemporaneous format would depict the president "in the manner in which he is most engaging and most effective: being himself." Johnson rejected each request.[21]

Another format which Kennedy had developed was *cinema verité,* allowing cameras to film "behind the scenes" glimpses of him working with his White House staff. Several films were aired on network television with considerable success. McPherson recommended that Johnson initiate similar programs, and he detailed a possible format. Busby rejected the suggestion, believing that the proposed program was unnecessary and too stagy. The president, however, was more accommodating. In January 1965 he agreed to narrate a television film project on the Texas hill country. He also accepted Robert Hunter's recommendation that he "prepare a televised program on 'the President at work,' similar to one prepared by President Kennedy." That summer Johnson permitted a production company to film his activities for one week. The subsequent one-hour film, *Seven Days in the Life of a President,* was produced by David Wolper, the same man who had produced *A Thousand Days.* Unlike Kennedy, Johnson did not allow microphones to record his conversations. He did, however, agree to act in staged scenes, accepting Valenti's suggestion that he participate in "the kind of shots that will get inside the hearts of the viewers." Johnson initially refused but then wrote next to the recommendation, "If you think [Wolper] is alright. O.K."[22]

Despite Busby's advice that the focus of Johnson's television strategy should be on substance, aides emphasized impressionistic matters rather than communication. He was inundated with favorable reviews of his television appearances and received a constant flow of theatrical suggestions. The staff engaged in lengthy debates about lighting, sound, settings, the proper height of the podium, the use of eyeglasses versus contact lenses, pacing, and appropriate humor. Once, Johnson was even urged to point his finger as Kennedy had done when responding to reporters' questions. Television was considered vital to image management. "I know that the only way that you can reach the country is by television—not by newspapers," Robert Kintner wrote. "I believe the President underestimates greatly the favorable impression he gives on television." Staff regularly sent him studies indicating television's importance and advised that he hire consultants.[23]

In general, the president dismissed aides' suggestions and complaints, but he did not neglect the medium. Indeed, he employed television in 1965 more extensively than any previous president. By the fall he had appeared on live television fifty-eight times in two years—nine times more than Eisenhower during his eight years in office, and twenty-five times more than Kennedy. But the manner in which he used television differed. Kennedy used it to convey a personal style of leadership but often eschewed substance. Johnson more often communicated the substance and activity of his presidency rather than his personality. In March he gave a powerful television address before a joint session of Congress, generating popular support for the 1965 Voting Rights Act. In the spring he appeared on television on three separate occasions to explain his military response to the Dominican Republic crisis. Of his thirty-seven live television appearances during the first nine months of 1965, only ten were press conferences. Thirteen of his appearances were special reports on foreign and domestic matters and thirteen pertained to formal addresses before various institutions, including Congress, Johns Hopkins University, and the United Nations. He also opened bill-signing ceremonies to live television.[24]

To some degree Johnson's television image reflected reality; he was a doer who wanted to publicize his achievements. Consistent with Busby's advice, his media techniques promoted issues, ideas, and programs rather than personality. Occasionally he returned to Kennedy-style formats, but his general strategy departed from the past standards. The change had mixed results. On the one hand, he was correct not to force on television a personal image with which he was uncomfortable. Such attempts would have appeared contrived. As it was, viewers regarded his television presence as "a little maudlin" and "two-faced." On the other hand, his effort to identify himself publicly with legislation often appeared self-indulgent. Thrusting himself into the limelight each time a bill was passed, Johnson generated criticism that he was using the occasions more to promote himself than to call attention to the nation's needs.[25]

The Johnson Men

The advice urging Johnson to use Kennedy-style strategies indicated that many aides resisted the president's movement away from the "mystique." "In 1965, one could still feel John Kennedy's presence in the White House," McPherson recalled. The "presence" was so strong that he once thought he saw Kennedy's "lithe figure" in the Oval Office, only to discover an aide of similar physique. The mirage revealed the staff's fixation on the past, an imprisonment compounded by competition with the idealized reputation of the New Frontiersmen.[26]

As the Johnson team evolved in 1964, the news media analyzed its composition and temperament, making inevitable and unflattering comparisons to the previous administration. When Eric Goldman was hired and Arthur Schlesinger resigned in January 1964, the *Washington Post* reported that he had "replaced" the Kennedy aide. "You are not the Johnson Arthur Schlesinger," Walter Jenkins lectured Goldman. "Nobody is going to be the Johnson Schlesinger. Nobody is going to be the Johnson anything of Kennedy. *This is a different Administration.*" Not all references to the previous staff were as curt as Jenkins's. On the day George Reedy replaced Pierre Salinger as press secretary, Busby wrote a teasing letter citing fictitious newspaper reports critical of Reedy's first press briefing: "I really feel that as your friend I should tell you that you should be thinking of moving on. Obviously you just don't have the touch with the press that Pierre had."[27]

Measured against the flamboyant reputation of the Kennedy staff, the Johnson team suffered severe problems in managing its reputation. McPherson summarized their popular image as "docile calves hustling around at the will of a singular bull." But their problem, he thought, rested less with the reality of the situation than with the Kennedy myth.

There was a mystique about the Kennedy staff, that it was a free-swinging, free-spirited collection of brilliant and independent intellects; each man became a personality, and oh what a good time they had running the government. On the other hand, we are rather bright, nice young men who lost our independence of mind the day we signed on. It wasn't true about the Kennedy staff, and it's not true about us, but it is a myth that dies hard.[28]

In general, the White House staff was fighting a losing battle, largely because of the president for whom they worked. They would likely have faced the criticism they did regardless of the administration that preceded them. The president's own dominating, insecure, and abrasive personality reflected negatively upon the people who surrounded him. The large turnover rate, knowledge of Johnson's intense involvement in White House details, the inordinate amount of time and energy that he demanded from his personnel, and his abusive behavior toward them prompted critics to assume that only a timid person or an absolute loyalist could withstand such treatment.[29]

The loyalist image of Johnson's staff peaked in July 1965 when Jack Valenti spoke before the Advertising Federation of America in Boston. Among his most unembarrassed observations was his belief that Johnson had "extra glands" that gave him "energy that ordinary men simply don't have." "I sleep each night a little better, a little more confidently because Lyndon Johnson is my President," he concluded. An avalanche of press ridicule soon followed. Sympathizers consoled Valenti by noting the unfairness of the media's "feeding frenzy." Lee White sent him a copy of an old speech by Sorensen which was similarly adulatory toward John Kennedy but which received little publicity. "I said a number of things which were laughed at," Valenti recalled years later, "but now have credence." Referring to Sorensen's speech, he noted, "nobody laughed at that."[30]

By the spring of 1965 staff members were becoming increasingly embittered by comparisons and offered biting comments to reporters aimed at their predecessors. "There are few brusque, abrupt people around now," one unnamed aide told *Newsweek*. "The place used to be crawling with them." "There's no more debating with kids," Johnson boasted. "I have the ablest staff that ever served any President in my memory. There's not a playboy among them. They aren't sitting around at Paul Young's drinking whiskey at 11 o'clock at night." Privately, however, the president sometimes measured his staff against the same idealized image that irked his aides. "How can you be so god-damn stupid!" he once berated a staff member. "Why can't I get men with the brains of the Kennedy bunch." He encouraged comparative analyses which may have been intended to foster pride but which likely heightened competition. After the 1964 election, for example, Moyers received instructions that the president was "insistent and adamant" that they "make a study—a thorough study—of the White House staff—who they are, what they are making—comparison between this staff and the last year of the Kennedy Administration—in toto. . . . And then to pare it. This is urgent and of the highest priority."[31]

Some Johnson aides sought to improve their reputation by mimicking the New Frontier image. Liz Carpenter wanted the administration to take the initiative on anticipated feature stories about the president's staff. She was uncomfortable with the emerging "Texas-look" and suggested "we could offset this with earlier staff stories about the able and intellectual people around the President." Hobart Taylor recommended that the administration duplicate the defunct New Frontier Club by forming an "LDJ Club," an organization in which "bright young men in the middle and upper echelons may come together."[32]

Johnson occasionally sought solutions to his staff's image problems, proposing, for example, that each staff member praise another aide to outsiders but do so anonymously. McPherson questioned the tactic. "[C]oupled with the power and dominance of your personality," he warned, "the prescription does not appear to welcome the emergence of your staff as a distinguished collection of individuals." He recommended instead that Johnson allow his most articulate aides to speak candidly at social functions. Admitting that he was unsure if this or any strategy would work, he warned nevertheless of a "danger" in their current image.[33]

No systematic attempt was made to encourage aides to speak independently of the president. Johnson was unlikely to be receptive to a plea that aides voice their opinions on their own in order to match the Kennedy "mystique," especially while he was trying to break free of past images. Nevertheless, he was accommodating. Moyers recommended that the administration approve a project by the ABC television network intended "to show the human side of the staff and dispel the image that the White House staff people are machines not men." Johnson acquiesced, writing on the memorandum, "Get good format [and] emphasize what is good." The program aired in the fall of 1965, featuring three former New Frontiersmen who had remained with the Johnson administration, and three Johnson men.[34]

Despite creative efforts at image management, staff members remained disgruntled by the public's continued poor perception of them. "I would match people like Bill Moyers against Ted Sorensen any day of the week," Kintner informed Johnson. "President Kennedy gained great personal mileage by the publicity given to his 'bright, young New Frontiersmen,'" newcomer Benjamin Wattenberg wrote in 1967. "Your staff is at least as bright and young—perhaps indeed brighter and younger but the public is generally unaware of them—to your disadvantage I believe." McPherson regularly complained that their "humor-less" and "frightened" image was "of course directly related to the image of the Kennedy staff—young, vibrant, light-hearted, Finding Government Fun." He later suggested sarcastically that the administration stage a fistfight between the Johnson staff and the president in the Rose Garden in order to offset their sycophant image. Former Kennedy aides could instruct the Johnson men "on how to fight against the President":

O'Donnell, Sorensen, Schlesinger, and Powers should describe their many vituperative encounters with President Kennedy, particularly during and after the Bay of Pigs affair. Their example should serve to strengthen our will, and give us a better understanding of the ways in which independent-minded, assertive assistants can promote national interest by standing their ground against the temporary occupant of the White House.[35]

The staff's long-term concerns illustrated the scope of the "mystique's" impact. Intellectually and charismatically they felt inadequate and reacted much as Johnson responded to John Kennedy's reputation. Their frustration was unfortunate. They were extremely able and bright individuals who were vital to the administration's achievements, and most of the public was less intrigued by the staff's image than they were. The progress of the wars against poverty and communism were more important to their reputation than their outward appearance. But the same "mystique" that elevated John

Kennedy's reputation extended to his staff, and the "Johnson men," like Johnson himself, perceived a need to compete against a myth.

Had the problem surrounding Johnson's staff centered only on its popular image, aides would have faced a relatively minor distraction. Unfortunately the "mystique" warped the substantive aspects of the president's staff as well. Directing his energy toward protecting himself from Robert Kennedy, Johnson adjusted the hiring procedures of his staff, removing aides whom he believed to be tainted by the senator.

Immediately after the assassination Johnson had given his own "loyalists" increasing responsibilities. Aides such as Walter Jenkins, Jack Valenti, George Reedy, Bill Moyers, Horace Busby, and Douglass Cater were vital to White House operations. They were included in social occasions and engaged in informal conversations with the president during off-hours. The resignation of Jenkins after his October 1964 arrest for homosexual solicitation in a Washington, D.C., mens room distanced relations between remaining Kennedy aides and Johnson's staff. "He was the only one who had both the entire staff's and Johnson's complete trust," Johnson's private secretary recalled. "He was a natural link between the Johnson and Kennedy men."[36]

By January 1965 few Kennedy holdovers remained on the White House staff. An offer by Theodore Sorensen to return to the administration was politely ignored. Meanwhile, Johnson brought in Harry McPherson from the State Department and hired another Texas friend, Marvin Watson, as his appointments secretary. Watson's arrival drove a further wedge between the Kennedy holdovers and the established Johnson team. "The truth is," Valenti noted, "Marvin never regarded Bobby and his people with anything other than mistrust and they responded in kind."[37]

McPherson's precarious beginnings with the White House in 1965 illustrated the extent of Johnson's obsession with loyalty. McPherson was a thirty-six-year-old native Texan who had graduated in 1956 from the University of Texas with a law degree. An intelligent, affable, and well-intentioned man, he secured a job as assistant counsel for the Senate Democratic Policy Committee in 1956, then headed by Senator Lyndon Johnson. By 1960 he had become general counsel to the committee, and in August 1963 he accepted a Pentagon post as Deputy Undersecretary of the Army for International Affairs. After the assassination McPherson neither joined the White House staff nor was invited to. Wary of the demands of working for Johnson, he was not eager to become involved in the White House's daily operations. In mid-1964 he accepted a position, with Johnson's consent, as Secretary of State for Educational and Cultural Affairs. There he utilized his intellectual interests.[38]

McPherson was in a unique position to observe Johnson's struggle with

Robert Kennedy. Well liked by Washington's social elite, he was frequently invited to Georgetown parties and was privy to circulating gossip. At the same time he was loyal to Johnson, having worked and socialized with him for the past nine years. Operating out of the State Department, he was removed from the daily events at the White House and avoided being consumed by Johnson's incessant demands on his staff.

In April 1965, four months before being officially appointed to the White House, McPherson informed Valenti about personnel problems in the State Department. He was particularly concerned about the "malaise" that had begun during the transition year. The poor attitude was attributed to Johnson's lack of interest in State Department personnel, his inadequate experience in foreign affairs, and his inferior educational and social background. "My guess is [Johnson would] like to wipe them all out and install bright young hard-hitting quick loyal aggressive Johnson men in their places." McPherson discouraged such a solution, suggesting instead that Johnson duplicate Kennedy's "legendary" interest in personnel. Kennedy once went to the State Department and had a candid, hour-long meeting with thirty or forty top officers. Johnson should follow suit: "If he wants better work out of them, he should tell them so. Kennedy did." Johnson was unreceptive. That spring he confided to aides that the Kennedy holdovers within the State Department were out to "get" him.[39]

McPherson's observations and Johnson's suspicions foreshadowed a more stressful occurrence. During the spring of 1965 Moyers cultivated McPherson in hopes of adding him to the White House staff. His youth and intelligence were qualities Johnson sought in his immediate team. In the summer of 1965 McPherson agreed to become Counsel to the President, but problems arose when he sought to enlist a "Kennedy man" as his replacement. Preparing for the transition, he "strongly" recommended that Patrick Moynihan fill his post as Secretary for Educational and Cultural Affairs. Moynihan was then Assistant Secretary of Labor and was having difficulty working under Secretary Willard Wirtz. His well-known affection for John Kennedy, however, made his appointment problematic. "There is the 'loyalty' problem, more fanciful than real," McPherson wrote Moyers. "How would you recommend I proceed to overcome it?"[40]

On June 24 McPherson wrote two memoranda to Johnson. The first sought "to put in context [Moynihan's] relationship to the Kennedys." He described Moynihan's background as a poor, working-class child, raised in New York City, who obtained scholarships from prestigious universities and had ambitiously advanced himself in the Labor Department since the 1950s. McPherson admitted that Moynihan was "crazy" about the late president, but he was also "the most imaginative thinker I know." Trying to reconcile

Moynihan's emotional ties to the Kennedys, McPherson recalled Moynihan's widely quoted statement made in the aftermath of John Kennedy's death, "We will never be young again." McPherson excused him for "speaking like an Irish poet straight from the heart." Moynihan had been unsure of Johnson's intentions, and the change "made him feel, not so much that the policies he wanted would be lost, as that he had lost a line of communication based on youth, love of things intellectual and Irishness." Nevertheless, he had come to respect Johnson and "believes that you will go farther than Kennedy ever could or would in achieving the social goals."

Next, McPherson put Moynihan's relationship with Robert Kennedy into perspective. Moynihan did not know Kennedy when the senator asked him to campaign for him in New York, and he helped only in order to defeat Keating. The rift between Wirtz and Moynihan stemmed from Wirtz's "paranoid" concern about Moynihan's ties to the senator. "Pat can develop the kind of loyalty to you that you must have" and would be able to "keep things within the family here. . . . I don't believe his relationship to Bobby Kennedy is deep enough to make him disloyal to you." Although Moynihan would never be "the man you need to keep Bobby in line—directly," it was more important that his "imagination and liberalism" be tapped by Johnson rather than Kennedy. These qualities, McPherson asserted, were required for "meeting and surpassing the 'Kennedy image.' "[41]

Five hours later McPherson sent a supplementary memorandum entitled, "Thoughts on Bobby Kennedy and Loyalty." He later described the memorandum as one which discussed "the whole Kennedy aperat [sic], call[ing] on the President to make a judgment on the basis of a man's merits and not his emotional absorption in the Kennedy mystique. It was a very tough, candid memorandum which set the President off." In general, it urged Johnson not to alienate the "Kennedy men" or to insist upon blind devotion from his own aides. Nor should Johnson "weed out" those who had worked for Kennedy. There were "squads of able men" who were inspired by John Kennedy and whose services Johnson should enlist. He could not "afford to give them a polygraph-loyalty test to determine whether they would go to the wall for you against Jack Kennedy." Johnson could develop "sufficient" loyalty among them without demanding it. "It is possible, in my opinion, for people to work hard for you, maintain confidences, and still find the Kennedys (including Bobby) attractive and adventurous."[42]

McPherson cautioned Johnson about the "greater danger" in demanding complete fidelity. "Most men of intellect and independent spirit" would be reluctant to take an oath never to talk to Kennedy, especially when he was espousing liberal ideals. "If the word gets around that one has to put on horse-blinders to work for you, you will probably come out with a bunch of clipped yes-men who are afraid of their own shadows and terrified of yours." Staff members could "talk to a great many people, including Bobby Kennedy" and still be committed to Johnson's policies. McPherson closed with a stark warning: "An obsession with Bobby and with the relationship of your best people to him may, I believe, distort policy and offend the very men you need to attract."[43]

McPherson's memoranda were ignored. Two weeks later he reiterated his arguments, asserting that Moynihan was not "Bobby Kennedy's man." He was "committed" to the administration and was an "honorable" and "brilliant" individual who "is too good to lose." That June, when Patrick Moynihan resigned from his Labor Department post, the president made no attempt to keep him. Moynihan eventually became heavily involved in New York City politics. Three years later he was hired by Robert Kennedy as an adviser to assist with his presidential campaign.[44]

McPherson began his new role in the White House under difficult circumstances. Johnson suspected that he was "in bed with all those bomb-throwing, ass-kissing, fuzzy-headed Georgetown liberals." Once officially assigned to the White House staff, he was approached by Moyers and informed that Johnson wanted him reassigned as chairperson of the Equal Economic Opportunities Administration. McPherson's distinct impression was that his memoranda had caused the president to distrust his loyalty. "I politely declined," he recalled, "and said that if the President wished me to be outside the White House that I would go back to the State Department rather than go do that."[45]

Although Johnson distanced himself from the "mystique" through personnel changes, he tried to convince the public that his hiring practices were consistent with McPherson's philosophy. In a July interview for *Newsweek* he argued that he was bringing the best people into his administration regardless of their relationship with Robert Kennedy. "Now they say that Bobby's against me, that he's my sworn enemy," Johnson told Charles Roberts. But he reminded the reporter that he had consented to Kennedy's request to appoint Nicholas Katzenbach as attorney general. And he did so "because I thought he was the best man I could find anywhere in the country." Indeed, Johnson argued, he had twenty-five lawyer friends in Texas who wanted to be attorney general, but he was determined to appoint the most qualified person. Johnson made a similar case for his appointment of Arthur Fowler as Treasury Secretary, claiming that he did not "care who appointed him originally."[46]

Nevertheless, loyalty began eclipsing talent in Johnson's personnel changes. Publicly the president could not bring himself to admit that he was moving beyond the "mystique"; he knew that the illusion of continuity would generate public support for his administration, but he could not accept the actual presence of potentially disloyal staff members, regardless of their "brilliance." As his struggle with Robert Kennedy intensified through the spring of 1965, he threatened to discharge people who were too close to the senator. "I can't trust anybody anymore," he remarked. He once instructed Moyers to fire McGeorge Bundy for disloyalty because he had committed himself to appear on television without permission. Moyers balked. "That's the trouble with all you fellows," Johnson responded. "You're in bed with the Kennedys." The lines were becoming more distinct. One was loyal to either Kennedy or Johnson but could not be faithful to both.[47]

Foreign Policy Departures

The tensions between Johnson and Robert Kennedy increased most noticeably in 1965 as the president embarked on his own foreign policy initiatives. In Latin America and Southeast Asia, Johnson used military power far beyond the commitment of his predecessor. In February he ordered air attacks against North Vietnam, and by July he committed 125,000 American combat troops to the war. That spring he dispatched additional troops to quell an uprising in the Dominican Republic. His willingness to deploy extensive military force contrasted to John Kennedy's propensity for low-scale counterinsurgency and provided Robert Kennedy with an opportunity to distance himself from Johnson's policies.

Since the beginning of the Johnson administration, Robert Kennedy and New Frontiersmen such as Arthur Schlesinger, Theodore Sorensen, and John Kenneth Galbraith had become increasingly dismayed by Johnson's foreign policy. Especially irritating to the Kennedy forces was his appointment of a fellow Texan, Thomas Mann, as Assistant Secretary of State and head of the Alliance for Progress. Many former Kennedy aides considered Mann a "reactionary" who was likely to undermine the late president's efforts at reform in Latin America. "President Johnson deliberately seized this occasion to make a declaration of independence," Schlesinger wrote Robert Kennedy, "to show that this is his administration and that he is master in his own house. . . ." Some holdovers tried to derail the appointment. Mann soon altered the focus of the Alliance for Progress by de-emphasizing its social and political components and increasing the involvement of North American business interests.[48]

Johnson deviated further from Kennedy's Latin American policies in the spring of 1964 after anti-American riots erupted in Panama. The Panamanian president, who was up for re-election, broke off diplomatic relations with the

United States and demanded a revision of the Panama Canal Treaty. While Mann negotiated with Latin American leaders, Johnson gave conflicting signals. He offered both conciliatory assurances and Cold War rhetoric as he consulted with Senate leaders. Kennedy aides called his policies and decision-making style contrary to the Kennedy legacy.[49]

Throughout the transition year Robert Kennedy refrained from publicly criticizing Johnson. Recuperating from the loss of his brother, he appeared indifferent to foreign policy matters and generally sought to maintain unity with the new administration. As an independent senator in 1965, however, he had a freer hand. He first challenged Johnson in late April, when the Dominican Republic suffered a military coup which overthrew a United States–supported government. The mounting tensions and violence had generated panicky reports from the American Embassy and the Central Intelligence Agency that a bloodbath was about to ensue, threatening American civilians. Johnson sent 22,000 combat troops to protect American lives and interests. "He had a sad example before him of the Bay of Pigs," Harry Ashmore recalled, "where they should either have stayed out or gone in but not done what they did, which was to go in half-way. I think he was determined not to repeat that error. . . ."[50]

Johnson explained his actions during three television appearances, maintaining that the extensive military response was appropriate. As part of a broad effort to rally support, he quoted "our beloved" President Kennedy, who, just one week before he died, declared the need to "use every resource at our command to prevent the establishment of another Cuba in this hemisphere." For the first time in his administration he confronted seriously divided public opinion. Opponents perceived his actions as "disorderly" and indicative of his lack of foreign policy experience. Some considered it a reversal of the principles promoted by Kennedy's Alliance for Progress. Robert Kennedy privately contended that Johnson's policy was an "outrage." Speaking before the Senate he was restrained, charging that Johnson's policies were "without regard to our friends and allies in the Organization of American States" and reminding the public that his brother had consulted the OAS during the Cuban missile crisis. Tom Wicker reported that some critics regarded Johnson as a "crude politician" who "doesn't understand foreign affairs (as Kennedy did and Bobby would)."[51]

Johnson grew wary of Kennedy's interest in Latin America. In the fall, as Robert prepared to travel to South America, he met with a State Department representative, Jack Hood Vaughn, the Assistant Secretary for Inter-American Affairs. Beforehand Jack Valenti spoke with Vaughn, who wanted to know how he should respond to Kennedy. "Should he discourage Kennedy from going to Argentina, Chile, and Venezuela?" Valenti asked Johnson.

"And what kind of briefing should he give Kennedy?" At the briefing later, Vaughn's demeanor was considered "hostile and bitter" by one attendant, an attitude that reflected Johnson's irritation at Kennedy's intrusion in Latin American foreign policy. Tension arose when Kennedy asked how, when addressing Latin American leaders, he might approach the topic of the Dominican Republic. Vaughn suggested that he cite his late brother's comments regarding United States policy toward Cuba. The implication irritated Kennedy. "I just hope you're not using anything that President Kennedy said to justify what you did in the Dominican Republic," he replied, "because you know I opposed that."[52]

Kennedy's Latin American tour bolstered his celebrity status, prompting one American newspaper to report that he had "opened his presidential campaign." Using mannerisms reminiscent of his brother's, he invoked President Kennedy's name and distributed PT-109 tie clips. He spoke favorably of Johnson, assuring Latinos that the president wanted to help Latin America's poor. He avoided criticizing Johnson's Dominican Republic policy, but the White House remained suspicious. Receiving an unsigned report from Peru entitled "Impressions of RFK in South American Tour," Johnson was informed that "Without actually saying so [Kennedy] disassociated himself from the Johnson Administration." He gave the impression of being "the complete liberal" while implying that Johnson was "an old-guard imperialist." Furthermore, the traveling press corps was "under his spell."[53]

Johnson was taken aback by Kennedy's Latin American welcome. During the following year he was reluctant to travel to Latin America in part because he feared he would not be as well received as his rival. He went to the region only after he felt Robert Kennedy had challenged his manhood. Johnson asserted that Kennedy had commented to others that the president's reluctance to go to the region resulted from a fear of being shot. "I'm going down there and show him," Johnson told his aides, before leaving for an overnight visit to Mexico City.[54]

Kennedy continued to search for opportunities to challenge Johnson on foreign policy issues. Frederick Dutton, an informal adviser, counseled him to deliver "a major, thoughtful talk on nuclear arms control" in order to "seize this moment and provide a striking, hopeful contrast to the military clanking and diplomatic grating of most of our present national efforts." He further recommended that Kennedy time the speech for "the day before the anniversary of President Kennedy's [American University] speech, so that you will be in the papers that day" and upstage Johnson or Vice President Humphrey, who would likely make passing note of the occasion. In June 1965, nearly two weeks after the anniversary of the American University speech, Kennedy expressed dissatisfaction with the administration's efforts at nuclear nonproliferation during his maiden address before the Senate. He was subsequently credited for moving within the idealistic framework bequeathed by his late brother, and, according to Tom Wicker, implied that "Mr. Johnson was not doing as much as he might—or as much as President Kennedy planned to do."[55]

Privately, White House reaction was mixed. McPherson viewed Kennedy as typically opportunistic. "A number of brave votes for pure liberalism, and a number of international, 'open' speeches such as the one on nuclear proliferation, and he will seem to them like St. George slaying the conservative dragons," he wrote Johnson. In a letter to Kennedy, however, Vice President Humphrey praised the speech as "excellent," characterizing it as "one that I wholeheartedly endorse and, as you know, vigorously support." Publicly, the administration worked to downplay Kennedy's criticism. Press secretary George Reedy told reporters that a commission proposed by the senator had long been established to examine the limitation of nuclear weapons. "Of course," he added, "we are glad Senator Kennedy is also interested in the field." Moyers cited an earlier address by Johnson that was consistent with Kennedy's comments. Johnson, meanwhile, instructed his speechwriter Richard Goodwin to edit out disarmament proposals from his scheduled address before the United Nations. "I want you to take out anything about the atom in that speech," he ordered. "I don't want one word in there that looks like I'm copying Bobby Kennedy."[56]

The most ominous foreign policy issue separating Johnson and Kennedy in 1965 concerned Vietnam. During the Kennedy administration Robert had not been briefed comprehensively about the military situation and had generally adhered to the hard-line policies of Defense Secretary Robert McNamara and General Maxwell Taylor, head of the Joint Chiefs of Staff. "We are going to win in Viet-Nam," the attorney general vowed when he visited Saigon in February 1962. "We will remain here until we do win." His involvement with the war was similarly sparse during the transition year. When he traveled to Indonesia and Malaysia in 1964, the topic was not even broached. His interest nevertheless grew. In June 1964 he wrote Johnson, volunteering to become Ambassador to Vietnam. Johnson rejected the curious offer with the calculated assertion that Robert might be killed in revenge for the CIA-sponsored assassination of South Vietnam's President Diem in 1963. During the remainder of the year Kennedy seldom discussed America's policy there.[57]

In light of Robert's few but "hawkish" comments on Vietnam, Johnson later claimed he was afraid he would be vulnerable to criticism if he withdrew American troops in 1965. "[T]here would be Robert Kennedy out in front leading the fight against me," he told Kearns, "telling everyone that

I had betrayed John Kennedy's commitment to South Vietnam. That I had let a democracy fall into the hands of the Communists. That I was a coward. An unmanly man. A man without a spine." He allegedly suffered nightmares in which he was tied to the ground while thousands of people advanced toward him, throwing stones, and shouting, "Coward! Traitor! Weakling!" But Johnson's fear of appearing weak in Robert's eyes was surely a minor factor in his decision to escalate the war. More important considerations pertained to North Vietnamese aggression, optimistic military advice, and his ideological commitment to contain communism. His professed fear of breaking continuity with the Kennedy administration had not prevented him from altering policies toward Latin America. Still, he may have felt intimidated by Robert. He often perceived the Vietnam War as a challenge to his manliness, once unzipping his pants and asking if Ho Chi Minh had anything that could compare with the length of his penis.[58]

Robert Kennedy moved cautiously in projecting a more "dovish" posture and challenging Johnson on the war. Visiting the president in late April, Kennedy recommended a temporary halt in the bombing of North Vietnam in order to encourage negotiations. Johnson told him the suggestion was already under consideration. Shortly thereafter he initiated a bombing pause but sent mixed signals of his ultimate intentions. He asked Congress for a $700 million appropriation for the war. Angered by the amount, Kennedy was assured by some senators of their support should he challenge the president. Speaking before the Senate, Kennedy took a moderate position, warning that an excessive commitment might lead to World War III but denouncing the idea of withdrawal. After asserting that the $700 million was not a "blank check," he joined eighty-seven other senators in passing the appropriation.[59]

By the summer of 1965 Johnson's Vietnam policies became increasingly unpopular among some editors, reporters, columnists, and academicians. Kennedy was well aware that he had a chance to build a liberal power base by aligning himself with those who questioned America's involvement. "Johnson is a very popular figure," he wrote columnist Anthony Lewis. "There is deep concern about Viet Nam and in my judgment the popularity of the Chief Executive will dissipate if the involvement and casualties grow to serious proportions." In July he continued to differ modestly with Johnson as he prepared for a commencement address at the International Police Academy. By that time the White House had grown increasingly impatient. "It will be another Kennedy v. Johnson issue," Watson told Johnson, and he suggested that, in the future, the administration demand that the IPA inform the White House as to whom they intended to invite. Kennedy's subsequent speech included numerous quotes from his brother, implying that Johnson had abandoned John's goals. He then inserted into the *Congressional Record* a statement expressing concern that the United States was assuming too much responsibility for the war.[60]

The White House seemed anxious to minimize Johnson's differences with Kennedy. At the invitation of the president, Kennedy attended an "off-the-record briefing" on foreign policy issues during the first week in April. "[T]here is quite a lot of work going on along lines which were strongly stimulated by your private talk with the President," McGeorge Bundy wrote Kennedy concerning the senator's interest in Algiers, "and it would be a very poor thing to knock that off the rails right now." In response to Kennedy's growing discomfort with the war, Lawrence O'Brien sent him a text of Johnson's opening remarks from his latest press conference which explained the nature of the conflict and its objectives. Robert had distanced himself enough to create his own base of support without incurring the full hostility of the White House.[61]

Kennedy's cautiousness in challenging Johnson on the war underscored the dilemma he faced in exploiting the war to his political advantage. Not only was there little evidence from his brother's presidency to challenge Johnson's policies, but he also had to be wary of offending former New Frontiersmen who were advising Johnson to escalate the war. Moreover, severe criticism would alienate him from the voters at large, who, in the summer of 1965, overwhelmingly approved of Johnson's handling of the war. His adversarial role was further hampered by the contention among some opinion-makers that the president was handling the war better than his predecessor. Cater recommended to Johnson that he cultivate Howard K. Smith of ABC News because "He thinks [John] Kennedy had reached an absolute stalemate on the domestic and foreign fronts, and that you have done an amazing job in getting the government moving again." Busby noted that Tony Day of the *Philadelphia Inquirer* had been a "reasonably strong supporter of Kennedy's policies" but "now believes Kennedy would have taken the same decisions in Viet Nam that you made."[62]

Suffering from increased criticism, Johnson returned to the "mystique" in an effort to neutralize opponents. In fact, former presidents, both living and dead, provided a valuable source of support. After deciding to bomb North Vietnam in February, Johnson consulted with Presidents Dwight Eisenhower and Harry Truman, who voiced public approval for escalation of the war. The administration also sought the posthumous support of President Kennedy. Three days before American combat troops first landed in South Vietnam in March, Busby sent Johnson a requested chronological summary of United States policy in Vietnam, listing public statements made by government officials. Busby lamented that "the record of President Kennedy's public statements is sparse in terms of current usefulness." Undaunted, Johnson defended his policy by noting, throughout a half-dozen press conferences in 1965, that his policy in Vietnam was in part a fulfillment of John Kennedy's commitment.[63]

Johnson's foreign policy advisers also sought to defend themselves by alluding to the late president. In late March Johnson planned a comprehensive speech at Johns Hopkins University explaining America's involvement in Vietnam. McGeorge Bundy sent the draft of the address to Johnson, along with a note apologizing for its length: the complexity of the subject required elaboration. "I have also wanted to include enough history to keep us straight in the line started by Eisenhower and continued by Kennedy." Of particular interest were the Kennedy references which were "designed to give us protection and encouragement with some of the 'liberals' who are falsely telling each other that your policy is different than his."[64]

Johnson's Johns Hopkins address was a pivotal moment in his explanation of the war. In the final draft Goodwin and Valenti added the proposal that, with North Vietnam's cooperation, the United States would devote its resources to reconstructing the Mekong River in order to provide food, water, and power "on a scale to dwarf even our own TVA." Johnson was enthusiastic about the idea. The historical context of the war was deemphasized in the final draft, and specific references to Eisenhower and Kennedy were deleted. Instead Johnson sweepingly claimed that, "Since 1954, every American President has offered support to the people of South Viet-Nam." He described their commitment as part of a "national pledge" which he would uphold. "To dishonor that pledge would be an unforgivable wrong." For the time being Johnson could plausibly portray the war as an extension of his predecessor's will.[65]

The Johnson Offensive

Johnson's effort to link his controversial foreign policies to John Kennedy was in part intended to maintain public support for the war and to neutralize wavering liberals. He needed desperately to maintain unity on Vietnam in order to move forward with his legislative agenda. Each time he escalated American involvement, he feared draining from his social programs the funds necessary to create the Great Society. His effort to minimize Kennedy's criticism, therefore, was part of a broad effort to protect larger goals. But because Kennedy was a particularly threatening critic, Johnson often targeted him. In challenging his rival, Johnson was caught in a dilemma: a direct assault against Robert could be viewed as a veiled insult to the memory of President Kennedy. In an attempt to minimize Robert's political maneuvers without offending the Kennedy legacy, Johnson resorted to tactics aimed more at Kennedy's supporters than at the senator himself.

In contrast to Johnson's rather defensive reaction in matters of foreign policy, party politics allowed him to be more aggressive. As president and leader of the Democratic party, Johnson had numerous levers with which to subtly diminish Kennedy's influence among rank-and-file party leaders. One tactic involved the withholding of patronage. Without consulting Kennedy, for example, Johnson installed his friend Edwin Weisl as New York's national committeeman, allowing the Johnson faction of the party to control federal appointments for the state. He also cultivated New York's Senator Jacob Javits, hoping to use the liberal Republican to challenge Kennedy as he sought to espouse progressive causes. And he financially impaired the state party and worked to defeat local candidates endorsed by Kennedy. During New York City's mayoral campaign in 1965, for example, when Robert backed the Democratic candidate Abraham Beame, a White House aide outlined for Bill Moyers the benefits and drawbacks of Johnson's involvement in the election, describing possible scenarios based on how each endorsement would affect Kennedy's political standing.[66]

Fearful that Kennedy might create his own Washington cadre, Johnson extended the scope of his offensive. Shortly after leaving the Justice Department in 1964, Kennedy renewed efforts to appoint Frank Morrissey, a long-time family friend, to the federal district court in Massachusetts. His poor qualifications made the nomination an obvious family favor. In a move that Robert considered both surprising and suspicious, Johnson sent Morrissey's name to the Senate for approval in 1965. Although Edward Kennedy thanked him for the nomination, insiders fancied that the president had cooperated in hopes that the family would be attacked for "cronyism." "Work hard on this one," Johnson instructed aide Joseph Califano. "Teddy's gonna get his ass beat on this one and I don't want him to accuse me of not helping him, 'cause he ain't going to blame himself when he loses." Johnson then called J. Edgar Hoover to request an FBI investigation of Morrissey. The nomination drew immediate criticism, and the embarrassed Kennedy brothers were forced to withdraw it. According to Schlesinger, "The only winner in this fracas was Lyndon Johnson."[67]

Other people were similarly victimized because of their relationship to the Kennedys. William Rivkin's nomination for an ambassadorship, for example, was delayed because of his suspected friendship with Robert. "He is a Johnson man," the White House was assured. "He is not a Kennedy man. . . . Once again, if anyone informed you that Rivkin is an RFK man, you were wrongly informed." Eugene Nickerson, the county executive for

Nassau County, New York, became the victim of an elaborate plot. In the spring of 1965 Kennedy contacted Arthur Hummel of the State Department, requesting that Nickerson be sent overseas to lecture in the Middle East and Africa as part of an exchange program. Nickerson was a political favorite of Kennedy, and the senator wanted to bolster his prestige in preparation for a gubernatorial campaign in 1966. McPherson informed Johnson of the exchange program and noted Nickerson's high qualifications as a "good speaker." "[U]nder ordinary circumstances," he wrote, "we would consider him a find." But the trip would help Nickerson politically and thus indirectly benefit Kennedy. McPherson listed various options, recommending that they send Nickerson abroad but not to all the locations Kennedy desired. Otherwise Kennedy could "stir up problems."

Johnson rejected the request outright. Arrangements were made for Hummel to explain to Kennedy through a telephone call that there were already too many speakers being sent abroad in areas of law and government. Kennedy balked at the explanation and requested a private meeting with Hummel. McPherson then advised Hummel to explain the program's nonpartisan flavor and the State Department policy that prohibited sending active candidates abroad. "We can't find any names on our past list to give the lie to this as a policy," he noted. "So it appears to be a sound answer." He assured Johnson that Hummel "will say that he has not spoken to me about it, and take responsibility for the decision himself." Kennedy again rejected the State Department's reasoning and suspected that there "must be more behind this than there appears to be." "At no time was my name or yours mentioned," McPherson informed Johnson, "but my deputy came away with the feeling that Kennedy's suspicions were sharply aroused."[68]

How effective were Johnson's attacks against Kennedy? As the Nickerson episode indicated, his actions were petty and mildly irritating. Robert's political strength (like his late brother's) derived from his popular appeal; his power rested more with his public image than with his governmental position. Accustomed to dominating political rivals through power plays, Johnson may have assumed that his actions were more successful than they were. When speaking to reporters he began to cite polls comparing himself favorably with John and Robert Kennedy. His delight in doing so prompted McPherson to warn him that the practice was "unwise." "I think there are plenty of ways for this stuff to get to the press other than your reading it out and describing yourself in third person," McPherson wrote. "It is valuable and encouraging information, but in my opinion it should not be delivered by you." While Johnson's efforts may have diminished Kennedy's authority within the party, they did not appear seriously to damage his national

reputation and long-term ambitions. The efforts simply and painfully reminded him of the president's power.[69]

Careful not to behave too aggressively toward Kennedy, Johnson projected
his hostility on those whom he imagined were aiding the senator's presidential ambitions. After the election many aides had wanted Johnson to reach
out to those favorable to the Kennedys rather than alienating them. Reflecting on the past campaign, for example, Robert Hunter discerned, "The
President's folksy approach has left him with an 'enthusiasm drain' with
many people who were most enthusiastic about President Kennedy." He
recommended a "vigorous imaginative program of action" in order to appeal
to "Eastern Liberals." Specifically, Johnson needed to conduct "high-
powered 'backgrounders' with the most liberal and most sophisticated
pressmen" as well as hold meetings with "various liberal opinion leaders."
The primary purpose would be to "permit something of the President's
personal touch—and sophistication—to get through."[70]

Johnson was unreceptive to such suggestions after the 1964 election. He
had won by the largest plurality in history, and his mandate was achieved
with little owed to "intellectuals" in the media, universities, or elsewhere.
Furthermore, many academicians, writers, editors, and government officials
had become increasingly outspoken against Johnson's foreign policies. But
his most immediate reason for excluding the intellectuals may have been
conditioned by his growing obsession with Robert Kennedy.[71]

During 1965 various writers and academicians grew more critical of
Johnson's foreign policies, comparing them poorly with his predecessor's
heralded skills at crisis management. Some contended that Johnson was not
as intellectually well equipped to deal with the issues, prompting Eric
Goldman to conclude that they were "determined to beat LBJ over the head
with JFK." "Until I got in this job," Johnson responded, "I didn't realize
you had to look down your nose to understand foreign policy." Goldman
interpreted Johnson's statement as indicating a new attitude; the intellectuals' attraction to the Kennedys and their lack of appreciation for the
president's efforts on their behalf prompted Johnson to let them "have it."[72]

Although Johnson continued to support intellectuals and artists by expanding federal programs and grants, he distanced himself from an image
associated with the Kennedy era. In May Douglass Cater recommended a
"useful project" to express the administration's interest in a peaceful foreign
policy: Johnson would meet with eight hundred foreign graduating seniors
and graduate students who were attending local universities. The president
was reminded that when he had met with a similar group the year before, he
had continued the custom initiated by John Kennedy. In 1965, however,
Johnson rejected the request.[73]

Johnson's animosity toward intellectuals became abundantly clear by June. Earlier that year Goldman had been advised to organize something "cultural" for the White House and reminded that John and Jacqueline Kennedy had once held a very successful dinner for Nobel prize winners and had invited Pablo Casals to perform at the White House. Goldman was asked to develop a similar idea without blatantly imitating the Kennedys; he subsequently recommended the "White House Festival of the Arts," a project consisting of one hundred writers, painters, musicians, and actors who would exhibit or perform their work during a twelve-hour festival on the White House grounds. The president was initially favorable to the proposal.[74]

The festival, however, was doomed in part by bad timing. Plans for the occasion originated in February, before Johnson had escalated America's involvement in the Dominican Republic and Vietnam. By June a number of those invited had grown publicly critical of Johnson's policies. As the festival neared, Johnson grew anxious and pessimistic, admonishing aides for proposing the idea in the first place. Although only a handful of guests had rejected their invitations, he believed they all disliked him, opposed his policies, and wanted to embarrass him. Some aides agreed, and the festival divided White House staff. Word circulated that novelist John Hersey intended to read a selection from his book *Hiroshima*. Some aides considered this a backhanded attempt to criticize the president's policies in Vietnam, prompting Marvin Watson to remark, "Fuck the intellectual community." Johnson considered canceling the festival, informing Goldman that he had "had enough of these people" and threatening that he "simply won't show up at the thing." The president sought to limit negative publicity by ordering a news blackout and trying to disassociate himself from the event. He also ordered the FBI to investigate the beliefs and associations of the invited guests.[75]

The June 14 festival did not desecrate the administration as Johnson and his aides had feared. Although moments of tension were reported, the news media initially responded favorably to Johnson's effort to emulate John Kennedy's promotion of the arts. Some political observers believed he had gained stature by demonstrating an ability to take criticism. The infighting and anxiety in the White House went largely unreported. "But enough had become public," Goldman recalled, "to make the wall [between Johnson and the intellectuals] seem as impassable as the barbed concrete between East and West Berlin."[76]

After the festival Johnson isolated Goldman from the administration's operations and stopped issuing the Medal of Freedom, an award initiated by John Kennedy and intended to recognize citizens who had contributed to the nation's intellectual and cultural well-being. Busby warned Johnson that a reporter had asked why no Medal of Freedom awards were issued, and he advised that the administration maintain that it did not give awards to "living citizens." Properly explained, the policy would be accepted by the public. "Unexplained, it may be turned into a distortion: e.g., a jab at Kennedy or at the 'press.' " The matter went unexplained.[77]

Throughout the remainder of his presidency Johnson continued to distance himself from the intellectual community. During a Princeton address in May 1966 he lectured "intellectuals" about the difference between "responsible criticism and heckling." After accepting the resignation of Goldman in September of that year, he announced that the position created during the Kennedy administration would be abolished altogether. That month the White House hired John Roche, a political scientist from Brandeis University. Roche was a strong supporter of the war, an intellectual who was contemptuous of the academic community, and a man who despised Robert Kennedy. Johnson's most blatant break with the intellectual community came during a speech in San Antonio in which he noted that "sometimes among our more sophisticated, self-styled intellectuals, some of them are more concerned with appearance than they are with achievement. They are more concerned with style than they are with mortar, brick, and concrete." According to one newspaper, the audience knew "very well whom he had in mind" and "cheered him to the echo. Perhaps it was L.B.J.'s way of serving notice on the world that it could take him or not, as it pleased. . . ."[78]

The departure from the Kennedy image was sometimes easier for Johnson than for his aides, some of whom regularly expressed frustration that his reputation with intellectuals compared poorly with the past. "President Kennedy has the reputation as the 'aesthete's President,' " McPherson lamented in 1966, "but as in so many other things, appearance and reality are different matters." Admitting defeat in terms of image, he sought to comfort Johnson with historical assurances; he and his staff would be remembered as "the most enlightened crowd to sit in this building," and Johnson had achieved more than his predecessor in "the world of cultural improvement and design." As valid as McPherson's observations were, the president's practical efforts on behalf of artists and intellectuals never compensated for the fundamental hostility revealed in the summer of 1965.[79]

During the first nine months following the election, Johnson's aggressiveness toward intellectuals was generalized and directed against those whom Johnson termed the "Georgetown crowd," a loose collection of government employees, academicians, publishers, columnists, and newspaper writers who socialized together in Washington. The precise composition of this nebulous in-crowd was difficult to discern. Most shared a common background: educated in the East, ostensibly "liberal," and with similar social interests. Among their binding characteristics, and the most troublesome to Johnson, was their affection for the Kennedys. Media personalities such as Rowland Evans, Philip Geyelin, Joseph Alsop, Joseph Kraft, Katharine Graham, Benjamin Bradlee, and Sander Vanocur had been closely identified with John Kennedy. Laced among them were such former New Frontiersmen as Theodore Sorensen, Arthur Schlesinger, Edwin O. Guthman, John Seigenthaler, and Burke Marshall. Former Kennedy aides who remained in the administration, such as Robert McNamara, McGeorge Bundy, Richard Goodwin, Nicholas Katzenbach, and Joseph Califano, also belonged. Even certain "Johnson men," such as Bill Moyers, Jack Valenti, and Harry McPherson, were regarded as members. "We were . . . white Jews to the Kennedys," McPherson noted. "We were acceptable."[80]

Robert Kennedy's social standing and political appeal made him the focal point of this inner circle. Journalists Joseph Alsop, David Brinkley, and Edwin Guthman frequently sent him congratulatory messages and offered informal advice. "Invitations to Hickory Hill [Robert Kennedy's home] were treasured," McPherson recalled. "The élan and glamour, which is very real, of the Kennedy world was the center of excitement and energy within the group." The president was well aware that his rival was perceived "as the man that most of this group looked to to save them from another four years of Lyndon Johnson." So he was alarmed by relationships among reporters and public officials within the "Georgetown crowd." Within this tightly knit social group, McPherson recalled, "it became de rigueur to attack President Johnson, and there was no social consequence attached to that. But one did not attack Bob Kennedy."[81]

Learning of the gossip that circulated at the various parties and gatherings, the president believed that the criticism and insults leveled against him ultimately impacted heavily on public opinion. He began to feel undermined by influential newspapers such as the New York Times and the Washington Post, and directed his anger against political columnists and editors, believing, according to McPherson, that "their devotion to John Kennedy's memory made them incapable . . . for fairness to him." Throughout the spring and summer of 1965 Johnson developed an "obsession" toward the press which aides and reporters had never before fully observed in him. As a senator he had treated journalists as he did his colleagues—with a mixture of cajolery and intimidation. But he had not appeared deliberately hostile. His attitude shifted drastically after the 1964 election. "I've been kissing asses all my life," he told George Reedy, "and I don't have to kiss them anymore. Tell those press bastards of yours that I'll see them when I want to and not before."[82]

Reporters wrote extensively about the change in Johnson's attitude. Articles depicted him as sensitive to criticism, moody, and humorless, some concluding that the change was a result of foreign policy problems. Certain reporters believed that the strain was the inevitable consequence of tensions between president and press. Some speculated about the president's psychological stability. While reporters were accurate about the general cause of Johnson's hostility, they failed to appreciate his growing concern for Robert Kennedy. As with other aspects of his presidency in 1965, Johnson's actions toward the press were subtly tied to his shifting concern for the Kennedy "mystique." According to Reedy, the president's growing desire to protect himself from Robert Kennedy prompted increased animosity toward the press, producing "some extraordinarily clumsy efforts" at trying to manage the news. One technique involved abolishing press pools. Rather than allowing selected reporters to fly aboard Air Force One during presidential trips, Johnson demanded that they fly separately. According to Reedy, he "insisted that they were 'spies' (his exact word) whose only purpose was to search out embarrassing secrets." He was also convinced that Pierre Salinger conceived the idea of press pools "at Bobby Kennedy's instigation." When Helen Thomas of the Associated Press wrote a quaint story on the president's impoverished cultural roots, Johnson considered it disparaging and charged that it had been inspired by Kennedy. His conspiratorial mind-set extended to numerous sympathetic reporters. In late June, for example, he asked Goodwin and Moyers "if we thought Tom Wicker was out to destroy him, if Wicker was caught up in some sort of conspiracy."[83]

In challenging Robert Kennedy by behaving more aggressively toward reporters, Johnson became strangely entrapped in the "mystique." He intended to protect himself against Kennedy's presidential ambitions by rejecting his alleged cohorts. But in the process he invited unfavorable comparisons with John Kennedy. Much to the irritation of Johnson aides, a resurgence of newspaper stories reminded the public that Johnson's rapport with the press contrasted poorly to the late president's. When *Newsweek* planned a cover story on Johnson's popular image, Cater spoke with the magazine's reporters and informed Johnson, "It will certainly *not* be a detailed comparison with Kennedy." Nevertheless, *Newsweek* reported that there had emerged a "Style Gap" since Kennedy's death, much of it founded on Johnson's manner of meeting with reporters. Two general criticisms were cited: the infrequency of live, televised press conferences, and Johnson's failure to give adequate warning of their scheduling.[84]

Rather than accommodating himself to the demands of the "mystique," Johnson became defensive, denying any significant change in his treatment of the press. In February he argued that he had given nine more news conferences than had Kennedy during his first fourteen months in office. While the figure was accurate, Johnson had in fact resisted live televised conferences. He was unable to counter reporters' criticism of his short advance notices but disputed other grievances. He pledged to use a variety of formats, including a televised press conference once a month "with ample advance notice, coverage by all media, full dress—even white tie if you choose." He also provided an elaborate list delineating every contact he had had with reporters since becoming president.[85]

Johnson's response seemed intended in part to assert that he was somehow "better" than Kennedy or at least no different in his treatment of reporters. He could not bring himself to admit publicly that he was moving beyond the Kennedy image. The administration compiled a twelve-page report entitled, "Various Editorials from [or for] the Press on President Kennedy's Press Conferences." The collection illustrated that the press problems for which Johnson was criticized had also been raised against his predecessor. Busby sent the president an article criticizing "news management." Summarizing the story, he wrote that it alleged "unfavorable facts suppressed, reporters reprimanded, favoritism promoted, courting is open. . . ." He ended the memorandum by surprising Johnson: the piece was written during the Kennedy administration. Johnson was also favorable to a letter from a reporter who noted that he "fared well" in comparison with Kennedy. Johnson wanted Moyers to read the letter to members of the press.[86]

Throughout his presidency Johnson tried to convince the press that he treated reporters as Kennedy had. He often requested tabulations comparing the number of press conferences each had given. On one occasion an aide manipulated the numbers to account for Johnson's illnesses, thus allowing him to "beat" Kennedy. On the bottom of one comparison sheet, Johnson wrote, "Bob. See that AP and UP 'Smitty' get this and ask for justice only." After complaints from reporters that his opening statements during press conferences were excessive, he called for a report detailing Kennedy's extensive use of opening statements. He also received "a summary of criticisms surrounding President Kennedy's press relations," a five-page summary of general criticism to which Kennedy was subjected, and a study which noted that Kennedy also faced a "credibility gap." The regular effort to draw parallels in press relations seemed intended to reassure Johnson. He could not admit that he was behaving differently toward the press. The problem, he believed, rested with the press's prejudice against him, not in his treatment of reporters.[87]

By July 1965 Johnson's press relations had seriously deteriorated. His Latin American and Vietnam policies were being criticized by prestigious newspapers, including the *New York Times* and the *St. Louis Post-Dispatch*.

His poor press relations were becoming major stories in themselves and were part of a broader array of threats to his presidency. That month Johnson intended to escalate America's commitment in Vietnam to 125,000 troops. Knowing that Vietnam would sidetrack his pursuit of a Great Society, he was anguished by the decision. Faced with potential political instability and internal anxiety about the future, he retreated to past tactics and sought reconciliation with the "Kennedy press."[88]

On July 8 press secretary George Reedy announced that he was taking a temporary leave of absence. Replacing him was thirty-one-year-old Bill Moyers. Johnson's choice was regarded as a conciliatory gesture designed to repair relations with reporters. Moyers and the president had shared a long and close relationship. "No one else, I believed, made Johnson think of himself when young," McPherson recalled. Aides often contended that he regarded Moyers as his "surrogate son," and Moyers held similar affection for Johnson.[89]

Johnson's decision to appoint Moyers as press secretary involved several considerations. Not only was he a popular choice among reporters and extremely loyal to the president, but, perhaps of more immediate importance, he was acceptable to the "Georgetown crowd." Since the 1960 campaign Moyers had worked closely with Kennedy aides, serving as a liaison between Johnson and the Kennedy organization. After John Kennedy's election, Moyers's relationship with the New Frontiersmen grew closer when he became deputy director of the Peace Corps and worked under the president's brother-in-law Sargent Shriver. During the transition year he served as an important link to the Kennedy team. Because of his affiliation with the Kennedys, his presence in the Johnson administration comforted the "Georgetown crowd." But his outside relations also made the president nervous. One aide believed that Moyers was "hypnotized" by Robert Kennedy and enchanted by the family's "jet set" image. The Kennedys, meanwhile, were attracted to Moyers. In time Johnson became anxious about Robert Kennedy's influence upon his aide. In July 1965, however, his trepidation seemed tempered by larger political concerns.[90]

The appointment of Moyers paid immediate dividends. Busby informed Johnson that reporters reacted "warmly and sympathetically" to the change and "seemed slightly flattered that a top, trusted aide had been made Press Secretary." After Johnson's next press conference he was told that reporters considered it a "good show" and his best session all year. They had "special applause" for his "responsiveness, crispness and, especially, the good humor of answers to questions." Some members of the "Kennedy press" sought reconciliation. Ben Bradlee of the *Washington Post* conveyed his desire to get off Johnson's "blacklist." He noted that both Robert and John

Kennedy had sometimes put him on their blacklists as well. Joseph Alsop reminded Johnson that he, too, was "one of your old friends and supporters, but is annoyed by the Drew Pearson attack on him, which he claims was sponsored by you." Johnson was unreceptive, writing on a memo, "Why see him?"[91]

In late July Johnson granted an interview with *Newsweek*'s Charles Roberts and reflected on several matters that had become sources of friction between himself and the press that year. He fluctuated among professed indifference, defensiveness, and hostility, arguing that despite criticism of his foreign policies, the public approved of his actions. Defending his Vietnam policy, he erroneously claimed that John Kennedy "put 33,000 American troops in there." In his animosity he exclaimed, "Somebody ought to do an article on you, on your damn profession, your First Amendment." A moment later he denied his anger. "The press helps me. I want to disabuse your mind that I'm worried about some rat terriers at my heels."[92]

During the first ten months after the election Johnson's behavior at times supported, on a surface level, the assessments of those who thought him "paranoid." Struggling to control his inner animosity and fear, he over-reacted to journalists and intellectuals who were drawn to Robert Kennedy. He responded as if each situation might have future catastrophic ramifications, alienating those opinion-makers who might have aided him in later years. Moreover, he permanently distanced himself from the Kennedy "mystique," for the more he challenged Robert and his supporters, the less he appealed to those who fondly remembered John Kennedy. And by moving against Robert, Johnson would later find it difficult to use John as a shield against his critics.

Publicly Johnson sought to maintain the illusion of harmony with Kennedy, appreciating that he was too strongly identified with the past to risk complete alienation. During the year he sent the senator a signed copy of his State of the Union Address, photographs of them taken during signing ceremonies, Christmas greetings, and a congratulatory message upon his first anniversary in the Senate. He thanked Kennedy for his occasional public support for his administration and invited the senator to attend a White House conference on education and various bill-signing ceremonies. Upon signing the Presidential Assassination Penalties Bill, Johnson was reminded that it "carries considerable emotional freight" and he should therefore consult Robert Kennedy. Kennedy, too, understood the need to defer to the president's authority, thanking him for his "courteous" treatment at the signing of the voting rights bill, his "thoughtfulness" during a memorial service for the late president, and wishing him a return to good health following gall bladder surgery. But the façade was weakening and could not compensate for underlying suspicions and underhanded efforts.[93]

For the moment, Johnson's continued legislative success and foreign policy adventures remained popular, partially obscuring a personal image and political style that were increasingly unappealing. In a *Time* magazine survey of Johnson's image that year, an auto worker praised him for his expertise: "He's not a glamour boy like Kennedy, and I think he has more on the ball." "Listen, the common man identifies with Lyndon," a salesman added, "and this is a big change from the smart jet-set image of the Kennedys." "[T]he difference between the two men," a reader wrote, "is the difference between form and substance." But Johnson's aggressive behavior in 1965 also emphasized an unflattering personal image that contrasted poorly to the public's fond memory of his predecessor. More and more, his unsavory reputation as a "politician" had proven out, prompting some Americans to describe him as "a common man with honey on his mouth," "a crook and a liar," "too fatherly," "a power-oriented egoist," and "a bit of a bully." Such attributes prevented much of the public from developing personal affection for him. "In his case," one person told *Time*, "we have to sacrifice love for accomplishment." As long as his achievements continued to impress enough of the public, Johnson was relatively capable of meeting challenges from a more charismatic rival. "The danger for the President," columnist Allen Otten noted in July, "is that with the undertone already there, some sudden reverses at home or abroad will result in a marked drop in popular support."[94]

From the fall of 1965 through December 1966, as Lyndon Johnson entered his third year in office, the Vietnam War beleaguered his administration. During those tense and difficult months he sought to induce North Vietnamese leadership into negotiations by simultaneously escalating the war and offering assurances that he would stop bombing if they halted communist infiltration into the South. The strategy was ineffective. The war dominated the news, and public support wavered as the fighting dragged on. By March 1966 Johnson had committed 250,000 troops to the war, and in late June the United States began bombing military targets in Hanoi and Haiphong. As "hawks" and "doves" expressed dissatisfaction with the president's middle-course strategy, his approval rating fell by more than twenty percentage points between June 1965 and September 1966. With Johnson increasingly ineffective and vulnerable, Robert Kennedy grew assertive, becoming a leading critic of the administration's foreign policies and prompting an open breach with the president.[1]

The Critic

In light of Johnson's difficulties, his ensuing struggle with Kennedy generated considerable speculation. A *Newsweek* cover story on Robert and Edward Kennedy in January 1966 noted the enormous attention that the brothers commanded. Their brief tenure should have made them politically irrelevant by traditional standards; but each was "the inheritor of a magic name, an uncompleted mission, a deep rooted family mystique of ambition, competition and power." As "the bearers of the name and looks and élan, double avatars of the late President," Robert and Edward received more mail, drew larger crowds, received more speaking invitations, and gained greater press attention than any member of Congress. The presidential implications were self-evident, though the precise timing of the intended "restoration" was speculative. Reporters predicted that developments in the Vietnam conflict might erode Congress's consensus on the war, prompting the Kennedys to lead the liberal opposition.[2]

Unlike Robert, Edward was generally supportive of Johnson's Vietnam policy. After traveling to Southeast Asia in October 1965 he gave an unqualified endorsement to America's effort there. Known as a "team member" by the Washington establishment, Edward was purportedly wary of right-wing congressmen who might pressure for a nuclear confrontation in the region. Because Edward was young and posed no immediate threat to displacing him as president, Johnson found him less threatening than Robert. He solicited his help on legislative matters and maintained privately that Edward had the potential to be "the best politician in the whole family."[3]

In late 1965 Robert Kennedy still confined his harshest comments about Johnson to private occasions. During a party at his Hickory Hill home in December he contrasted the president's mishandling of peace overtures with his brother's diplomatic skill during the Cuban missile crisis. He assured guests that he was "upset" with Johnson's policies. "I'd like to speak out more on Vietnam," he lamented. "But if I broke with the administration it might be disastrous for the country." Occasionally he could not restrain himself. One month earlier he had carelessly told reporters that it was "a good idea" for Americans to donate blood to the Viet Cong. Widely criticized for aiding and abetting the enemy, Kennedy shrugged off the political damage, joking privately with columnists about his laxity.[4]

On December 18 Johnson suspended American bombing of North Vietnam, hoping to encourage negotiations. The Kennedy brothers sought to pressure him to continue the pause as long as possible. In January 1966 Robert told reporters that the administration might face new challenges if the president resumed escalation of the war. "Appropriate committees should be consulted," he noted. "Administration witnesses should testify." Edward's approach was more private. Calling Bill Moyers, he conveyed his "hopes" that Johnson would prolong the pause and explore contacts with the National Liberation Front (NLF), a guerrilla resistance force formed in South Vietnam in 1960 to oppose the Diem government. Edward noted that he intended to make a speech on the Senate floor "which will strongly support the

President." Moyers warned Johnson that the senator would probably "raise these two points" of contention.[5]

Robert Kennedy next sent a letter to the president noting how "impressed" he was with his latest effort to resolve the conflict peacefully. He encouraged Johnson not to be pressured by military advice to resume bombing. Enclosing a copy of Bruce Catton's *Never Call Retreat,* Kennedy referred to select passages showing that Abraham Lincoln faced "identical problems and situations" during the Civil War. In a reply drafted by Jack Valenti, Johnson thanked Kennedy for his "warm letter" and expressed gratitude for having received it during "one of those hours when I felt alone, prayerfully alone." He recalled President Kennedy's difficulties during the Cuban missile crisis, and because of Robert's closeness to his brother he knew that the senator understood "better than most the gloom that crowds in on a President." He also noted that he had read the Catton passages during a meeting with congressional leaders. He did not mention that the reading was delivered in the context of his decision to resume bombing on January 31, 1966.[6]

The Senate circulated a petition opposing the renewed escalation. Robert and Edward Kennedy signed it, but at the last moment Edward withdrew his name. Robert, meanwhile, increased public pressure, warning from the Senate floor that the resumption of bombing "may become the first in a series of steps on a road from which there is no turning back—a road which leads to catastrophe for all mankind." Frederick Dutton, one of his chief advisers, privately praised Kennedy for asserting his independence from Johnson. "[T]he really significant base you are developing throughout the nation to augment the hard-core Kennedy following you already have," Dutton wrote Kennedy, "is slightly to the left of Johnson philosophically and politically." For this reason he advised Robert against planning a trip to South Vietnam because, in part, an interest in Johnson's recent pacification program there would make him appear to be "Me-Tooing LBJ."[7]

But Kennedy's effort to distance himself further from Johnson's policies became careless. During Senate Foreign Relations Committee hearings on Vietnam in February, he sought to exploit Johnson's vagueness about conditions for negotiations by implying that one condition for a settlement might be the acceptance of "a compromise government" involving the NLF. He privately deleted from his statement references praising Johnson's pacification program. Kennedy warned Bill Moyers of the impending news conference and statement, and sent Robert McNamara an advance copy. "I don't believe it causes problems," he wrote McNamara, "—but then I've been wrong about that before."[8]

The Johnson administration responded swiftly and aggressively to Kennedy's proposal. John Connally warned the president that Robert was "the motivating force behind the Senate hearings and the Saturday statement was only his climax." Vice President Humphrey stated publicly that Kennedy's idea to involve the NLF was like putting "a fox in a chicken coop." Speaking on *Issues and Answers,* Undersecretary of State George Ball argued against a coalition government: historically they either turned communist or self-destructed. Appearing on *Meet the Press,* national security adviser McGeorge Bundy countered Robert's proposal by quoting John Kennedy, who opposed popular-front governments: "I do not believe that any democrat can successfully ride that tiger." "I initially planned to quote Bobby himself on our side of the question," Bundy recalled, "and it was the President who told me not to do that if I valued my friendship with the Senator." Johnson, meanwhile, indirectly challenged Kennedy. At the National Freedom Award ceremony he quoted at length from John Kennedy's Inaugural Address, pledging America's commitment to "pay any price, bear any burden, meet any hardship, support any friend, oppose any foe to assure the survival and the success of liberty." Robert attended the function and was visibly uncomfortable with the innuendo. The Kennedy staff was taken aback by the intensity of the White House reaction. "[I]t sounded as if they all decided they had found Bobby in bed with the Communists," an aide lamented, "and were determined to pin him there."[9]

Publicly Kennedy retreated on the matter, claiming that he had been misinterpreted. He did not favor the NLF "automatically" sharing power in the interim government. He meant that the NLF should not be "automatically excluded," a point which Bill Moyers noted was acceptable to the administration. Privately he thought the White House had overreacted and wrote Bundy to express dissatisfaction: "Perhaps a [telephone] call [to me] would not have taken any more time than for someone to look up the quote of President Kennedy to use against my position." He deleted this comment from his final letter. Bundy assured Robert that he had tried to avoid directly criticizing him and offered publicly to retract any inaccurate comments. He added that the senator should have contacted the administration before attacking it. George Ball, meanwhile, having been informed by Bundy that he misinterpreted Kennedy's proposal, sought to clarify the criticism expressed on *Issues and Answers.* "[I]f I had understood that you were suggesting only that the Viet Cong be permitted to participate in an election," Ball wrote Kennedy, "my comments would have taken quite a different course." The rift which Kennedy had perpetrated on Saturday was "papered over" by Tuesday. Nevertheless, tensions remained. On the *Today Show,* Kennedy contended that his main purpose was to clarify the "confusion" of the White House. "I don't think it is the administration that is confused," Moyers responded.[10]

Kennedy's attack and retreat stalled his political momentum. Although he received support from several prominent newspapers, Dutton roundly criticized him for his "muddled handling" of the situation. He accused the senator of appearing "contradictory" and of injecting "confusion and off-handedness about a critical issue. . . ." Seeking to repair the damage, he advised Kennedy to "comment about the subject on a high, solid level," to avoid a "running attack," to appear on television to discuss the substance of his criticism, to infuse "a little more patriotic rhetoric" when addressing Vietnam, and to engage in a media blitz by calling columnists, editors, and reporters. Finally, Dutton recommended that Kennedy "Find a low key, early public opportunity to comment favorably about President Johnson personally in some newsworthy way."[11]

The White House continued to monitor Kennedy's comments and assess his motives. Joseph Alsop told Harry McPherson that Robert had said he called for a coalition government because he believed the president would seek a negotiated settlement rather than "stay the long course." He did not want to appear as a hard-liner if Johnson's negotiations proved successful. Kennedy's conversation with Alsop, McPherson informed the president, was a convenient "covering position" to protect him from criticism by the *New York Times*.[12]

Before the end of the spring Kennedy again chastised Johnson for his handling of the war. In April the administration announced that Chinese air bases would not be immune from military retaliation if planes operating from such bases attacked American planes. Speaking on the Senate floor, Kennedy argued against further escalation of America's military involvement until the South Vietnamese government was stable enough for "the successful prosecution of our efforts," and he called upon them to "organize their society and government if they are to wage a successful war." Coverage of Kennedy's criticism impressed White House aide Robert Kintner, who assessed the speech as "quite effective" and "so uncomplicated" that it would have wide appeal to the public and liberal press. "The picture he is painting of you as President, without mentioning you, is the opposite of what I think is the right public posture—namely, a President being very careful of the use of the Armed Forces in Viet Nam."[13]

Although Johnson was not silent against his critics, he avoided openly challenging Kennedy, hoping to maintain a fragile consensus on the war. He occasionally lashed out in a general fashion, labeling "doves" as "Nervous Nellies" and criticizing "hawks" for confusing policy and indirectly costing American lives. But in contending with Kennedy he relied on oblique strategies. Johnson forwarded to Senator George Smathers, a close friend of the Kennedys, four pages of quotes by John and Robert Kennedy dating back to the 1950s, in which they expressed support for America's commitment in Southeast Asia. The quotations implied that Johnson's policy was consistent with John Kennedy's legacy and Robert's earlier, less tainted opinions. Other strategies involved criticizing Kennedy through third parties. Kintner recommended that Johnson get "an offset to Kennedy," convincing someone outside the administration, such as Senator Jacob Javits, to challenge his colleague on Vietnam. Dean Rusk could attack Kennedy "on a confidential basis at the highest level," and Moyers might arrange for a Kennedy critic to appear on the *Today Show*. Whatever tactic Johnson used, "the response to Kennedy should come from someone outside of the administration, but who was also liberal and Eastern."[14]

Johnson himself sought to diminish Robert Kennedy's position against the war by drawing on John Kennedy's memory. Sometimes he linked President Kennedy's policy to broad historical trends. In his State of the Union Address, for example, he claimed agreement with "lines of policy that America has followed under its last four Presidents," and when tracing the history of U.S. involvement during a Democratic fund-raiser in Chicago, he erroneously asserted that President Kennedy "began to send American forces [to Vietnam] as early as 1962." On other occasions, including his speech at the National Freedom Award ceremony, Johnson directly quoted John Kennedy in Robert's presence. And at a Memorial Day ceremony at Arlington, he emphasized John Kennedy's commitment to Vietnam by citing a quote from the late president made two months before his death: "We want the war to be won, the Communists to be contained, and the Americans to go home."[15]

By drawing on John Kennedy's memory, Johnson implied that Robert was outside the mainstream and (unlike John) was "soft" on communism. But Johnson was at a distinct disadvantage in trying to use President Kennedy for his own purposes. Logic dictated that, as a Kennedy himself, Robert, not Johnson, best understood John's intentions. He was the true spokesperson for the "mystique"—an image that was difficult, if not impossible, to challenge. Furthermore, it was becoming incredible to identify Johnson's policies with John Kennedy's: the war in 1966 hardly resembled the conflict that Johnson had inherited in 1963. The "present tangle is not the direct legacy of President Kennedy or Eisenhower," Dutton reminded Robert. "It is a whole new mess that responsible Americans like yourself ... need to help get us out of, despite the growing self-righteousness and simplistic Texas nationalism of the White House." Perhaps sensing the distinctions, Johnson did not quote the late president as much as he could have or planned to when defending his Vietnam policies, seldom drawing on the extensive lists of quotes available to him. As John's avatar, Robert was slowly denying him access to the "mystique," thus widening the gap between them.[16]

Relinquishing the "Mystique"

In 1966 Robert Kennedy began more fully to identify himself with his brother's memory. In January he recalled publicly that he had run for the Senate in order to follow John's lead and to pursue his unfulfilled dreams. He tended to measure Johnson's performance against his brother's and attached himself to issues with which John was associated, such as nuclear testing, the Alliance for Progress, and American relations with the Third World. Kennedy frequently invoked the late president's name, injected literary flourishes into his speeches, and adopted a 1960 campaign theme that promised to "keep this country moving." His mirroring seemed more deliberate in 1966 than it had in the past. He assumed his brother's gestures, including the jabbing finger and the hands inside the sport jacket with thumbs inside. Like John, Robert was often seen in the company of scholars, celebrities, and artists. His Senate office was crowded with photographs of the late president, his brother's favorite paintings, and framed notes from his last cabinet meeting. *Life* described his home as "a virtual museum of J.F.K. memorabilia." By October *Newsweek* reported that he possessed "a new appearance of ease and grace and openness that reminds people of his brother's style and less of his own old image as the ruthless Little Brother." Richard Goodwin praised Kennedy for having become "a romantic figure—not because people liked the way you looked, but because you conveyed the impression of a man of great dedication, conviction, a worthy heir to his brother. That is the way you acted, thought and spoke."[17]

Robert's transformation was tied to a pessimistic perspective. Asked in June whether he intended to run for president, he responded introspectively: "Who knows where either of us will be six years from now." Later that year he described his popularity as a "fad." "Existence is so fickle," he noted, "fate is so fickle. Not only can this feeling [of sudden popularity] pass but also your existence can pass." It was reported that he was reading Camus and was a self-professed existentialist. His repeated references to death and his emotional bond to his late brother suggested that he had reinterpreted John's fate as his own.[18]

While cultivating a new image, Robert continued to court Johnson's dissenters within the Democratic party, the news media, and academia. His most publicized effort consisted of seminars held in his home at Hickory

193

Hill. It was there that he regularly complained about Johnson's policies and used personal contacts to develop arguments against the administration. John Roche, a former president of Americans for Democratic Action, recalled a "very substantial disaffection" of liberals to the Kennedys during the summer of 1966. Indeed, the ADA became "the bastion of the Kennedys in exile," whose only interest was in "trying to figure out how to get Johnson out and Kennedy in."[19]

Johnson received disquieting reports about Kennedy's influence upon opinion-makers. In April, Kintner warned that Kennedy and David Brinkley "have become close friends," and that the senator used his social relationships "to keep his lines open to key commentators, columnists, and editors." Kintner also noted that Joseph Alsop, who strongly supported Johnson's Vietnam policy, had become "very close" to the senator. "While Joe was not a close friend of Bobby Kennedy when President Kennedy was alive, Bobby Kennedy has made a point of seeing and talking to Alsop, particularly during the last few months." Indeed, Alsop perceived himself as Kennedy's "affectionate, admiring, and deeply concerned uncle" and regularly advised him about career decisions. The columnist's attraction to Kennedy alarmed Johnson, for it suggested that anti-Vietnam sentiment and support for Robert were not necessarily related. Even some who approved of Johnson's Vietnam policy still found Kennedy an appealing figure. By the summer, press reports became more disturbing when Moyers warned that a journalist friendly with the Kennedys might have an "inside" source acting against the administration. Although Moyers was unsure about the informant's identity, "some circumstantial evidence" pointed to an "outside friend who is most likely to see the President in off-hours over the weekend."[20]

By the summer of 1966 Kennedy's influence on the Washington news media seemed insurmountable. Moyers sent the president an article by Peregrine Worsthorne, a noted British journalist who had recently come to Washington and was "wined and dined at one dinner party after another by the Kay Grahams, Joe Alsops, etc." In his piece Worsthorne expressed surprise at the prevailing notion that Johnson was a pretender to the throne: "[T]he impression, of course, is that if only John F. Kennedy was still alive, or the country was in better hands now than those of L.B.J., then all would be well. The Washington pundits love to dilate on how brilliantly 'Bobby' has put this idea across." Recalling his evenings in the capital, Worsthorne was disturbed by "Washington liberals" who "bemoaned President Johnson's lack of idealism and nobility, and lauded the Senator for precisely these qualities." Worsthorne distrusted Robert's professed liberalism, warning British readers against being blinded by the Kennedy image. "The outside world played an important part in building up the original John F.

Kennedy mystique," he concluded. "The Americans love to be loved, and our passionate willingness to love the late President added immeasurably to his stature at home. In my view, we should be profoundly chary to do the same for his brother."[21]

Because Kennedy was exploiting contacts with reporters and fortifying a "government-in-exile," numerous columnists speculated that he was preparing to run for president. "Quite literally," Emmet John Hughes wrote in March, "nothing is missing":

[The government-in-exile] has its cherished heroes, and its appointed heirs. It has its shining myths and its tragic memories. It has its historians to popularize its tale as poetically as Camelot, and its agents to recruit its forces. . . . It has its battles to plan and its scores to settle. And with discipline and discernment, it views the present as a menial pause between power wrecked and power reconquered. . . . It privately confesses the certitude that nothing is being done as wisely as it might be done. . . . And it avows the return of the dispossessed to fulfill all promise of the past—as can be done only by the true believers.

The formal organization of such a collection of politicians, intellectuals, and former officials with a distinct purpose was questionable. Considering the diversity of people associated with Kennedy, the "government-in-exile" was not as cohesive as Hughes alleged. Had Johnson's political fortune improved, it was unlikely that these ambitious individuals would have waited for the next President Kennedy. Nevertheless, Kennedy advisers were keenly aware of their support. "Emmett [sic] Hughes was not completely off base," Dutton wrote Kennedy, "in suggesting you are a one man government in exile, whether you or President Johnson like that or not."[22]

Kennedy's affiliation with a "glorious" past created anxiety in the White House, prompting aides to urge Johnson to take initiatives to counter his influence over the press. Kintner advised Johnson to be accessible to "the opposition," including David Brinkley and Walter Cronkite. Kintner, along with Moyers, Rostow, and Rusk, might be able to tap into the ideas of publishers, columnists, and editors through amiable contacts. "Let's start working to soften up the Kennedy columnist set," Liz Carpenter, Lady Bird's secretary, added, "subvert them from 'buying' everything Bobby does." She was especially anxious to exploit those occasions when Kennedy misspoke on Vietnam. "If *they* point out his error, it's twice as effective." She also wanted to invite some members of the "jet set" to the next White House social event, "even though they are personally obnoxious." After receiving the memorandum, Johnson wrote a curious response: "Tear this up and flush it down the toilet."[23]

Johnson initiated several covert measures in an attempt to undermine

Kennedy's growing appeal. One strategy involved renewed efforts to diminish the senator's standing within the New York Democratic party. In June Marvin Watson informed the president of his discussions with Mike Pendergast, whom Robert had removed as state chairperson of the Democratic party when he was attorney general. Watson and Pendergast discussed "ways in which your Administration can properly recognize the Democratic Party machinery there and therefore take away the separate organization which Senator Kennedy is planning."[24]

Johnson also tried to cultivate personnel leaning toward the Kennedy camp. Although McPherson had failed in his attempt to hire Patrick Moynihan in 1965, he continued similar recruitment practices. In August he informed Johnson that Kennedy had been trying unsuccessfully to recruit Berl Bernhard, McPherson's law partner who had known Kennedy "only as an occasional adversary" when he worked on the Civil Rights Committee in the early 1960s. "But Kennedy recognizes talent and is obviously after it in Berl." McPherson advised that Bernhard be given a post at the White House, suggesting that Johnson speak with him and that he and his wife be invited to White House social occasions. Bernhard was "one of the brightest and most honorable young men around. He is also a team player and very much a Johnson man." Johnson responded favorably to McPherson's advice, and in 1966 Bernhard participated in a White House conference promoting constitutional rights.[25]

Publicly Johnson usually responded with "backdoor" strategies, indirectly challenging his rival in order to avoid an open rift. In the summer of 1966 Kennedy tried to lead Democratic senators in an effort to infuse more money into the War on Poverty, threatening to adopt the president's cause as his own and further strain the administration's budget. Johnson countered by summoning Senate leaders to the White House and encouraging Minority Leader Everett Dirksen to lead the fight to defeat Kennedy's proposal. The collusion between Johnson and Dirksen prompted Kennedy to accuse the administration of having "turned our backs . . . on those who need help so desperately." Distressed by the comment, Johnson implicitly challenged Kennedy during his next press conference, arguing that he had increased the budget by $5 billion since the Kennedy administration. Later, in a Baltimore speech, he avoided mentioning Kennedy by name while charging that "you just can't push a button and have a whole working program. . . . [W]e shall not be stampeded into unwise programs."[26]

Johnson's ambivalence sometimes revealed itself on less volatile issues. In April Dutton had suggested that Kennedy associate himself with more idealistic issues such as nuclear nonproliferation. He further advised Kennedy to consider a "major, exciting personal adventure" in order to exploit his image as an "existential" politician "in contrast to the dull middle aged tone that President Johnson and Hubert [Humphrey] have hanging like a pall over the country." In June Kennedy embarked on a two-week tour of South Africa, Tanzania, Kenya, and Ethiopia, combining images of adventure and idealism. He was warmly greeted by crowds of blacks, scenes which played well in the American press. Speaking before African political leaders, he encouraged them to place greater pressure on nations with nuclear weapons in order to limit proliferation. Initially Johnson had sought to neutralize the political implications of the tour. A week before the senator's scheduled departure, he condemned South Africa's apartheid policies during his only speech on the matter. The timing of the address prompted speculation by reporters that he was trying to deflate the significance of Kennedy's visit. When Kennedy returned to the United States, however, Johnson summoned him to the White House for a rare visit, thereby increasing the prestige of the trip.[27]

Privately Johnson sought to reduce tensions between himself and Kennedy. In June he instructed Kintner to call Kennedy about a foreign policy report to which the senator had contributed. Kintner pretended to be circumventing Johnson's authority by privately telling Kennedy that the president was "extremely complimentary about the character of the report, the Senator's helpful suggestions and the atmosphere of the talk." "I told him," Kintner reported to Johnson, "that you had said he had helped you more with advice on how to be President than you had helped him on how to be a Senator."[28]

As Kennedy gained momentum, Johnson expressed confidence in his ability to meet the challenge, but he appeared defensive. During a press conference a reporter noted that the senator had a two-to-one edge over the president among California Democrats for the next presidential election. In response, Johnson cited polls that showed him leading Kennedy and accused the press of selectivity. He then detailed numerous polls in different states showing the extent of his support. "So we are not upset," he insisted. After polls showed Kennedy leading Johnson nationwide among Democratic voters, Kintner sent Johnson a preferred response to anticipated questions from reporters. He should note courteously that, although he has no comment about the recent poll, he "considers [Kennedy] able, alert, and an important national figure and that the President has worked closely with him . . . [and] the President always likes to receive his ideas and suggestions." Asked at the subsequent news conference about the possibility of a Johnson-Kennedy ticket in 1968, Johnson smiled coyly. "I think the people of the country have a pretty good estimate of that," he replied. "And I will just leave it at that." Asked if he had any explanation for Kennedy's surge in the polls, Johnson was evasive: "No, I don't have an explanation for it."[29]

Johnson's congeniality toward Kennedy was generally successful at keeping their true hostilities private. *Life*'s Hugh Sidey described their relationship in November as "proper, and almost affable." The two posed together for photographs during ceremonies and political gatherings. It was reported that the president sent Kennedy a birthday card and twice forwarded messages that they should "be tolerant and understanding" about press reports alleging a feud. "Bob," Johnson wrote, "what will they be writing about us next?" He blamed the press for exaggerating their differences. "I have no quarrel with Bobby," he insisted, "and he should have no quarrel with me. He is of a different generation." "[T]he battle has been an exquisitely modulated one," *Newsweek* reported in September. Kennedy's criticism "has been just enough to make itself felt, not enough to force an open break. And the president's counterattacks have been just as subtle—so subtle that few have noticed them."[30]

Anticipating re-election in 1968, Johnson could not afford to alienate the Kennedy wing of the party and risk a challenge to his nomination. Moreover, he sought to maintain a fragile Democratic consensus on the war. But his reluctance publicly to confront Kennedy may have also reflected the political predicament inherent in the "mystique." As Robert embraced his brother's idealism and image and received the attention and praise of John's former supporters, he encouraged followers to transfer their affections from his late brother onto himself. For Johnson, Robert's emulation produced two consequences. First, Robert may have inhibited Johnson from attacking him, for the president could not be critical of the senator without implicitly attacking John. "It's impossible to separate the living Kennedys from the Kennedy legend," a Johnson aide lamented. "I think President Kennedy will be regarded for many years as the Pericles of a Golden Age. He wasn't Pericles and the age wasn't golden, but that doesn't matter—it's caught hold." Thereafter, the more Robert promoted himself as John's avatar (and the more he posed a serious threat to Johnson's presidency), the less Johnson seemed inclined to counterattack. Second, Robert's full embodiment of his brother's legacy severely limited Johnson's own access to the "mystique." Johnson could not compete against the flesh-and-blood heir to the Kennedy legacy. By exalting John Kennedy, he would indirectly enhance a myth that was ultimately more beneficial to Robert than to himself.[31]

Throughout 1966 Johnson slowly relinquished his claim to the "mystique." In December 1965 he rejected a request that he appear in a memorial film on John Kennedy. After placing a wreath at the Tombs of the Unknowns on Memorial Day, he made a brief visit to Kennedy's grave at Arlington, but the gesture was unplanned and received little media attention. Unlike previous years, Johnson made no formal recognition of John Kennedy's birthday. Indifference to the occasion was reflected by staff members. Kintner informed the president of NBC's two-part film biography on John Kennedy, *The Age of Kennedy*. Kintner considered the film "well done" and "a very favorable portrayal" but resented the media's excessive attention. In August aides deliberated about the benefits and drawbacks of conducting a public signing ceremony for the John F. Kennedy Library Bill. Some argued that participation in the occasion presented Johnson with an opportunity "to identify with President Kennedy and force the Senator [Robert Kennedy] onto neutral ground." Lawrence O'Brien did not favor Johnson's attendance because "the bill is so unimportant that this will appear to be an obvious attempt at trying to drive a wedge into the Kennedy camp." Johnson decided against the idea.[32]

When Johnson mentioned John Kennedy, as he did when defending his Vietnam policy, the invocation was usually in the context of a larger, historical theme rather than an independent, spiritual force with which he was keeping faith. He continued to mention Kennedy during ceremonies, proclamations, anniversaries of programs, and announcements of appointments, but he less frequently praised our "beloved late President." Indeed, by the summer he seemed less willing to mention John Kennedy by name, usually referring to "the previous administration." Whereas he had previously contrasted the "Kennedy-Johnson administration" to Eisenhower's, he began to compare "this" administration with "the previous one" or with a particular time during the Kennedy years. Assessing Johnson's relations with the Kennedys, *Newsweek* reported that, while Robert Kennedy was moving farther from the Johnson administration, Johnson was seeking "to disassociate himself from the late John F. Kennedy."[33]

Johnson's detachment from John Kennedy's memory had offsetting results. On the one hand, he sacrificed an image with which he had previously won vicarious approval. On the other hand, he was liberated from the past. If, in Johnson's mind, John Kennedy became less significant or mystical, Robert became more mortal and frail. And with John's mythic being pressing him less, Johnson could more easily assail Robert.

Crises

During the summer of 1966 Johnson's presidency rapidly deteriorated. Rampant inflation hampered domestic programs, civil rights violence erupted in cities across the country, and the Vietnam War drained the economic resources and executive attention necessary to achieve the Great Society that Johnson once envisioned. Moreover, the war itself evolved into a serious political liability. A March Gallup poll indicated that 49 percent of the public approved Johnson's handling of the war, a decline of fourteen points from January. The American people seemed torn between the desire for a peaceful resolution and an unlimited war. While an increasing number favored United States withdrawal, a growing percentage supported a more aggressive response.[34]

The combination of foreign and domestic problems brought Johnson to a crisis point. Characterizations of a "credibility gap" became pervasive, and loyal aides began resigning from the administration. By June the president's popularity had fallen to its lowest point in two and a half years. Only 46 percent approved of his handling of the presidency, a loss of seventeen points in six months. Johnson learned that the Kennedy staff was propagating the rumor that the president would "honorably settle" the war by 1968 and then decline the nomination for reasons of poor health. "They are saying that therefore the time to get on the Kennedy bandwagon is now," Johnson was informed. White House aides gave an air of cool concern. "The President is an earthy, sentimental man," an aide told *Newsweek*. "He fully understands the desire of the Kennedy family to regain what was torn from them at Dallas."[35]

Overwhelmed by events, Johnson frantically searched for scapegoats. When the Ambassador to India, Chester Bowles, visited the White House in the summer of 1966, he recalled that "Literally half our time was taken up by almost paranoiac references to Bobby Kennedy, Wayne Morse, Bill Fulbright and others." Bowles sensed that Johnson was "headed for deep trouble with the probability of an increasing obsession with his 'enemies.' " The president's political fears distracted from daily chores. When Kennedy criticized an administration witness during a committee hearing on the prevalence of rats in slums, Johnson transformed a cabinet meeting into an hour-long debate about federal rodent control simply because his rival had raised the point. "Johnson's paranoia used to get on my nerves," Roche noted. "There was not a sparrow fell from a tree but what he was convinced that it was the intervention of a Kennedy."[36]

Johnson was not completely unjustified in his concern. By the end of 1966, after his public approval rating declined to 43 percent, memories of the Kennedy administration assumed greater significance. "With the passage of time," pollster Lou Harris assessed, "the President seems to be haunted more rather than less by the image of his predecessor." John Kennedy's "memory seems to stand at his elbow—posing to many a contrast of calm elegance with crudity and corn." Moreover, Johnson was losing hold of the one element that had traditionally brought him approval—his achievements. The fraction of people who had praised him as one who "gets things done" had declined by one-third in two years, and, within the last year, three times as many people defined him as a political opportunist. "Unless events themselves in Vietnam miraculously solve the whole problem for him," Harris concluded, "the challenge to Lyndon Johnson thus is to restore public faith in him as a candid leader who can be trusted."[37]

Robert Kennedy, who had spent his first year in the Senate placing greater distance between himself and the administration, now inspired a wave of enthusiasm for the "restoration" of John Kennedy's unfinished presidency. For the first time an August Gallup poll showed voters favoring him over Johnson as the 1968 Democratic nominee. Forty percent of Democratic voters supported Kennedy; 38 percent favored Johnson. Among independent voters, the disparity was greater: 38 percent wanted Kennedy while only 24 percent chose Johnson. Gallup described Kennedy's rise in appeal as "spectacular"; he now posed a threat to Johnson himself.[38]

The temperament in Washington was also changing. "[T]he notion that [Kennedy] might actually 'take over' in 1968 instead of waiting until 1972," Tom Wicker reported in August, "now is being taken seriously, at least at dinner-table conversation." Joint appearances between the two rivals prompted comparisons of crowd reaction. When Johnson traveled to New York for an off-year election swing, Kennedy joined him in Syracuse, where banners asking, "Where's Bobby?" were removed before the president's speech. The Kennedy staff took delight in noting that crowds for Johnson's visit were smaller than expected. They mocked newspaper reports that exaggerated the crowd reaction to Johnson, and they expressed satisfaction that Kennedy had received "almost deafening" applause.[39]

Kennedy's momentum continued into the fall. A September Harris poll among Democrats showed him leading Johnson 47 to 41 percent for the 1968 nomination. "Fate and Gallup," columnist Kenneth Crawford wrote, "decree that Robert F. Kennedy shall be the next President of the U.S." In October *Newsweek* devoted a cover story to "The Bobby Phenomenon," referring to Kennedy as "the first politician in U.S. history who seems so plainly headed for the White House so long in advance of when he can get there." He was "the inheritor of a myth that refuses to die" and embodied "the dream of Camelot." Political pundits, as well as the Kennedy organization, speculated on the possible scenarios for the 1968 campaign: Johnson might be forced to offer him the vice-presidential nomination; Kennedy might run for the presidency himself in 1968; Johnson might remove himself from contention if his chances for re-election were poor. By December 1966 a national Harris poll showed Kennedy leading Johnson 54 to 46 percent.

Johnson aides offered weak assurances. "Bobby is reaching his peak too early," the president was informed, "and runs the risk of becoming a bore."[40]

It was only two years since Lyndon Johnson had been elected president by the largest plurality in history. By the end of 1966, however, Hugh Sidey reported that the president seemed to be "drifting on an island of time between Kennedys." Robert offered those who yearned for the past an alternative to the future; Americans could either continue the "perverted" course set by the usurper or turn its affairs over to the man who would return the nation to Camelot. "Bobby hasn't made a mistake," a high-ranking Republican aide noted. "His touch has been perfect. But how long can he keep it up?"[41]

In the midst of this remarkable political reversal, Kennedy suffered serious setbacks. His struggle with Johnson followed two courses. First, Kennedy became vulnerable. In December, Robert and Jacqueline Kennedy made serious public relations blunders, one of which made them appear mean-spirited toward Johnson. Second, the struggle between Kennedy and Johnson became more personal. Until that time Kennedy's personal animosity for Johnson had been reserved for the company of trusted aides and journalists. In late 1966, however, he publicly insulted Johnson's character and intruded into one of the president's most valued relationships.

Shortly before Christmas, Johnson's protégé, Bill Moyers, announced his resignation in order to become publisher of a Long Island newspaper, *Newsday*. He was replaced by George Christian, Johnson's fourth press secretary in three years. Moyers's reasons for leaving were complex, but in general he felt emotionally drained. His brother had committed suicide the previous September, and he had become increasingly frustrated in trying to deal constructively with the President. "I thought I could make [Johnson] more like me," he explained privately, "but I've found in the last several months that I'm becoming more like him; so I got out."[42]

Johnson initially wished Moyers luck in his new career, but tensions soon arose. As the press secretary prepared to announce his resignation, Robert Kennedy called him, inviting him for lunch at the Capitol building. After accepting the offer, Moyers received a second call; Kennedy preferred to meet at a popular Washington restaurant instead. John Roche charged that Kennedy arranged to have a photographer from the *Washington Star* at the restaurant in order to photograph them together. Whether or not Kennedy's public appearance with Moyers was intentionally divisive, the White House believed it was, and, according to Roche, Johnson "just went right up the wall" upon receiving publicity of the rendezvous. The incident prompted a wave of rumors suggesting that Moyers was moving permanently into the

Kennedy camp. "Jesus Christ! It was such a set-up too," Roche recalled. "[Kennedy] was a demonic little bastard. You've got to hand it to him. That was a beauty. Of course, nothing would ever convince Johnson that Moyers really hadn't been on the Kennedy payroll for years and years. He was crazy."[43]

Thereafter Johnson maintained that "the Kennedys had sucked Bill away." Hurt by the incident, he tried to convince himself that Moyers had been detrimental to the administration, requesting information on his public approval rating during Moyers's stewardship compared with George Reedy's. Predictably, the figures were higher under Reedy, due less to the different press secretaries than to Johnson's faltering policies. Johnson's animosity toward Moyers was encouraged by old political allies. McPherson informed him that Governor John Connally and his friends "celebrated [Moyers's departure] as if a new day had dawned." They argued that Johnson's difficulties stemmed from "being too kind to the Kennedy people." As a liaison with the Kennedys, Moyers "conveyed their wishes and your 'acquiescence.'" Six months later Moyers assured Johnson of his continued respect and explained that he had come to appreciate his leadership more clearly since leaving the White House, especially in comparison with John Kennedy's. Despite such efforts, the two men remained estranged, and Moyers eventually developed a closer relationship with Robert Kennedy.[44]

That same month the Moyers incident was punctuated by another personal affront by the Kennedys when Jacqueline Kennedy announced a lawsuit to stop publication of the serialization of William Manchester's *Death of a President*. Shortly after the assassination the Kennedy family had wanted to avoid sensational treatments of the murder by authorizing Manchester to write an "official" account. He had previously written an adulatory biography of John Kennedy during the 1960 campaign. Manchester signed an agreement giving the family final approval of the book's content and was granted access to unique information, including private interviews with Jacqueline. In the summer of 1966 he sold excerpts of the manuscript to *Look* magazine. Upon examining the manuscript, Kennedy aides were alarmed about its political implications, initially fearing that a careless reading might incite public anger against President Johnson. The draft of Manchester's manuscript, for example, began with Johnson pressuring John Kennedy to shoot a deer while at his Texas ranch after the 1960 convention. Another story depicted him arguing with Kennedy about the need to visit Texas in November 1963. President Kennedy was against the trip, but Johnson successfully pressured him, citing the need to repair a party feud within the state. Manchester also portrayed Johnson after the assassination as power-hungry and insensitive. The depiction was so harsh that some Kennedy aides worried about being accused of character assassination. Editing the *Look* galleys that fall, Richard Goodwin sought to remove 50 percent of the material. Arthur Schlesinger complained in a letter to Manchester that the deer hunt scene had the effect of "defining the book as a conflict between New England and Texas, decency and vulgarity, Kennedy and Johnson." He feared that the symbolism generated by the depictions would prompt criticism that "the unconscious argument of the book is that Johnson killed Kennedy. . . ."[45]

The Kennedys' suit against Manchester pertained only to the personal material that Jacqueline had revealed to the author. Unlike Robert's aides, she was less concerned about the text's political implications and more disturbed that Manchester intended to publish revelations disclosed during their emotionally difficult interview sessions. Robert, meanwhile, was unhappy with the depiction of Johnson but was willing to have it published. One chapter "will injure both Johnson and me," he told Manchester, "but apparently it's factually correct and a contribution to history. I'd like you to change it, but I guess you won't." Publicly the Kennedys attempted to avoid responsibility for any unkindness to the president, claiming they were powerless to alter the book's political content. Jacqueline's public statement maintained that the manuscript's "inaccurate and unfair references to other individuals" were "perhaps beyond my prevention." The Kennedys' willingness to allow the publication of Manchester's insulting depiction of Johnson heightened the president's unsavory reputation and reinforced his image as an ogre and implicit murderer.[46]

The administration responded with public and private stances. Less than a week after the suit was filed, Johnson sent a Christmas card to Jacqueline, noting that he and Lady Bird were "distressed to read the press accounts of your unhappiness about the Manchester book." "Some of these accounts attribute your concern to passages in the book which are critical or defamatory of us. If this is so, I want you to know while we deeply appreciate your characteristic kindness and sensitivity, we hope you will not subject yourself to any discomfort or distress on our account." Johnson assured her that he had learned to live with slander and that "your own tranquility is important to both of us, and we would not want you to endure any unpleasantness on our account. We are both grateful to you for your constant and unfailing thoughtfulness and friendship." After wishing her a Merry Christmas, he closed with an uncharacteristic salutation, "Sincerely, Lyndon Johnson." He had usually signed personal notes to Jacqueline, "Love, Lyndon."[47]

White House aides had traditionally monitored and planned strategies to counter publications that were either favorable to the Kennedys or disparaging of Johnson. Some aides now urged the president to respond more aggressively to the Manchester affair. Kintner implored Johnson to plant an article that would give his version of events, and he asked permission to convince either *Time* or *Newsweek* to interview two conflicting sources who were witness to events aboard Air Force One. The differing accounts would imply that Manchester was selective in his sources and "offset what I believe will be a very damaging impression." Kintner was also angered that the Kennedys had not tried harder to edit political content from the manuscript.[48]

Although Kintner's advice was not followed, aides leaked to the press that the president had private letters from Jacqueline thanking him for his kindness and thoughtfulness during the days after the assassination. Johnson's supporters, meanwhile, spoke out in his defense. After criticizing Manchester's allegations, John Connally called the White House and relayed a message to the president, informing him that reaction to "his statement on [the] Manchester book had been highly favorable." Connally noted that the consensus among his contacts was that "you should remain silent on the controversy. [Connally] has the definite feeling that you have gained from a 'gentlemanly attitude' toward the whole thing."[49]

On December 21 the Kennedys abruptly settled their suit out of court. *Look* agreed to remove or modify passages relating to Jacqueline's personal life. Approximately sixteen hundred words were excised, none of which pertained to Johnson. The agreement would make a settlement between Manchester and his publishers, Harper and Row, easier. The family, however, could not halt the interest which their suit brought to Manchester's work or the negative implications of trying to censor the author. "The Kennedys thus had won all the battles," *Newsweek* assessed, "—but they seemed more than ever to be losing the war."[50]

Officially the White House had refused public comment about the lawsuit, prompting *Newsweek* to conclude that Johnson had "maintained a dignified if hurt—silence" about the controversy. But his side of the story, as well as his anger, were conveyed when he gave *Newsweek* an exclusive interview. His recollection of the events aboard Air Force One differed from Manchester's version. Johnson claimed that the Secret Service wanted him to fly aboard the president's plane and that President Kennedy's body was to return on the vice president's plane, but he refused to have Jacqueline return alone with the remains. The president also claimed that he had asked Robert Kennedy if he should take the oath immediately in Dallas. He admitted calling Jacqueline "honey" but explained, "It's a word that comes easy to me as a Texan." He also noted that he was "as puzzled as anyone else" about the Manchester affair. He was unhappy with his depiction but understood that the Kennedys would have resented anyone new coming into office. The White House later denied that the president had spoken to *Newsweek*.[51]

Johnson was satisfied that the Kennedys bore the brunt of the bad publicity. Aides forwarded memoranda noting White House mail on the subject. Only one of fifty letters was anti-Johnson. Twenty-two letters were "sympathetic and laudatory" toward him. Kintner sent Johnson an editorial from the *Washington Star* characterizing the president as a "victim" for having experienced a "very real injustice." Jack Valenti, who had resigned from the administration six months before, forwarded a letter from a *Time/Life* reporter who blamed the Kennedys for the fiasco and felt they had used Manchester to "get even" with the president for "replacing their fallen idol." Johnson had "never handled himself better."[52]

The Manchester affair dimmed the noble aura from which the Kennedys had benefited. The news media put the lawsuit into perspective by examining other attempts by the family to mold history. "The tragedy of Dallas belongs to history," Kenneth Crawford wrote, "it is not the negotiable property of the Kennedys." Critics charged that the entire project was misconceived to begin with and that the attempt to "censor" Manchester was poorly handled. The family missed opportunities for reconciliation, appeared insensitive toward Johnson, and brought increased attention to the manuscript through the lawsuit. With little effort on Johnson's part, they appeared manipulative and mean-spirited—characteristics which were antithetical to the Kennedy "mystique" and more reminiscent of Johnson.[53]

For the first time since the assassination, Jacqueline Kennedy's public stature was diminished. "It is almost as if there had been a vast well of envy and dislike for Jackie waiting to be tapped," *Newsweek* observed. According to Crawford, she was perceived by many as "an imperious woman of fashion who has always had her own way and means to go on having it, regardless of consequences. And, anyway, she wears her skirts too short. So much for Camelot." In February Manchester told the *New York Times* that "Mao Tse-tung and Jackie are the most inscrutable people I know." A Gallup poll showed that 44 percent of the public thought she was hurt by the Manchester affair.[54]

Having taken an active and visible role in his sister-in-law's defense, Robert Kennedy suffered repercussions as well. One reporter charged him with trying to "gut Johnson," and Arthur Schlesinger acknowledged that the lawsuit enhanced Kennedy's reputation for being "ruthless." A February Harris poll indicated that 20 percent of the public "thought less" of Robert because of the controversy. He was politically distressed by an unrelated matter when it was revealed that, as attorney general, he had approved wiretapping of telephones and the illegal use of listening devices. Receiving information from his friend, Supreme Court Associate Justice Abraham Fortas, Johnson seized the opportunity to embarrass Kennedy by associating him with the wiretapping revelations. A January Gallup poll conducted before the full impact of the incidents had been felt showed Kennedy leading Johnson, 48 to 39 percent. By February a Harris poll indicated that Kennedy trailed Johnson by ten percentage points. By March a Gallup poll showed Kennedy with a higher unfavorable rating than Johnson. Although the precise reasons for the juxtaposition rested with a variety of broad political concerns, part of Kennedy's decline in the polls was likely associated with the Manchester affair. Disheartened by events, Kennedy wrote to journalist Edward Lewis that his problems "will never be over."[55]

Johnson was assured privately that Kennedy was in political trouble. New York business leaders reportedly felt that his "popularity in New York and his 'control' was exaggerated." Kennedy was also known to have "plenty of problems with middle-class and independent voters." The president was reminded that Kennedy did "very poorly" during the previous election "not only with those [candidates] he spoke for, but with those he contributed to." In the past Johnson had refrained from challenging his rival because he feared alienating Kennedy supporters or indirectly insulting John Kennedy's memory. But Kennedy had transformed the conflict into a highly personal and public battle, and he had tarnished the "mystique" in the process. With the semblance of political and personal courtesies now undone, and Robert behaving less like his mythical brother, Johnson could more freely challenge him with less fear of repercussion.[56]

The Break

On February 6, 1967, the public deference between Johnson and Kennedy shattered. In large part the immediate cause was associated with events in Vietnam. Since the fall of 1966 Kennedy had restrained his criticism of Johnson's policy. The one exception came in late October when he disparaged South Vietnam's leadership during Johnson's meeting with South Vietnam's prime minister. Kennedy lamented to friends that his criticisms hurt him politically and goaded Johnson to do the opposite of what he advised. "He hates me so much that if I asked for snow, he would make rain, just because it was me." In reality Kennedy had never been anxious to become a leading spokesperson of the "doves." Seeking to appeal to a broad political base, he did not wish to alienate the majority of moderates and conservatives who believed that the United States should pursue an aggressive military posture. Furthermore, if Kennedy criticized Johnson amidst the Manchester revelations, it would have magnified his image for "ruthlessness."[57]

In late January 1967 Kennedy traveled to Europe, generating suspicion that he was trying to boost his declining popularity. "The grand tour," *Newsweek* reported, "had all the earmarks of a Presidential procession." He was well received in Europe, and his appeal there was in sharp contrast to Johnson's ebbing popularity. He met with a variety of people, including movie stars and such foreign leaders as the Pope and French President Charles de Gaulle. Kennedy gave de Gaulle a deluxe edition of *Profiles in Courage,* inscribed by Jacqueline Kennedy.[58]

The administration was disturbed by Kennedy's trip, especially in light of recent signs that a peaceful settlement to the war was near. Aides believed the visit to be politically motivated and diplomatically awkward. Two incidents in particular provoked their anger. During a question-and-answer period at a seminar on Anglo-American affairs at Oxford, Kennedy noted that he had "grave reservations" about Johnson's decision to renew bombing in Vietnam. He conceded that the president sincerely wanted a negotiated settlement, then implied that secret talks were taking place: "I think the next three or four weeks are critical and crucial." A White House spokesperson charged Kennedy with "mischievous interference." "If he didn't know what he was talking about then he was acting irresponsibly," Walter Rostow responded angrily. "But if he did know what he was talking about, then he was acting irresponsibly."[59]

Kennedy's second exercise in foreign policy was more serious. During his stay in Paris he participated in a discussion with a North Vietnamese representative and an embassy expert on Vietnam, John Gunther Dean. During their talk the North Vietnamese official told Kennedy of Hanoi's "complete mistrust" of United States peace gestures but stressed his nation's desire to negotiate. He mentioned that an "indispensable condition" for negotiations was a cessation of American bombing. Dean considered the emphasis upon a bombing halt a change in North Vietnam's conditions. Believing that the representative was using Kennedy as a conduit, Dean forwarded a cable to the State Department describing the supposed peace overture. The message was mishandled by the State Department and released to *Newsweek*'s contributing editor Edward Weithal.[60]

Kennedy returned from Europe on February 4, before the *Newsweek* exclusive was published. The next day Johnson received an advance copy of the magazine and was convinced that Kennedy had leaked the story. For weeks the United States had been toughening its negotiating position toward Vietnam, prompting suspicion that Kennedy was forcing the president's hand in negotiations just as the policy was taking effect. Or, Johnson speculated, Kennedy might be building up hopes of peace in order to spread dissension if talks broke down. The president called Undersecretary of State Nicholas Katzenbach, demanding to know why he had not been informed by the State Department of the supposed "peace signals." He instructed Katzenbach to talk with Kennedy. Kennedy, meanwhile, had told his aides that he was confused by the *Newsweek* story. The notion of a "peace feeler," he argued, was rooted in Dean's interpretation of events and not his own. Speaking with Katzenbach, he maintained that he had not understood the implications of his conversation and denied responsibility for the leak. A late afternoon meeting was arranged between Kennedy and the president. Katzenbach and Rostow were also present.[61]

Although there is no available record of the conversation, accounts of the February 6 meeting indicate that it "ended in a complete rupture." "It was rough," Rostow told reporters. "It was very rough." Two matters concerned Johnson: Kennedy's intrusion into the peace process and the leaking of the story. "Bobby, who had not done it, could not understand what he was being accused of," Katzenbach recalled. "They were both bristling, really bristling." Defending himself, Kennedy told Johnson that the leak had come "from your State Department." Johnson responded angrily: "It's not *my* State Department, God damn it. It's *your* State Department." He proceeded to lecture Kennedy about the ineffectiveness of calls for negotiations, contending that the war would be won militarily by June or July. He then threw down the gauntlet that he had carried so uncomfortably for years. "I'll destroy you and everyone of your dove friends in six months," Johnson vowed. "You'll be dead politically in six months."[62]

The conversation degenerated rapidly. Kennedy offered his advice on the war, suggesting a number of conciliatory measures which might encourage negotiations. "There just isn't a chance in hell that I would do that," Johnson responded, "not the slightest chance." Accusing Kennedy of prolonging the war, the president decreed, "The blood of American boys will be on your hands." "I never want to hear your views on Viet Nam again," Johnson told him. "I never want to see you again." Kennedy reacted furiously. News reports surfaced alleging that he called the president a "son of a bitch" and tried to leave the room stating, "I don't have to sit here and take that shit." Those present denied that Kennedy used profanity, but they agreed that the meeting had collapsed. "[Johnson] was very abusive," Kennedy later told a reporter. "He was shouting and seemed very unstable." Katzenbach and Rostow sought to restore order and limit the damage. They asked Kennedy to inform the press that there was no "peace feeler" in Paris. Kennedy refused, explaining that he first wanted to see all the relevant documentation of the Paris discussions. "I'm telling you that you can [state publicly that no "peace feelers" were conveyed]," Johnson responded. Kennedy balked again, implying that he did not trust the president's assurances or his interpretation of the data. After further hedging he met with reporters in the White House lobby to deny he had brought home any "peace feelers."[63]

In the aftermath of the furor, both sides made futile attempts to cover the rift. Johnson reportedly told intimates that he was satisfied Kennedy did not leak the original report. A Johnson aide commented to *Newsweek* that the meeting was "correct, proper" and polite. The magazine's publisher, Katharine Graham, recalled that Johnson "claimed that nothing but sweetness and light had happened in this meeting. Since only he and Kennedy were in the meeting, I guess he thought we were taking Kennedy's word against his." "I wouldn't say [the meeting] was amiable," a Kennedy press aide added. "But just because it wasn't amiable doesn't mean that they were shouting insults at each other."[64]

During the annual Gridiron Banquet in Washington, Kennedy made light of the confrontation. "We had a long serious talk," he told his audience, "about the possibility of a cease-fire, the dangers of escalation, and the prospects for negotiations—and we agreed that the next time we met, we'd talk about Vietnam." Despite efforts at damage control, neither Johnson nor Kennedy was able to offset the wave of speculative stories about the content and consequences of the confrontation. Publicly the two rivals dismissed inquiries about their personal hostility. They assured reporters that their dispute was political, not personal. But insiders knew that their relationship would never be the same. It "was the final break between Bobby and LBJ," a Kennedy aide recalled. "If there had been any chance for reconciliation between the two men, there was certainly no chance after that."[65]

END OF THE ORDEAL

Lyndon Johnson's February 6 meeting with Robert Kennedy was an important transition in his struggle with the "mystique." For the first time since Robert had tried to remove him from the 1960 Democratic ticket, the president vented deep and long-standing hostility. Earlier private meetings between the two men had been tempered by deference. Even when Johnson eliminated Kennedy from vice-presidential contention before the 1964 convention, their meeting had been civil. The February 6 meeting broke new ground, but Johnson's private hostility was not entirely transferred to the public arena. He remained trapped between two Kennedys. He could not openly attack Robert without implicitly attacking John. Conversely, he could not exalt John for his own purposes, because to promote the Kennedy myth would indirectly help Robert. Despite the difficulty of the strategy, Johnson sought to undermine Robert while drawing on his predecessor's memory.

Johnson's vow to destroy Kennedy politically within six months rested on an assumption that the war would be resolved by the fall of 1967; Kennedy would then lack the most viable issue with which to challenge the president. Certainly the settlement of the war was important to Johnson for other reasons. The lives of hundreds of thousands of American soldiers as well as the advancement of Great Society programs demanded a resolution. But his political survival also hinged upon the progress of the war. During the half-year following the February 6 meeting Johnson employed various tactics to induce Hanoi to negotiate. He twice sent personal letters to Ho Chi Minh requesting evidence of de-escalation in return for a bombing halt. In February he encouraged British Prime Minister Harold Wilson to mediate a solution with the Soviet Union. In June the president met with Soviet

Chairman Aleksei Kosygin in Glassboro, New Jersey, and again tried to broach an agreement. In general he sought assurances that North Vietnam would not take advantage of an American bombing halt to escalate its infiltration into the South. Hanoi rebuffed each effort, insisting upon an unconditional cessation of American bombing before negotiations.[1]

Johnson also employed military pressure to encourage negotiations. "By early 1967," he recalled in his memoirs, "most of my advisers and I felt confident that the tide of war was moving strongly in favor of the South Vietnamese and their allies, and against the Communists." Encouraged by "heartening signs of progress," he expanded the bombing of North Vietnam in the spring of 1967 and increased the number of American soldiers in Vietnam to 525,000 by August.[2]

Kennedy, meanwhile, was inundated with conflicting advice as he tried to recover from the Manchester affair as well as the "peace feeler" and wiretapping episodes. Playing the role of devil's advocate, Richard Goodwin urged Kennedy to run for president in 1968 and discussed his chances with Edward Kennedy. They agreed "you werent [sic] too good at handling [his recent setbacks] and [Johnson] had all the machinery of govt. press at his command and was pretty good." Rather than challenging the president on specific issues, they advised that should Robert enter the race, "the only campaign you could run would be one squarely against LBJ." Edward recommended that Robert postpone his presidential ambitions, but he told Goodwin, "Jack would probably have cautioned against [running], but he might have done it himself."[3]

Frederick Dutton displayed more caution than Goodwin. Although he advised Kennedy not to challenge Johnson, he outlined a flexible, long-term strategy should Johnson suffer a setback in the next year's New Hampshire primary and "unexpectedly give one of his out-of-the-air explanations that he will only serve out his present term." Kennedy needed to avoid political confrontations. "[T]he country is now evidently in a period in which it sharply demeans politics and politicians," he explained. "The aura President Kennedy brought to the art has largely been displaced by what the public dislikes about the Johnson administration." He recommended that Kennedy appear philosophical in his political approach: "[Y]our pacesetters are not Lyndon Johnson, Hubert Humphrey, Chuck Percy and other aspirants for the Presidency but, quite frankly, Ghandi, John F. Kennedy, Pitt the Younger, Alexander the Great, Pope John, and others. . . ." Kennedy should "avoid appearing the politician," exude his "existential" qualities, and hold off "the kind of comments which, rightly or wrongly, are construed by the press as needling" the president. Because of "the country's deep dislike for President Johnson's personality," Kennedy had to exhibit "qualities of the spirit" that voters desired "in their alternative choices."[4]

After the February 6 meeting Kennedy continued to question the war but refrained from personal criticism of Johnson. At the University of Chicago on February 8 he reprimanded the administration for an incoherent China policy and urged it to move beyond "sweeping statements, pious hopes, [and] grandiose commitments." When questioned about Johnson's handling of the war, however, Kennedy conceded that the president had "inherited a situation that was very complex—and he has acted with courage." The next day McPherson noted journalist Rowland Evans's recent assertion that Kennedy's "restlessness" was damaging his career and America's foreign policy efforts. McPherson rejected Evans's offer to do a ten-minute interview on a local Washington television program. In the past the president had been reluctant to allow staff members to speak on his behalf. His attitude was changing. "Go on," Johnson instructed.[5]

By now Johnson regarded Kennedy's criticisms, no matter how mild, as indicating an impending presidential bid. "Throughout 1967," Lawrence O'Brien recalled, "whenever Bob criticized the Administration, Johnson regarded it as the start of his presidential candidacy. Bob knew this and got a certain grim pleasure out of the thought that he was annoying Johnson." Aides heightened Johnson's anxiety with ominous warnings. Kennedy's actions since January, John Roche insisted, were part of "a full-court press aimed at discrediting the Administration." Roche sensed that Kennedy was "increasingly desperate," and he doubted that the senator had the patience to wait until 1972 before running for president. "In short," he warned, "I am beginning to think that he has moved up his time-table, that he may be just demonic enough to go for broke in 1968."[6]

In the weeks following the Johnson-Kennedy confrontation, third- and fourthhand conversations speculating about Kennedy's intentions were summarized and forwarded to the president. Roche informed him of his talk with a drunken friend from Harvard who related a story about a man present at a cocktail party in Cambridge. According to the friend, an aide to Kennedy announced that "Bobby's Master Plan" was to "pull a Kefauver in New Hampshire." The comment referred to Senator Estes Kefauver's successful challenge of President Harry Truman in the 1952 New Hampshire primary, a victory which prompted Truman to announce two weeks later that he would not be a candidate for re-election. Although Roche urged Johnson to be cautious about the story, he advised "to plan for the worst" and to be wary of Kennedy's activities in the state.[7]

While Kennedy privately considered his political options, Johnson aides debated his intentions. Marvin Watson, Lawrence O'Brien, and George

Christian suspected that Kennedy was preparing to challenge Johnson immediately. Roche's opinions ranged from alarm to certainty that he would not risk an open conflict. Johnson was anxious to hear all points of view. Hugh Sidey reported that he "probes his visitors these days. Eyes narrowed, hunched forward, LBJ asks: 'What's Kennedy really up to?' "[8]

Kennedy, meanwhile, prepared to make a clean break with the administration. Dutton had advised him against isolating himself from the political scene, fearing he would convey the impression that "you are brooding, scheming or just a spoil-sport in regard to '68." Rather than making "occasional digs" at Johnson, Kennedy needed to confine criticism to select Senate speeches on major subjects. "[Y]ou have not established yourself in the public mind as the leading authority . . . on a single major area," Dutton assessed. "I urge that you make that one of your top priorities during the next year and a half." In February Kennedy and his aides began drafting a speech in which they outlined a proposal for a peaceful resolution to the war. He consulted with Robert McNamara and Maxwell Taylor, two former New Frontiersmen still counseling the president. Much to the administration's delight, he also spoke with such leaders of the "New Left" as Tom Hayden and Staughton Lynd. Roche sent an article to the president in which Kennedy stated that Hayden's and Lynd's ideas on Vietnam were "in the same ballpark" as his own. "Neither of them could lead a parade let alone a revolution," Roche noted. "If Bobby is going to play in that 'ballpark,' he is going to have some real problems."[9]

Nevertheless, Kennedy's impending address seriously threatened Johnson's delicate consensus. Politically he could not afford further discord. His approval rating was declining along with public support for the war. Although other notable Democratic senators had spoken out against the war, Kennedy was the Democrats' most viable potential challenger to Johnson, and he could deeply divide the party. Robert's open opposition would also make it difficult for Johnson to assert that his policies were in keeping with John Kennedy's.[10]

Johnson sought to dissuade Kennedy from presenting the policy address, dispatching Averell Harriman to urge him to cancel the speech "in the national interest." Kennedy contended that it was too late; he had already released the speech's details to the press. Johnson next sought to minimize the speech's impact, directing General William Westmoreland, commander of American forces in Vietnam, to denounce any call for a bombing pause. "I don't want to pay one drop of blood for a pig in a poke," the general remarked from the front. James Farley, the Democratic party's elder statesman and Johnson's long-time political ally, criticized Kennedy in advance of his Senate address. During the Jefferson-Jackson Dinner in Hartford, Farley condemned Kennedy's "soaring ambition" and claimed that if John Kennedy were alive he would support the president. "Insulting, belittling and interfering with the office of the President," he noted, "is not the act of a mature citizen let alone a United States Senator."[11]

On March 2, 1967, Kennedy broke officially with Johnson, sending a draft of his speech to the White House only hours before the address. Speaking on the Senate floor, he protected himself from accusations that he was motivated by personal animosity toward Johnson. He was united with the president in seeking an end to the conflict and expressed sympathy for his military dilemma. Recalling that Vietnam was the product of three administrations, Kennedy disarmed critics by confessing guilt. "As one who was involved in many of those decisions," he noted, "I can testify that if fault is to be found or responsibility assessed, there is enough to go around for all—including myself." Implicitly he linked himself to his brother, who was also an interventionist.[12]

Kennedy proceeded to describe the history of America's involvement in Vietnam. He accused the North Vietnamese of continuing the war but spoke at length of the need to "look at ourselves." He urged listeners not to reflect upon the justification or the importance of the war but, for the moment, to consider "the horror." He used emotionally charged descriptions and noted that the destruction was "partly our responsibility." He then outlined a three-point peace proposal. First, the United States would initiate a bombing halt in order to encourage negotiations. On this matter Kennedy directly criticized Johnson's effort, noting that his announced objectives in 1965 were unfulfilled. Second, he proposed that during the negotiations neither side would engage in a "substantial increase" of arms. Finally, an international presence would replace American forces while a settlement was concluded with North Vietnam.[13]

Kennedy received considerable praise for his proposal. "You are absolutely right," Rowland Evans's wife wrote Kennedy. "Keep at it." Hugh Sidey informed him that his speech reminded him of the "sensations" he had once felt when listening to John Kennedy. "There was a lot of him last Thursday [in your address.]" In breaking with the administration, Kennedy used a carefully constructed position paper. The American people had been losing confidence in both the war and its leadership. Gallup polls indicated that more than 40 percent of the public disapproved of Johnson's handling of the war. But there was a widespread belief that *all* political leaders had lost control of events. Indeed, before Kennedy's speech, only one-quarter of the public thought *he* could do a "better job" than Johnson in dealing with the war. If Kennedy intended to lead the growing discontented, he needed to demonstrate leadership beyond the glib comments he had made in the past.[14]

Johnson worked to minimize Kennedy's impact with a flurry of activity. A few hours before the address he held a press conference to announce that the Soviet Union had agreed to talks on arms limitations. He gave two unscheduled speeches, one at Howard University in which he re-committed himself to civil rights and another before a congressional reception. Johnson then allowed others to question Kennedy's proposal. Dean Rusk argued that Kennedy's solutions were "substantially similar" to those "explored" by the administration, "all without result." Senator Henry Jackson claimed that the administration had already attempted an unsuccessful bombing pause. He read a pre-dated letter from the president on the Senate floor, explaining the necessity of bombing. Administration officials told reporters that Kennedy's plan would allow North Vietnam to regroup just at a time when military pressure was forcing the enemy to negotiate. White House criticism was augmented by reporters and congressional colleagues who opposed the senator for their own reasons.[15]

Defending Kennedy, Arthur Schlesinger accused the administration of deliberately misrepresenting North Vietnam's peace initiatives because it "does not wish to negotiate now." McPherson assured Johnson that the former special assistant would not go unpunished. Representative Sam Stratton planned to "attack" Schlesinger on the House floor. "He will say that as a former member of the Harvard faculty, he is shocked by Schlesinger's inability to understand the English language." The congressman would accuse him of failing to make critical distinctions in the administration's conditions for negotiations, and that "his recommendations add up to a goose egg."[16]

Johnson's own response came during a press conference one week later. Privately he felt victimized by the "mystique." "Bobby wouldn't be talking that way if Jack Kennedy were still president," he confided to a reporter. "I kept faith with Jack Kennedy on Vietnam." Rumors circulated that he was preparing to carry out his threat to destroy Robert. But Johnson took the high ground. A press briefing paper avoided any personal criticism of either Kennedy or Schlesinger. Several reporters had privately suggested that Johnson downplay the conflict. "[Mel] Elfin, who is anti-Kennedy," Douglass Cater wrote, "advised that the best way to handle this story is to ignore it as much as possible. He said he hoped you would 'keep your cool' at the press conference—that the Kennedy clique enjoys the prospect of irritating you." Charles Bartlett "didn't think you were handling Kennedy correctly. He said the press corps was alive with stories about your 'over reaction' —that these stories tended to build Kennedy up, even among those who dislike him."[17]

During the news conference Johnson checked his anger, contending that he was not offended by "individuals" having "different approaches" to the war. "I have no particular fault to find, or criticism to make, of others." He was acting in the best interests of the country, "without regard to personalities or politics," and was always prepared to negotiate with North Vietnam. But he also noted that five previous bombing pauses had proven ineffective, and he remained "very sure of victory." "I don't want to quarrel with anyone," he added. "I must grant [critics] the same sincerity that I reserve for myself."[18]

Afterwards Bartlett relayed the message that Johnson's tempered response was "nothing short of genius and did more than anything to halt the onward rush of LBJ vs. RFK writings in the press." Robert Novak expressed weariness with the entire story, privately telling McPherson that he was "bored with the whole Kennedy operation." Johnson's downplaying of the conflict yielded unanticipated benefits as well. Several weeks after the news conference, Hanoi released a letter from the president dated February 8, 1967. It noted that negotiations would be likely if North Vietnam demonstrated good faith by halting its supplies to the South. Inadvertently, Johnson had shown his good intentions at a time when the Kennedy camp criticized the president's unwillingness to negotiate. Columnists commended the president for not revealing the letter beforehand and for keeping negotiation efforts properly private. He had positioned himself above the political fray.[19]

Johnson could not entirely hide his indignation. He revealed more authentic feelings during a dinner speech before the Democratic National Committee. Without mentioning Kennedy by name, he accused critics of selfish motives. "Peace . . . must not be bought at the price of a temporary lust for popularity," he declared. The public would reject "a dishonorable settlement disguised as a bargain for popularity purposes eighteen months before the election." He concluded by reading a letter written to the grieving sister of a soldier killed in Vietnam: "Your brother was in South Vietnam because the threat to the Vietnamese people is, in the long run, a threat to the free world community." The letter, Johnson announced, had been written four years before by President John F. Kennedy. The implication was clear: Johnson was a more legitimate servant of the Kennedy legacy than Robert.[20]

The day after the news conference and dinner, Johnson and Kennedy met through an accident of protocol while attending the swearing-in ceremony of Ramsey Clark as attorney general. "They peered at each other," *Newsweek* reported. "They nodded. And they shook hands, so fleetingly that photographers almost missed the picture. . . ." Although annoyed by the criticism he had faced since the previous December, Kennedy tried to assume a carefree attitude. Dutton advised him to avoid a "slugging match" and warned that, in comparison with President Kennedy, "there is a considerable question whether you have as much 'cool' " and "detachment." Moreover, a rivalry with Johnson risked making Robert appear too "political." Dutton recommended that he *use an early opportunity to make some tangible gesture to the White House entirely on your own initiative* [emphasis Dutton's].[21]

On the defensive, Kennedy sought conciliation on March 17 by announcing his support for President Johnson's presumed re-election bid in 1968. The White House received assurances that Kennedy was seeking to lessen tensions between himself and the president. "[Bartlett] is urging Bobby to de-escalate," McPherson wrote Johnson, "—and Bobby's TV appearance of two nights ago where he called the President 'an outstanding President and leader' and pledges his support of the President in 1968 maybe [sic] the first result of Charlie's importuning."[22]

Johnson had successfully played the role of the rational, tolerant leader and seemed content to let others in the administration, Congress, and the news media criticize his rival. Robert's conciliatory gestures suggested that the strategy had worked. Moreover, the senator *felt* defeated. "An indefinable sense of depression hung over him," Schlesinger wrote in his journal, "as if he felt cornered by circumstance and did not know how to break out." "How can we possibly survive five more years of Lyndon Johnson?" Kennedy asked the historian. "Five more years of a crazy man?"[23]

Although the public remained dissatisfied with Johnson, polls indicated that they were unwilling to abandon him for Kennedy. To be sure, the president continued to have problems. A mid-March Gallup poll showed that two-thirds of the public did not believe the administration was forthcoming about Vietnam. In April Johnson's public approval remained below 50 percent. But Kennedy also faced serious problems. Gallup reported that the "ranks of Kennedy supporters have steadily declined." By April Johnson led him as the favorite for the 1968 Democratic nomination, 49 percent to 37. And Kennedy's "unfavorable" rating was higher than Johnson's. Unsure of the precise reasons for the president's resurgence, Kennedy and Johnson aides concurred independently that a combination of Johnson's proper handling of criticism and Kennedy's "overassertiveness" had worked to the president's advantage. Johnson might still deflect Kennedy's presidential aspirations.[24]

Crisis and Confidence

Despite signs of retreat by Kennedy, White House aides were convinced that the respite was temporary and that he remained a serious threat. They urged Johnson to take the offensive while the senator reflected on his political problems. Roche wanted Johnson to threaten Kennedy with political reprisals if he challenged him for the nomination. Kennedy had "a vested interest in the defeat of the national ticket in 1968," and Johnson could expect attacks from Republicans, George Wallace, and Martin Luther King, with "the Kennedy Corporation as interested spectators." Opponents, therefore, needed to be divided into "manageable chunks" with the greatest concern reserved for Kennedy. They should convince his organization that "if we go down in bankruptcy, *they will go down with us.* This is the only argument that will have the slightest impact on them." If they dared to divide the party, the Republicans would control the White House for a prolonged period, and former Johnson aides would launch a public relations offensive to undermine the senator's presidential hopes for 1972. The Kennedy camp was already keenly aware of this possibility.[25]

Roche was one of several White House aides intent on an aggressive posture. In February he had asked Johnson's permission to "put on the knuckles" against Schlesinger, who had been regularly defending the Kennedy administration before "liberal audiences." "If those of us who do share your ideals stand silent," he reasoned, "the opposition among the intellectuals wins by default." A few days later, after appearing in public with Richard Goodwin, he noted that only the concern for bad press prevented him from "belting" the former New Frontiersman. In the late spring McPherson wanted Johnson to launch a public relations campaign to undermine Kennedy's initiative on domestic issues. Kennedy had recently participated in highly publicized tours of poverty areas and was exploiting the Kennedy image to deny Johnson the constituency that the president had tried to call his own. "The fact that [Kennedy] looks bored [during the tours], and probably doesn't give a damn about what he is seeing, is beside the point. To the concerned voter, certainly to the young, he is 'out among us.' " Johnson, therefore, should tour a Job Corps camp or selected poverty areas. He needed to "get out more among the people" and to "use the occasion to fight for your legislative program—the new program, and funding the old." "It's in bad trouble," McPherson warned, "and you ought not let it go down without an open, vigorous fight to preserve it."[26]

Johnson ignored McPherson's advice. By 1967 his "populist" image had worn thin as he de-emphasized the Great Society in order to concentrate on the Vietnam War. Existing programs were rife with corruption and mismanagement. Moreover, certain poverty areas were increasingly hostile to the administration, a pessimism underscored by the eruption of urban riots in July. Aides nevertheless encouraged public relations gambits in an attempt to neutralize Kennedy's "existential" image. Benjamin Wattenberg, a native Texan and a new member of the White House staff, contended that Johnson's "image problem" stemmed from the public's "derogatory" perception of "politics" and "politicians." There was no way to "escape from the political image," he wrote Johnson, without heightening "the so-called credibility gap." Johnson should redefine the image into an "asset" by presenting a speech before "a university audience, preferably Ivy League or New York City, dealing with the art and craft of politics" and stressing that "vigorous, hardnosed political activity is necessary to achieve social and economic goals." While promoting himself as a "technician and tactician," he could "obliquely" note that the nation is better served by a practical politician than by "a man who is selling a classic profile and nothing more." "The 'political image' is here to stay," he argued. "The challenge is whether it can be made a *plus* rather than a *minus*."[27]

While Wattenberg sought to highlight Johnson's genuine qualities, other aides looked to appeal to those Kennedy supporters who had perhaps grown disillusioned with Robert. With Robert behaving as a "ruthless" opportunist, Johnson could remind the public that John Kennedy's idealism and values survived through his successor. In late January, for example, Roche urged him to cultivate the intellectuals. The Manchester episode proved that it was a mistake to "overrate the genius of 'the Kennedys.' " But "it is also unfortunate to underestimate them, particularly in their appeal to the 'intellectuals.' " Johnson needed to reward intellectuals through ceremonial recognitions and appointments to various advisory commissions. Roche provided a list of those who might be rewarded for their loyalty.[28]

In May McPherson sought to bridge the gap between Johnson and "literary" people such as journalists, professors, historians, and sociologists. He cited Kennedy's Hickory Hill seminars as successful in "acknowledging the primacy of the literary intellectual" and in gaining the senator favor. These seminars also heightened the impression that "our policy is supported only by the Yahoos; that thinking people question it or reject it altogether." To counter this, he recommended that Johnson demonstrate a "closer association" with his own intellectuals by meeting with a small, preferably younger group to discuss their experiences and to recommend how to "improve relations." Less than two weeks later a well-publicized luncheon was arranged between the president and sixteen administration intellectuals. Before the meeting McPherson reminded the president that he was contributing to a worthwhile tradition. "Since 1960," he wrote, "more and more scholars and intellectuals have come into government. We want that trend to continue and expand. . . ."[29]

During the meeting Johnson conveyed his desire to renew dialogue with the intellectual community, acknowledging that "personality factors" may have contributed to his problems with them in the past. In September Roche arranged for Johnson to meet with a group of distinguished academicians, assuring that there was "not a Kennedy flunky in the crowd." After meeting the group, Johnson was informed that he had done "an extraordinary job" and may have made inroads with the Kennedy intellectuals. "As you know," James MacGregor Burns told McPherson in late 1967, "I was more or less identified with the Kennedy people. But I have watched President Johnson carefully, and he has simply met every issue squarely and rightly, and I have come to admire him greatly." Johnson was also assured that John Kennedy had suffered from similar image problems with intellectuals when he was president.[30]

During the spring of 1967 Johnson also sought to appeal to young adults. An article from the *Boston Globe* entitled, "Think Young, Mr. President," reported that he had hired a Madison Avenue advertising "glamour girl" to "shine up" his image with young people in order to counter Robert Kennedy's appeal. The piece was forwarded to the White House, along with a cartoon of Johnson trying on a toupee fashioned in the likeness of a Kennedy hairstyle. Aware that the president's attempt to appeal to young adults appeared contrived, the administration vetoed a proposal to establish a Special Assistant for Youth Affairs. The creation of "a new post with a lot of fanfare," an aide argued, "would appear to the press as being an overly as well as overtly calculated attempt to counter Senator Kennedy's appeals to youth." He recommended, instead, more subtle strategies.[31]

The difficulty of trying to mold Johnson in the image and likeness of his predecessor illustrated the paradox of the Kennedy "mystique" which had plagued him since 1964. By presenting himself as an intellectual or youth-oriented president, he elevated the prestige of those attributes that were related more to the Kennedys than to himself. He ran the risk of suffering by comparison, especially when such efforts appeared alien to his own character. And his promotion of such images ultimately benefited Robert. Johnson was wedged between two brothers whom he could neither emulate nor attack without suffering repercussions.

In late May 1967 this dilemma was illustrated by an event that brought together Lyndon Johnson, Robert Kennedy, and John Kennedy's memory. Two months earlier, at Robert and Jacqueline Kennedy's invitation, Johnson had attended a private ceremony consecrating John Kennedy's new and permanent grave at the Arlington National Cemetery. He shared an umbrella with the senator and, according to a Kennedy aide, their exchange during the brief sunrise ceremony was relaxed. The commemoration, conducted in secrecy, received little coverage in the news media but served as a prelude to a highly publicized meeting between Johnson and the Kennedys.[32]

On the anniversary of John Kennedy's birthday, Johnson was scheduled to speak at the christening of an aircraft carrier named in the late president's honor. Wattenberg characterized the occasion as *the most dramatic single appearance you will make all year.*" He agonized over the event's political implications, noting that it was both "a great opportunity and a great hazard." There was inherent drama in having the nation's attention focused on Johnson, but there were risks concerning how much the president should praise his predecessor. He anticipated "problems" if Johnson focused solely on "the legacy of John F. Kennedy." If he noted that his predecessor was "a man of *peace*, and that he brought a *new* style of politics to America—you are, by indirection, almost saying what your critics say, that you are a man of *war* with *old* style politics." Because of "the absurd way the press has dealt with Johnson vs. Kennedy," he would be vulnerable to unfair comparisons. "On the other hand, if you don't talk about 'the legacy of JFK'—the question arises, why not?, how ungracious, etc." Meanwhile, Robert Kennedy's presence made it inappropriate to talk about Vietnam, or to quote, for example, the late president's letter to the sister of the soldier killed in the war. Wattenberg therefore enclosed an outline which fulfilled the goals of a "good" speech: "broad in scope, for world consumption, considerate of the Kennedys, and paying authentic homage to the memory of JFK." It stressed John Kennedy's belief in America's "strength and preparedness" and its duty to defend freedom abroad. "Outline is a good speech," Johnson wrote on the memorandum, but he wanted a more "euphonious" tone.[33]

Cater, Roche, McNamara, and others refined the speech's message and style, making it "short, eloquent, and just right for the occasion." Although Johnson was allowed twenty minutes to give his address, his remarks that day were brief. Noting that John Kennedy died "at the pinnacle of national affection," he reminded the audience that his predecessor "saw the failure of appeasement." *Newsweek* reported that he "looked careworn and uneasy." "Meetings with the Kennedys," it reminded readers, "are always difficult for him. . . ." News reports of a "visible strain" between the president and the Kennedy family filtered to the White House. "Everyone smiled a great deal," one newspaper reported, "but not at each other."[34]

Despite underlying tensions, Johnson had handled the event gracefully. Aides forwarded to him flattering remarks from former Kennedy aides; "even Arthur Schlesinger thought it was excellent." During the next several weeks Johnson sent photographs of the christening to various members of the Kennedy family. "Thank you again, dear Mr. President," Rose Kennedy replied, "for all you have done to perpetuate [John's] memory." He also compelled deference from Robert. Appearing together at a Democratic dinner in New York one week later, Johnson and Kennedy spoke of the past and future concerns of the party. The president reaffirmed John Kennedy's promise to "get the country moving again." Robert returned favor, praising the "height" of Johnson's aim, "the breadth of his achievements, the record of his past, the promises of the future." "In 1964," he recalled, "[Johnson] won the greatest popular victory in modern times, and with our help he will do so again in 1968." He credited Johnson for having "never failed to spend [his popularity] in the pursuit of his beliefs or in the interest of his country."[35]

Privately Kennedy resented having to speak as he did. "If I hadn't said those things," he remarked afterwards, "that would give Lyndon Johnson the opportunity to blame everything that was going wrong . . . on that son of a bitch Bobby Kennedy." Schlesinger assessed the comments as Kennedy's "one mistake." "They seemed out of character," he wrote, "and that is the one thing you must never be." For Johnson, Robert's observations became a source of pride. Four years later, when writing his memoirs, he quoted at length from Robert's speech. The comments were "nearer to what I believe is the truth" about the nature of the 1964 victory "than any others."[36]

By early summer Johnson appeared politically stable again. Following the Glassboro summit in June his approval rating jumped to 62 percent. In July Harris polls indicated that 70 percent of the people supported his effort at a negotiated settlement of the war, and that Johnson could beat any of the major Republican challengers in 1968. Peace Democrats seemed to be losing support. Indeed, half the American people favored a ground invasion of North Vietnam. Although the polls were extremely sensitive to political conditions and suggested only temporary moods, they indicated that Johnson might salvage his presidency provided he could quickly end the war.[37]

As the summer wore on, however, the president found it increasingly difficult to ward off a Kennedy threat. In mid- and late July, race riots erupted in Newark and Detroit, leaving scores dead. The percentage of people who approved of Johnson's handling of civil rights fell from 50 percent in June to 32 percent in August. Meanwhile, a Harris poll indicated that, despite optimistic military reports, two-thirds of the public believed that the progress of the war was no better than it had been six months before. Johnson bore the brunt of public criticism. The boost he received from the Glassboro summit deteriorated, and his approval rating fell to 39 percent, the lowest presidential approval rating since the last year of the Truman administration.[38]

Some of Johnson's most loyal supporters in Congress began to desert him, and Kennedy supporters used the opportunity to renew criticism. Long-time party chief Joseph Rauh publicly urged that a peace plank be incorporated into the 1968 Democratic platform. Fifty-one former Democratic party delegates appealed to Johnson to withdraw from the 1968 presidential race in favor of a Kennedy-Fulbright ticket. Critics within the Democratic party were stinging in their attacks. Senator William Fulbright remarked that "The Great Society has become a sick society." Kennedy called the recent elections in South Vietnam "a fraud and a farce."[39]

With deteriorating domestic conditions, Kennedy found new opportunities to distinguish himself from the president. Throughout early 1967 the war had compelled Johnson to devote staggering time and energy to foreign policy concerns at the expense of his domestic agenda. "With the administration otherwise engaged," Schlesinger recalled, "Kennedy moved out on his own." Like Johnson, Kennedy condemned the violence erupting in the cities, but he spoke more deliberately about the need to emphasize domestic reform. That summer he sought to create an expanded federal version of the Bedford-Stuyvesant project—a Brooklyn slum rehabilitation project funded through tax incentives. Johnson responded by introducing a comparable program, killing Kennedy's proposal.[40]

Although faced with enormous policy setbacks, the White House seemed relatively confident of meeting Kennedy's challenges. The senator continued to struggle with his own difficulties. Reports filtered into the White House that he was meeting with journalists and asking, "What am I doing wrong?" One reporter accused him of running for the presidency by "standing on Jack Kennedy's casket." Roche assured Johnson that Kennedy was aware "that if we go down, he goes with us." Kennedy, meanwhile, was regularly informed by trusted aides that it was in his best long-term political interest not to challenge Johnson in 1968.[41]

Although aides expressed confidence that Kennedy was manageable, Johnson could not be saved from himself. Facing overwhelming foreign and domestic crises, he became increasingly anxious and intolerant. Aides and cabinet officers leaked to the press that the situation in the White House was "dreadful" and degenerating. Johnson's personality became an issue in itself, generating as much press criticism as his foreign or domestic concerns. He was described as impatient, brusque, tired, and worn. His manner during meetings with reporters was secretive and glib. Between June and September a Harris poll indicated that one of five Americans had reversed his once positive opinion of the president. "In short," *Newsweek* concluded, "the report for Johnson about Johnson showed what everybody around Johnson already knows: that Lyndon Johnson is his own worst enemy."[42]

It had been six months since Johnson issued his February 6 threat to Kennedy. By September, however, it was he, not Kennedy, who faced political destruction. A "Dump Johnson" movement was established by a loose coalition of groups including "Dissenting Democrats" and "Citizens for Kennedy." Gallup reported that Kennedy was making "steady gains in public appeal." In an open field, Democrats preferred him over Johnson 39 percent to 37 percent, and 51 percent to 39 percent in a two-person race. By October, Harris polls showed Kennedy leading Johnson 52 percent to 32 percent. In November Johnson was painfully informed that polls showed a continuation of a year-long trend: "RFK benefits when LBJ declines." He sought desperately for favorable polls, at one point wanting to leak to the press a survey of high school students showing him more popular than John and Jacqueline Kennedy. "Find a way to get this out," he ordered on the memorandum, "—Drew Pearson or somehow."[43]

Publicly Johnson tried to appear unconcerned by the new Kennedy threat. Speaking before reporters and visitors, he complained of unfair press coverage and charged that the public was poorly informed about the complexity of the problems at home and abroad. He rebuffed criticism of his urban programs and indirectly accused Senators Abraham Ribicoff and Kennedy of opportunism. "What did they do or propose for the cities and the slum dweller when they were in the Cabinet?" he asked. "If some folks think a fellow is winged or cripple, they pile into him. If you've got an enemy, it gives him a lot of hope." He insisted that the 1968 presidential election and history would redeem him.[44]

During the early fall of 1967 Kennedy held a series of meetings to discuss his political options. He did not want to appear motivated by "ambition and envy." At the same time he implied that he might run if someone else within the party first declared his candidacy: "I think Johnson might quit the night before the convention opens. I think he is a coward." Other Kennedy aides concurred. "I have always speculated [Johnson] is a highly insecure man inside himself," Dutton wrote Kennedy. He predicted that it was "close to probable" that Johnson would not seek re-election but warned that "your pressing him would only firm up his resolve" and would evoke a "ruthless" image. Because of the fickleness of public opinion polls, Kennedy should "keep cool for now" and "even public[ly] fraternize with LBJ a little" by inviting him to Hickory Hill. At the same time he should covertly develop a power base in New Hampshire, refine his television skills, cultivate intellectuals, exploit his friendly relations with reporters, and give a "Camus-like style" speech on "the state of mankind" in "an implicit contrast" to Johnson.[45]

Johnson's aides and friends privately feared that he would not seek re-election. Of particular concern was his unwillingness to organize the various committees and factions of the Democratic party. Indeed, Roche discussed the president's "inexplicable" behavior with McPherson, who suggested in jest that Johnson might not run again. Others, however, noted that although Johnson was politically wounded and emotionally distraught, he still possessed formidable power with which to regain support, and he remained in vital control of the country's majority party. Only the polls showed Johnson to be weak. They did not necessarily indicate that support for Kennedy was firm, a point that Kennedy was well aware of. In September, *Newsweek* reminded readers that Johnson's political intelligence, skill, and experience could not be underestimated. "He has a string of legislative achievements . . . that puts his predecessor's record in the shade," it asserted. "Despite the Kennedyites' dreams of restoration, . . . [Johnson] is the quintessential politician, and he is already shaping his 1968 campaign."[46]

That fall Johnson seemed suddenly inspired, behaving more like a candidate than a president. During a press conference he reproached congressional opponents of his model cities program and was sarcastic toward Vietnam critics. Speaking before a thousand representatives from sixty-three local, state, and national consumer organizations, he attacked Congress for not passing his proposed tax bill and promised to veto protectionist legislation on imports. He also spoke harshly against "crime in the streets" and maintained that the Great Society was not dead. Appearing before one thousand trade unionists, he charged it was "pure bunk" to believe that, due to the war, progress at home was impossible. "The President is simply going to fight for his program and for what's right," an aide told reporters. "If that means talking tougher, then he's going to talk tougher."[47]

White House officials augmented the president's assertiveness, especially in defending the war. Dean Rusk argued that by fighting in South Vietnam the United States was defending its own vital security. A withdrawal of American troops would place the United States in "mortal danger" that could lead to "catastrophe for all mankind." Vice President Humphrey reminded audiences of the cost of appeasement during the 1930s and attacked critics for "bad-mouthing our cause." In his latest defense of his foreign policy, Johnson had imprecise targets. They included Congress, the news media, and "intellectuals." In dealing with Kennedy, Johnson struggled for rights to the Kennedy "mystique." Earlier in the year, Roche had been frustrated by Kennedy aides "inventing quotes—mostly on Vietnam— by John Kennedy" to criticize Johnson's escalation of the war. In early September 1967, when public support for the war rapidly declined, the prospect of invoking the late president was reconsidered. Johnson secured transcripts of John Kennedy's two network interviews from September 1963, when he had articulated the "domino theory." Recalling the lessons of 1930s appeasement, the late president had argued that immediate force was required to stop the spread of "evil" before large territories came under an enemy's control. It was therefore imperative that the United States use force against North Vietnam now rather than having to contend with a broader conflict later. John Kennedy had also charged that those opposed to America's effort were aiding communism. A Johnson aide noted that some of the statements could be very effective in "bringing back into the fold some of the doves in the Democratic Party."[48]

Nine days later national security adviser Walter Rostow sent Johnson a forty-one-page text containing "a rather full compilation of statements by President Kennedy regarding Viet Nam and U.S. interest and commitments in Southeast Asia." Expediting the review of the material, Rostow used a coloring system to mark specific passages. Yellow highlight designated "the most significant passages" while red markings emphasized "items particularly quotable." Rostow was surprised by Kennedy's "explicit linkage" of the U.S. commitment in Vietnam to the SEATO treaty, his "flat acceptance of the domino theory," his linkage of events in Vietnam to Berlin, and his general contention that American self-interest was at stake. "I don't believe any objective person can read this record without knowing that President Kennedy would have seen this through whatever the cost." The late president had made one particularly important comment: "In my opinion for us to withdraw from that effort would mean a collapse not only of South Vietnam, but Southeast Asia. So we are going to stay there." "That," Rostow concluded, "is the nut of the story."[49]

Hesitantly, Johnson reminded partisan audiences of John Kennedy's commitment to interventionism. He quoted his predecessor three times when speaking before the National Legislative Conference in San Antonio. During a "Salute to the President" Democratic Party Dinner, Johnson expressed hope that the United States "will have enough of that bravery, unselfishness, and wisdom that Jack Kennedy said we would need—to see it through all the way." Speaking on the telephone to the Regional Democratic Conference in West Virginia, he quoted from a speech that the late president had intended to give on the night of his death, referring to Americans as "the watchmen on the wall of world freedom."[50]

Despite his staff's elaborate preparation and the volume of Kennedy quotes available to him, Johnson recalled his predecessor's commitment to Vietnam only periodically and continued to mix his references with quotes from other presidents. During two highly publicized television appearances in November and December he failed to cite the late president when asked about America's commitment to the war. Aides planned to use John Kennedy's letter to the dead soldier's sister, but Johnson did not insert it into any of his speeches that fall. Similar to his earlier reluctance to link his policy with Kennedy's, Johnson likely understood the incredulousness of the analogy; the war was quite different from the one Kennedy had left behind. And by 1967 he may have further realized that no matter how much he invoked John Kennedy, Robert's opposition to the war and his own invocations were more powerful persuaders.[51]

Johnson's self-restraint was not easy. Privately he was embittered by the public's failure to acknowledge John Kennedy's role in Vietnam. Years later, in retirement, he vented his resentment during an interview with Mike Wallace of CBS. Johnson noted that wars were often labeled by a president's name, but Kennedy was "spared that cruel action." Wallace was "struck by the bitter, derisive tone that came into his voice" when he mentioned President Kennedy. "[H]e obviously felt that he had been unjustly blamed," he recalled, "that it was Kennedy who had set the course [in Vietnam], and that he, Johnson, had merely followed it."[52]

Idealized memories of John Kennedy intruded into Johnson's communications strategies. During a November 17 press conference, for example, the president wore a lavaliere microphone, allowing him to step out from behind the podium and walk freely and gesture broadly. "[T]his was the Lyndon Johnson of the Congressional cloakroom coming to the nation live on television," *Newsweek* assessed. Johnson conveyed warmth, sincerity, and conviction. He joked about dissenters, patiently explained reasons for slow progress in Vietnam, and used humor to deflect questions about his political future. He was flooded with memoranda praising his appearance as "a masterpiece," "a morale booster," and "a turning point." A Harris poll afterwards showed that the decline in his popularity had reversed.[53]

Johnson's rare media triumph, however, was soon dampened by the "mystique." Extensive newspaper attention to the press conference emphasized Johnson's theatrical talents. While clearly appreciative of the power of television politics, Johnson had often disparaged television's tendency to favor style over substance. According to one of his media advisers, Robert Fleming, the president was offended by a supposed *New York Times* story which likened his press conference "performance" to John Kennedy's. There was no story in the *Times* that compared the two presidents, though one aide had obliquely compared Johnson's appearance with Kennedy's address during the Cuban missile crisis. Johnson likely felt that the attention to his "performance" made him appear an "actor" and hence an extension of Kennedy. He never again wore the lavaliere microphone and returned to the practice of remaining behind the lectern.[54]

Fighting for his political life, Johnson could not afford to abandon television. After years of prodding from his aides he conducted another

"Conversation with the President" interview in December 1967. The program depicted Johnson as "scrappy," "happy in his work," and "combative toward his tormentors." Sitting in a rocking chair as John Kennedy had during his 1962 program, Johnson admitted to gathered reporters that his "biggest problem" was in communicating with the public. He confessed frustration with the war and North Vietnam's unwillingness to negotiate. Although he was hostile to Republican critics, he was sterner toward the "Kennedy-McCarthy movement," of which he claimed to have only a vague understanding. "I do know of the interest of the both of them in the presidency and the ambitions of both of them." He was later informed that the show's Nielsen rating was higher than John Kennedy's earlier program.[55]

Johnson's newfound aggressiveness extended to his treatment of administrative officials. Those who had once worked for John Kennedy and were potentially loyal to Robert faced renewed persecution. In November 1967 Johnson announced that Defense Secretary Robert McNamara had been nominated director of the World Bank. Political pundits speculated that Johnson's action was motivated by several factors. Because McNamara had become disillusioned with the escalation of the war, Johnson wanted to insulate himself from doubters. Johnson and others were also concerned that McNamara was suffering from acute depression. A less discussed factor, however, pertained to his relationship with Robert Kennedy. "McNamara's problem," Johnson recalled, "was that he began to feel a division in his loyalties. He had always loved and admired the Kennedys; he was more their cup of tea, but he also admired and respected the Presidency [in general]." Johnson believed that his Defense Secretary had "deep affection" for him, "not so deep as the one he held for the Kennedys but deep enough." But, as Johnson explained, McNamara became tainted by surrounding intellectuals. "Then the Kennedys began pushing him harder and harder. Every day Bobby would call up McNamara, telling him that the war was terrible and immoral and that he had to leave." Plagued by guilt, McNamara felt like a "murderer." "I loved him and I didn't want to let him go," Johnson recalled, "but he was just short of cracking. . . . I had no choice."[56]

Curiously absent from Johnson's recollection was any overt hostility toward McNamara. As one of the chief architects of the war, he had contributed significantly to the demise of the Johnson presidency. But Johnson transferred his anger onto Robert Kennedy. Unable to accept that McNamara was sincerely distraught by the lack of progress in the war, Johnson conjured up demons. Although Kennedy had indeed discussed the war with McNamara, the notion that he had meddled with McNamara's mind reflected Johnson's deeper fears. His suspicions were heightened when he learned that, on the eve of McNamara's resignation, Kennedy met with him for more than an hour. Johnson alluded to Kennedy's role in manipulating McNamara when he was asked by reporters if other members of the cabinet were about to resign. "No," he replied, "I am told that 'some kids' have been calling around some of your [news] bureaus predicting that. . . ." " 'Some kids,' " *Newsweek* qualified, "spelled Kennedy to most newsmen present."[57]

The departure of one of the few remaining Kennedy holdovers made some Johnson aides anxious to prove their loyalty. Robert Kintner felt compelled to repledge his support to the president and to detail his thirty-three-year personal history with the Kennedys, "since I am convinced that the bitterness and antagonism between supporters (reporters, political figures, etc.) of the President and of Senator Robert Kennedy will increase with intensity." By March 1968 Harry McPherson reiterated his concern about Johnson's excessive demands for loyalty. "Half-way support for you is to be preferred to total support for Bobby," he argued, "and our rejectees may very well end up over there."[58]

Politically Johnson seemed more defensive than aggressive. He nevertheless appeared to be making some progress. By November 1967 his approval rating had increased by three percentage points over the preceding month. Two-thirds of the people favored continuing the war effort or stepping up the military offensive. A majority of Americans also agreed with his decision not to initiate an unconditional bombing halt. Unfortunately, his combativeness was not coordinated with deliberate attempts to organize his presidential campaign. Aides remained dismayed by Johnson's failure emphatically to announce his candidacy for 1968.[59]

In late November 1967 Senator Eugene McCarthy became the first Democrat to openly challenge Johnson for the nomination. Low on funding and limited in national appeal, his candidacy was regarded by the news media and White House more as a symbol than a real threat. McCarthy had considerable but narrow appeal among former supporters of Adlai Stevenson, especially young adults and the academic community. Still, he was expected to gain support by exploiting the "mood of discontent," and his candidacy demonstrated division within the party. Although few pundits believed he could win the nomination, some speculated that he might compel Johnson's withdrawal if he did well in the early primaries.[60]

The Kennedy camp reacted with mixed emotions. Robert had gained a required "stalking horse" who might diminish his image as an ambitious malcontent if he entered the race. But with McCarthy as the hero of the anti-war movement, Kennedy's candidacy could also appear opportunistic. He had pledged his support to Johnson but stood closer to McCarthy on the issue of Vietnam. And he knew there was no guarantee that Johnson would back him in 1972. "He would die and make Hubert President rather than let me get it," he remarked.[61]

The White House, meanwhile, was nominally concerned about McCarthy. According to O'Brien, Kennedy, not McCarthy, "worried" Johnson. A Harris poll in early December showed the president beating McCarthy 63 percent to 17. By January a Gallup poll showed no movement toward the challenger. Publicly, aides expressed only modest concern, seemingly relieved that the threat came from McCarthy rather than Kennedy. Johnson, too, appeared more anxious about his unannounced challenger. "That little runt will get in," he remarked. "The runt's going to run. I don't care what he says now."[62]

The Kennedy Challenge

Monitoring Kennedy's activities early in 1968, White House aides forwarded assurances and warnings about the prospect of him challenging Johnson for the nomination. Sometimes they felt confident. Roche reminded Johnson that Kennedy risked "total obliteration" if he pursued his presidential ambitions in 1968. The "civil war" within the Democratic party during 1968 would make the nomination in 1972 "worthless." His "new Bobby" image would "go up in smoke" in favor of the "old Bobby" image of "the ruthless, unscrupulous schemer who will stop at nothing in his drive for power." "By 1976," Roche reasoned, "it would be a whole new ballgame—the *Camelot* records will be gathering dust in the attic—and a new generation of Democratic leaders would seek a non-controversial compromise candidate." Although Kennedy was "an arrogant little schmuck," he was sufficiently astute to "play it safe."[63]

At other times aides feared that Kennedy's emotionalism might blind him to political reason. Wattenberg noted that Richard Scammon, the director of the Elections Research Center, thought "Bobby Kennedy would be 'crazy' to challenge you in 1968—and then we all speculated as to whether or not he was crazy." "Bobby is an emotional fellow," James Rowe warned. "He is quite capable of jumping off the deep end." Roche pondered, "How rational is Bobby?" Uncertain, he urged Johnson to take further measures to protect himself. Kennedy was "sponsoring a 'War of Liberation' against you and your administration," but he was still undecided about moving from "random guerrilla attacks" to organizing his "Main Force Units." Noting that "Bobby is no more decisive than you are when torn by conflicting sentiments," Roche suggested that precautionary "actions" might dissuade him while Johnson's inattention to the Democratic party machinery only encouraged him. By challenging McCarthy, Johnson might discourage Kennedy from announcing his candidacy. If McCarthy suffered "a couple of real beatings" in the early primaries, Kennedy would likely "keep his cool." Johnson needed to "take charge, get on those ballots, reorganize the DNC, and we will break their backs." Rowe concurred that "we are doing *nothing*" to remind Kennedy that his own ambitions might destroy the party as well as his own career. He recommended that someone "open conversations" with Kennedy.[64]

Considering Johnson's chronic fear of elections, the memoranda likely heightened his anxiety. He began to consider withdrawing from the race. In January 1968 he wrote a statement which he planned to read at the end of his State of the Union Address, announcing his intention not to seek re-election. An old political friend, John Connally, supported the move, arguing that a "delay in announcement helps Bobby, who is already free to operate while others are not." Several aides sensed the end was near. "Should you decide not to run," Roche wrote, "I hope you will give a few of us enough advance notice so we can escape from the country."[65]

At the last moment Johnson decided against the announcement. He had received assurances that the war of attrition in Vietnam was taking its toll. Polls indicated that the only Republican challenger who could defeat him was Nelson Rockefeller, but political pundits speculated that the party would likely turn to Nixon. Johnson felt relatively confident that he could defeat Nixon in a general election. His reluctance therefore to announce his withdrawal in January 1968 may have been prompted by signs of hope. "When a great ship cuts through the sea," he noted in his State of the Union Address, "the waters are always stirred and troubled. And our ship is moving—and it's moving through troubled new waters, and it's moving toward new and better shores."[66]

Whatever hope Johnson sustained, it dissolved on January 31, 1968. On the first day of the Vietnamese New Year, or Tet, Viet Cong forces launched a concerted attack upon principal American strongholds in South Vietnam. Although American forces inflicted significant casualties upon the Viet Cong and regained most of the positions lost, the enemy's surprising strength shattered public support for the war. Over the next several weeks, approval of Johnson's handling of the war dropped from 40 percent to 26 percent. Seven major newspapers, including the *Wall Street Journal*, *New York Post*, and *St. Louis Post-Dispatch*, turned against the administration's policy. So did such major newsweeklies as *Life*, *Look*, *Time*, and *Newsweek* as well as CBS and NBC television.[67]

As the party's only announced peace candidate, McCarthy stood to gain considerably from events. But a poll conducted by *Time* two weeks before the March New Hampshire primary showed him with only 11 percent support. Kennedy, meanwhile, found it difficult to remain neutral. Dutton advised him to assert publicly that Saigon must "broaden its popular base—in effect, the real problem remains in South Viet Nam. . . ." Speaking in Chicago on February 8, Kennedy contended that the Tet offensive had "shattered the mask of official illusion." He called on the nation to free itself from "wishful thinking, false hopes, and sentimental dreams." He argued that the "current regime in Saigon is unwilling or incapable of being an effective ally" and demanded that the nation "be told the truth about this war." Kennedy's latest barrage, *Newsweek* reported, was his "bitterest broadside yet at the President's conduct of the Vietnam War."[68]

White House aides were disturbed by Kennedy's attack, especially his questioning of the legitimacy of the South Vietnamese government. McPherson contended that South Vietnam's stability was not properly recognized by either the press or congressional supporters. Those with whom he had spoken believed that "Kennedy's attack was absolutely irresponsible." He acknowledged that the government there was flawed, but chaos would ensue if it were dissolved. He wanted the White House to launch a public relations counteroffensive to convey these points.[69]

Johnson did not choose to criticize Kennedy and was instead consoled by selected polls showing him leading both McCarthy and Kennedy. He learned, for example, that he had outpolled McCarthy seventy to five among Iowa Democratic county chairmen; he also led Kennedy fifty-nine to ten. On the memorandum Johnson scribbled, "Send to Drew Pearson, Winchell & Spivak." Dissatisfied with Johnson's mild response, Roche requested permission to appear on television with Pierre Salinger in order to debate the topic, "The Liberals and the President." "[W]e can't let these programs be monopolized by our opponents—by default," he reasoned.[70]

Amidst the latest political struggle, a controversy arose which underscored Johnson's dilemma with the Kennedy "mystique." In February 1968 Johnson became alarmed by the publication of Evelyn Lincoln's *Kennedy and Johnson*. In her book the late president's secretary asserted that she had heard John Kennedy say in late October 1963 that he intended to deny Johnson the vice-presidential nomination in 1964 and select North Carolina Governor Terry Sanford. The accusation carried two implications. First, its timing was suspicious in light of Kennedy's anticipated candidacy. Second, her account threatened Johnson's linkage to John Kennedy.[71]

Johnson's perception of events had always held that John wanted him as his running mate; it was only Robert who wanted him off the ticket. After receiving a *New York Times* clipping, Johnson ordered a check on a small factual matter contained within Lincoln's account, hoping to use the error to discredit the broader charge. "*An interesting question, to me,*" Marvin Watson responded, "*is whether this is one of the '12 anti-LBJ books' Bobby's people have reported were in preparation for 1968*" [emphasis Watson's]. Watson believed that the idea of Sanford replacing Johnson could "only come from Bobby's camp." Johnson later received an article from the *Houston Post* disputing Lincoln's allegation and noting that John Kennedy had wanted to fire her. "This is delightful," George Christian wrote the president. "But, alas, it got all too little coverage."[72]

Kennedy, meanwhile, persisted in challenging the president on the war. By early March rumors circulated that Johnson would request more American troops for Vietnam. The Senate debated the wisdom of escalation, prompting Kennedy to declare that it would be a mistake to do so without first consulting the Senate and gaining public "support and understanding." He charged that "victory is not just ahead of us" and disparaged the South Vietnamese government as corrupt. "When this [corruption] was brought to the attention of the President," Kennedy noted, "he replied that there is stealing in Beaumont, Texas. If there is stealing in Beaumont, Texas, it is not bringing about the death of American boys." He stopped short of calling for a unilateral withdrawal.[73]

While Kennedy attacked, Johnson withdrew into seclusion. In early March *Newsweek* reported an assertion by Kennedy's aides that unless Johnson emerged from the confines of the White House, the senator might challenge him for the nomination. Johnson, meanwhile, received ominous warnings. "I am told that Robert Kennedy is giving out PT boat tie clasps," one aide wrote. "Very interesting. "[Hugh] Sidey said that Kennedy has almost a mystique about his future," another memorandum read, "that he has it 'all inside him' that he has to do it."[74]

The Kennedy camp felt increasingly confident about challenging Johnson. On March 12, the day of the New Hampshire primary, Schlesinger spoke with Bill Moyers, who surmised that the president would avoid a confrontation with Kennedy if he declared his candidacy. Although Moyers had left the White House in 1967, he knew Johnson well enough to sense that he was removed from reality and perhaps "paranoid." Johnson "flees from confrontations," Moyers told Schlesinger. "He is willing to take on people like Goldwater or Nixon, to whom he feels superior. But he does not like confrontations when he does not feel superior."[75]

That night Johnson "lost" the New Hampshire primary when Eugene McCarthy received 42.4 percent of the vote compared with Johnson's 49.5 percent. "I must admit," Johnson recalled, "that the results . . . surprised me." He had not visited the state, knowing it would be interpreted as a sign of panic for an incumbent president to campaign in a primary. Nevertheless, few pundits expected McCarthy to receive the percentage of votes that he did, and consequently the media quickly declared him the "victor."[76]

McCarthy's "victory" had serious implications for Kennedy. "I just don't know what Johnson is thinking," Kennedy wrote columnist Anthony Lewis the next day. "My basic inclination and reaction was to try and let the future take care of itself." Publicly he announced that he was "reassessing the possibility" of running for president. The White House offered no official response and aides affected an air of "stoic unconcern." Staff members reviewed possible scenarios and concluded that McCarthy had served as Kennedy's "stalking horse." Continuing to regard Kennedy as their more serious threat, some urged Johnson to enter the next several primaries. They set about collecting old McCarthy and Kennedy quotes. McCarthy's record was intended to portray him as unpatriotic. The Kennedy quotations showed him "a vigorous defender of the Administration's Vietnam policy when his brother sent the first American troops." Advisers also planned for John Connally to arrange a press conference with a planted question about Kennedy's anticipated candidacy. He would note that it was "not the least bit surprising because Senator Kennedy has a long and proven record of treachery." Although Connally's known disdain for Kennedy could make his criticism moot, it might "give the press terminology to use."[77]

Aides continued to assure Johnson that Kennedy would suffer severe repercussions if he announced his candidacy; many reporters felt that Kennedy would be "stabbing" both Johnson and McCarthy "in the back" if he entered the race. George Reedy argued that Kennedy would appear as a "peace-at-any-price" candidate. Although the senator would be difficult to beat in the upcoming Wisconsin primary, "At most he can be a 'spoiler' who tears up the Democratic Party." Johnson needed to "play it cool" and to concentrate on clear declarations of policy. "This situation is not good right now, but *it can be mastered.*"[78]

Johnson, meanwhile, tried to strike a private deal with Kennedy. In previous months the two camps had privately discussed the possibility that Johnson might appoint a commission to review American policy in Vietnam. In return, Kennedy would not declare his candidacy. The day after the New Hampshire primary, Johnson requested from Kennedy a list of prospective appointees to such a commission. On Thursday Robert Kennedy, Edward Kennedy, and Theodore Sorensen met secretly with Johnson's liaison Clark Clifford. The three men proposed a list of former New Frontiersmen, including Robert, to be named to the commission. Robert also insisted that Johnson declare American Vietnam policy a failure. A White House aide called Kennedy's proposal "the damnedest piece of political blackmail" he had ever heard. Johnson rejected the idea, believing it would appear to be a blatant "deal."[79]

Two days later Kennedy announced his candidacy, issuing his statement in the Senate caucus room, the same place his late brother had announced his candidacy eight years before. Aides had regularly reminded Kennedy of his duty to carry on his brother's legacy. A draft of Kennedy's announcement underscored the purpose of the campaign for many of his supporters. "When he took office," it read, "President Johnson said 'let us continue.' For a brief period that was our course. . . . It is time once again to go to the American people—to point to that proud heritage—and say this time truly, 'let us continue.' " Although the passage was not included in Kennedy's announcement, enough of the Kennedy image was evoked to remind observers distinctly of John's earlier campaign.[80]

For Johnson the 1968 campaign appeared to be a horrid re-run of 1960. An article by Louis Harris was sent to the president drawing parallels between the two campaigns. Polls indicated that, like his brother, Robert had the support of blue-collar and minority voters. McCarthy's appeal to intellectuals and suburbanites was comparable to Adlai Stevenson's. Johnson, meanwhile, was burdened by the same ambivalence and disorganization that had marked his 1960 bid. "Kennedy's hopes," *Newsweek* reported, "hinge on the calculation that LBJ may turn out to be as much of a paper tiger this time as he proved to be in Los Angeles eight years ago."[81]

Aides forwarded encouraging messages to the president. Associated Press reporter Jim Marlow "despises Bobby Kennedy, and thinks he is the most contemptible political figure he has ever known." Anna Rosenberg Hoffman, a congressional liaison under Roosevelt, maintained that "many newspaper people . . . feel that Bobby is cheap and crooked." Johnson received articles comparing him favorably with both Kennedy and McCarthy. On Monitor radio Al Capp contended that the "only thing wrong with Lyndon Johnson is that 'he has done everything right but with the wrong accent.' "[82]

Other letters indicated private support. A long-time Kennedy acquaintance wrote to assure Johnson that he was "unalterably opposed" to Kennedy's candidacy. Congressman Richard Bolling informed Johnson that he would announce his support for the president by declaring that "Bob Kennedy is an old and close personal friend of his, sincere, patriotic, but wrong." Sources outside the White House cited widespread anti-Kennedy sentiment in various parts of the country; the senator's "vitriolic attacks" on the president had hurt his candidacy. "You are the most popular living figure on college campuses today!!" exclaimed an assessment of a recent poll. "A certain young candidate with a youthful haircut was not mentioned at all."[83]

There were further signs of encouragement. A Gallup poll indicated Kennedy was only slightly ahead of Johnson, 44 to 41 percent. Analyzing the data, an aide noted that Kennedy's announced candidacy "gained him little support" among Democrats. A Harris poll conducted on the day of the New Hampshire primary indicated that Johnson and Kennedy each had 40 percent of the national vote. More important, there had been a "continuing decline for Kennedy since October." Fifty-eight percent of the nation perceived him as "opportunistic." Whereas 38 percent of the public agreed with Johnson's Vietnam position, only 29 percent supported Robert's. It was Johnson's leadership, not his position on Vietnam, to which large segments of the electorate objected. And he still had considerable authority as commander-in-chief and leader of the party with which to manipulate events.[84]

Other news was less encouraging. Johnson was reminded that many factions of the press, such as the *Washington Post*, were partial to Kennedy. McPherson called attention to a *New York Times* story about a meeting of Johnson's "big contributors" in the state. The story "typifies what's wrong with our campaign," McPherson wrote. "We have a few fat-cats in New York; Kennedy has the bosses, the reformers, the young people, etc. It's a 'bad image for Johnson.' " He was also informed that the Kennedy camp was trying to win over Johnson supporters. A *Newsweek* poll of potential delegates to the convention revealed that Johnson "is markedly vulnerable to a Kennedy-McCarthy challenge" and "may be in real danger of being dumped by his party." By late March public opinion reflected the full impact of Kennedy's announced candidacy. A Gallup poll indicated that Kennedy now led Johnson by 13 percentage points. "Psychologically," Fred Panzer warned the president, "the release date will give Bobby a lift."[85]

At times Johnson seemed inspired by Kennedy's challenge. "If he wasn't in this before Bobby announced," James Rowe told reporters, "he's in it up to his neck now. He will not turn this country over to Bobby—not a chance." Aides contended that Johnson's passivity was temporary; he was allowing the "excitement over Kennedy" to die down. "The President doesn't intend to lie down and get run over by Bobby Kennedy," an aide asserted. "When the President decides that the timing is right you are going to see him put up one hell of a fight." In the days following Kennedy's announcement, Johnson encouraged administration representatives to defend his policies in Wisconsin, and he directed his New York forces, led by Edwin Weisl, to pressure uncommitted party leaders. Johnson himself utilized several ceremonial occasions to attack his rival. "We love nothing more than peace," he noted before the National Farmers Union convention, "but we hate nothing more than surrender. . . . We don't plan to let people

. . . pressure us and force us to divide our nation in a time of national peril." "Lyndon B. Johnson had wasted no time hacking out a strategy for the campaign months ahead," *Newsweek* reported: "whirlwind forays into the heartland, paced by a rhetorical barrage aimed ostensibly at Ho Chi Minh but really designed to bring down Kennedy."[86]

Johnson's efforts were illusory. Beyond occasional tough talk before selected audiences, he did little else to help himself. When asked about Kennedy's candidacy he feigned indifference. "I would have no comment on Senator Kennedy's entrance other than to say I was not surprised," he told reporters. "And I could have made this statement to you this time last year." As in 1960 he acted as the dutiful public servant with little time for the trivialities of a political campaign. Instead of barnstorming the country he dispatched cabinet officials to defend the administration. Some aides were alarmed that he was handing over "center stage" to Kennedy. "He's trying to hold a sort of Maginot Line against a blitzkrieg," one aide told *Newsweek*. "Sometimes I wonder if he really might be thinking of not running."[87]

Trying to re-direct the president, McPherson sent a ten-page memorandum criticizing the current strategy; it "will lead either to Kennedy's nomination or Nixon's election, or both." Johnson needed to show that he, too, was "restlessly eager to change things." McPherson noted that on Vietnam, Kennedy "offers the change to a dove policy, together with the reputation of a tough guy who could somehow prevent us from being hurt by following a softer line." On domestic matters, Kennedy proposed "radical changes" designed to unify the young, old, and blacks. "He will try to occupy the same relation to you that his brother Jack occupied to the Eisenhower-Nixon Administration: imagination and vitality vs. staleness and weariness, movement vs. entrenchment, hope of change vs. more of the status quo." And although Kennedy had been criticized as opportunistic, he was "cynical enough to believe that [young liberals] will forget, given time, razz-ma-tazz, and the development of momentum behind his candidacy. He is right about that."

To meet the Kennedy challenge, McPherson recommended that Johnson move to the left on both foreign and domestic issues by de-escalating the war and showing greater concern for urban violence; thus preventing Kennedy from appearing as the "responsible politician who cares." Meanwhile, Johnson should court coalitions that were anti-Kennedy, work to nullify Kennedy's and McCarthy's "sex appeal," cultivate support in Congress, and travel to cities lacking strong anti-war movements in order to "create the impression that you can go anywhere." "The purpose of this memorandum," he concluded, "is to suggest that a moving target is better than a stationary one—on the issues and physically."[88]

Other aides devised a scathing television campaign. "Kennedy lends himself to satire and ridicule, at top level," an aide wrote Johnson. "Others can deal with his record of ingratitude, treachery, backstabbing and self-ishness. Both ought to be pressed hard and quickly, before mothers begin feeling motherly towards him." One proposed commercial was intended to mock his appearance: "Today we saw Senator Bugs Bunny playing Hamlet. Yesterday he was offering his blood to the Vietcong. He's certainly a *boy* for all seasons." Another voice-over consisted of a two-pronged attack against Kennedy's wealth and manhood: "It's not that Bobby's a bad *boy*—he means well—but he just doesn't know any better. *That's the way it always is with the rich.*" "A Strong Man in a Tough Job" read a proposed Johnson slogan. The strategy illustrated Johnson's unresolved struggle to reconcile his own insecurities with the "mystique." Reminiscent of his attacks against John Kennedy in 1960, Johnson sought to disparage Robert's youth, inexperience, and privilege. "Young Jack" had been replaced by "a bad boy."[89]

In contending with the "mystique," Johnson received assurances that John and Robert were not interchangeable. "As you so well know," wrote a long-time associate of Robert, "Bobby is not of equal character and standing as that of his distinguished brother, the late President Kennedy." Johnson received an article by Roscoe Drummond which disparaged Robert's attempt to campaign "in a manner to evoke the image and memory" of John. Drummond criticized those who would vote for Robert based on his identification with the late president. "A legend cannot serve as President of the United States," he concluded. "Robert F. Kennedy is not John F. Kennedy. Bobby is not Jack." He noted that John would not have reversed course on Vietnam as easily as his brother had. "It seems unlikely," Drummond wrote, "that John F. Kennedy would ever attack the President as Robert attacked Mr. Johnson."[90]

In an attempt to minimize the impact of the "mystique," the White House staff sought to publicize the "darker" elements of Robert's image. One proposal to "seriously damage the RFK image" consisted of publicizing his attempt to censor books about his brother. McPherson also wanted to parallel Robert's attacks on Vietnam policy with Joseph Kennedy's defeatist attitude toward Hitler in the 1930s. Another aide thought that "the present idolatry of Bobby could be turned against him." "Can you imagine John F. Kennedy permitting people to ruffle his hair and manhandle him?" he asked. "Do people really want a President whom they can pinch, pull, squeeze and hug?"[91]

As part of the effort to gauge the "mystique," aides assessed Robert's telegenic skills. During the past year Kennedy had devoted considerable energy to refining his television image, and he searched for opportunities to promote his personality. He was well aware that his popularity owed much to "impressionistic" elements fostered by television. Dutton had regularly advised him to participate in visually "interesting human situations" and "action" shots in order to strengthen his "nonpolitical impression." He recommended consultations with television specialists in order to appear less "hot" and more "cool," as his brother had. "The new politics must think pictures, not words," Dutton asserted, a fact that Johnson understood but could seldom bring himself to practice effectively.[92]

Johnson's aides were divided in their assessment of Kennedy's television presence. Analyzing his announcement of his candidacy, Reedy noted that, on the surface, it was "forceful," "professional and well staged." "However, he is *NOT* an imposing figure and nothing can make him into one. He has charm but does not give the feeling of wisdom and reassurance that people like to see in a President." He noted a number of image problems haunting Kennedy, most notably his opportunism. "Finally," Reedy assured, "despite all of his assets (name, money, experience, ability to command headlines, close relationships with publicists, organization, etc.) it is still difficult to see Kennedy as President. He just doesn't look big enough and regardless of what the newspapers may say, I have a feeling that his TV appearances accentuated this point."[93]

Other assessments were less assuring. Although Kennedy appeared in a "highly nervous condition" during public appearances, aides warned that his appeal transcended such inadequacies. "Bobby did 'very poorly' on the *Meet the Press* 'by logical standards,'" read one assessment, "but this campaign is not logical. Many people—not ordinary Kennedy partisans— thought he was great. 'It's the way people come across to the nerve ends, not to the brain, that counts.'" Updates on Kennedy's appearances on the nightly news confirmed his ability to use television as an emotional device. One summary noted that he had received a "wild welcome" in Watts, gained "remarkable momentum," and "acquired the mystical Kennedy magic."[94]

While some White House aides assessed Kennedy's appeal, others sought to lay claim to the "mystique." When Lawrence O'Brien toured Wisconsin he reminded audiences that Johnson was "John Kennedy's choice for Vice President and thus the true inheritor of the New Frontier." McPherson wanted to use recordings of "two or three most forthcoming [Robert] Kennedy endorsements of the President," especially his laudatory comments at the New York Democratic dinner the previous June. Another aide wanted to exploit Robert's quote from Theodore White's 1964 campaign book in which he had stated "that if he could not be President himself he thought Lyndon B. Johnson better qualified for the Presidency than any other man he knew." By using Robert to endorse Johnson, aides wanted to demonstrate his two-faced opportunism. But they may also have valued the senator's praise; an endorsement by any Kennedy seemingly increased Johnson's stature.[95]

Johnson was also advised to appropriate certain Kennedy images for his own purposes. Cater recommended the creation of a band of intellectual supporters called "Thinking People for LBJ" to serve as "the counterpart" of a similar group formed four years earlier. A full-page advertisement listing its members would "counteract the bandwagon psychology of the Kennedy group." Young people were also targeted. Except for being drafted, Rostow noted, college students felt generally "ignored" by the administration and were therefore drawn to McCarthy and Kennedy. Johnson should consider using a special assistant to renew dialogue with young adults and sponsoring a rock'n'roll band to play at political rallies. "It is not difficult," Reedy observed, "to get some kids with long hair and fancy clothes and give them a title such as 'The Black Beards' or 'The White Beards' and turn them loose."[96]

Johnson was sent four pages of recommendations, many of which appeared to mirror the Kennedy image. Cater had been disturbed by Johnson's poor image, warning the president that he should not try to "counteract Bobby by impassioned stump speeches." Thus far, Johnson's television sound bites projected "an angry, embittered and isolated leader. This is not the best image to put up against Kennedy's emotional one." Seeking to evoke a more visceral appeal, Cater recommended "a series of *action images of the President at work*." He suggested eighteen photo-opportunities, including walking tours of urban and rural poverty areas, meetings with young staff members, being surrounded by his grandchildren in the Oval Office, a museum tour or attendance at a cultural event, and an appearance with Kennedy's brother-in-law Sargent Shriver.[97]

Johnson himself may have intended to partially evoke the "mystique" when he traveled to Dallas in February for the first time since the assassination and passed within two hundred yards of the Texas School Book Depository. Aides had warned him that, because it was his first trip to the city since the assassination, press attention would be high. A draft of his scheduled speech was "strong on praise for President Kennedy—if it were not, there would certainly be adverse comment." Johnson subsequently made reference to "that great President John Fitzgerald Kennedy," but the need for such heedfulness was increasingly difficult. He had been receiving newspaper clippings noting that Kennedy's death "created a myth [that] put the subsequent President at a disadvantage" and referring to him as a "second husband."[98]

The debate over Johnson's image-management strategy illustrated his entrapment in the "mystique." Aides advised Johnson to attack Kennedy and to undermine the "mystique." But they also suggested that he adopt Robert Kennedy's stance on issues and emulate John Kennedy's image. The advice that Johnson embody the "mystique," however, was poorly considered. In 1968 it would have been folly for him to have presented himself as John Kennedy's surrogate. Vietnam was a policy disaster while poverty and urban violence at home persisted. To try to link mortal failures to a myth would have drawn attention to Johnson's limitations and fallibility. Moreover, Robert's television expertise, his ability to manipulate reporters, his charisma, and his "Kennedy magic" designated him as John's proper surrogate. Indeed, Robert was perhaps even more threatening than John had been in 1960. John was at least required to behave deferentially, respecting Johnson's power as Senate Majority Leader. By 1968, however, Johnson, though president, was highly unpopular and faced insurmountable domestic and foreign policy problems. Vulnerable to attack, he now confronted a Kennedy bolstered by myth and motivated by seeming hatred. Even if he survived Robert's challenge, he would likely face Nixon in the fall—the man who had lost to John Kennedy by only 119,000 votes.

Johnson never emerged from his passive state, squandering his power and resources and enabling Kennedy and others to attack without fear of retribution. In late March he lamented to a friend Kennedy's expert organization and media skills. "However, I can't do anything about it," he explained. "I've got too much to do here. . . . If they want Bobby Kennedy, that's what they'll get; and they may wind up with Nixon in the end." On March 31, 1968, Johnson announced on television steps to de-escalate the war. After reaffirming his commitment to John Kennedy's inaugural pledge to "bear any burden" to ensure the defense of liberty, Johnson asserted that military commitments abroad required unity at home. In that spirit he announced that he would neither seek nor accept the nomination of his party for a second term. He would instead concentrate on seeking a peaceful solution to the war.[99]

In a short press conference that followed, Johnson maintained that his decision was "completely irrevocable" and had been under consideration since the previous November. Asked if Kennedy's entrance contributed to the timing of the announcement, he acknowledged that "it added to the general situation [of disunity] I talked about that existed in the country." Aides informed reporters that, although many factors contributed to Johnson's decision, the division within the party had "hurt him most." "The

President would have had to go out and plead with the people and defend himself, and try to raise money, and try to round up delegates," one aide told a reporter. "He just didn't have the time—and he didn't have the stomach for it." "I'm tired," Johnson told a friend immediately after his speech. "I'm tired of feeling rejected by the American people. I'm tired of waking up in the middle of the night worrying about the war. I'm tired of all these personal attacks on me."[100]

Years later Lyndon Johnson confided to Doris Kearns why he did not seek re-election. The Tet offensive, the pyrrhic New Hampshire victory, and the criticism of the Kerner Report on civil rights violence overwhelmed him. He had suffered from dreams, one of which placed him paralyzed in bed while he listened to his assistants in the next room dividing up his power. He was unable to talk or walk, and no aide was there to comfort him. The dream reflected the realities of 1968 and his belief that everyone had turned against him: "rioting blacks, demonstrating students, marching welfare mothers, squawking professors, and hysterical reporters." "And then the final straw," he told Kearns. "The thing I feared from the first day of my Presidency was actually coming true. Robert Kennedy had openly announced his intention to reclaim the throne in the memory of his brother. And the American people, swayed by the magic of the name, were dancing in the streets. The whole situation was unbearable for me."[101]

Scholars, journalists, and White House aides have debated the source of Johnson's resignation. Kearns concluded that it was a shrewd political ploy; if he could create an image of putting himself above politics and find a peaceful solution to the war, the party would nominate him by acclamation. Others cited his serious heart problems and his desire to become better acquainted with his family and grandchildren. Still others believed that Johnson's "resignation" was intended to undermine Kennedy. Columnist Carl Rowan, for example, noted that Johnson's speech portrayed the senator as an "overambitious young man who has put his lust for power above his country's future." Kennedy would find it difficult to contend that he had a greater desire for peace than Johnson when the latter "has made the ultimate political sacrifice in an effort to end the war." Moreover, Kennedy had an easier target in Johnson than either McCarthy or Humphrey.[102]

Reflecting on Johnson's withdrawal statement twenty years later, the president's chief of staff, James Jones, contended that Johnson wanted to be free of partisan handicaps which might deter his effort to end the war. "I can state categorically," he wrote, "that fear of losing the 1968 election was not the reason he retired." In recalling Johnson's decision-making process, however, Jones confirmed the atmosphere of fear that Kennedy's candidacy had brought to the White House. Before Johnson announced his decision, he met with Vice President Humphrey and showed him a copy of the withdrawal statement. "When [Humphrey] got to the final paragraph," Jones wrote, "the Vice President's face flushed, his eyes watered and he protested that Mr. Johnson could not step down." Humphrey looked "pathetic at that moment." "There's no way," he said softly, "I can beat the Kennedys."[103]

Humphrey knew that he would not be running only against Robert. He would be opposing "the Kennedys"—an enigmatic force composed of Robert, John, Edward, the widow, the New Frontiersmen, the media, the magic, the legacy, the "mystique." Like Johnson, Humphrey had once been humiliated by the Kennedys, losing to John during the crucial 1960 West Virginia primary. What had immediately distressed the vice president was not the enormity of the task before him but the thought of serving as Johnson's surrogate in a battle against John's avatar.

Coming Home

The day after Johnson's withdrawal from the 1968 campaign, Robert Kennedy sent the president a telegram calling the decision "truly magnanimous" and requesting a private conference "in the interest of national unity during the coming months." Johnson was hostile: "I won't bother answering that grand-standing little runt." The last time the two men had met, he had vowed to destroy Kennedy. Fourteen months later Johnson himself had self-destructed. Nevertheless, having removed himself from the race and no longer fearful of Robert, Johnson appeared "relieved" and "relaxed." He acquiesced to a meeting.[104]

The conference took place on April 3 in the cabinet room and included Theodore Sorensen as well as White House staff member Charles Murphy and national security adviser Walter Rostow. Johnson began by noting the nation's troubled time and the need for unity. He briefed Kennedy about the Vietnam War, the explosive Middle East situation, and problems concerning the budget, noting the difficulty of coping with these problems while under attack from political opponents. He doubted that their opinions would be far apart if they "sat at the same table." Johnson explained that he had withdrawn from the race to avoid the impression that his actions in Vietnam were motivated by self-interest. He planned to remain out of the campaign and had "no desire to be a political boss or to determine the Senator's future."

Kennedy called Johnson's speech "magnificent," "unselfish," and "courageous." He appreciated the briefing and suggested that subsequent discussions be arranged to avoid future misunderstandings. Kennedy regretted that "we have not had closer contact." Much of their miscommunication "was my fault." "People try to divide us," Johnson conceded, "and we both suffer from it." He, too, wanted to renew their dialogue.

Curious about the "political situation," Kennedy tried to gauge Johnson's intentions. "Where do I stand in the campaign?" he asked. "Are you opposed to my effort and will you marshal forces against me?" Johnson assured him that he wanted to avoid politicizing the presidency. "I'm not that pure," he noted, "but I am that scared. The situation of the country is critical." He did not know if Humphrey would run and said he would not offer advice on the matter. Although he had affection for the vice president, he reminded Kennedy that it would defeat his purpose to campaign for someone else. Johnson did, however, offer a cautionary note: "future developments" could change his thinking. "I might have to disagree with you tomorrow," he warned. "I might say who I'm going to vote for, but I do not plan to do so. I do not want to mislead or deceive you, and I must preserve my freedom of action. . . ." Kennedy asked Johnson to talk with him first should he decide to endorse a candidate. "Yes," Johnson replied, "unless I lose my head and pop off. I will try to honor your request."

Next, Johnson spoke "very eloquently and movingly" about the 1960 Democratic convention. Claiming that he had been reluctant to seek the presidential nomination or to accept the vice presidency, Johnson would have preferred to remain Senate Majority Leader—"the best job he ever had." But Sam Rayburn and Philip Graham had persuaded him otherwise, and he wanted to help the late president carry the South. He reminded Robert that John "had always treated him well as Vice President," despite their differences. Robert agreed that Johnson had served loyally.

Reflecting further on the past, Johnson linked himself to the Kennedy legacy. He had tried to avoid running for president in 1964. Indeed, he had never wanted to be president "and had been counting the days to the end of his term ever since the beginning." Believing that Robert "did not understand his feelings about President Kennedy," he elaborated on the bond he felt toward John. As vice president he had entered into a "partnership" with President Kennedy, a partnership that continued into his own presidency. Indeed, it blossomed into a deep sense of "duty to look after the family and the members of the firm, which they had formed together." He had never fired a New Frontiersman and felt "no bitterness or vindictiveness" toward Robert. The press, he contended, "greatly exaggerated the differences" between them. Attempting to reach out and belong, Johnson said he had "never thought of his Administration as just the Johnson Administration, but as a continuation of the Kennedy-Johnson Administration. It was carrying on a family matter."

245

Johnson's reference to "a family matter" carried important connotations. He spoke not only of his wish to attach himself to the "mystique" but of his resolve in coming to terms with John and Robert Kennedy. In defeat he may have been able to reconcile his feelings toward the Kennedys. Having previously perceived the two brothers as two polarities, Johnson, by bowing out, had now linked them directly. John and Robert were bonded into a single entity of which Johnson was a vital component, for he served as an interlude between two Kennedy presidencies. John and Robert were neither "good" nor "bad"; they were "family." As a member of the "family," Johnson could neither lose to the Kennedys nor beat them because he was among them.

Next, Johnson explained that he had "done his best" to "carry on policies and programs," and believed he had done "reasonably well." He told Robert that "as President Kennedy looked down at him every day from then until now, he would agree that he had kept the faith." He conceded that his efforts "had not been good enough." Perhaps alluding to Robert, he noted that, in light of the current difficulties, the "next man who sits in this chair will have to do better." Kennedy responded: "You are a brave and dedicated man." According to Sorensen, these words "stuck in his throat, and Johnson asked him to repeat it." Kennedy had said what Johnson had longed to hear; he had received the sympathy and approval of the heir to the Kennedy legacy. Cementing the bond, Johnson again denied any hostility toward Robert and disavowed the anguish that had consumed him for eight years: "He wants Senator Kennedy to know that he doesn't hate him, he doesn't dislike him, and that he still regards himself as carrying out the Kennedy/Johnson partnership." Later that day Johnson met informally with two old friends, Drew Pearson and David Karr, and reiterated the "partnership" he felt with John Kennedy as vice president. Karr found Johnson's delusional behavior "terrifying."[105]

The sincerity of Johnson's conversation is questionable. Although Kennedy, who was always wary of his rival's emotional manipulations, seemed persuaded of his genuineness, Johnson was much too shrewd a politician not to have appreciated the meeting's larger implications. By withdrawing from the race he was forced to acknowledge a direct line from John to Robert—a line to which he never truly belonged. His claim of a partnership likely reflected a desperate search for approval as he sought to convince himself and others that he was an extension of a more glorious past. His claim to family membership was transparent. Part of him had always been contemptuous of the Kennedys. He had been bitter toward Robert, disdainful of New Frontiersmen, and determined to distinguish himself from the Kennedys. But with an eye toward history, Johnson "wheeled and dealed" the "mystique," hoping to restore his name. Indeed, he included verbatim notes of the meeting in the text of his memoir.[106]

In terms of his immediate concerns, Johnson's reflections on the "family" and "partnership" may also have been sentimental trimmings, intended perhaps to lure Kennedy into complacency. By assuring Kennedy that he felt no animosity toward him, he may have sought to dissuade him from attacking the administration, making it easier to maneuver Vice President Humphrey's nomination. Kennedy did indeed ease his public criticism of Johnson, while Johnson sometimes seemed to flirt with the idea of re-entering the race. A Draft Johnson for President Committee was formed in Virginia, and conservative Democratic members of Congress commented publicly about the possibility of drafting the president. Reporters speculated that he could become a compromise candidate if the Democratic National Convention resulted in a stalemate. By late April the Associated Press characterized Johnson as "a most tantalizing noncandidate." At a fund-raising dinner in Chicago he teased an audience by periodically flirting with a dramatic announcement declaring his candidacy. He reminded the public that his withdrawal "does not mean that I am just going to be an uninterested or passive bystander."[107]

Johnson also continued to monitor Kennedy's campaign. He was briefed on television appearances by Kennedy spokespersons and provided with the assessments of political columnists. A report from Pennsylvania noted that the senator had been losing strength since entering the race. Although the Kennedy name remained popular, "the more he exposes himself the more people realize he is not Jack Kennedy." After Kennedy condemned the Vietnam War in late April, Johnson's staff assistant, Fred Panzer, recommended "letters to the editor, floor speeches, and column plants to offset Senator Kennedy's great retreat." He also suggested that critics quote John Kennedy's statements supporting the Vietnam War. Just days before the California primary, Johnson boasted that the record of his administration was accomplished without benefit of "charisma and style."[108]

Johnson's political interest in Kennedy became moot on June 5 when the senator was shot in Los Angeles shortly after winning the California primary. "Oh my God!" Johnson responded. "Not again. Don't tell me its happened all over again." He received numerous "gloomy" updates about Kennedy's condition and sent administration officials friendly with the Kennedys to the hospital to "signify your personal concern to the family." He arranged to have members of the Kennedy family flown to Los Angeles and assigned Secret Service protection to the senator and other candidates. Johnson's concern seemed genuine. He rejected a request to help generate "a good feature" story on his response to the assassination and his effort to assist the Kennedy family.[109]

While Kennedy lay unconscious, the president spoke to the nation in a televised address. He expressed remorse and joined the American people in prayers for the senator's full recovery—for the country's sake, for his family's sake, and "in memory of his brother, our beloved late President." After Kennedy's death on June 6 Johnson again addressed the nation, calling the occasion "a time of tragedy and loss." He spoke in glowing terms about the senator's dedication to the people and declared a national day of mourning. He also arranged to have Kennedy's body flown to New York City. The Kennedy organization questioned whether to invite Johnson to the funeral, but the president nevertheless attended services at St. Patrick's Cathedral, consoled members of the immediate family, and was present at the burial at Arlington. Jacqueline, Ethel, and Rose Kennedy later sent letters of gratitude.[110]

Johnson was visibly disturbed by the events. McPherson remembered him being "terribly agitated" and "filled with a hundred competing emotions." Lady Bird recorded in her diary a sense of "unreality about the whole thing. . . . It had all happened before." She and the president watched replays of the assassination on television for hours at a time. But competing with Johnson's emotions were the political implications of Kennedy's death—what might have happened had he not withdrawn from the race. With Robert Kennedy gone, Johnson, as the incumbent, would have been difficult to beat at the convention. His own favorite, Humphrey, was assured the nomination.[111]

Johnson also felt curiously cheated by Kennedy's death. McPherson recalled that Johnson had been "resigned" to a Kennedy presidency. Having struggled for five years under illusions of what the future might hold based on a glorified sense of the past, Robert's presidency would have finally revealed the "mystique" for what it was. "It would have been hard on me to watch Bobby march to 'Hail to the Chief,'" Johnson recalled, "but I almost wish he had become President so the country could finally see a flesh-and-blood Kennedy grappling with the daily work of the Presidency and all the inevitable disappointments, instead of their story book image of great heroes who, because they were dead, could make anything anyone wanted happen."[112]

Johnson resisted the open displays of grief he had shown after John Kennedy's death. "This nation," Reedy advised, "cannot afford to wallow in another orgy of self-flagellation." On the day the senator was buried, Liz Carpenter expressed concern that the nation might "be permanently brainwashed by high drama." "The spectacular we have just watched must not make hollow your five years of real progress in the presidency, nor must it make hollow a victory by the Vice President." She called for "some quick dramatic actions" to show the president's ability to handle "the issue of violence" and to "provide some *other* kinds of stories." Although ambivalent, press secretary George Christian also recommended "high impact" dramatic actions.[113]

Robert's death complicated Johnson's struggle with the Kennedy "mystique." Now two martyred Kennedys would haunt the administration through its final days. As in 1963, Johnson heard oblique accusations that he was somehow responsible for Robert's death. Why, it was asked, had he not assigned Secret Service protection to the senator earlier? Letters to the White House demanded that he resign and relinquish the presidency to Edward Kennedy. Robert's death seemed to re-fortify the "mystique." A new wave of articles comparing Johnson's achievements with the previous administration crossed the president's desk. Political strategies designed to identify Humphrey with the Kennedy legacy were debated. Rumors circulated that Humphrey might choose Edward Kennedy as his running-mate. When Jacqueline Kennedy married Aristotle Onassis in October 1968, a sense of relief was felt at the White House. "That'll sure take its toll on the Kennedy myth," Johnson remarked to Joseph Califano. "I feel strangely freer," Lady Bird wrote in her diary. "No shadow walks beside me down the hall of the White House or here at Camp David. I wonder what it would have been like if we had entered this life unaccompanied by that shadow?"[114]

Except for his obligatory comments following Robert's death, Johnson did not mention the senator in his remaining public addresses. Although his memoir sought to downplay the friction between himself and Robert, he reflected little on his rival's passing. "When tragedy struck him down," he wrote simply, "I was glad that my last meeting with Bobby Kennedy had been friendly." Whereas Robert remained absent from Johnson's public and private expressions, John became his refuge. From June 1968 through January 1969 he reaffirmed his identity with the late president. He reminded audiences of John Kennedy's resolve in Berlin and Cuba as indicative of the United States' determination to stand firm around the world. He noted that during these times of trouble he was frequently reminded of Kennedy's plea for Americans to "Ask not what your country can do for you; ask what you can do for your country." As he campaigned for Humphrey in the fall of 1968 he invoked the name of "our beloved late President, John Kennedy" and reminded audiences of Humphrey's help in the Senate in passing the "Kennedy-Johnson" legislation. "When President Kennedy and I came into office in 1961, the choice that we faced together was quite clear," Johnson told an audience. They could choose either to close their eyes to the nation's problems, "or we could get this country moving toward meeting those needs. I think everyone in this room knows the choice we made. And for all the Gallup polls and all the pundits in the world, I would not take back that choice we made."[115]

On the fifth anniversary of John's assassination, Johnson spoke nostalgically to some military advisers and remembered once seeing "poor President Kennedy" sit in the White House "in the evening sometimes for an hour while three [military] aides reviewed details in each department with him." He considered laying a wreath at Kennedy's grave, and a month later, speaking before a group of black presidential appointees, he referred to himself as John Kennedy's "trustee." In his final State of the Union Address, Johnson cited two people who had influenced his presidency. "I have been guided by the memory," he noted, "of my pleasant and close association with the beloved John F. Kennedy, and with our greatest modern legislator, Speaker Sam Rayburn."[116]

The tragedies of Lyndon Johnson were many. From the standpoint of the Kennedy "mystique" his most unfortunate fate was to survive. "The only difference between the Kennedy assassination and mine," he told reporters in the spring of 1968, "is that I am alive and it has been more torturous." Unlike John of the mythic past and Robert of the mythic future, Johnson was condemned to the present, wedged between two illusions and forced to deal with harsh realities. Retreating to fantasy, he sought his own place in the Kennedys' "story book image of heroes." Better to reside in Camelot than reality, for myths had won the power, approval, and love that had eluded him.[117]

EPILOGUE

Lyndon Johnson's attempt to renew his identity with the Kennedy "mystique" continued through his retirement. From January 1969, when he relinquished the presidency to Richard Nixon, until his death four years later, Johnson regularly depicted himself as John Kennedy's surrogate. "And every moment of sorrow, I've been by [the Kennedy family's] side," he told Walter Cronkite in the spring of 1970. "And every decision I made with the feeling that this is what I believe [John] would have done. And I don't want anyone to ever say that I ever let him down for a moment." "John Kennedy had died," he further explained to Doris Kearns. "But his 'cause' was not really clear. That was my job. I had to take a dead man's program and turn it into a martyr's cause. That way Kennedy would live on forever and so would I." "I never lost sight of the fact," he wrote in 1971, "that I was the trustee and custodian of the Kennedy administration." Johnson's memoir was roundly criticized for its transparent embrace of the Kennedy legacy and its attempt to deflect criticism about Vietnam.[1]

Johnson's ambivalence toward the "mystique" remained as strong in retirement as it did when he was president. He was bitter that John Kennedy had not received his share of blame for the war. "[Kennedy] was a great public hero," he explained to Cronkite, "and anything I did that someone didn't approve of, they would always feel that President Kennedy would have done it a different way, that he wouldn't have made that mistake." He insulted Kennedy's memory by confiding to reporters about Kennedy's alleged involvement in CIA attempts to kill Fidel Castro. "I'll tell you something [about the Kennedy assassination] that will rock you," he told Howard K. Smith. "Kennedy was trying to get Castro, but Castro got him first." Occasionally he diminished the quality of his relationship with Kennedy. "We were not like brothers," he told Cronkite. "We were not constant companions. . . . We were friendly, cordial, but not personally intimate."[2]

Consistent with his past behavior, Johnson reserved his harshest animosity for the Kennedy staff, the news media, and family members. Kennedy holdovers had tried to "undermine the Administration and bored from within

251

to create problems with us and leaked information that was slanted, and things of that nature." "Influential molders of opinion" doggedly maintained that his policy failures would not have occurred if Kennedy had lived. Although he had once felt close to Jacqueline Kennedy, after the assassination "it seemed like she and the other Kennedys seemed to somehow blame me for it." Edward Kennedy, whom Johnson had admired as a professional politician, was scorned after his Chappaquiddick accident. "He's still the fair-haired boy where the national press is concerned," he observed. "You know, if I'd killed a girl like he did then they'd have wanted to send me to the electric chair."[3]

In retirement Johnson was a recluse on his ranch outside of Johnson City. His personality fluctuated as usual. He appeared relaxed and friendly for days, but at other times he brooded silently. Occasionally he went across the Pedernales River to the welcoming center of the LBJ State Park and escorted guests through a slide show and exhibit on the hill country. During more productive moments he devoted time to farming and became extensively involved in the construction of his presidential library on the University of Texas campus in Austin.[4]

The museum portion of the Lyndon B. Johnson Library displays only a few artifacts associating Johnson with the Kennedys. The vice-presidential section contains two telegrams from Texas constituents protesting his acceptance of the nomination, but placards note that Johnson was "an integral part" of the administration. Jacqueline Kennedy's sentimental letter to Johnson written after her husband's death is exhibited, as is the statement that Johnson read at Andrews Air Force Base upon his return from Dallas. As might be expected, the Vietnam portion contains a quote from John Kennedy expressing his determination to secure victory in the region. Nowhere in the museum is Robert Kennedy mentioned. Ironically, souvenirs associating Johnson with the Kennedys sell faster in the museum gift shop than the Johnson material alone.[5]

The library staff, workers, and the people of Austin are determinedly forgiving of their protagonist, just as the personnel at the Kennedy Library and the people of Boston ignore the shortcomings of their champion. Indeed, there is virtually no mention of Lyndon Johnson in the entire museum portion of the Kennedy Library. The disparity that popular opinion holds for each man is more accurately conveyed in Washington, D.C., a city which likely reflects greater historical objectivity than Boston or Austin. After twenty-five years John Kennedy's grave at Arlington continues to receive a steady stream of visitors—schoolchildren, vacationing families, senior-citizen tour groups—most of whom also make a brief stop at Robert Kennedy's less conspicuous grave. During a recent visit I overheard a teacher explain softly to an eight-year-old girl, "The flame above President

Kennedy's grave will burn forever and ever." Several carnations dotted both John's and Robert's marker, and one middle-aged woman wept openly. Not all the attention is solemn. A teenage girl stood with her back to President Kennedy's grave, looking into her compact mirror and combing her hair. A young security guard joked privately about how he had once lit his cigarette off the eternal flame because he was short on matches. True to Tom Wicker's prediction in 1964, however, John Kennedy remains "one of those sure-sell heroes out of whose face or words or monuments a souvenir dealer can turn a steady buck." His image graces postcards, coffee mugs, and facsimile campaign buttons. In specialty shops, authentic Kennedy campaign memorabilia carries the highest price of all contemporary presidents. At the house in which Lincoln died, visitors can purchase a brochure comparing Kennedy with the Great Emancipator.[6]

In marked contrast to the abundant memorials to Kennedy, Lyndon Johnson barely receives notice in the town he dominated for nearly two decades. The only available Johnson souvenir I saw was an eleven-by-fourteen-inch print of Peter Hurd's portrait of the president. The reproduction of the painting, which Johnson himself despised, was reduced from a dollar to twenty-five cents.

Locating artifacts of Johnson requires considerable effort. In an obscure hallway of the Capitol sits a bust of the president, but it could not be displayed until the late 1970s for fear it would be vandalized. Since then someone has taken a chip out of the statue's chin. A dining hall dedicated to Lyndon Johnson is located in a dark corner of the Capitol, across the hall from the John F. Kennedy Room. Those who tour the White House will see a portrait of Kennedy but not Johnson. And the portrait of Johnson at the National Portrait Gallery stares pensively at a painting of Kennedy, who looks outward to images of Nixon, Carter, and Reagan. While John Kennedy is memorialized by the Kennedy Center for the Performing Arts, Johnson is bestowed an obscure park which receives few visitors. Not only is he passed over as an icon, but, more tragically, the programs which he once worked so diligently to pass and which he hoped would be his most lasting legacy have vanished to the eye; the Great Society is mocked by scores of homeless people who sleep in the parks and on the curbs of the city.

Scorned in the last years of his life, Johnson likely knew that memorials to him would be sparse. During the 1972 presidential campaign he was politely informed that it would be best if he did not appear at the Democratic National Convention in Miami Beach. Politically dead, Johnson seemed to anticipate physical death as well. He became strangely obsessive about attending funerals, and despite having suffered a massive heart attack in the spring of 1972, he continued to gain weight and chain-smoke cigarettes.

Self-destructiveness finally won out. In January 1973 Lyndon Johnson died of a heart attack alone in the bedroom of his Texas ranch.[7]

There were subtle parallels in the services that followed. The same plane that had carried John Kennedy's body from Dallas to Washington, D.C., and Robert Kennedy's from Los Angeles to New York, transported Johnson's remains from Austin to a full-dress funeral in the nation's capital. Like John Kennedy's casket, Johnson's was mounted on a horse-drawn caisson and pulled through crowd-lined streets. The twenty-six-year-old gelding that walked riderless during Kennedy's funeral played the same role during Johnson's. As the coffin was taken out of the Capitol rotunda, Johnson's little grandson, Lyn Nugent, snapped his hand to a salute—a scene reminiscent of John Kennedy, Jr.'s reaction nine years earlier. At the services, Sargent Shriver, the former director of the Peace Corps and the War on Poverty, represented the Kennedy family.[8]

Johnson's body was flown back to Texas and buried in the family cemetery on his ranch. During my visit there in the summer of 1987, tour buses stopped for an obligatory remembrance outside its stone wall. None of the visitors wept, and none left flowers. Most stared stoically from a distance at his grave. "President Johnson could have been buried in Washington, D.C., with some big eternal flame," the tour guide explained cheerfully, "but he wanted to be buried near the people he loved and who loved him." After the passengers re-boarded the bus and it wove its way off the ranch, the guide played a recording of one of Johnson's favorite songs—a song, he explained, which the former president liked to listen to when he inspected his land at the end of the day. Visitors were invited to join in a sing-along of *Raindrops Keep Falling on My Head*. While Lyndon Johnson chain-smoked himself to death, he had found pleasure in a song that blissfully rejoiced in freedom and lack of worry. Some tourists obliged the request, but participation was awkward. They strained to celebrate a man who had inspired little affection when he was alive and little emotion in death. As the bus circled one last time past the cemetery, passengers stared out the window and sang the song's most familiar chorus with slightly more enthusiasm: "... Because I'm free, nothing's worrying me." By the end of the second verse they were talking among themselves. Lyndon Johnson's grave was behind them.

NOTES

Introduction

1. The Mount Rushmore poll was reported July 19, 1990, on *CBS This Morning*. Thirty-five percent chose JFK. The *Newsweek* polls were reported in *Newsweek*, "Kennedy Has Become America's Favorite President," November 28, 1983, 64. The survey asked, "Of all the presidents we have ever had, who do you wish were president today?" Thirty percent chose JFK. One percent chose LBJ. Three percent chose Richard Nixon.

2. For discussions of LBJ's alleged involvement with the JFK assassination, see Thomas Brown, *JFK: History of an Image* (Bloomington, Indiana University Press, 1988), 24; Rowland Evans and Robert Novak, *Lyndon B. Johnson: The Exercise of Power* (New York, New American Library, 1966), 354–355; Joachim Joesten, *The Dark Side of Lyndon Baines Johnson* (London, Dawnay, 1968). The story of LBJ sitting on JFK's coffin was related to me by a student at Bowling Green State University. Barbara Garson, *The Complete Text of MacBird* (New York, Grove Press, 1966). The comment on Robert Caro's work was noted by Robert Wilson, "LBJ's Ascent to Power: A Critical View," *USA Today*, March 6, 1990, Section D, 1–2.

3. Tom Wicker, "Lyndon Johnson vs. the Ghost of Jack Kennedy," *Esquire* 64 (November 1965), 85 ff. Wicker was a native of North Carolina, where, for most of the 1950s, he worked for local newspapers and earned his way up the ranks of the *Winston-Salem Journal*. In early 1960 the *New York Times* hired him to cover regulatory agencies in Washington. He soon became a congressional reporter and later covered parts of the 1960 presidential campaign. In June 1961 he replaced William Lawrence as the *Times*'s White House correspondent. During Wicker's early years covering the White House, he, like many correspondents, was courted by President Kennedy. After Kennedy's death Wicker later admitted having an affinity for Lyndon Johnson. "Perhaps because as a Southerner myself," he wrote in 1978, "I was sympathetic to Johnson and privately hoped for his continuing success...." He remained as White House correspondent until 1965 when he became Washington bureau chief. Although he believed that Johnson's perception of the press was erroneous and distorted, Wicker was considered by the Johnson staff to be among the fairest reporters to cover the administration. See Tom Wicker, *On Press* (New York, Viking, 1978).

4. The past-future dialectic of the Kennedy "mystique" is noted in Vincent L. Toscano, *Since Dallas: Images of John F. Kennedy in Popular and Scholarly Literature, 1963–1973* (San Francisco, Robert J. Reed, 1978), 47–48.

5. William E. Leuchtenburg, *In the Shadow of FDR: From Harry Truman to Ronald Reagan* (Ithaca, Cornell University Press, 1983); Doris Kearns, *Lyndon Johnson and the American Dream* (New York, Harper and Row, 1976); Robert A. Caro, *The Years of Lyndon Johnson: The Path to Power* (New York, Alfred A. Knopf, 1982). Merrill D. Peterson, *The Jefferson Image in the American Mind* (New York, Oxford University Press, 1962); John William Ward, *Andrew Jackson: Symbol for an Age* (New York, Oxford University Press, 1955).

6. Otis L. Graham, Jr., and Meghan Robinson Wander, eds., *Franklin D. Roosevelt: His Life and Times* (Boston, G. K. Hall, 1985), 374–375. James L. Golden, "FDR's Use of the Symbol of TR in the Formation of His Political Persona and Philosophy," and John Robert Greene, "The Men in the Arena: Presidential Use of the Image of Theodore Roosevelt, 1916–1989," both presented as papers at "Theodore Roosevelt and the Birth of Modern America" Conference, April 19–21, 1990, Hofstra University, Hempstead, N.Y. Wilson's concern about being unable to match Theodore Roosevelt's image is noted in George Juergens, *News from the White House: The Presidential-Press Relationship in the Progressive Era* (Chicago, University of

Chicago Press, 1981), 128. Hoover's concern noted in Craig Lloyd, *Aggressive Introvert: A Study of Herbert Hoover and Public Relations Management, 1912–1932* (Columbus, Ohio State University Press, 1972), 171. Truman's difficulty in following FDR is noted in Leuchtenburg, *In the Shadow of FDR*, 1–40.

7. Material discussing Gary Hart's attraction to JFK noted in Michael Kramer, "Hart Stopper," *New York*, March 12, 1984, 32–38; Michael Kramer, "Falling in Love Again," *New York*, March 19, 1984, 28 ff; Morton Kondracke, "Hart's Long March," *New Republic*, April 2, 1984, 14–17; Morton Kondracke, "Hart Line, Soft Line," *New Republic*, April 9, 1984; William Lee Miller, "Remembering Gary," *New Republic*, April 16, 1984, 11–12; Interview, "A Talk with Gary Hart," *Newsweek*, March 26, 1984, 26–27, 32; "In Search of the Real Hart," *Newsweek*, March 26, 1984, 32–33; *New York Times*, "Hart Finds You Can Go Home Again," January 18, 1984; Hart's supplanting of his personality and refusal to alter his media techniques was conveyed to me in two separate "off-the-record" conversations with a reporter who covered his campaign in 1984 and a key adviser to Hart during the same campaign. The reporter characterized Hart as having "schizophrenic tendencies."

8. Gary Warren Hart, *Right from the Start: A Chronicle of the McGovern Campaign* (New York, Quadrangle, 1973), 267–269. Reagan's excessive use of JFK quotes is noted in Paul D. Erickson, "The Once and Future President: John F. Kennedy in the Rhetoric of Ronald Reagan," in Paul Harper and Joann P. Krieg, eds., *John F. Kennedy: The Promise Revisited* (New York, Greenwood, 1988), 313–320.

9. Nixon's ambivalent feelings for the Kennedys are noted in Garry Wills, *Nixon Agonistes: The Crisis of the Self-Made Man* (Boston, Houghton Mifflin, 1970), 7, 29, 422–428; Dan Rather and Gary Paul Gates, *The Palace Guard* (New York, Harper and Row, 1974), 5, 38, 40, 57, 73, 77–78, 166, 168–173; William Safire, *Before the Fall: An Inside View of the Pre-Watergate White House* (Garden City, Doubleday, 1975), 63, 152–153. Jimmy Carter's ambivalence is noted in David Halberstam, "The Coming of Carter," *Newsweek*, July 19, 1976, 11; Martin Schram, *Running for the President: The Carter Campaign* (New York, Stein and Day, 1977), 25–26; Garry Wills, *The Kennedy Imprisonment: A Meditation on Power* (Boston, Little, Brown, 1981), 192–194; Robert S. McElvaine, "Franklin and Jack . . . and Jimmy?" *America*, October 23, 1976, 246–248.

CHAPTER I
Prologue: The Johnson Personality

1. For a critique of the major scholarly, journalistic, and staff literature on LBJ, see Robert A. Divine, "The Johnson Literature," in Robert A. Divine, ed., *The Johnson Years: Foreign Policy, the Great Society, and the White House* (Lawrence, University Press of Kansas, 1981), 3–23. See also Divine, "The Johnson Revival: A Bibliographical Appraisal," in Robert A. Divine, ed., *The Johnson Years, Volume Two: Vietnam, the Environment, and Science* (Lawrence, University Press of Kansas, 1987). Moyers quoted in Bernard J. Firestone and Robert C. Vogt, eds., *Lyndon Baines Johnson and the Uses of Power* (New York, Greenwood, 1988), 349. The difficulty of categorizing LBJ and the disparagement of "psychobiographical" interpretations is discussed in Paul K. Conkin, *Big Daddy from the Pedernales: Lyndon Baines Johnson* (Boston, Twayne, 1986), ix–xii.

2. Personal material available on LBJ's early life is discussed in Robert A. Caro, "A Note on Sources," in *The Years of Lyndon Johnson: The Path to Power* (New York, Alfred A. Knopf, 1983), 775–780. Caro discusses LBJ's capacity for secrecy on 183–188, 200, 205, 235, 262, 280, 485–486, 495, and 600–602. The destruction of yearbooks noted on 198.

3. For LBJ's distortion and storytelling ability, see Caro, *Path*, 153–156, 159, 454, 482, 573. For LBJ's manipulation through flattery, see 109–110, 149–153, 174, 192, 194, 198–199, 231, 271, 449, 665–666. LBJ's skills as a braggart are depicted on 153–155, 156, 160, 185, 200. For a description of the Johnson Treatment, see Rowland Evans and Robert Novak, *Lyndon B.*

Johnson: The Exercise of Power (New York, New American Library, 1966), 115–117. For Johnson's suspected manipulation of aides and scholars, see Garry Wills, "Singing 'Mammy' to Doris: *Lyndon Johnson and the American Dream* by Doris Kearns and *LBJ: An Irreverent Chronicle* by Booth Mooney," *New York Review of Books*, June 24, 1976, 8–11.

4. Divine, "The Johnson Literature," in *The Johnson Years*, 3–23. Bill Moyers offers a poignant assessment in Firestone and Vogt, eds., *Lyndon Baines Johnson*, 349–362. Two researchers in particular who have written extensively on LBJ but have avoided lengthy discussions of his personality are Kathleen J. Turner, *Lyndon Johnson's Dual War: Vietnam and the Press* (Chicago, University of Chicago Press, 1985), and Vaughn Davis Bornet, *The Presidency of Lyndon B. Johnson* (Lawrence, University Press of Kansas, 1983).

5. The three "psychobiographical" works discussed here are Doris Kearns, *Lyndon Johnson and the American Dream* (New York, Harper and Row, 1976); Caro, *Path*; and Hyman Muslin and Thomas Jobe, "The Tragic Self of Lyndon Johnson and the Dilemma of Leadership," *Psychohistory Review* 15 (Spring 1987), 69–119.

6. For a unique but jaded inside, scholarly account of LBJ, see Eric Goldman, *The Tragedy of Lyndon Johnson: A Historian's Interpretation* (New York, Alfred A. Knopf, 1969). Kearns explains her background with LBJ in Kearns, *Lyndon Johnson*, 1–5, 11–15. LBJ quote on "teaching" Kearns is on 5.

7. Kearns, *Lyndon Johnson*, 11–13.

8. LBJ's "confessional" with Kearns in Kearns, *Lyndon Johnson*, 15–18. For a brief explanation of Kearns's "psychobiographical" approach toward her writings, see Jeane Kirkpatrick, "*Lyndon Johnson and the American Dream* by Doris Kearns," *Commentary* (August 1976), 75–80.

9. Kearns's summary of LBJ's personality structure is discussed in Kearns, *Lyndon Johnson*, 369–375. LBJ's violin lessons and Rebekah's withdrawal discussed on 25. Rebekah's rejection of LBJ because of his bad grades or refusal to go to college on 39–40.

10. Kearns, *Lyndon Johnson*, 37–39.

11. Kearns, *Lyndon Johnson*, 23–25, 28–29. Johnson's trip to California discussed on 42–44. His decision to enter politics discussed on 44–45.

12. Divine, ed., *The Johnson Years*, 19.

13. Kearns's methodology noted in *Lyndon Johnson*, 16–18. Kearns's account of LBJ's breakup with Carol Davis on 56–60 differs markedly from Caro's account in *Path*, 161–165. LBJ's fabrication of the California trip can be shown by contrasting Kearns, *Lyndon Johnson*, 42–45, to Caro, *Path*, 123–129. Kearns's description of LBJ's work for the college newspaper in Kearns, *Lyndon Johnson*, 46, 53–56, differs from Caro, *Path*, 147–151, 195. Sam's disparagement of intellectuality in Kearns, *Lyndon Johnson*, 33, 39–42, differs from the depiction in Caro, *Path*, 40–42. Sam urged his son to go to college in Caro, *Path*, 119–121. Sam and Rebekah were also more compatible than Kearns suggests. See Caro, *Path*, 50–65.

14. Wills, *New York Review of Books*, 8–11. Kearns's doubt about LBJ's information and her assessment of his reasons for talking to her in Kearns, *Lyndon Johnson*, 17–18.

15. Kearns, *Lyndon Johnson*, xi.

16. Caro's previous work and background in *Newsweek*, "The Power and Dubious Glory of Lyndon Johnson," November 29, 1982, 100–103. See also Caro, "A Note on Sources" in *Path*, 775–780.

17. Background on Sam and Rebekah in Caro, *Path*, 50–65. LBJ's rejection of their values on 119–120, 136–137.

18. Caro, *Path*, 66–78. LBJ's need to "be somebody" on 70.

19. Sam's downfall is discussed in Caro, *Path*, 79–97. LBJ's changing regard for his father discussed on 110–111. LBJ's personality change is discussed on 98–122. LBJ misrepresents his father as a drunk on 543. LBJ's decision to go to college noted on 122–137. LBJ's unsavory behavior in college is discussed on 150–160, 174–201. Caro's quote on 199.

20. Caro's thesis is neatly synthesized in *Newsweek*, November 29, 1982, 100.

21. Caro's discussion of LBJ as "professional son" noted in *Path*, 27, 294, 445; with Cecil Evans, 144–145, 151–153, 192; with Charles Marsh, 477, 486–488; with Sam Rayburn,

333–334, 452–453, 757–762; with Franklin Roosevelt, 668, 742; with Alvin Wirtz, 373, 392–393.

22. Robert A. Caro, *The Years of Lyndon Johnson: Means of Ascent* (New York, Alfred A. Knopf, 1990), xxvi–xxvii. For criticism of *Means of Ascent*, see David S. Broder, "How 'Landslide Johnson' Earned his Nick-name," *Guardian Weekly*, April 15, 1990, 20; Ronald Steel, "The Long Shadow of Ambition," *New York Times Book Review*, March 11, 1990, 1, 24–25; Tom Mathews, "Loathing Lyndon, Part II," *Newsweek*, March 19, 1990, 66ff; Sidney Blumenthal, "Getting It All Wrong: The Years of Robert Caro," *New Republic*, June 4, 1990, 29–36. The responses of several Johnson aides to Caro's second volume are in an Associated Press wire story by Mike Feinsilber, March 8, 1990. For a criticism of Caro's reductionist interpretation in the first volume of his biography, see Geoffrey C. Ward, "A One-sided Johnson," *American Heritage*, July/August 1990, 10, 12.

23. For Caro's discussion of LBJ's motives, see *Path*, 110–112. See also his chapter "The Bunton Strain," 3–32.

24. Caro discusses numerous "needs," including a need for affection, 228; need for attention, prominence, 68–70, 106–108, 110, 185, 458–459, 552; need for respect, 110–112, 170, 171, 195, 196, 552; need to dominate: as a child, 70, 71, 76, 99, 100, 110; as a college student, 153–154, 175, 194, 200; as a congressional secretary, 227, 275; as a congressman, 533–534, 552; at parties, 457–458, 552, 659.

25. Heinz Kohut, *The Restoration of the Self* (New York, International Universities Press, 1977). See also Hanna Segal, *Introduction to the Work of Melanie Klein* (New York, Basic Books, 1964, 1973), and Melanie Klein, *Contributions to Psychoanalysis, 1921–1945* (London, Hogarth Press, 1968).

26. For Muslin's and Jobe's psychohistorical methods, see Muslin and Jobe, "The Tragic Self," *Psychohistory Review* 15 (Spring 1987), 69–72.

27. Alice Miller, *The Drama of the Gifted Child* (New York, Basic Books, 1981), 14–21, 30–48. Muslin and Jobe, 72–79, 103, 107–108.

28. Muslin and Jobe, 72–77, 77–79.

29. Muslin and Jobe, 80–88.

30. Muslin and Jobe, 86–87, 88–95, 103–113.

31. Muslin and Jobe, 75, 80–88, 103. They discuss Rebekah's withdrawal from LBJ on 75. For Rebekah's illnesses, see Caro, *Path*, 58, 62, 94.

32. LBJ's effort to get Sam's advice in Caro, *Path*, 398–399. Sam's role in LBJ's campaigns discussed on 399–402, 428–429, 442–443, 444.

33. Of their sixty-three endnotes, twenty-three came from Kearns's biography and twenty-four were derived from Caro's work. For a quantitative breakdown of Muslin's and Jobe's end notes, see Muslin and Jobe, 113–116.

34. For an alternative perspective of "neurotic" behavior, see Robert C. Tucker, "The Georges' Wilson Reexamined: An Essay on Psychobiography," in Geoffrey Cocks and Travis L. Crosby, eds., *Psycho/History: Readings in the Method of Psychology, Psychoanalysis, and History* (New Haven, Yale University Press, 1987), 157–176.

35. Muslin and Jobe, 72.

CHAPTER II

From Senate to White House

1. The contrast between Johnson and Kennedy is cited in *Time*, "The Reverberating Issue," July 18, 1960, 10.

2. LBJ's political career until 1946 is discussed thoroughly in Robert A. Caro, *The Years of Lyndon Johnson: The Path to Power* (New York, Alfred A. Knopf, 1983). Caro devotes a chapter to Johnson's World War II experience in *The Years of Lyndon Johnson: Means of Ascent* (New York, Alfred A. Knopf, 1990), 35–53. For LBJ's early career, World War II experience, and role as Senate Majority Leader, see Merle Miller, *Lyndon: An Oral Biography* (New York,

Putnam, 1980), 3–231. A brief summary of LBJ's career is available in William D. De-Gregorio, *The Complete Book of Presidents* (New York, Dembner Books, 1984), 567–569.

3. Among the best scholarly accounts of JFK's early career is Herbert S. Parmet, *Jack: The Struggles of John F. Kennedy* (New York, Doubleday/Dial, 1977). JFK's initial reluctance to enter politics and the PT-109 episode are discussed thoroughly in Joan Blair and Clay Blair, *The Search for JFK* (New York, Berkeley, 1976), 5–61, 178–202. See also DeGregorio, *Complete*, 550–551.

4. Miller, *Lyndon*, 141–231. For a detailed account of the 1948 election, see Caro, *Means of Ascent*.

5. DeGregorio, *Complete*, 551. Theodore C. Sorensen, *Kennedy* (New York, Harper and Row, 1965), 43–70. Paul K. Conkin, *Big Daddy from the Pedernales: Lyndon Baines Johnson* (Boston, Twayne, 1986), 148–149, contrasts JFK and LBJ in the Senate. Kenneth P. O'Donnell, *"Johnny, We Hardly Knew Ye"* (Boston, Little, Brown, 1972), 117–118.

6. For a brief discussion of LBJ's effort concerning the 1957 civil rights bill, see Miller, *Lyndon*, 185–191; Rowland Evans and Robert Novak, *Lyndon B. Johnson: The Exercise of Power* (New York, New American Library, 1966), 131–153; Doris Kearns, *Lyndon Johnson and the American Dream* (New York, Harper and Row, 1976), 144–153. For LBJ's leadership qualities in the Senate, see Kearns, *Lyndon Johnson*, 135–159, 379–384.

7. LBJ's regard for JFK in Lyndon B. Johnson, *The Vantage Point: Perspectives of the Presidency 1963–1969* (New York, Holt, Rinehart and Winston, 1971), 4. "Telephone conversation of Senator Lyndon Johnson with Mr. Joseph Kennedy," November 10, 1951, White House Famous Names—John F. Kennedy (WHFN-JFK), box 4, Lyndon B. Johnson Library (LBJL).

8. JFK to LBJ, December 1, 1954, Sorensen, box 9, John F. Kennedy Library (JFKL). Theodore Sorensen to JFK, December 20, 1954, Sorensen, box 9, JFKL. LBJ to JFK, January 7, 1955, Sorensen, box 9, JFKL. LBJ to JFK, January 11, 1955, WHFN-JFK, box 4, LBJL.

9. JFK to LBJ, July 8, 1955, WHFN-JFK, box 4, LBJL. LBJ to JFK, September 26, 1955, WHFN-JFK, box 4, LBJL.

10. Joseph P. Kennedy's telephone call is noted in Johnson, *Vantage Point*, 3. JFK's list of arguments is noted in "Memorandum on Committee Status of Senator John F. Kennedy," January 1956, Sorensen, box 9, JFKL. JFK to LBJ, May 3, 1956, Sorensen, box 9, JFKL. LBJ's nomination of JFK to the Historical Sites Commission is noted in Theodore Sorensen to JFK, n.d., Sorensen, box 7, JFKL.

11. JFK's work with LBJ on USIA bill noted in Evans and Novak, *Lyndon B. Johnson*, 202; McClellan bill, 230–232; rejection of Lewis Strauss as Secretary of Commerce, 230; Lee White noted that JFK thought LBJ was "always very sound, very reliable" in Lee White, LBJL–Oral History (OH), 4. LBJ's appreciation of JFK noted in LBJ to JFK, August 3, 1956, Presidential Office Files (POF), box 30, JFKL.

12. LBJ's declaration of support of JFK at 1956 convention noted in Arthur M. Schlesinger, Jr., *A Thousand Days: John F. Kennedy in the White House* (Boston, Houghton Mifflin, 1965), 8.

13. LBJ to JFK, August 23, 1956, WHFN-JFK, box 4, LBJL. See also Johnson, *Vantage Point*, 3–4. JFK to LBJ, n.d, 1956, WHFN-JFK, box 4, LBJL. Arthur Schlesinger questioned LBJ's contention that Joseph enlisted his son's support in 1956. See Arthur M. Schlesinger, Jr., LBJL-OH, 2.

14. LBJ to JFK, November 6, 1956, WHFN-JFK, box 4, LBJL. LBJ to JFK, September 28, 1958, WHFN-JFK, box 4, LBJL.

15. LBJ to JFK, December 3, 1956, WHFN-JFK, box 4, LBJL. JFK to LBJ, December 11, 1956, WHFN-JFK, box 4, LBJL. LBJ to JFK, December 17, 1956, WHFN-JFK, box 4, LBJL. LBJ's manipulation of committee seat noted in Evans and Novak, *Lyndon B. Johnson*, 112–113. Doris Fleeson's observations noted in *Time*, "Restless Estes," January 21, 1957, 14. JFK's letter of gratitude in JFK to LBJ, January 26, 1957, WHFN-JFK, box 4, LBJL. George Reedy contended that LBJ developed affection for JFK. See George Reedy, LBJL-OH, part II, 22. Lee White noted that the appointment was "a very happy day in [JFK's] life . . . he just thought it was the best thing that had ever happened to him." See Lee White, LBJL-OH, 1–2.

16. JFK to LBJ, April 5, 1957, WHFN-JFK, box 4, LBJL.

17. LBJ to JFK, April 9, 1957, WHFN-JFK, box 4, LBJL. LBJ's Diary, WHFN-JFK, box 4, LBJL, 7 pages, listed all contacts between himself and JFK via telephone calls and visits between 1956 and 1960. On the average, they talked "officially" about a dozen times a year.

18. JFK's efforts on the 1957 civil rights act noted in *Time*, "Man Out Front," December 2, 1957, 20, and Evans and Novak, *Lyndon B. Johnson*, 148–149. LBJ's admiration of JFK on civil rights bill noted in Eric Goldman, *The Tragedy of Lyndon Johnson* (New York, Dell, 1969), 26. JFK's appeal to LBJ in JFK to LBJ, June 11, 1957, WHFN-JFK, box 4, LBJL. JFK to LBJ, September 4, 1957, WHFN-JFK, box 4, LBJL. LBJ to JFK, September 10, 1957, WHFN-JFK, box 4, LBJL. *Time*, "On to the Midwest," November 18, 1957, 27.

19. *Time*, June 9, 1958, 15; "Retreat and Defeat," June 16, 1958, 12–13; "Shattered Peace," June 23, 1958, 15; "Don't Blame Me," August 11, 1958, 15. LBJ to JFK, August 24, 1958, POF, box 30, JFKL. LBJ to JFK, September 5, 1958, Pre-Presidency Papers (PPP), box 964, JFKL.

20. LBJ to JFK, telegram, November 14, 1958, POF, box 30, JFKL. JFK to LBJ, telegram, November 21, 1958, POF, box 30, JFKL. JFK to LBJ, November 17, 1958, Sorensen, box 9, JFKL. LBJ to JFK, November 19, 1958, Sorensen, box 9, JFKL. JFK to Mike Mansfield, January 13, 1959, Sorensen, box 9, JFKL.

21. LBJ thanked JFK for the book and inscription in LBJ to JFK, January 12, 1956, PPP, box 964, JFKL. LBJ praised JFK for his book on JFK's birthday. See LBJ to JFK, May 29, 1956, POF, box 30, JFKL. JFK's "state document" analogy and need to express deference noted in Schlesinger, *A Thousand Days*, 703–704.

22. Mary to LBJ, January 12, 1956, WHFN-JFK, box 4, LBJL. LBJ to JFK, May 29, 1956, POF, box 30, JFKL. LBJ to JFK, May 29, 1957, POF, box 30, JFKL. A description of the Johnson Treatment is found in Evans and Novak, *Lyndon B. Johnson*, 115–117.

23. Harry McPherson, LBJL-OH, 41–42. Robert Kintner noted LBJ's jealousy of JFK's war heroics in Miller, *Lyndon*, 343. Bobby Baker, *Wheeling and Dealing: Confessions of a Capitol Hill Operator* (New York, W. W. Norton, 1978), 76–77.

24. Kearns, *Lyndon Johnson*, 201. LBJ's envy of JFK for embodying the traits that Rebekah admired is noted in Kearns, *Lyndon Johnson*, 165–166.

25. Leonard Baker, *The Johnson Eclipse: A President's Vice-Presidency* (New York, Macmillan, 1966), 52.

26. For a brief summary of the changing political structures by 1960 and JFK's adaptation, see Theodore Sorensen, "Election of 1960," in Arthur M. Schlesinger, Jr., ed., *History of American Presidential Elections: 1789–1968*, vol. IV (New York, McGraw-Hill, 1971), 3449–3460. See also Miller, *Lyndon*, 240. *Time*, "The Reverberating Issue," July 18, 1960, 9.

27. LBJ's feelings toward love and votes noted in Kearns, *Lyndon Johnson*, 209, 378–379.

28. "In almost every . . ." quoted from Herbert S. Parmet, *JFK, The Presidency of John F. Kennedy* (New York, Doubleday/Dial, 1983), 14. LBJ's illnesses noted in Kearns, *Lyndon Johnson*, 59, 88–89, 101, 125; Caro, *Path*, 423, 434, 494, 339. LBJ's desire to withdraw from the 1964 race noted in Johnson, *Vantage Point*, 93–98. Reedy, LBJL-OH, 16. "I don't want . . ." in Evans and Novak, *Lyndon B. Johnson*, 261. LBJ's health problems and fear of defeat noted in Baker, *Wheeling and Dealing*, 43–45. LBJ's "deep fear of defeat" noted in Evans and Novak, 119. "This is impossible . . ." cited in Miller, *Lyndon*, 236.

29. O'Daniel's early career noted in Caro, *Path*, 695–698. LBJ emulated O'Daniel's campaign tactics in Caro, 706. LBJ's illness noted in Caro, 703–704.

30. For a discussion of LBJ's regional handicaps, see Johnson, *Vantage Point*, 95–96; *New York Times*, June 11, 1964, 22; *Wall Street Journal*, "The 'Regional' Candidate," July 10, 1959. *Time*, "The Men Who," November 24, 1958, 18. *Time*, July 18, 1960, 9.

31. LBJ's political strengths noted in *Wall Street Journal*, "The 'Regional' Candidate," July 10, 1959.

32. LBJ to JFK, April 21, 1959, POF, box 30, JFKL. LBJ to JFK, May 19, 1959, POF, box 30, JFKL. LBJ to JFK, September 16, 1959, POF, box 30, JFKL. JFK to LBJ, October 29, 1959, PPP, box 964, JFKL. JFK to LBJ, November 1959, PPP, box 964, JFKL. *Time*, "Nine Days of Labor," May 4, 1959, 12. *Time*, "Strictly for the Bird," May 18, 1959, 22.

33. Rayburn's committee cited in Theodore White, *The Making of the President 1960* (New York, Atheneum, 1961), 47. LBJ's comment on "gray in the hair" noted in *Time*, July 18,

1960. LBJ's actions in West Virginia and New Hampshire noted in Evans and Novak, *Lyndon B. Johnson*, 262; tour of Appalachia, 274. LBJ's newsletters are found in PPP, box 1046, JFKL.

34. JFK to LBJ, November 17, 1959, WHFN-JFK, box 4, LBJL. LBJ to JFK, November 27, 1959, WHFN-JFK, box 4, LBJL. Copies of the same letters are found in PPP, box 964, JFKL.

35. John Connally to JFK, January 4, 1960, PPP, box 964, JFKL. See also Price Daniel to John Hynes, September 10, 1959, PPP, box 964, JFKL and John Connally to Hynes, September 8, 1959, PPP, box 964, JFKL. LBJ loses supporters in Evans and Novak, *Lyndon B. Johnson*, 261.

36. Evans and Novak assessment cited in Evans and Novak, *Lyndon B. Johnson*, 272. LBJ's strategy noted by James Rowe in Miller, *Lyndon*, 236. LBJ's "tending the store" in Evans and Novak, *Lyndon B. Johnson*, 265. LBJ's assumptions about the Kennedys' Catholicism is noted by Bill Moyers in Miller, *Lyndon*, 242. See also Reedy, LBJL-OH, 16. Rayburn pleads with LBJ in Evans and Novak, *Lyndon B. Johnson*, 263–264. *Time*, July 18, 1960, 9.

37. Rowe noted LBJ's ignorance of national politics in Miller, *Lyndon*, 236. Jack Bell noted LBJ's mishandling of JFK in Miller, *Lyndon*, 240. JFK's belief that LBJ was "surprised" noted in Jacqueline Kennedy, LBJL-OH, 11.

38. LBJ's power play and resentment noted in Evans and Novak, *Lyndon B. Johnson*, 281–282. *Time*, July 11, 1960, 18.

39. LBJ's and Rayburn's discussion with Eisenhower noted in Evans and Novak, *Lyndon B. Johnson*, 271. JFK a "dangerous man," see Parmet, *JFK*, 72. Peter Lisagor, John F. Kennedy Library—Oral History (JFKL-OH), 25-26. See also Miller, *Lyndon*, 241. Hugh Sidey, JFKL-OH, 9. Arthur Krock noted LBJ's ingratitude in Miller, *Lyndon*, 241. LBJ's response to polls noted in Hugh Sidey, *A Very Personal Presidency: Lyndon Johnson in the White House* (New York, Atheneum, 1968), 169.

40. *Time*, July 18, 1960, 10–11.

41. George Reedy, LBJL-OH, tape 2, 16, 22. Baker, *Wheeling and Dealing*, 120, 121.

42. LBJ's strategy outlined in Evans and Novak, *Lyndon B. Johnson*, 285–286.

43. LBJ's use of the U-2 incident as a campaign ploy against JFK noted in Evans and Novak, *Lyndon B. Johnson*, 238. The authors noted that LBJ excluded JFK from a Democratic parlay of foreign policy advisers. See also Theodore White, *The Making 1960*, 146–147 on the U-2 incident and JFK's Catholicism. *Time*, "The Candidates' Health," July 18, 1960, 12. LBJ's belief that JFK alluded to him noted in Parmet, *JFK*, 17.

44. *Time*, July 18, 1960, 12. Clifford's observations noted in Miller, *Lyndon*, 246. RFK's response cited in Parmet, *JFK*, 18. Evans and Novak, *Lyndon B. Johnson*, 289.

45. Reedy, LBJL-OH, tape 2, 22. Myer Feldman recalled tracing rumors in Miller, *Lyndon*, 246. Evans and Novak, *Lyndon B. Johnson*, 286, noted LBJ did not have a role in the health accusations.

46. "Telephone conversation on Senator Lyndon Johnson with Mr. Joseph Kennedy, father of Senator Kennedy, November 10, 1954, at 4 o'clock p.m.," WHFN-JFK, box 4, LBJL. Arthur Krock recalled in an oral history interview for the John F. Kennedy Library that Joe had told him "Jack's dying." See Peter Collier and David Horowitz, *The Kennedys: An American Drama* (New York, Summit, 1984), 202–204.

47. JFK's health discussed in Parmet, *JFK*, 17–18, 119–124. Kennedy's comment to Joseph Alsop noted in Schlesinger, *A Thousand Days*, 95–96. LBJ proves his good health in Hugh Sidey, *A Very*, 169. "Chicago (UPI)," July 10, 196?, Watson, box 25, LBJL.

48. LBJ's tactics noted in Evans and Novak, *Lyndon B. Johnson*, 279. "This young fellow . . ." cited in Goldman, *Tragedy*, 454–455. LBJ's comment on Joseph P. Kennedy noted in Evans and Novak, 289.

49. Evans and Novak, *Lyndon B. Johnson*, 278. O'Donnell quoted in Lester David and Irene David, *Bobby Kennedy: The Making of a Folk Hero* (New York, Dodd, Mead, 1986), 152. See also p. 113. Baker's conversation with RFK noted in Baker, *Wheeling and Dealing*, 118.

50. See Evans and Novak, *Lyndon B. Johnson*, 289–291. LBJ taught debate to high school students before launching a political career. See Caro, *Path*, 207–209, 211. JFK to LBJ, July 12, 1960, PPP, box 1046, JFKL.

51. Philip Graham's observations about the debate are noted in Miller, *Lyndon*, 249. LBJ's

fear of debates noted in Caro, *Path*, 431–432. Jack Valenti, LBJL-OH, 7–8. See also *Time*, "The Organization Nominee," July 25, 1960, 15.

52. Videotape, NBC News, July 12, 1960. See also *New York Times*, July 13, 1960, 1. LBJ traditionally debated by finding an opponent's weak points and shaming him. See Caro, *Path*, 154, 432.

53. Videotape, NBC News, July 12, 1960. LBJ's poor speaking style noted in Caro, *Path*, 693–695. See also White, *The Making 1960*, 144–145.

54. JFK's nervousness noted in *Time*, "The Organization Nominee," July 25, 1960, 15. Videotape, NBC News, July 12, 1960.

55. *Time*, July 25, 1960, 15. See also Miller, *Lyndon*, 249. John Roche, LBJL-OH, 3.

56. LBJ's recollection of the debate in Doris Kearns Goodwin, *The Fitzgeralds and the Kennedys* (New York, Simon and Schuster, 1987), 780–781. LBJ's failure to grasp new trends noted in Evans and Novak, *Lyndon B. Johnson*, 291. Harry McPherson, *A Political Education* (Boston, Little, Brown, 1972), 178–179.

57. Johnson quoted in *New York Times*, October 28, 1964, 33. Evans and Novak noted LBJ's "half-hearted" effort in Evans and Novak, *Lyndon B. Johnson*, 265. Johnson's aide quoted in Parmet, *JFK*, 24. See also Miller, *Lyndon*, 253.

58. Pierre Salinger, *With Kennedy* (Garden City, Doubleday, 1966), 40–46. RFK quoted in Edwin O. Guthman and Jeffrey Shulman, eds., *Robert Kennedy in His Own Words: The Unpublished Recollections of the Kennedy Years* (New York, Bantam, 1988), 21. His account of the decision to nominate LBJ noted on 19–26. For a good summary of the events in Los Angeles, see Parmet, *JFK*, 21–30.

59. JFK's comment to reporter Carroll Kilpatrick in Miller, *Lyndon*, 235–236. For Sorensen's and Feldman's advice, see Parmet, *JFK*, 23. For Graham's and Alsop's consultation with JFK see Schlesinger, *A Thousand Days*, 42–43. See also Katharine Graham, LBJL-OH, 10. Joseph Alsop to LBJ, n.d., March 1964, PL1, box 78, LBJL. LBJ to Joseph Alsop, March 23, 1964, PL1, box 78, LBJL. Joseph Alsop to LBJ, March 25, 1964, PL1, box 78, LBJL. See also Arthur M. Schlesinger, Jr., LBJL-OH, 2.

60. Benjamin C. Bradlee, *Conversations with Kennedy* (New York, W. W. Norton, 1975), 30–31. Guthman and Shulman, eds., *Robert Kennedy*, 20. According to Hugh Sidey, Kennedy intended to nominate Missouri Senator Stuart Symington but asked Johnson out of courtesy and fear that Johnson might respond negatively as Senate Majority Leader if he were not asked. "We'll have to offer the job to Lyndon, that's for sure," Kennedy told Sidey several days before the convention. "He's a proud man, and he'd be mad if we didn't. He's too big a figure in the party and in the country. He'll enjoy turning it down; then we can make our choice." See Hugh Sidey, "Boston-Austin Was an Accident," *Time*, July 25, 1988, 23.

61. See Miller, *Lyndon*, 254. McPherson, *A Political Education*, 178, notes LBJ's reluctance to serve under JFK as Senate Majority Leader. See also Schlesinger, *A Thousand Days*, 32.

62. Kearns, *Lyndon Johnson*, 90–91, 102–107. Caro, *Path*, 272. Divine notes "political daddys" in Robert Divine, ed., *The Johnson Years: Foreign Policy, the Great Society, and the White House* (Lawrence, University Press of Kansas, 1981), 7. "Power is . . ." quoted in Evans and Novak, *Lyndon B. Johnson*, 298, 304–306. LBJ and Kleberg noted in Caro, *Path*, 217–223.

63. Parmet, *JFK*, 24–25. LBJ to JFK, July 13, 1960, PPP, box 1046, JFKL. JFK to LBJ, n.d., PPP, box 1046, JFKL.

64. Jenkins quoted in Miller, *Lyndon*, 257. RFK's version in Guthman and Shulman, eds., *Robert Kennedy*, 21. JFK's comment noted in Schlesinger, *A Thousand Days*, 48.

65. RFK's recollection noted in Guthman and Shulman, eds., *Robert Kennedy*, 19–22. Salinger's objection to LBJ noted in Salinger, *With Kennedy*, 46. General opposition noted in Parmet, *JFK*, 27.

66. Rayburn's conditions noted in Schlesinger, *A Thousand Days*, 49. See also Evans and Novak, *Lyndon B. Johnson*, 300.

67. Guthman and Shulman, eds., *Robert Kennedy*, 21–23.

68. LBJ packed to go home in Parmet, *JFK*, 28–29.

69. Guthman and Shulman, eds., *Robert Kennedy*, 22; Parmet, *JFK*, 28–29.

70. Graham memorandum published in Theodore White, *The Making of the President 1964*,

(New York, Atheneum, 1965), 434. See also James Rowe in Miller, *Lyndon*, 261. LBJ comment on reading his statement noted in White, 434. LBJ called RFK a "little shitass" in Baker, *Wheeling and Dealing*, 130.

71. Joseph Alsop to LBJ, n.d., March 1964, PL1, box 78, LBJL. LBJ to Joseph Alsop, March 23, 1964, PL1, box 78, LBJL. Joseph Alsop to LBJ, March 25, 1964, PL1, box 78, LBJL.

72. White, *The Making 1964*, 434. Katharine Graham, LBJL-OH, 16. Jacob Jacobsen to LBJ, August 12, 1965, FG2, box 40, LBJL. Guthman and Shulman, eds., *Robert Kennedy*, 24–25. McPherson also prepared for LBJ a summary of the convention events. See Harry McPherson to Bill Moyers, August 15, 1965, McPherson, box 51, LBJL.

73. Johnson, *Vantage Point*, 91–92. See also Michael Janeway, "LBJ and the Kennedys," *Atlantic* 229 (February 1972), 51–52.

74. Kearns Goodwin, *The Kennedys*, 781. Evans and Novak, *Lyndon B. Johnson*, 312.

75. Evans and Novak, *Lyndon B. Johnson*, 312.

CHAPTER III
The Lost Frontiersman: Kennedy's Vice President

1. LBJ's sense of rejection noted in Rowland Evans and Robert Novak, *Lyndon B. Johnson: The Exercise of Power* (New York, New American Library, 1966), 307–308. RFK's embitterment noted in Peter Lisagor, JFKL-OH, 24–25. Lester David and Irene David, *Bobby Kennedy: The Making of a Folk Hero* (New York, Dodd, Mead, 1986), 153, and Paul K. Conkin, *Big Daddy from the Pedernales: Lyndon Baines Johnson* (Boston, Twayne, 1986), 155.

2. Merle Miller, *Lyndon: An Oral Biography* (New York, Putnam, 1980), 263–264.

3. Miller, *Lyndon*, 264. *New York Times*, August 1, 1960. "Letter from Lyndon Johnson," circular, August 2, 1960, Pre-Presidency Papers (PPP), box 1046, John F. Kennedy Library (JFKL). JFK to LBJ, August 1, 1960, PPP, box 1046, JFKL. LBJ's description of JFK's heroics noted in Miller, 262. JFK's emotional reaction noted in Miller, 269.

4. Miller, *Lyndon*, 268. Insults at LBJ noted in Evans and Novak, *Lyndon B. Johnson*, 239. LBJ's insults toward JFK in Evans and Novak, 239. LBJ's drinking cited in George Reedy, *Lyndon B. Johnson: A Memoir* (New York, Andrews and McMeel, 1982), 54.

5. LBJ's experience at Adolphus Hotel cited in Miller, *Lyndon*, 270–272.

6. Arthur M. Schlesinger, Jr., *A Thousand Days: John F. Kennedy in the White House* (Boston, Houghton Mifflin, 1965), 702–704, 1018. Schlesinger acknowledged that Johnson "proved a powerful and tireless campaigner, especially in the South."

7. Miller, *Lyndon*, 273.

8. LBJ's plotting with Baker noted in Bobby Baker, *Wheeling and Dealing: Confessions of a Capitol Hill Operator* (New York, W. W. Norton, 1978), 133–134. See also Evans and Novak, *Lyndon B. Johnson*, 324. "It's gonna be . . ." quoted in Baker, *Wheeling*, 134–135.

9. LBJ's response to rejection noted in Baker, *Wheeling*, 134–135. See also Miller, *Lyndon*, 305, and Leonard Baker, *The Johnson Eclipse: A President's Vice-Presidency* (New York, Macmillan, 1966), 28.

10. LBJ's executive order noted in Doris Kearns, *Lyndon Johnson and the American Dream* (New York, Harper and Row, 1976), 165; Evans and Novak, *Lyndon B. Johnson*, 326–327; Arthur M. Schlesinger, Jr., Lyndon B. Johnson Library—Oral History (LBJL-OH), 5; Schlesinger, *A Thousand Days*, 704.

11. Richard E. Neustadt to Bill Moyers, February 28, 1961, White House Name File—Bill Moyers, JFKL. See also Schlesinger, LBJL-OH, 8, and Schlesinger, *A Thousand Days*, 702–707. Nicholas deB. Katzenbach, the assistant attorney general, believed that Kennedy "tried very hard to remember the vice president and tried to create something for him that would use his abilities." See Kenneth W. Thompson, ed., *The Johnson Presidency* (Lanham, Md., University Press of America, 1986), 210. See also Kearns, *Lyndon Johnson*, 162–163. Message to Kennedy is noted in Villard to Secretary of State, April 10, 1961, President's Office Files (POF), box 30, JFKL.

12. Lee White, LBJL-OH, 12–13. Staff forgetfulness noted in Horace Busby to Sorenson [sic], March 20, 1961, White House Name File—Horace Busby, JFKL. LBJ thanked another JFK aide for informing him of the existence of interdepartmental meeting in LBJ to Frederick Dutton, April 19, 1961, Robert Kennedy Senate Files Personal Correspondences (RFK-SF/PC), box 4, JFKL. JFK's preference to use O'Brien noted in Schlesinger, LBJL-OH, 5. Fear that LBJ might circumvent JFK noted in Harry McPherson, LBJL-OH, 9–10. Baker, *Wheeling*, 143–146. See also Miller, *Lyndon*, 305, and Baker, *Johnson Eclipse*, 48. Carpenter's effort noted in Charles Bartlett, LBJL-OH, 5.

13. Edwin O. Guthman and Jeffrey Shulman, eds., *Robert Kennedy in His Own Words: The Unpublished Recollections of the Kennedy Years* (New York, Bantam, 1988), 151–153. The president was also dismayed by Johnson's absence of leadership in the space committee. See White, LBJL-OH, 15; Bartlett, LBJL-OH, 7; Baker, *Johnson Eclipse*, 28–31, 47.

14. Baker, *Wheeler*, 115–117.

15. JFK to LBJ, August 27, 1962, White House Famous Names—John F. Kennedy (WHFN-JFK), box 4, LBJL. JFK's consideration of LBJ noted in Bartlett, LBJL-OH, 7, and Tom Wicker, "Lyndon Johnson vs. the Ghost of Jack Kennedy," *Esquire* 64 (November 1965), 146. JFK once congratulated LBJ on a speech in JFK to LBJ, April 1, 1963, POF, box 30, JFKL. Duke quoted in Miller, *Lyndon*, 278–279. "The real problems," Duke recalled, "were when the President would have some of the 'in-group' parties for Arthur Schlesinger, [McGeorge] Bundy, Kenneth Galbraith, and his friends that would come down from New York." Evelyn Lincoln, *Kennedy and Johnson* (New York, Holt, Rinehart and Winston, 1968), 151, 153. For discussions of JFK's private regard for LBJ, see Arthur M. Schlesinger, Jr., *Robert Kennedy and His Times* (Boston, Houghton Mifflin, 1978), 621; Guthman and Shulman, eds., *Robert Kennedy*, 23; Bartlett, LBJL-OH, 4, 6–7.

16. Wicker, *Esquire*, 141. LBJ at the Taj Mahal in Miller, *Lyndon*, 285–286. Elizabeth Gatov, a United States treasurer, was uncomfortable with the gossip that circulated at social occasions. "Really, it was brutal, the stories that they were passing, and the jokes, and the inside nasty stuff about Lyndon," she noted. "I didn't protest—I don't want to pretend that I did—but it seemed unnecessary to me at the time." See Miller, 279. Plans to exclude LBJ from photographs noted in Nancy Tuckerman to Evelyn Lincoln, n.d., POF, box 67, JFKL. McPherson quoted in McPherson, LBJL-OH, 9–10. See also Bartlett, LBJL-OH, 10–14. Once, the vice president received an envelope and letterhead stationery from the "John F. Kennedy Philatelic Society" in Canton, Texas. Written in large capital letters beneath Johnson's name was the inscription "S.O.B." LBJ's early social behavior noted in Robert A. Caro, *The Years of Lyndon Johnson: The Path to Power* (New York, Alfred A. Knopf, 1983), 455–457, 659. During his early years in Congress, Johnson was similarly snubbed and ridiculed for his overbearing and boorish behavior at Washington gatherings. Lacking power, he had tried too hard to be liked, desperately seeking to be the center of attention. When he was rebuffed, however, he would brood in a corner.

17. Guthman and Shulman, eds., *Robert Kennedy*, 23–26, 46, 178. Kenneth O'Donnell, David Powers, and Joe McCarthy, *"Johnny, We Hardly Knew Ye"* (Boston, Little, Brown, 1972), 6. Krock quoted in Miller, *Lyndon*, 280. Benjamin C. Bradlee, *Conversations with Kennedy* (New York, W. W. Norton, 1975), 194. See also Bartlett, LBJL-OH, 7.

18. LBJ's usual reaction to rejection noted in Caro, *Path*, 337. LBJ's boredom in meetings noted in Caro, 548, 552–553. LBJ's nonparticipation in the House noted in Caro, 273–275. See also Kearns, *Lyndon Johnson*, 164–165. Caro notes that after Johnson lost an election as head of the Little Congress in 1935, he resigned. Schlesinger, LBJL-OH, 9. Bradlee, *Conversations*, 226. LBJ's trips overseas noted in Miller, *Lyndon*, 280, 291. Bartlett, LBJL-OH, 5–6. LBJ's passivity during the Cuban missile crisis noted by RFK in Guthman and Shulman, eds., *Robert Kennedy*, 16. JFK frequently sent memos to LBJ asking the vice president to travel overseas. See JFK to LBJ, September 30, 1961, POF, box 30, JFKL; JFK to LBJ, September 27, 1961, POF, box 30, JFKL; JFK to LBJ, September 26, 1961, POF, box 30, JFKL; JFK to LBJ, March 31, 1961, POF, box 30, JFKL.

19. Baker, *Wheeling*, 117. See also Richard Harwood and Haynes B. Johnson, *Lyndon* (New York, Praeger, 1973), 139. JFK sometimes appreciated LBJ's self-restraint. See Schlesinger, *Robert Kennedy*, 621. Miller, *Lyndon*, 279. Baker, *Wheeling*, 145.

20. Bradlee, *Conversations*, 194. Steven F. Lawson, "I Got It from the New York Times: Lyndon Johnson and the Kennedy Civil Rights Program," *Journal of Negro History* 67 (Summer 1982), 159–172. Bell quoted in Miller, *Lyndon*, 288. LBJ's initial reluctance to travel to Berlin noted in Conkin, *Big Daddy*, 168–169. See also Kearns, *Lyndon Johnson*, 167–168.

21. Baker, *Wheeling*, 116. Kearns, *Lyndon Johnson*, 165–167. Reedy, *Lyndon B. Johnson*, 21–22, 127.

22. Wicker, *Esquire*, 147. Baker, *Wheeling*, 145. Miller, *Lyndon*, 279, 307.

23. Jack Valenti, LBJL-OH, 27. See also Baker, *Wheeling*, 116, 144–145. McPherson, who had worked for Johnson since the mid-1950s, believed he was "very scrupulous" in criticizing the president. "He did not talk with anybody who might have published any of his negative thoughts about Kennedy," McPherson recalled. "He would tell me how Jack Kennedy and Bobby had failed to do whatever it was to meet congressional problems." He would also complain that the well-publicized Kennedy parties were not in the administration's best interest. See Miller, *Lyndon*, 305.

24. LBJ to JFK, September 6, 1961, WHFN-JFK, box 4, LBJL. LBJ to JFK, August 30, 1963, POF, box 30, JFKL. LBJ to JFK, January 1, 1962, WHFN-JFK, box 4, LBJL. Consideration of a luncheon invitation noted on attached letter, LBJ to JFK, January 1, 1962, POF, box 30, JFKL. JFK's discomfort for LBJ's adulation noted in Bradlee, *Conversations*, 217. For other expressions of affection from LBJ, see J. C. Kellan to Walter Jenkins, May 30, 1961, WHFN-JFK, box 4, LBJL; LBJ to JFK, August 30, 1960, POF, box 30, JFKL.

25. Ralph Dungan to JFK, October 3, 1962, POF, box 30, JFKL.

26. Miller, *Lyndon*, 280.

27. Baker, *Wheeling*, 116. LBJ to JFK, September 25, 1962, WHFN-JFK, box 4, LBJL. Contrary to his comments to Baker, Johnson claimed that he often enjoyed relaxed conversation with JFK. His recollection was consistent with his post-presidential attempts to appear closer to JFK than he actually was. See Lyndon Johnson, *The Vantage Point: Perspectives of the Presidency 1963–1969* (New York, Holt, Rinehart and Winston, 1971), 4.

28. Kearns, *Lyndon Johnson*, 164. JFK and LBJ quoted in Baker, *Wheeling*, 116–117. LBJ's desire to retire from vice presidency noted on 144. See also Schlesinger, *Robert Kennedy*, 622–623; Miller, *Lyndon*, 309; and Harwood and Johnson, *Lyndon*, 139.

29. Reedy, *Lyndon B. Johnson*, 127. Miller, *Lyndon*, 305. Baker discusses LBJ's drinking habits in Baker, *Wheeling*, 75–76. LBJ's dreams noted in Kearns, *Lyndon Johnson*, 167.

30. Reedy, *Lyndon B. Johnson*, 121.

31. Thompson, ed., *The Johnson Presidency*, 210. Reedy, *Lyndon B. Johnson*, 133. See also George Reedy, LBJL-OH, 22. "He's done much better by me," LBJ noted, "than I would have done by him under the same circumstances." Once in 1963, Bartlett suggested to Kennedy that he "dump" Johnson. Kennedy was "furious" at the suggestion and briefly lectured the columnist on the political foolishness of the proposal. See Bartlett, LBJL-OH, 12. Schlesinger, *Robert Kennedy*, 621–622. Baker, *Wheeling*, 274.

32. *Time*, "What Happened to LBJ," April 5, 1963, 27–28. See also Evans and Novak, *Lyndon B. Johnson*, 332.

33. Reedy quoted in Thompson, ed., *The Johnson Presidency*, 100.

34. Guthman and Shulman, eds., *Robert Kennedy*, 417. White, LBJL-OH, 15. Hugh Sidey, "He Makes a Truce . . . ," *Life*, November 18, 1966, 39. Eunice Kennedy to RFK, n.d., RFK-SF/PC, box 8, JFKL.

35. Miller, *Lyndon*, 305. Wechsler's meeting with LBJ in Schlesinger, *Robert Kennedy*, 625.

36. Baker, *Wheeling*, 144–146; Thompson, ed., *The Johnson Presidency*, 240; Schlesinger, *Robert Kennedy*, 623–624; and Reedy, *Lyndon B. Johnson*, 4, 56–57, 63–64, 122, 124–125, have various notations about LBJ's paranoia as vice president. See especially Reedy, 123, 134.

37. Baker, *Wheeling*, 175–176. See also Miller, *Lyndon*, 298. Reedy, *Lyndon B. Johnson*, 123–124.

38. For a discussion of JFK's various intentions in 1964, see Guthman and Shulman, eds., *Robert Kennedy*, 46, 389–390; Bartlett, LBJL-OH, 12; Bradlee, *Conversations*, 216, 227; Schlesinger, LBJL-OH, 12. See also Miller, *Lyndon*, 308; Schlesinger, *Robert Kennedy*, 604–605; Baker, *Wheeling*, 117; Wicker, *Esquire*, 147; McPherson, LBJL-OH, tape 2, 10; Thompson, ed., *The Johnson Presidency*, 266–267.

39. In 1984 Billy Sol Estes told a grand jury that about the time Johnson was inaugurated as vice president, Johnson had ordered Marshall's murder. Johnson allegedly feared that Marshall might link him to Estes's financial dealings. The accusation was unsubstantiated and brought immediate condemnation from Johnson's associates. Walter Jenkins characterized the charge as "so far-fetched it's sick." The jury brought no indictments, in part because the participants in the alleged conspiracy were all dead. See *Newsweek*, "Did LBJ Order a Murder?" April 2, 1984, 37. Bradlee's conversations with Kennedy noted in Bradlee, *Conversations*, 105, 215–216, 228.

40. James Wechsler, "The Two-Front War: Johnson vs. Kennedy," *The Progressive* (May 1967), 23.

41. Schlesinger, *Robert Kennedy*, 623–624.

42. Schlesinger, *Robert Kennedy*, 624. "The last thing…" in Harwood and Johnson, *Lyndon*, 139. Johnson, *Vantage Point*, 2.

CHAPTER IV
The Caretaker: President Johnson and the Kennedy Family

1. For Johnson's sense of feeling a usurper, see Merle Miller, *Lyndon: An Oral Biography* New York, Putnam, 1980), 336. Doris Kearns, *Lyndon Johnson and the American Dream* (New York, Harper and Row, 1976), 170.

2. For Johnson's reactions to death, see Robert A. Caro, *The Years of Lyndon Johnson: The Path to Power* (New York, Alfred A. Knopf, 1983), 542–543. FDR's death noted in William E. Leuchtenburg, *In the Shadow of FDR: From Harry Truman to Ronald Reagan* (Ithaca, Cornell University Press, 1983), 121–122. Rayburn's death noted in Bobby Baker, *Wheeling and Dealing: Confessions of a Capitol Hill Operator* (New York, W. W. Norton, 1978), 148–149. See also, Miller, *Lyndon*, 290.

3. Miller, *Lyndon*, 315.

4. George W. Ball, *The Past Has Another Pattern: Memoirs* (New York, W. W. Norton, 1982), 313. Rowland Evans and Robert Novak, *Lyndon B. Johnson: The Exercise of Power* (New York, New American Library, 1966), 363–364. Robert McNamara, however, thought LBJ was "surprisingly stable" in William Manchester, *The Death of a President* (New York, Harper and Row, 1967), 402. LBJ quoted in Miller, *Lyndon*, 324–325.

5. Johnson quoted in Kearns, *Lyndon Johnson*, 164. See also Thomas Brown, *JFK: History of an Image* (Bloomington, Indiana University Press, 1988), 24, and Evans and Novak, *Lyndon B. Johnson*, 354–355. A book attempting to link Johnson to the assassination is Joachim Joesten, *The Dark Side of Lyndon Baines Johnson* (London, Dawnay, 1968). Robert Kennedy once received an incoherent letter from author Taylor Caldwell asserting that Johnson had sponsored his brother's murder. See Taylor Caldwell to RFK, December 16, 1966, Robert Kennedy Senate Files/Personal Correspondences (RFK-SF/PC), box 2, JFKL.

6. Evans and Novak, *Lyndon B. Johnson*, 366–370.

7. LBJ quoted in Kearns, *Lyndon Johnson*, 172. Lyndon Johnson, *The Vantage Point: Perspectives of the Presidency, 1963–1969* (New York, Holt, Rinehart and Winston, 1971), 18.

8. Johnson's dual role is noted in Evans and Novak, *Lyndon B. Johnson*, 11. "What can I do…" noted in Manchester, *Death*, 387.

9. Jacqueline Kennedy's popularity was so high that several Democratic county chairmen wanted her to be Lyndon Johnson's running mate in 1964. See *New York Times*, January 3, 1964, 1.

10. LBJ to Jacqueline Kennedy, July 23, 1962, White House Famous Names—Mrs. John F. Kennedy (WHFN-Mrs. JFK), box 4, Lyndon B. Johnson Library (LBJL). "The Vice-President and Mrs. Kennedy," n.d., WHFN-JFK, box 4, LBJL. Jacqueline Kennedy, Lyndon B. Johnson Library—Oral History (LBJL-OH), 6–7. Miller, *Lyndon*, 335.

11. Miller, *Lyndon*, 335–336, 444–446. Harry McPherson, LBJL-OH, Tape 3, 24.

12. Jacqueline Kennedy, LBJL-OH, 1, 3, 13. LBJ to Jacqueline Kennedy, n.d. President's Office Files (POF), box 30, John F. Kennedy Library (JFKL).

13. LBJ's romance with Lady Bird noted in Caro, *Path*, 294, 298–301. See also Robert A. Caro, *The Years of Lyndon Johnson: Means of Ascent* (New York, Alfred A. Knopf, 1990), 54–71.

14. Caro, *Path*, 478–485.

15. *Newsweek*, "LBJ on the Assassination," May 11, 1970, 41. Manchester, *Death*, 317–318, 346. Jacqueline Kennedy, LBJL-OH, 4–5.

16. Manchester, *Death*, 402. *New York Times*, March 16, 1964, 18–19. Arthur M. Schlesinger, Jr., *Robert Kennedy and His Times* (Boston, Houghton Mifflin, 1978), 646–647, notes Lady Bird's contention: "Lyndon would like to take all the stars in the sky and string them on a necklace for Mrs. Kennedy." Pierre Salinger, *With Kennedy* (Garden City, Doubleday, 1966), 336.

17. Jacqueline Kennedy, LBJL-OH, 7–8. LBJ to Jacqueline Kennedy, November 29, 1963, FG2, box 40, LBJL.

18. Jacqueline Kennedy to LBJ, October 26, 1964, WHFN-Mrs. JFK, box 4, LBJL. *New York Times*, March 8, 1964, 54. Jacqueline Kennedy to LBJ, May 16, 1964, WHFN-Mrs. JFK, box 4, LBJL.

19. Jacqueline Kennedy, LBJL-OH, 6–7, 13–14.

20. For a discussion of Jacqueline's manipulation of history after the assassination, see Theodore H. White, *In Search of History: A Personal Adventure* (New York, Harper and Row, 1978), 518–524. Charles Bartlett, LBJL-OH, 8.

21. Jacqueline Kennedy, LBJL-OH, 13.

22. Johnson appeared at various dedication ceremonies in John Kennedy's honor and often assumed responsibility for preserving his predecessor's memory. In December 1963 he approved an act authorizing a fifty-cent coin engraved with the late president's profile. That month Johnson awarded John Kennedy the Medal of Freedom. In January 1964 he signed a bill authorizing federal participation in the construction of the John F. Kennedy Center for the Performing Arts. In May he authorized Kennedy's portrait to be printed on the seventy-five-dollar United States Savings Bond. See *Public Papers of the Presidents of the United States: Lyndon B. Johnson, 1963–64* (Washington, Government Printing Office, 1965), 26, 29, 41, 46, 598.

23. Manchester, *Death*, 318–322.

24. Salinger, *With Kennedy*, 336. *New York Times*, February 26, 1964, 14; February 27, 1964, 18.

25. Charles Roche to Jack Valenti, September 24, 1964, PL2, box 84, LBJL. Jack Valenti to Charles Roche, September 29, 1964, FG2, box 40, LBJL. Jacqueline Kennedy, LBJL-OH, 9. *New York Times*, October 15, 1964, 1.

26. Jacqueline Kennedy, LBJL-OH, 15–18. *New York Times*, April 23, 1965, 1. Robert and Ethel Kennedy, as well as Jacqueline Kennedy's mother, did attend the dedication of the garden. Lady Bird noted that the garden reflected "the unfailing taste" of the former First Lady. Johnson's equating of love and votes noted in Kearns, *Lyndon Johnson*, 58–60.

27. Schlesinger, *Robert Kennedy*, 647. Kearns, *Lyndon Johnson*, 9–11.

28. LBJ to Jacqueline Kennedy, December 15, 1964, WHFN-Mrs. JFK, box 4, LBJL. *New York Times*, December 30, 1964, 10.

29. Dean Markham to Robert Kennedy, November 28, 1963, Robert Kennedy, Attorney General Files, box 7, JFKL. Richard N. Goodwin, *Remembering America: A Voice from the Sixties* (Boston, Little, Brown, 1988), 246. Clark Clifford, LBJL-OH, part II, 5. Jacqueline Kennedy, LBJL-OH, 5. RFK's responsibility to the Kennedy legacy and its implications for Johnson are also noted in Anthony Lewis column, *New York Times*, March 22, 1964.

30. Eric Goldman, *The Tragedy of Lyndon Johnson* (New York, Dell, 1969), 92–93. Clifford, LBJL-OH, 5. Theodore H. White, *The Making of the President 1964* (New York, Atheneum, 1965), 312.

31. Miller, *Lyndon*, 601. Manchester, *Death*, 476. Schlesinger, *Robert Kennedy*, 627.

32. Schlesinger, *Robert Kennedy*, 626–627. Manchester, *Death*, 476.

33. Kenneth W. Thompson, ed., *The Johnson Presidency* (Lanham, Md., University Press of America, 1986), 148. Schlesinger, *Robert Kennedy*, 627. Manchester, *Death*, 477–478.

34. Schlesinger, *Robert Kennedy*, 627–628.

35. Schlesinger, *Robert Kennedy*, 628, 648. Edwin O. Guthman and Jeffrey Shulman, eds., *Robert Kennedy in His Own Words: The Unpublished Recollections of the Kennedy Years* (New York, Bantam, 1988), 407.

36. Dean Markham to Robert Kennedy, November 28, 1963, Robert Kennedy, Attorney General Files, box 7, JFKL. Schlesinger, *Robert Kennedy*, 627, 647. See also Miller, *Lyndon*, 331. Guthman and Shulman, eds., *Robert Kennedy*, 407, 415.

37. Goldman, *Tragedy*, 91–92. Jack Valenti, *A Very Human President* (New York, W. W. Norton, 1976), 123.

38. Goldman, *Tragedy*, 93. Schlesinger, *Robert Kennedy*, 649. Guthman and Shulman, eds., *Robert Kennedy*, 326–327.

39. Stewart Alsop, "Only Johnson Can Beat Johnson," *Saturday Evening Post*, January 4, 1964, 12. Johnson quoted in Evans and Novak, *Lyndon B. Johnson*, 459. In Kenneth P. O'Donnell, David Powers, and Joe McCarthy, *"Johnny, We Hardly Knew Ye"* (Boston, Little, Brown, 1972), 391, Johnson told O'Donnell, "I don't want history to say I was elected to this office because I had Bobby on the ticket with me. But I'll take him if I need him." See also *U.S. News and World Report*, " 'Bobby' Kennedy on LBJ's '64 Ticket?" March 23, 1964, 42–44, for early speculation of RFK's chances of being selected. See also *Newsweek*, "The No. 2 Man," January 13, 1964, 17–18.

40. *Newsweek*, "Bobby's Back," January 20, 1964, 14. *New York Times*, March 11, 1964, 19. Goldman, *Tragedy*, 92, 233. Miller, *Lyndon*, 387.

41. Schlesinger, *Robert Kennedy*, 646. White, *The Making 1964*, 312–313.

42. Kearns, *Lyndon Johnson*, 199–200. Schlesinger, *Robert Kennedy*, 647. Goldman, *Tragedy*, 233. Lawrence O'Brien, *No Final Victories: A Life in Politics from JFK to Watergate* (Garden City, Doubleday, 1974), 174. Valenti, *A Very*, 128.

43. Goodwin, *Remembering*, 295, notes that Robert Kennedy wanted to be offered the vice-presidential nomination. Schlesinger, *Robert Kennedy*, 651–652. *Newsweek*, "A Vice Presidential Skirmish," March 16, 1964, 27–28.

44. *New York Times*, March 16, 1964, 18. Schlesinger, *Robert Kennedy*, 651–652. Guthman and Shulman, eds., *Robert Kennedy*, 406–407.

45. *Newsweek*, "What's Bobby Going to Do?" July 6, 1964, 24–26.

46. *Newsweek*, "Tour Time," July 13, 1964. O'Donnell, *"Johnny,"* 458. Schlesinger, *Robert Kennedy*, 666.

47. *Newsweek*, "Periscope," August 31, 1964, notes that Higgins was helping Rose Kennedy to write an autobiography. Horace Busby to Walter Jenkins, July 7, 1964, Busby, box 19, LBJL. Memorandum from Chicago, July 23, 1964, FG, box 183, LBJL.

48. Schlesinger, *Robert Kennedy*, 662. White, *Making, 1964*, 314. Goldman, *Tragedy*, 234. *Newsweek*, "LBJ and RFK," August 10, 1964, 19.

49. Evans and Novak, *Lyndon B. Johnson*, 465–466.

50. Evans and Novak, *Lyndon B. Johnson*, 460. Miller, *Lyndon*, 386–387.

51. O'Brien, *No Final*, 174. Evans and Novak, *Lyndon B. Johnson*, 467. Nancy Dickerson, *Among Those Present: A Reporter's View of 25 Years in Washington* (New York, Random House, 1976), 123. Goldman, *Tragedy*, 234.

52. Horace Busby to LBJ, August 16, 1964, Busby, box 54, LBJL.

53. Kathleen Turner, *Lyndon Johnson's Dual War: Vietnam and the Press* (Chicago, University of Chicago Press, 1985), 88. Schlesinger, *Robert Kennedy*, 658. Goldman, *Tragedy*, 231. Miller, *Lyndon*, 603.

54. Goldman, *Tragedy*, 231. Jack Valenti, LBJL-OH, part II, 8. *Newsweek*, July 7, 1964, 24–26. Guthman and Shulman, eds., *Robert Kennedy*, 414. Johnson's concern for RFK is also noted in O'Donnell, *"Johnny,"* 455.

55. Kearns, *Lyndon Johnson*, 199–200.

56. Miller, *Lyndon*, 388.

57. "The President's Campaign Objectives," July 1964, PL/Kennedy, box 26, LBJL. Although the memorandum is unsigned, Clifford discussed preparing a memorandum to LBJ before the meeting. See Clifford, LBJL-OH, part II, 8.

58. "Memorandum," n.d., WHFN-RFK, box 6, LBJL.

59. "DT to vm," September 30, 1964, WHFN-RFK, box 6, LBJL. Johnson, *The Vantage Point*, 98–100.

60. Schlesinger, *Robert Kennedy*, 659–661.

61. Schlesinger, *Robert Kennedy*, 661. *Newsweek*, August 10, 1964, 19. Evans and Novak, *Lyndon B. Johnson*, 469–470.

62. *New York Times*, July 31, 1964, 8. Kearns, *Lyndon Johnson*, 202.

63. *New York Times*, July 31, 1964, 1. *Newsweek*, August 10, 1964, 19. *Newsweek*, "Now—A Lyndon Johnson Party," August 10, 1964, 18–19. *U.S. News and World Report*, "Why the President . . . ," August 10, 1964, 14–15. See also Clifford, LBJL-OH, part II, 8; Goldman, *Tragedy*, 235; Evans and Novak, *Lyndon B. Johnson*, 469.

64. Goldman, *Tragedy*, 236. White, *The Making 1964*, 317. Miller, *Lyndon*, 389.

65. Schlesinger, *Robert Kennedy*, 662.

66. Goldman, *Tragedy*, 233.

67. O'Brien, *No Final*, 174–176. Richard Gid Powers, *Secrecy and Power: The Life of J. Edgar Hoover* (New York, Free Press, 1987), 390–399, 433–434. Guthman and Shulman, eds., *Robert Kennedy*, 132. Schlesinger, *Robert Kennedy*, 662–664.

68. Johnson's concern for the publication of the Warren Report and the long-term political implications of the report for him is noted in Michael Schuyler, "The Bitter Harvest: Lyndon B. Johnson and the Assassination of John F. Kennedy," *Journal of American Culture* 88 (Fall 1985), 101–109. Bundy's memorandum to Johnson noted on 102–103. Schuyler also notes memoranda that was sent to LBJ about accusations that he was responsible for the Kennedy assassination. The administration debated the wisdom of responding publicly to such critics.

69. Goldman, *Tragedy*, 226. *New York Times*, August 23, 1964, 82, 83. *Newsweek*, "It's LBJ Week in Atlantic City," August 31, 1964, 15. Douglass Cater to Bill Moyers, July 15, 1964, Cater, box 13, LBJL.

70. Douglass Cater to LBJ, July 21, 1964, Cater, box 13, LBJL. Memorandum to Moyers, August 5, 1964, PL1, box 78, LBJL. Douglass Cater to Bill Moyers, August 5, 1964, Cater, box 13, LBJL.

71. "Schedule for Atlantic City," August 27, 1964, Statements File, box 117, LBJL.

72. Evans and Novak, *Lyndon B. Johnson*, 465. George Reedy, *Lyndon B. Johnson: A Memoir* (New York, Andrews and McMeel, 1982), 55–56.

73. Miller, *Lyndon*, 390–391. Johnson, *The Vantage Point*, 93–94, 97–98.

74. *New York Times*, August 28, 1964, 1, reported, "If Mr. Johnson is identified with an older generation of Democrats, Mr. Humphrey is somewhat nearer to the younger men and women who found a new hero in John F. Kennedy." *Newsweek*, "In Love with Night," September 7, 1964, 27–29. *New York Times*, August 23, 1964, 84. *New York Times*, August 28, 1964, 1. *New York Times*, August 26, 1964, 1. *New York Times*, August 17, 1964. Goldman, *Tragedy*, 252. "Signs of continued loyalty—at least to the Kennedy name—struck the eye and ear throughout the convention city," *Newsweek* reported.

75. *New York Times*, August 28, 1964, 1. NBC news broadcast.

76. Theodore Sorensen to RFK, August 25, 1964, phone dictation, Attorney General File, box 3, JFKL. RFK deleted references to his brother's support of LBJ in "Dictated over phone RFK," August 26, 1964, text of speech, Attorney General File, box 3, JFKL, and "Final Draft," August 26, 1964, Attorney General File, box 3, JFKL. Those who sent drafts of various speeches or offered suggestions included Theodore Sorensen, Joseph Kraft, and Edwin Guthman. *New York Times*, August 28, 1964, 1. *Newsweek*, September 7, 1964, 27–29. Schlesinger, *Robert Kennedy*, 664–665.

77. *Newsweek*, September 7, 1964, 27–29. *Newsweek* reviewed the Kennedy film as "a fresh—and artfully edited—reminder of JFK's style . . . recreat[ing] the spirited beginning, the tragic end of the brief Kennedy Administration."

78. Diary Entry, August 27, 1964, Daily Diary, box 2, LBJL. Goldman, *Tragedy*, 255–258. White, *The Making 1964*, 348, characterized Johnson's speech as the "poorest he made in the campaign."

79. *Public Papers, 1963–64*, 541. *Newsweek*, "LBJ: 'I Ask for a Mandate to Begin,' " September 7, 1964, 16.

CHAPTER V
Managing the White House: Johnson and the New Frontiersmen

1. McGeorge Bundy, "Opening Address," Presidential Conferences, John F. Kennedy, The Promise Revisited, Hofstra University, New York, March 28, 1985. The importance of Johnson's relationship with the Kennedy staff is noted in Anthony Lewis column, *New York Time*, March 22, 1964.

2. Doris Kearns, *Lyndon Johnson and the American Dream* (New York, Harper and Row, 1976), 174–178. Johnson reiterated his feelings in his memoir, claiming "a deep-rooted sense of responsibility" to his predecessor. Lyndon Johnson, *The Vantage Point: Perspectives of the Presidency, 1963–1969* (New York, Holt, Rinehart and Winston, 1971), 19.

3. Eric Goldman, *The Tragedy of Lyndon Johnson* (New York, Dell, 1969), 26. Kenneth W. Thompson, ed., *The Johnson Presidency* (Lanham, Md., University Press of America, 1986), 49. Rowland Evans and Robert Novak, *Lyndon B. Johnson: The Exercise of Power* (New York, New American Library, 1966), 358. Johnson, *Vantage Point*, 19.

4. Harry McPherson, Lyndon B. Johnson Library—Oral History (LBJL-OH), tape 3, 17. Bundy noted in a memorandum to LBJ that many of the staff "are quite numb with personal grief, and in keeping with your own instinct of last night you will wish to avoid any suggestion of over-assertiveness." See McGeorge Bundy to LBJ, November 23, 1963, Cabinet Papers, box 1, LBJL. "Suddenly..." noted in Kearns, *Lyndon Johnson*, 175. For an account of the first cabinet meeting, see Merle Miller, *Lyndon: An Oral Biography* (New York, Putnam, 1980), 330. "Remarks to the Cabinet," November 23, 1963, Cabinet Papers, box 1, LBJL. "Summary Remarks to the Cabinet," November 23, 1963, Cabinet Papers, box 1, LBJL. See also William Manchester, *The Death of a President* (New York, Harper and Row, 1967), 475. The rough draft of Johnson's prepared statement contained an additional plea, reflecting his underlying confidence in Kennedy's people and the humility he was willing to express: "I am looking to all of you for your wisdom, your talent, your counsel, and your help." Bundy wrote later that it was "typical of [Johnson] that he made [the memorandum] his own in action."

5. Goldman, *Tragedy*, 29. Evans and Novak, *Lyndon B. Johnson*, 364. Lawrence O'Brien, *No Final Victories: A Life in Politics from JFK to Watergate* (Garden City, Doubleday, 1974), 169. Johnson, *Vantage Point*, 21.

6. Arthur M. Schlesinger, Jr., LBJL-OH, 15–16.

7. Richard N. Goodwin, *Remembering America: A Voice from the Sixties* (Boston, Little, Brown, 1988), 247.

8. For a discussion of the division between Johnson and Kennedy staff members, see Miller, *Lyndon*, 330–331; Charles Bartlett, LBJL-OH, 8–9; Johnson, *Vantage Point*, 18. For a discussion of staff complaints against LBJ after the assassination, see Arthur M. Schlesinger, Jr., *Robert Kennedy and His Times* (Boston, Houghton Mifflin, 1978), 626–627; Goldman, *Tragedy*, 20; Miller, *Lyndon*, 601; Schlesinger, LBJL-OH, 16–17. For a defense of Johnson's actions after the assassination, see Johnson, *Vantage Point*, 16. Miller, *Lyndon*, 315, 320. O'Brien, *No Final*, 164. Rose Kennedy to LBJ, February 21, 1964, White House Famous Names (WHFN)—Ambassador and Mrs. Joseph P. Kennedy, LBJL.

9. Patrick Anderson, *The President's Men* (Garden City, Doubleday, 1968), 213–217.

10. *Playboy* Interview with Arthur M. Schlesinger, Jr., *Playboy* 13 (1966), 209.

11. Anderson, *President's Men*, 276–286. Herbert Parmet, *Jack: The Struggles of John F. Kennedy* (New York, Doubleday/Dial, 1977).

12. Anderson, *President's Men*, 233–234.

13. Anderson, *President's Men*, 239–242. John Roche, LBJL-OH, 55–56.

14. Manchester, *Death*, 449–450, 474. John Kenneth Galbraith, *Ambassador's Journal: A Personal Account of the Kennedy Years* (Boston, Houghton Mifflin, 1969), 519. Miller, *Lyndon*, 308. Arthur M. Schlesinger, Jr., *A Thousand Days: John F. Kennedy in the White House* (Boston, Houghton Mifflin, 1965), 18–19. Schlesinger, LBJL-OH, 1. Horace Busby to LBJ, January 23, 1964, FG/RS/PR18, box 9, LBJL. Evans and Novak, *Lyndon B. Johnson*, 361.

15. Johnson, *Vantage Point*, 21. Jack Valenti, LBJL-OH, 27–29. In December 1963 Sorensen was irritated that Johnson planned to present awards at the Presidential Medal of

Freedom ceremony. Bickering also erupted between Sorensen and Valenti, who recalled that Sorensen was angry with Johnson for "turning his back on one of President Kennedy's great efforts."

16. Pierre Salinger, *With Kennedy* (Garden City, Doubleday, 1967), 331–333. Evans and Novak, *Lyndon B. Johnson*, 311. Pierre Salinger to White House Press Staff, February 10, 1964, FG2, box 40, LBJL.

17. Arthur Schlesinger to Bill Moyers, January 27, 1964, Moyers, box 10, LBJL. *New York Times*, January 29, 1964, 16. Arthur Schlesinger to Bill Moyers, January 29, 1964, Moyers, box 10, LBJL. Schlesinger also told Moyers that it was "inevitable and right" that Johnson "place his own stamp on the Administration." Schlesinger suggested he would be more useful working from the "outside."

18. *New York Times*, January 16, 1964, 1. Goldman, *Tragedy*, 95–96. The *New York Times* noted that the White House "sought to emphasize that there was no personal or policy differences between them." Nor was Sorensen's resignation "expected to set off a round of resignations from other former Kennedy assistants." But the departure "might force the President to begin what he has so far refrained from doing, reorganizing the White House staff to suit his own operating methods."

19. *New York Times*, March 20, 1964, 1. Kathleen Turner, *Lyndon Johnson's Dual War: Vietnam and the Press* (Chicago, University of Chicago Press, 1985), 63. Anthony Lewis column, *New York Times*, March 22, 1964. James Reston column, *New York Times*, March 22, 1964. *New York Times*, March 22, 1964, 44. James Reston wrote an obituary for Johnson's commitment to the Kennedy legacy: "Both the period of mourning for President Kennedy and of experimentation for President Johnson are over. . . . The nostalgic pretense of the first three months of the Johnson Administration is vanishing."

20. Clark Clifford, LBJL-OH, part II, 4–5. Roche, LBJL-OH, 10. Goldman, *Tragedy*, 18. Kenneth O'Donnell, *"Johnny, We Hardly Knew Ye": Memories of John Fitzgerald Kennedy* (Boston, Little, Brown, 1972), 452, 456, 469. Valenti, LBJL-OH, 30. Anderson, *President's Men*, 244.

21. Anderson, *President's Men*, 197–198.

22. Anderson, *President's Men*, 290. Jack Valenti to LBJ, September 3, 1964, PL2, box 83, LBJL. *New York Times*, January 17, 1965.

23. Anderson, *President's Men*, 220–226. Goldman, *Tragedy*, 131–132. Valenti, LBJL-OH, 13.

24. Goodwin, *Remembering*, 271. Schlesinger, LBJL-OH, 14–16. Tom Wicker, "Johnson's Men: 'Valuable Hunks of Humanity,'" *New York Times Magazine*, May 3, 1964, 11ff.

25. Goldman, *Tragedy*, 19. Harry McPherson, *A Political Education* (Boston, Little, Brown, 1972), 247. O'Brien, *No Final*, 180. Schlesinger, *Robert Kennedy*, 632.

26. Luman H. Long, ed., *The World Almanac 1967* (New York, Newspaper Enterprise Association, 1966), 718. *Newsweek*, "Echoes," October 19, 1964, 34–35. *Newsweek*, "Now There Are Two Senators Kennedy," November 9, 1964, 35–36. Andy Logan, "The Stained Glass Image," *American Heritage* (August 1967), 5–7, 75–78. McGeorge Bundy, "The History-Maker," *Massachusetts Historical Society* (December 1978), 78. A review of the "loyalist" literature as well as other accounts of the Kennedy administration are noted in Donald C. Lord, *John F. Kennedy: The Politics of Confrontation and Conciliation* (Woodbury, N.Y., Barron's, 1977), 295–320.

27. When Sorensen resigned, critics soon sensed a "word gap" and contended that Johnson's speeches suffered from "clumsy images and poor metaphors." See *Newsweek*, "JFK's Alter Ego," January 27, 1964. *Newsweek*, "Closing the Word Gap?" April 13, 1964, 23.

28. Anderson, *President's Men*, 245–249.

29. Goldman, *Tragedy*, 95. O'Brien, *No Final*, 11–14.

30. Anderson, *President's Men*, 261–263, 271. Nelson Lichtenstein, ed., *Political Profiles: The Johnson Years* (New York, Facts on File, 1976), 75–77.

31. Thompson, ed., *The Johnson Presidency*, 139, 142. Lichtenstein, ed., *Political Profiles*, 390–394.

32. Lichtenstein, ed., *Political Profiles*, 535–537. Schlesinger, *A Thousand Days*, 435–437, 1017.

33. O'Brien, *No Final*, 164–166. Anderson, *President's Men*, 257.

34. Anderson, *President's Men*, 257–258. O'Brien, *No Final*, 178, 199. Goldman, *Tragedy*, 95.

35. *Newsweek*, "Periscope," April 20, 1964. Evans and Novak, *Lyndon B. Johnson*, 359–360. Lichtenstein, ed., *Political Profiles*, 265–266. Goldman, *Tragedy*, 94–95. Anderson, *President's Men*, 292. Johnson persuaded other important members of the Kennedy administration to remain as well. Treasury Secretary Douglas Dillon also remained temporarily with the Johnson administration. Perceived by Johnson as an Ivy League, Eastern Establishment Republican, the conservative banker and former undersecretary during the Eisenhower administration did not inspire Johnson's trust. He remained until after Johnson's election in 1964, but his departure was due less to questions of loyalty to Kennedy than to his conservative political background.

36. Miller, *Lyndon*, 321–322. George Ball, *The Past Has Another Pattern: Memoirs* (New York, W. W. Norton, 1982), 313.

37. Evans and Novak, *Lyndon B. Johnson*, 359. Anderson, *President's Men*, 271–274. *Newsweek*, "The Austin-Boston Axis," January 13, 1964, 20. Jack Valenti, *A Very Personal President* (New York, W. W. Norton, 1976), 61.

38. Henry L. Trewhitt, *McNamara* (New York, Harper and Row, 1971), 255. Goldman, *Tragedy*, 94. Kearns, *Lyndon Johnson*, 177. Johnson, *Vantage Point*, 20.

39. Goldman, *Tragedy*, 93–94. Schlesinger, LBJL-OH, 24–25.

40. George Reedy, *Lyndon B. Johnson: A Memoir* (New York, Andrews and McMeel, 1982), 146. Thompson, ed., *The Johnson Presidency*, 13, 89, 244. McPherson, LBJL-OH, 32–33. Clifford, LBJL-OH, part II, 15.

41. Thompson, ed., *The Johnson Presidency*, 89, 261.

42. Lichtenstein, ed., *Political Profiles*, 32. Ball, *The Past*, 317, 425.

43. Thompson, ed., *The Johnson Presidency*, 50.

44. McGeorge Bundy to LBJ, December 3, 1963, FG/RS/PR18, box 9, LBJL. Anthony Lewis column, *New York Times*, March 22, 1964. Schlesinger, *Robert Kennedy*, 648. Lichtenstein, ed., *Political Profiles*, 75–77.

45. Richard Tanner Johnson, *Managing the White House: An Intimate Study of the Presidency* (New York, Harper and Row, 1974), 178.

46. Speech to the Cabinet, May 28, 1964, Moyers, box 127, LBJL. *Public Papers of the President of the United States: Lyndon B. Johnson, 1963–64* (Washington, Government Printing Office, 1965), 370.

CHAPTER VI

"Let Us Continue":
Johnson's Legislative Record and the Kennedy Shadow

1. *Public Papers of the Presidents of the United States: Lyndon B. Johnson, 1963–64* (Washington, Government Printing Office, 1965), 8–10. Doris Kearns, *Lyndon Johnson and the American Dream* (New York, Harper and Row, 1976), 173–174. The construction of the November 27 speech and reaction to its message is summarized in Patricia D. Witherspoon, " 'Let Us Continue': The Rhetorical Initiation of Lyndon Johnson's Presidency," *Presidential Studies Quarterly* 17 (Summer 1987), 531–539. See also George Reedy, *Lyndon B. Johnson: A Memoir* (New York, Andrews and McMeel, 1982), 15–16; Merle Miller, *Lyndon: An Oral Biography* (New York, Putnam, 1980), 337; Jack Valenti, Lyndon B. Johnson Library—Oral History (LBJL-OH), part II, 25.

2. William Leuchtenburg, *In the Shadow of FDR: From Harry Truman to Ronald Reagan* (Ithaca, Cornell University Press, 1983), 123–130, 137. For a discussion of Johnson's sincerity toward domestic reform, see Robert A. Caro, *The Years of Lyndon Johnson: The Path to Power* (New York, Alfred A. Knopf, 1983), 273–275, 547–549, 766–767.

3. Memorandum to Bill Moyers, November 23, 1963, FG1, box 10, LBJL. "In Los Angeles, I helped to draft that program," the statement read. "As the Vice Presidential candidate, I endorsed that program. In the last campaign, I explained that program. And, in office, I helped to implement that program." Robert Sherrill, *The Accidental President* (New York, Grossman, 1967), 194.

4. Kenneth W. Thompson, ed., *The Johnson Presidency* (Lanham, Md., University Press of America, 1986), 6–7, 11–12. Richard N. Goodwin, *Remembering America: A Voice from the Sixties* (Boston, Little, Brown, 1988), 257. See also Arthur M. Schlesinger, Jr., LBJL-OH, 16.

5. Thompson, ed., *The Johnson Presidency*, 229.

6. Rowland Evans and Robert Novak, *Lyndon B. Johnson: The Exercise of Power* (New York, New American Library, 1966), 131–134.

7. For discussions regarding Johnson's sincerity toward civil rights, see Goodwin, *Remembering*, 257–258; Steven F. Lawson, "Civil Rights," in Robert A. Divine, ed., *The Johnson Years: Foreign Policy, the Great Society, and the White House* (Lawrence, University Press of Kansas, 1987), 93–97; Miller, *Lyndon*, 365–369; Monroe Billington, "Lyndon B. Johnson and Blacks: The Early Years," *Journal of Negro History* 62 (1), 1977, 26–42; Sidney Blumenthal, "Getting It All Wrong: The Years of Robert Caro," *New Republic*, June 4, 1990, 32.

8. Evans and Novak, *Lyndon B. Johnson*, 132–134.

9. Evans and Novak, *Lyndon B. Johnson*, 134–137.

10. Kearns, *Lyndon Johnson*, 144–151.

11. Edwin O. Guthman and Jeffrey Shulman, eds., *Robert Kennedy in His Own Words: The Unpublished Recollections of the Kennedy Years* (New York, Bantam, 1988), 149.

12. Nicholas deB. Katzenbach, LBJL-OH, 14–15. Guthman and Shulman, eds., *Robert Kennedy*, 211–212. Lawson, in *Johnson Years*, 98. Lyndon Johnson, *The Vantage Point: Perspectives of the Presidency, 1963–1969* (New York, Holt, Rinehart and Winston, 1971), 157. For a transcript of Johnson's conversation with Sorensen, see Steven F. Lawson, " 'I Got It from the New York Times': Lyndon Johnson and the Kennedy Civil Rights Program," *Journal of Negro History* 67 (2), 1982, 159–172. For an argument that contends that JFK pursued LBJ's advice, see Michael P. Riccards, "Rare Counsel: Kennedy, Johnson, and the Civil Rights Bill of 1963," *Presidential Studies Quarterly* 11 (Summer 1981), 395–398.

13. Goodwin, *Remembering*, 257–258. Kearns, *Lyndon Johnson*, 191. See also Katzenbach, LBJL-OH, 5.

14. Kearns, *Lyndon Johnson*, 191–193. Johnson, *Vantage Point*, 29. *Public Papers, 1963–64*, 113, 170. *New York Times*, May 10, 1964, 73. Arthur M. Schlesinger, Jr., *Robert Kennedy and His Times* (Boston, Houghton Mifflin, 1978), 644–645. Guthman and Shulman, eds., *Robert Kennedy*, 211–212. Miller, *Lyndon*, 367.

15. Goodwin, *Remembering*, 313–314. Miller, *Lyndon*, 369. Johnson, *Vantage Point*, 158. Russell quoted in Thompson, ed., *The Johnson Presidency*, 143.

16. Goodwin, *Remembering*, 315. Johnson, *Vantage Point*, 158–160. *Public Papers, 1963–64*, 842–844. Guthman and Shulman, ed., *Robert Kennedy*, 210–212.

17. Schlesinger, *Robert Kennedy*, 645. Days after he signed the Civil Rights Act, Johnson discussed with Nicholas Katzenbach his plans for an even more impressive act for 1965: "I want you to write me the goddamndest, toughest voting rights act that you can devise." See also *Public Papers, 1963–64*, 258, 842–844.

18. Bradley S. Greenberg and Edwin B. Parker, eds., *The Kennedy Assassination and the American Public: Social Communication in Crisis* (Stanford, Stanford University Press, 1965). Arthur M. Schlesinger, Jr., *A Thousand Days: John F. Kennedy in the White House* (Boston, Houghton Mifflin, 1965), 949. Thomas Brown, *JFK: History of an Image* (Bloomington, Indiana University Press, 1988), 8, 25. The notion that civil rights violence would not have occurred had John Kennedy lived is noted in Louis Heren, *No Hail, No Farewell* (New York, Harper and Row, 1970), 249. Other assertions that the assassinations of John and Robert Kennedy created a seedbed for upheaval are noted in Alfred John Farrari, "Kennedy Assassinations and Political Detours (A Possibly Romantic Posthumous Speculation)," *Minority of One*, November 1968, 7–9.

19. Memorandum to Bill Moyers, November 23, 1963, FG1, box 10, LBJL. Nicholas Lemann, "The Unfinished War," *Atlantic* 262 (December 1988), 38–39. Mark I. Gelfand,

"The War on Poverty," in Robert A. Divine, ed., *The Johnson Years: Foreign Policy, the Great Society, and the White House* (Lawrence, University Press of Kansas, 1987), 127–128.

20. Memoranda to Bill Moyers, November 23, 1963, FG1, box 10, LBJL. Richard Goodwin to LBJ, n.d., 1964, FG1, box 10, LBJL.

21. Goodwin, *Remembering*, 257, 269–270, 317.

22. Jack Valenti to LBJ, January 4, 1964, PR18, box 367, LBJL. Jack Valenti to LBJ, January 11, 1964, PR18, box 367, LBJL.

23. Lemann, *Atlantic*, 40–44. Miller, *Lyndon*, 363. Kearns, *Lyndon Johnson*, 188. Johnson, *Vantage Point*, 104.

24. *U.S. News and World Report*, "The 'Image' Johnson Is Trying to Create," February 3, 1964, 33. Goodwin, *Remembering*, 244. Lemann, *Atlantic*, 39. Schlesinger, *Robert Kennedy*, 637.

25. Lemann, *Atlantic*, 43–44.

26. Lemann, *Atlantic*, 47–48. Gelfand, in *The Johnson Years*, 130–131.

27. Valenti, LBJL-OH, 30.

28. Miller, *Lyndon*, 357–358. Johnson, *Vantage Point*, 37.

29. *Public Papers, 1963–64*, 115. Valenti, LBJL-OH, 30. *New York Times*, February 27, 1964.

30. Lemann, *Atlantic*, 47–49. Jules Witcover, *Marathon: The Pursuit of the Presidency, 1972–1976* (New York, Viking, 1977), 152, on Kennedy family resentment toward Shriver.

31. Gelfand, in *The Johnson Years*, 132–133. O'Brien quoted in Goodwin, *Remembering*, 260.

32. *Newsweek*, "LBJ: Perpetual Motion," May 4, 1964, 17–18. *Newsweek*, "Mr. Johnson: Larger than Life," August 31, 1964, 17. *Newsweek*, "The LBJ Image," August 31, 1964, 27. A comparison of Johnson's legislative record with Kennedy's is noted in Russell D. Renka, "Comparing Presidents Kennedy and Johnson as Legislative Leaders," *Presidential Studies Quarterly* 15 (Fall 1985), 806–825. Milton C. Cummings, Jr., ed., *The National Election of 1964* (Washington, Brookings Institution), 1966, 261–262.

33. *Newsweek*, "The LBJ Image," August 31, 1964, 27.

34. *Newsweek*, "The Brand of LBJ," August 17, 1964, 32, 34.

35. *New Republic*, "T.R.B. from Washington," May 2, 1964. James Reston column, *New York Times*, March 22, 1964, IV, 8.

36. *Public Papers of the Presidents of the United States: Lyndon Baines Johnson, 1963–64* (Washington, Government Printing Office, 1965), 1145, 1152, 1158–1159, 1248, 1275, 1287, 1466–1470, 1523–1529.

37. *Public Papers of the Presidents of the United States: Lyndon Baines Johnson, 1965* (Washington, Government Printing Office, 1966), 408–412. Evans and Novak, *Lyndon B. Johnson*, 10–11. Johnson made frequent references to Doris Kearns concerning his dedication to JFK's domestic policies. See Kearns, *Lyndon Johnson*, 178, and Johnson, *Vantage Point*, 19, 41. At a dedication of a JFK memorial park in Lewiston, Maine, in 1966, LBJ noted, "We have tried to carry forward his programs, put it on the statute books, and execute it as he would have us do." See Vaughn Davis Bornet, *The Presidency of Lyndon B. Johnson* (Lawrence, University Press of Kansas, 1983), 50. During his last meeting with Robert Kennedy in April 1968, Johnson told him that John Kennedy was watching him from heaven and approved his actions. See "Memorandum of Conversation," April 3, 1968, White House Famous Names—Robert F. Kennedy (WHFN-RFK), box 6, LBJL. "Notes on Meeting of the President with Senator Robert Kennedy," April 4, 1968, WHFN-RFK, box 6, LBJL.

38. Kearns, *Lyndon Johnson*, 340–341.

39. LBJ to Robert Kintner, November 24, 1966, Ex WE9, box 28, LBJL. Fred Panzer to Jake Jacobsen, November 26, 1966, Ex WE9, box 28, LBJL. Charles Maquire to Robert Kintner, November 25, 1966, CF FG/RS/PR18, box 16, LBJL. Bornet, *The Johnson Presidency*, 22. Robert Kintner to LBJ, August 10, 1966, CF FG1, box 16, LBJL. Robert Kintner to LBJ, August 17, 1966, CF FG/RS/PR18, box 16, LBJL. Joseph Califano to LBJ, November 7, 1967, FG2, box 41, LBJL. Bob Faiss to Jim Jones, December 10, 1968, FG2, box 41, LBJL. Goldman notes that JFK's memory goaded Johnson to achieve more legislation. See Eric Goldman, *The Tragedy of Lyndon Johnson* (New York, Dell, 1969), 21–22.

40. Goldman, *Tragedy*, 26–27. John Roche, LBJL-OH, 4. Evans and Novak, *Lyndon B. Johnson*, 10. Tom Wicker, "Lyndon Johnson vs. the Ghost of Jack Kennedy," *Esquire* 64 (November 1965), 148.

CHAPTER VII
Projecting the Johnson Image

1. Rowland Evans and Robert Novak, *Lyndon B. Johnson: The Exercise of Power* (New York, New American Library, 1966), 56. *Newsweek*, "Closing the Word Gap," April 13, 1964, 23. Tom Wicker, "Johnson's Men: 'Valuable Hunks of Humanity,'" *New York Times Magazine*, May 3, 1964, 11ff. According to Wicker, Busby was "a trusted associate of the President and his advice [was] listened to with respect."

2. Horace Busby to LBJ, January 14, 1964, Busby, box 53, Lyndon B. Johnson Library (LBJL).

3. Johnson's capacity for emulation noted in Robert A. Caro, *The Years of Lyndon Johnson: The Path to Power* (New York, Alfred A. Knopf, 1983), 695–698, 703–704, 706, 75–76, 98; George Reedy, *Lyndon B. Johnson: A Memoir* (New York, Andrews and McMeel, 1982), 21, 39; Kenneth W. Thompson, ed., *The Johnson Presidency* (Lanham, Md., University Press of America, 1987), 254–256; Doris Kearns, *Lyndon Johnson and the American Dream* (New York, Harper and Row, 1976), 103–106; William E. Leuchtenburg, *In the Shadow of FDR: From Harry Truman to Ronald Reagan* (Ithaca, Cornell University Press, 1983), 121 160; Merle Miller, *Lyndon: An Oral Biography* (New York, Putnam, 1980), 342–343; Paul K. Conkin, *Big Daddy from the Pedernales: Lyndon Baines Johnson* (Boston, Twayne, 1986), 157–158.

4. *Newsweek*, "Mr. Johnson: Larger than Life," August 31, 1964, 18. LBJ's use of media is discussed in David Culber, "Johnson and the Media," in Robert A. Divine, ed., *The Johnson Years: Foreign Policy, the Great Society, and the White House* (Lawrence, University Press of Kansas, 1987), 214–248. Harry McPherson, Lyndon B. Johnson Library—Oral History (LBJL-OH), tape 5, 26.

5. David Riesman, *The Lonely Crowd: A Study of the Changing American Character* (New Haven, Yale University Press, 1950). William H. Whyte, *The Organization Man* (Garden City, Doubleday, 1957).

6. Thomas Brown, *JFK: The History of an Image* (Bloomington, Indiana University Press, 1988), 12–13. Tom Wicker, "Lyndon Johnson vs. the Ghost of Jack Kennedy," *Esquire* 64 (November 1965), 149.

7. Michael Maccoby, *The Gamesman: Winning and Losing in the Career Game* (New York, Simon and Schuster, 1976), 26.

8. Maccoby, *Gamesman*, 73–83, 255. Brown, *JFK*, 25. Kathleen Turner, *Lyndon Johnson's Dual War: Vietnam and the Press* (Chicago, University of Chicago Press, 1985), 42. See also Wicker, *Esquire*, 148.

9. William Rivers, "The Correspondents After 25 Years," *Columbia Journalism Review* 1 (Spring 1962), 4–10. Tom Wicker, *On Press* (New York, Viking, 1978), 3.

10. Lyndon Johnson, *The Vantage Point: Perspectives of the Presidency, 1963–1969* (New York, Holt, Rinehart and Winston, 1971), 95.

11. Ben H. Bagdikian, "JFK to LBJ: Paradoxes of Change," *Columbia Journalism Review* (Winter 1964), 36. Harry McPherson, *A Political Education* (Boston, Little, Brown, 1972), 248. Thompson, ed., *The Johnson Presidency*, 106–107. Conversation with Tom Wicker, November 19, 1987. See also Turner, *Lyndon Johnson's*, 42; Sam Kinch, LBJL-OH, 17; "The Press and Government: Who's Telling the Truth," in Warren K. Agee, ed., *Mass Media in a Free Society* (Lawrence, University Press of Kansas, 1969), 19; Katharine Graham, LBJL-OH, 35; Charles Bartlett, LBJL-OH, 16–17.

12. Frank Luther Mott, *American Journalism: A History* (New York, Macmillan, 1962), 824. David Halberstam, *The Powers That Be* (New York, Alfred A. Knopf, 1979), 316.

13. Wicker, *On Press*, 94. Arthur M. Schlesinger, Jr., *A Thousand Days: John F. Kennedy in*

the White House (Boston, Houghton Mifflin, 1965), 716–717. For a simple and enjoyable assessment of the impact of television, see Neil Postman, *Amusing Ourselves to Death: Public Discourse in the Age of Showbiz* (New York, Viking, 1985). A more complex assessment of television's impact on politics is noted in Joshua Meyrowitz, *No Sense of Place: The Impact of Electronic Media on Social Behavior* (New York, Oxford University Press, 1985).

14. Thompson, *The Johnson Presidency*, 221. Jack Valenti, LBJL-OH, part v, 27, 30, 33. Reedy, *Lyndon B. Johnson*, 22. Turner, *Lyndon Johnson's*, 107. According to Reedy, television "gave him an opportunity to study his public appearances and, Pygmalion-like, seek to change his image." LBJ continuously re-evaluated and adjusted his hair style and the cut of his clothes. Johnson and his staff also engaged in "interminable arguments over the merits of horned rim versus rimless glasses."

15. Pierre Salinger, *With Kennedy* (Garden City, Doubleday, 1966), 337. Bill Moyers to LBJ, December 5, 1963, PR18-2, box 374, LBJL. Valenti, LBJL-OH, part v, 27. See also Bartlett, LBJL-OH, 16; Wicker, *On Press*, 86–87; Turner, *Lyndon Johnson's*, 43.

16. Bill Moyers to LBJ, December 7, 1963, PR18-2, box 374, LBJL, noted the reaction to Johnson's first press conference. "The excitement is unbelievable," Moyers wrote. "Some of the people are still in a daze.... You should dominate Sunday's papers." In early January Valenti sent Johnson a memorandum relaying the observations of a reporter who praised his press conferences as "exceptional—but he thinks you will have to expose yourself to TV conferences." See Jack Valenti to LBJ, January 8, 1964, PR18-2, box 374, LBJL. Tom Wicker, "Johnson Seeks Policy on Press," *New York Times*, February 9, 1964, part v, 8. *Newsweek*, "If I Do Run," March 9, 1964, 17. News release of ABC Network Radio Broadcast of Edward Morgan, April 16, 1964, PR18-2, box 374, LBJL.

17. Kearns, *Lyndon Johnson*, 315. Evans and Novak, *Lyndon B. Johnson*, 375. Turner, *Lyndon Johnson's*, 96. Turner contended that Cormier never said the quote often attributed to him. Nevertheless, the point that Johnson felt in competition with JFK is clear. See also Evans and Novak, *Lyndon B. Johnson*, 499; John Roche, LBJL-OH, 38.

18. Thompson, ed., *The Johnson Presidency*, 88. Reedy, *Lyndon B. Johnson*, 62, 67–68.

19. William Spragens interview with George Christian, 2. Conversation with Tom Wicker, November 19, 1987. LBJ noted the competition he felt with JFK, saying in an interview, "I had my problems in my conduct of office being contrasted with President Kennedy's conduct in office, with my accent and his accent, with my background and his background." See "LBJ: Tragedy and Transition," broadcast, Saturday, May 2, 1970, produced by CBS News with Walter Cronkite.

20. *U.S. News and World Report*, "The 'Image' Johnson Is Trying to Create," February 3, 1964, 32–33. *Newsweek*, "Mr. Johnson: Larger Than Life," August 31, 1964, 16–17.

21. Horace Busby to LBJ, April 1964, Busby, box 52, LBJL.

22. Jack Valenti to LBJ, January 4, 1964, PR18, box 367, LBJL. Jack Valenti to LBJ, January 11, 1964, PR18, box 367, LBJL. Reston's suggestion noted in Eric Goldman to LBJ, March 4, 1964, PR18, box 367, LBJL.

23. Robert A. Divine, "The Johnson Literature," in Divine, *The Johnson Years*, 14–15. Reedy, *Lyndon B. Johnson*, 138. *U.S. News and World Report*, "On a Poverty Trip with LBJ," May 25, 1964, 58. *Newsweek*, "Tours de Force," May 18, 1964, 33–34. *Time*, "The Presidency," May 1, 1964, 17–21. *Newsweek*, "Love in November," June 8, 1964, 16–17. *Newsweek*, "April and November," April 27, 1964, 26–28. *Newsweek*, "LBJ: Perpetual Motion," May 4, 1964, 17–18.

24. Conversation with Tom Wicker, November 19, 1964. *Newsweek*, "Sparerib Summit," January 6, 1964, 12. *Newsweek*, "The Austin-Boston Axis," January 13, 1964, 20. *U.S. News and World Report*, "Diplomacy at LBJ Ranch," January 6, 1964, 26. *Newsweek*, "Workweek," January 27, 1964, 16. *U.S. News and World Report*, "There's a New Social Style at the White House," February 17, 1964, 60–61, 63.

25. *U.S. News and World Report*, "New Social Style," 61. *Newsweek*, "Still Lyndon Johnson," April 20, 1964, 36–37. One aide argued against the pretentiousness of the past administration: "President and Mrs. Johnson are trying to humanize White House entertainment. ... Have you ever tried to entertain your friends in a national museum and make them feel at home there?" *Newsweek*, "In the Driver's Seat," April 13, 1964, 22–23. *New York Times*,

April 7, 1964, 20. *Time*, "Mr. President, You're Fun," April 10, 1964, 23–23A. *Time*, "Letters to the Editor," 25, noted that the story was "disconcerting at a time when the nation is still adjusting to the tragic loss of President Kennedy." *Time*, "Letters to the Editor," May 8, 1964, 13, notes, "What puzzles me is the fact that Johnson is making a joke of being President. His driving escapade in Texas . . . and his crude conversations are not characteristic of a good President." *U.S. News and World Report*, "Why Press Reports Irk Johnson," April 20, 1964, 21. *Newsweek*, "By the Ears," May 11, 1964, 21. *U.S. News and World Report*, "As Dog Lovers Took Pen in Hand," May 11, 1964, 6. Kenneth Crawford column, *Newsweek*, May 11, 1964, 34.

26. *Newsweek*, "Still Lyndon Johnson," 36.

27. Miller, *Lyndon*, 342–346.

28. For a discussion of Johnson's intellectual abilities, see Bernard J. Firestone and Robert C. Vogt, *Lyndon Baines Johnson and the Uses of Power* (New York, Greenwood, 1988), 356; James David Barber, *The Presidential Character: Predicting Performance in the White House* (Englewood Cliffs, N.J., Prentice-Hall, 1972), 74; Thompson, ed., *The Johnson Presidency*, 254; Roche, LBJL-OH, 3, 8–9. Milton Gordon, *Assimilation in American Life: The Role of Race, Religion, and National Origins* (New York, Oxford University Press, 1964), 224–232. Brown, *JFK*, 8–12. Frederick Dutton to RFK, December 8, 1966, Robert F. Kennedy–Senate Files/Personal Correspondence (RFK-SF/PC), box 3, John F. Kennedy Library (JFKL).

29. Kearns, *Lyndon Johnson*, 41–42. Johnson's exaggeration of IQ scores in Caro, *Path*, 154. Busby quoted in Thompson, ed., *The Johnson Presidency*, 254. See also George Ball, *The Past Has Another Pattern: Memoirs* (New York, W. W. Norton, 1982), 319; Miller, *Lyndon*, 284.

30. Kearns, *Lyndon Johnson*, 122–123. Eric Goldman, *The Tragedy of Lyndon Johnson* (New York, Dell, 1969), 26. Miller, *Lyndon*, 420. For discussions of Johnson's bathroom conversations, see Caro, *Path*, 239; Richard N. Goodwin, *Remembering America: A Voice from the Sixties* (Boston, Little, Brown, 1988), 257, 267–269.

31. Horace Busby to LBJ, January 23, 1964, FG/RS/PR18, box 9, LBJL.

32. Jackson J. Benson, *The True Adventures of John Steinbeck, Writer* (New York, Viking, 1984), 545, 877, 925, 955–961. See also John Steinbeck to Bill Moyers, September 3, 1966, FG1, box 13, LBJL.

33. For LBJ's relationship with Leinsdorf, see Caro, *Path*, 481. *New York Times*, August 27, 1964, 26. Goldman, *Tragedy*, 8–9. *Newsweek*, "Stand In," February 17, 1964, 14.

34. *New York Times*, January 24, 1964, 29. *New York Times*, March 15, 1964, vi, 75. *New York Times*, August 30, 1964, vi, 15. McGeorge Bundy to LBJ, February 17, 1964, FG/RS/PR18, box 9, LBJL.

35. Horace Busby to LBJ, "Image Assessment and Suggested Activities," April 1964, Busby, box 52, LBJL. Busby also wanted LBJ to allow staff greater access to reporters, as Kennedy had, in order to provide "background" material. See Horace Busby to LBJ, April 11, 1964, Busby, box 53, LBJL. Horace Busby to LBJ, May 14, 1964, Busby, box 52, LBJL.

36. Horace Busby to LBJ, April 29, 1964, Busby, box 52, LBJL. Horace Busby to LBJ, April 30, 1964, Busby, box 53, LBJL.

37. Eric Goldman to LBJ, June 16, 1964, FG1, box 10, LBJL.

38. Jack Valenti to LBJ, January 8, 1964, PR 18-2, box 374, LBJL. Bill Moyers to LBJ, May 15, 1964, Moyers, box 10, LBJL.

39. *Newsweek*, "Sunny Side Up," March 2, 1964, 17–18. *Newsweek*, "Periscope," May 11, 1964, 15. *Newsweek*, "Love in November," June 8, 1964, 16. *Newsweek*, "Johnson and Johnson," June 22, 1964, 29–30. *Newsweek*, "April and November," April 27, 1964, 26–28. Douglass Cater to LBJ, November 21, 1964, Cater, box 13, LBJL.

40. Wicker, *New York Times Magazine*, May 3, 1964, 11. Patrick Anderson, *The President's Men* (Garden City, Doubleday, 1968), 317.

41. Brown, *JFK*, 6–23.

42. Horace Busby to LBJ, January 23, 1964, FG/RS/PR18, box 9, LBJL.

43. See photographs of Johnson in *Newsweek*, January 16, 1964, 13; January 20, 1964, 16–17, and April 27, 1964, 26–27. *U.S. News and World Report*, "Now It's Teentime at the

White House," February 3, 1964, 14. *Look,* "Teen-age Party in the White House," March 10, 1964, 22–23. *Life,* "Texas Team Makes Its Musical Bow," August 7, 1964, 53–54. *Time,* "Yes, My Darling Daughters," April 17, 1964, 35. *New York Times,* February 15, 1964, 26. *New York Times,* February 17, 1964, 14. *New York Times,* February 27, 1964, 41. *New York Times,* August 6, 1964, 19. *New York Times,* August 11, 1964, 30. *Newsweek,* "The 5-Gallon Hat," February 10, 1964, 68. *Business Week,* "Fashion Czar in the White House," March 21, 1964, 94, 99, 100, 102. Johnson was photographed bowling in 1968 in *Sports Illustrated.* See Liz Carpenter to LBJ and Lady Bird, March 19, 1968, FG1, box 17, LBJL.

44. Horace Busby to LBJ, July 19, 1964, Busby, box 52, LBJL.

45. Letter from Charles King to Hal Pachios, August 18, 1965, FG1, box 12, LBJL.

46. Bill Moyers to LBJ, August 31, 1965, FG1, box 12, LBJL. Charles King to Hal Pachios, September 23, 1965, FG1, box 12, LBJL. Hal Pachios to Charles King, September 28, 1965, FG1, box 12, LBJL. Charles King to Hal Pachios, December 3, 1965, FG1, box 12, LBJL. *New York Times,* December 9, 1965, 73.

47. *Life,* July 17, 1964, 38–39. *Life,* "Letters to the Editor," August 7, 1964, 18. The twenty-eight-foot cabin cruiser was laden with fifteen passengers. Johnson was pictured in a plaid swim suit. One reader remarked that the scene was "a perfect example of overloading, one of the major causes of boating accidents," Others were more critical of Johnson's "form." "As a teenager," a reader wrote, "saturated with the physical fitness campaign propaganda and after study of the spread, I would respectfully suggest Mr. Johnson participate in a program his staff advises, or camouflage his adipose physique."

48. Burton Berinsky, "Photographer's Panel," Presidential Conference: John F. Kennedy, The Promise Revisited, Hofstra University, Hempstead, N.Y., March 30, 1985. During campaigns Kennedy took precautions not to be photographed smoking a cigar, eating food, or wearing a hat or eyeglasses. See Paul B. Fay, Jr., *The Pleasure of His Company* (New York, Harper and Row, 1966). Bradlee found Kennedy to be one of the vainest men he knew and discovered that "few things interested the President more than a discussion of his own weight." According to Bradlee, Kennedy was once "horrified" by a photograph of himself sailing at Hyannis Port because it revealed "the Fitzgerald breasts." See Bradlee, *Conversations,* 29, 69, 151. See also Elmer Cornwell, Jr., *Presidential Leadership of Public Opinion* (Bloomington, Indiana University Press, 1965), 280. Robert MacNeil, *The People Machine: The Influence of Television on American Politics* (New York, Harper and Row, 1968), 295–296. Hugh Sidey, *John F. Kennedy, President* (New York, Atheneum, 1963), 50. William Spragens interview with George Christian.

49. See David Donald, *Lincoln Reconsidered: Essays on the Civil War Era* (New York, Vintage Books, 1961), Chapter 1, "Getting Right with Lincoln," 3–18.

50. *Public Papers of the Presidents of the United States: Lyndon B. Johnson, 1963–64,* (Washington, Government Printing Office, 1965), 64. *Newsweek,* "Stand-in," February 17, 1964, 14–15. *Public Papers, 1963–64,* 174. *New York Times,* February 7, 1964, 1. LBJ ordered "no partisan political speeches of any sort" during the first thirty days after the assassination. See Theodore Reardon to Departments and Agencies, November 29, 1963, FG2, box 40, LBJL. Johnson also approved a quote to be issued by the White House upon commemorating a JFK stamp. See George Reedy to LBJ, July 1, 1964, PL2, box 83, LBJL. LBJ also made it a point to buy the first Kennedy savings bond. See *New York Times,* May 2, 1964, 9. *New York Times,* June 17, 1964, 34. LBJ visits to JFK's grave noted in *New York Times,* January 27, 1964, 5; *New York Times,* May 29, 1964, 12; *New York Times,* July 22, 1964, 14. LBJ's birthday tribute to JFK noted in *New York Times,* May 29, 1964, 12. Tom Wicker, "Lyndon Johnson vs. the Ghost of Jack Kennedy, *Esquire* 64 (November 1965), notes that RFK was almost moved to tears during the tribute. In late January, for the first time since Kennedy's funeral, Johnson paid his respects, standing before the grave with his head bowed for about thirty seconds. Authorities at Arlington were not notified until minutes before Johnson arrived and had no time to make special preparations. It is not known what provoked Johnson's action.

51. George Reedy to LBJ, December 3, 1963, PA2/D, box 3, LBJL. Horace Busby to LBJ, May 15, 1964, Busby, box 19, LBJL. "The question cannot—and should not—be raised," Busby qualified, "but I hardly share the AEC's conclusion that the dedication to President

Kennedy—for next September—is really appropriate. At that point in time, such emphasis is backward-looking."

52. Goldman, *Tragedy*, 25–26. William Manchester, *The Death of a President* (New York, Harper and Row, 1967), 482. Tip O'Neill, *Man of the House: The Life and Political Memoirs of Speaker Tip O'Neill* (New York, Random House, 1987), 183. "[T]here must have been some degree of reluctance on his part to go along with it quite as much as he was required to," Harry McPherson recalled. See McPherson, LBJL-OH.

53. Stanley Kelley, Jr., "The Presidential Campaign," in Milton C. Cummings, Jr., ed., *The National Election of 1964* (Washington, Brookings Institution, 1966), 43–47. Stewart Alsop, "Only Johnson Can Beat Johnson," *Saturday Evening Post*, January 4, 1964, 12. Emmet John Hughes column, *Newsweek*, February 24, 1964, 17, notes, "Politically and emotionally, [Johnson] possesses one formidable asset wholly beyond the reach of JFK—namely, the memory of JFK." Edward T. Folliard, "The President Will Run Scared," *America*, July 11, 1964, 32, comments about LBJ's willingness to use JFK as a political vote-getting symbol. LBJ's speech noted in *New York Times*, March 20, 1964, 14. Johnson, *Vantage Point*, 104. *Newsweek*, August 31, 1964, cover shows Johnson sitting in a Kennedy-style rocking chair. See also Goldman, *Tragedy*, 4, for a discussion of LBJ's uncomfortable use of a JFK-style rocking chair.

54. Horace Busby to Bill Moyers, September 5, 1964, Busby, box 20, LBJL. For a review of the speech, see *Time*, "Above the Battle," September 18, 1964, 30. The text is printed in *Time*, September 18, 1964, 30. *Public Papers, 1963–64*, 1049–1052.

55. Theodore Sorensen to Jack Valenti, September 14, 1964, PL2, box 84, LBJL. Jack Valenti to Theodore Sorensen, October 3, 1964, PL2, box 84, LBJL. W. J. Jorden to Douglass Cater, September 18, 1964, PR3, box 11, LBJL.

56. Evans and Novak, *Lyndon B. Johnson*, 499–500. Johnson, *Vantage Point*, 105. Johnson also noted that he visited Senator Edward Kennedy in the hospital during his swing though New England. The senator "was expecting me and wanted to see me." See p. 107.

57. Horace Busby to LBJ, October 1964, Busby, box 52, LBJL. LBJ's depression noted in Evans and Novak, *Lyndon B. Johnson*, 490–492, 496, 498, 501–502, 507. Goldman, *Tragedy*, 21, notes that JFK's memory goaded Johnson to win by a wide margin. See also memorandum comparing votes, n.d., FG2, box 41, LBJL.

58. For a complete listing, see index to *Public Papers, 1963–64*, Kennedy, John F., Campaign Remarks on, A-54. Johnson frequently adopted JFK's theme promising to keep the country moving. See *Public Papers, 1963–64*, 1134, 1145, 1248, 1271, 1292, 1373. See also LBJ's speeches in Buffalo, Akron, Bellville, Ill., and Detroit. In Dayton, Johnson reasserted, "We are proud that John Fitzgerald Kennedy said, 'We are going to get America moving,' and she is on her way." LBJ commercial noted in Kathleen Hall Jamieson, *Packaging the Presidency: A History and Criticism of Presidential Campaign Advertising* (New York, Oxford University Press, 1984), 202. LBJ's praise of JFK's Test Ban Treaty noted in *Public Papers, 1963–64*, 1254, 1329. At the Alfred E. Smith Memorial Foundation in October he noted, "[I]t is with the deepest pride that I participated in helping our late beloved President, John Fitzgerald Kennedy, prove to the world that there are no religious bars to the highest office in the land."

59. *New York Times*, September 10, 1964, 17. See also September 12, 1964, 10, for Salinger's reaction. Dick Scammon to Douglass Cater, September 10, 1964, FG2, box 40, LBJL. Clark Clifford to LBJ, September 11, 1964, Busby, box 52, LBJL. Horace Busby to LBJ, September 11, 1964, Busby, box 52, LBJL.

60. *Public Papers, 1963–64*, 1162, 1177. Edwin O. Guthman and Jeffrey Shulman, eds., *Robert Kennedy in His Own Words: The Unpublished Recollections of the Kennedy Years* (New York, Bantam, 1988), 16, 23, 411.

61. *Public Papers, 1963–64*, 1260, 1315–1316, 1324, 1352, 1414, 1522, 1534, 1550.

62. *Public Papers, 1963–64*, 1260, 1275, 1294, 1469–1470, 1498, 1507.

63. *New York Times*, November 22, 1964, 74, noted that 7,740,000 people had visited Kennedy's grave. Forty thousand visited the grave on the first anniversary.

64. Horace Busby, "The Campaign," October 1964, Busby, box 52, LBJL. *New York Times*, June 14, 1964. *New York Times*, June 29, 1964.

65. *New York Times*, October 15, 1964, 1, 30. *Newsweek*, "Back to Dallas," October 19, 1964, 30–31. *New York Times*, October 14, 1964, 30. *New York Times*, October 20, 1964, 1. LBJ eventually returned to Dallas in 1968 and drove within sight of the Texas School Book Depository. See *New York Times*, February 28, 1968, 1.

66. *Newsweek*, "Robert Kennedy and New York: Decision Point," August 24, 1964, 22–25, 27. *New York Times*, September 4, 1964, 1. RFK to LBJ, September 3, 1964, WHFN-RFK, box 6, LBJL. LBJ to RFK, September 3, 1964, WHFN-RFK, box 6, LBJL. Stewart Alsop, "The One Weakness of LBJ," *Saturday Evening Post*, September 19, 1964, 12.

67. Johnson, *Vantage Point*, 100. *New York Times*, October 15, 1964, 1, 30. Schlesinger, *Robert Kennedy*, 674.

68. *Public Papers, 1963–64*, 1337–1340, 1341–1347. Schlesinger, *Robert Kennedy*, 674.

69. *New York Times*, September 5, 1964, 1. *New York Times*, October 15, 1964, 1.

70. *Newsweek*, "Now There Are Two Senators Kennedy," November 9, 1964, 35–36. Schlesinger, *Robert Kennedy*, 675. Jack Valenti, *A Very Human President* (New York, W. W. Norton, 1976), 114–115.

71. Cummings, *The National Election*, 261–262. Stewart Alsop, "Uncle Lyndon," *Saturday Evening Post*, October 24, 1964, 16.

72. *Public Papers, 1963–64*, 1580. The desire to move forward into the future was also noted in an earlier speech in Texarkana on September 25, 1964, while LBJ was dedicating John F. Kennedy Square: "He would want us to honor him as he always honored us: by thinking about tomorrow." See *Public Papers, 1963–64*, number 599.

CHAPTER VIII

Emerging from the Kennedy Shadow

1. Doris Kearns, *Lyndon Johnson and the American Dream* (New York, Harper and Row, 1976), 313–317. Johnson's erratic mood swings and illness during the inauguration were perhaps among the earliest indications of depression. See *Newsweek*, "Hail to the Chief," February 1, 1965, 12. *Newsweek*, "The Uncommon Cold," February 1, 1965, 17. *Time*, "After the Ball," January 29, 1965, 9.

2. Kearns, *Lyndon Johnson*, 315–316. See Kearns's endnote number 8 on 418 for reference to Goodwin and Moyers.

3. Richard N. Goodwin, *Remembering America: A Voice from the Sixties* (Boston, Little, Brown, 1988), 393, 400, 402–403.

4. Goodwin, *Remembering*, 392–394, 416.

5. *New York Times*, August 24, 1988. John Roche, Lyndon B. Johnson Library—Oral History (LBJL-OH), 42. Jack Valenti, *New York Times Magazine*, "Letters," September 11, 1988, 8.

6. Goodwin, *Remembering*, 396.

7. Goodwin, *Remembering*, 396. *Newsweek*, "The Senators Kennedy," January 18, 1965, 21. *Newsweek*, "The 99th Senator," March 15, 1965, 29–30. Arthur M. Schlesinger, Jr., *Robert Kennedy and His Times* (Boston, Houghton Mifflin, 1978), 687. Kenneth Crawford column, *Newsweek*, September 5, 1966, 24. George Gallup, *The Gallup Poll: Public Opinion, 1935–1971* (New York, Random House, 1972), 1972–1973.

8. *Newsweek*, "The Senators Kennedy," 21. *Newsweek*, "The 99th Senator," 29–30. *Newsweek*, "The Climber," April 5, 1965, 29–30. *Newsweek*, "Newsmakers," May 24, 1965, 63. Appraising Robert's first year in office, James Reston wrote that he was "doing nothing to discourage the thought that he would like to be President." Kennedy was also willing to use the "mystique" for his own ends. Evoking past memories, he frequently mentioned his brother during prepared remarks and embarked on a number of highly publicized events which reinforced his public commitment to his brother's legacy. In March 1965 he participated in a climbing expedition on Mount Kennedy in Canada and was the first to reach the peak of the mountain named in honor of his brother. At the summit he left three PT-109 tie clips and a copy of John Kennedy's Inaugural Address. Robert was often photographed in the company of

280

Jacqueline Kennedy and traveled with her to England in May to attend a dedication of a memorial honoring the late president. RFK Clubs noted in Marvin Watson to LBJ, May 18, 1965, White House Famous Names—Robert Kennedy (WHFN-RFK), box 6, LBJL.

9. Harry McPherson to LBJ, June 24, 1965, McPherson, box 21, LBJL.

10. Eric Goldman, *The Tragedy of Lyndon Johnson* (New York, Dell, 1969), 20. He notes that most Johnson staff members considered RFK "the perfect model of the liberal fascist."

11. Chester Clifton to George Reedy and Horace Busby, November 18, 1964, FG2, box 40, LBJL. *Public Papers of the Presidents of the United States: Lyndon B. Johnson, 1964* (Washington, Government Printing Office, 1965), 1596–1597. *New York Times*, November 23, 1964, 1. *New York Times*, December 3, 1964, 58. *Public Papers, 1964*, 1624–1626. Later in 1965 the December 2 speech was requested for use as an introduction to a documentary on John Kennedy's life. See Roger Stevens to Bill Moyers, December 27, 1965, FG2, box 40, LBJL.

12. Jack Valenti to LBJ, November 16, 1964, FG2, box 40, LBJL. RFK to LBJ, November 17, 1964, WHFN-RFK, box 6, LBJL.

13. *Newsweek*, "For LBJ—A Texas Size Inaugural," January 25, 1965, 21–22. *Newsweek*, "Lyndon Johnson's Pledge," February 1, 1965, 10–11. *U.S. News and World Report*, "Johnson Era Starts," February 1, 1965, 29. "The Inaugural would seal, finally and formally, Lyndon Johnson's clear title to the world's most important job," *Newsweek* reported, "—and he plainly meant to impress it with his own style." See also the official inaugural program published by the Democratic National Committee.

14. Horace Busby to LBJ, December 9, 1964, Busby, box 52, LBJL. Busby argued that the anniversary theme was noncontroversial, nonpartisan, and would encourage the news media to view the Johnson administration in a broad historical context.

15. *New York Times*, January 4, 1965, 18. Goldman, *Tragedy*, 333. *Newsweek*, February 1, 1965, 11–12. "[H]is language was plain," *Newsweek* noted, "his style bland, his delivery slow and prosy." The *London Times* noted, "It was plain to see that warmhearted, middle-aged, and middle-class America was again in charge at the White House." *New York Times*, January 21, 1965, 19.

16. *Time*, "Coonskins on the Wall," February 26, 1965, 21. *Public Papers of the Presidents of the United States: Lyndon B. Johnson, 1965* (Washington, Government Printing Office, 1966), 730, 811, 415, 667, 885, 746, 766, 641, 462–463, 1121–1122, 1123. Goldman, *Tragedy*, 433. Johnson's concern for publications questioning his rights to the Kennedy legacy were especially aroused by the publication of Theodore White's book, *The Making of the President 1964*. See *Time*, "When Bobby Gulped," July 2, 1965, 17; Douglass Cater to LBJ, June 8, 1965, Cater, box 13, LBJL; Horace Busby to LBJ, June 22, 1965, Busby, box 51, LBJL; Horace Busby to LBJ, July 20, 1965, Busby, box 51, LBJL. These memoranda expressed concern about White's account of LBJ's decision not to bring RFK onto the 1964 ticket. It should be noted that White allowed RFK to edit that portion of the manuscript in such a manner as to "cover the truth and yet protect you at the same time." See Theodore White to RFK, March 25, 1965, and April 5, 1964 [sic], Robert F. Kennedy–Senate Files/Personal Correspondence (RFK-SF/PC), box 12, John F. Kennedy Library (JFKL). See also Arthur Schlesinger to RFK, February 23, 1965, RFK-SF/PC, box 11, JFKL.

17. Tom Wicker, "Lyndon Johnson vs. the Ghost of Jack Kennedy," *Esquire* 64 (November 1965), 149. William E. Leuchtenburg, "A Visit with LBJ," *American Heritage*, May/June 1990, 47–52ff.

18. Horace Busby to LBJ, December 4, 1964, Busby, box 52, LBJL.

19. Press conference advice is noted in Douglass Cater to LBJ, December 26, 1964, Cater, box 13, LBJL. Jack Valenti to LBJ, February 13, 1965, PR 18-2, box 375, LBJL. Douglass Cater to LBJ, February 4, 1965, Cater, box 13, LBJL. Memorandum for Jack Valenti, April 25, 1965, PR18-2, box 375, LBJL. Jack Valenti to LBJ, March 10, 1965, Moyers, box 9, LBJL.

20. *Newsweek*, "End of the Honeymoon," February 15, 1965, 62–63. The place and times of LBJ's press conferences are noted in *Public Papers, 1965*, January 16, 54; February 4, 131; March 13, 274; March 20, 299; April 1, 364; April 8, 402; April 27, 448; June 1, 609; June 17, 669; July 13, 735; July 28, 794; August 25, 917; August 29, 943; December 6, 1138.

21. James Reston noted the success of LBJ's first "Conversation with the President" program in *New York Times*, March 16, 1964, 1. Later advice noted in Douglass Cater to LBJ,

November 27, 1964, Cater, box 13, LBJL. "Report to the President," from Cater, Busby, Reedy, Carpenter, Goldman, Watson, and Valenti, February 19, 1965, PR18, box 367, LBJL. Robert Hunter first noted LBJ's need to appear sophisticated on handling foreign policy in Robert Hunter to Douglass Cater, November 20, 1964, PR19-2, box 374, LBJL. Jack Valenti to Bill Moyers, July 14, 1965, PR18, box 367, LBJL. Moyers responded, "I'm for it."

22. JFK's earliest programs included "Eyewitness to History," broadcast on CBS on February 17, 1961; "Adventures on the New Frontier," broadcast on ABC on March 28, 1961; and "Just Plain Jack," broadcast on NBC on February 28, 1961. Also, "Crisis: Behind a Presidential Commitment" was produced by Robert Drew and aired on October 21, 1963. For discussions of JFK's television exposure in this regard, see John Cogley, "The Presidential Image," *New Republic*, April 10, 1961, 29–31; *Time*, "Exposure," April 21, 1961, 16–17. Douglass Cater, "Mr. Kennedy's Open Door Policy," *Reporter*, April 27, 1961, 33; Jack Gould, "TV: Too Many Cameras," *New York Times*, October 22, 1963, 27. Advice urging LBJ to participate in documentaries noted in Harry McPherson to Horace Busby, July 6, 1965, Busby, box 19, LBJL. Horace Busby to Harry McPherson, July 7, 1965, Busby, box 19, LBJL. "Such may be good theater and good prestige promotion," Busby noted. "But in my own judgment, permitting such eavesdropping has a reverse psychology because the public know, automatically, that such an activity is either staged or controlled—and the result is likely to be an impression of the President trying too hard to over-correct a bad image." Horace Busby memorandum, January 27, 1965, PR18, box 367, LBJL. The "President at Work" program was recommended by Robert Hunter to Douglass Cater, November 12, 1964, PL2, box 86, LBJL. Johnson's earlier interest in documentary films is noted in Robert Fleming to Pierre Salinger, January 24, 1964, FG/RS/PR18, box 9, and Robert Fleming to Andrew Hatcher, January 27, 1964, FG/RS/PR18, box 9, LBJL. Two occasions on which Johnson staged shots are noted in Jack Valenti to LBJ, March 25, 1965, FG1, box 11, and Jack Valenti to LBJ, July 7, 1965, FG1, box 12, LBJL.

23. For examples of advice that Johnson received, see Robert Kintner to LBJ, July 23, 1966, UT1-1, box 3, LBJL; Hal Pachios to Bill Moyers, August 10, 1966, FG1, box 12, LBJL; Robert Kintner to LBJ, June 22, 1966, CF PR18, box 83, LBJL; William Connell to Marvin Watson, March 7, 1967, UT1-1, box 3, LBJL; Robert Hunter to LBJ, October 6, 1966, PR18-1, box 368, LBJL; Robert Hunter to LBJ, October 13, 1966, PR18-2, box 375, LBJL; Robert Hunter to LBJ, November 4, 1966, PR18-2, box 375, LBJL; Robert Fleming to LBJ, February 3, 1967, PR18-1, box 368, LBJL; Robert Kintner to LBJ, February 18, 1967; PR18-1, box 368, LBJL; Liz Carpenter to LBJ, June 17, 1965, UT1-1, box 3, LBJL. Kintner wanted LBJ to point his finger at reporters, noted in Robert Kintner to LBJ, February 18, 1967, PR18-1, box 368, LBJL.

24. *Broadcasting*, "The Brand That's Being Burned in TV," November 8, 1965, 54–56, 58.

25. Criticism of LBJ's TV personality noted in *Time*, "Mover of Men," August 6, 1965, 22.

26. Harry McPherson, *A Political Education* (Boston, Little, Brown, 1972), 245.

27. For comparison of staffs, see Tom Wicker, "Johnson's Men: 'Valuable Hunks of Humanity,'" *New York Times Magazine*, May 3, 1964, 11ff. See also *Newsweek*, March 1, 1965, 27–29, 32–33. Goldman, *Tragedy*, 38–39. Horace Busby to George Reedy, April 17, 1964, Busby, box 20, LBJL. *Newsweek*'s feature story on the Johnson staff in March 1965 described staff members as "faithful," "deferential," and having an "unswerving commitment" to the president. After fifteen months Johnson had assembled his own team—"ready, willing, and able to do things the LBJ way." "Mr. Johnson has surrounded himself with determinedly self-effacing men content to submerge their egos and ambitions for the greater glory of the Great Society," *Newsweek* reported.

28. Harry McPherson to LBJ, July 13, 1965, McPherson, box 52, LBJL. McPherson also noted, "The press believes we lack 'gaiety,' and are a bunch of drones who are afraid to step out of line. We don't go out for lunch; we don't play touch football or softball; we just work. Our only relaxation is complaining about the hours. . . . I don't know what the prescription is, or even whether there should be one but I do think the press—a cynical crowd who had rather destroy a stuffed shirt than eat—will continue to sneer so long as we show thin skins, fear, and the kind of sanctimony people display who never enjoy themselves."

29. *Newsweek*, March 1, 1965, 27–29, 32–33.

NOTES

30. *New York Times*, August 28, 1965, 7. *Newsweek*, "A Loyal Lieutenant Views LBJ," July 12, 1965, 12–13. Valenti, LBJL-OH, part v, 20. Harry McPherson to Jack Valenti, July 6, 1965, McPherson, box 51, LBJL. The most scathing criticism was a cartoon by the *Washington Post*'s Herblock, illustrating Johnson with a whip in hand, walking away from brutalized staff members on the White House lawn. It was entitled, "Happy Days on the Old Plantation."

31. *Newsweek*, March 1, 1965, 27. *Newsweek*, "An Interview with LBJ," August 2, 1965, 20–21. See also Goldman, *Tragedy*, 18, 20, 120. "[Johnson] doesn't want cold intellectuals, without commitment to his programs," Valenti noted. "To most LBJ men," Goldman observed, "JFK and his group were a band of clever, opportunistic sophomores who had taken on a man's job and settled for a patina of style." Jack Valenti to Bill Moyers, December 11, 1964, FG2, box 40, LBJL.

32. Liz Carpenter to Jack Valenti, November 24, 1964, PR18-2, box 374, LBJL. Hobart Taylor to LBJ, January 13, 1965, FG1, box 10, LBJL.

33. Harry McPherson to LBJ, July 13, 1965, McPherson, box 52, LBJL.

34. Bill Moyers to LBJ, August 24, 1965, Moyers, box 11, LBJL. *New York Times*, October 15, 1965, 91. Three of the aides (Bundy, O'Brien, and Califano) were Kennedy men. The other three (Moyers, Watson, and Valenti) were Johnson men.

35. Robert Kintner to LBJ, April 27, 1966, FG/RS/PR18, box 16, LBJL. Harry McPherson to Bill Moyers, March 8, 1966, McPherson, box 21, LBJL. See also Harry McPherson to LBJ, May 23, 1966, McPherson, box 32, LBJL. Ben Wattenberg to LBJ, January 6, 1967, McPherson, box 51, LBJL. Harry McPherson to George Christian, February 28, 1967, McPherson, box 22, LBJL.

36. *U.S. News and World Report*, "The Johnson Staff," December 2, 1963. *U.S. News and World Report*, "How the White House Is Changing," December 23, 1963, 34–36. Goldman, *Tragedy*, 96, 122–123. Rowland Evans and Robert Novak, *Lyndon B. Johnson: The Exercise of Power* (New York, New American Library, 1966), 364–365. *Newsweek*, "Inside the White House," March 1, 1965, 27–29, 32–33. According to Eric Goldman, "It was the LBJ men whom the President tended to draw into everything and to include in a way which made their influence pervasive." Kearns, *Lyndon Johnson*, 176. See also Jack Valenti, LBJL-OH, part v, 18.

37. O'Donnell, Powers, Feldman, and Travell resigned in January 1965. See *New York Times*, January 17, 1965, 1. Sorensen's desire to return to the White House noted in *Newsweek*, "Periscope," June 21, 1965, 17. Jack Valenti, *A Very Human President* (New York, W. W. Norton, 1976), 73. See also McPherson, *A Political*, 251–252.

38. Patrick Anderson, *The President's Men* (Garden City, Doubleday, 1968), 374–375.

39. Harry McPherson to Jack Valenti, April 20, 1965, McPherson, box 51, LBJL. Goodwin, *Remembering*, 394–396.

40. Harry McPherson to Bill Moyers, May 19, 1965, McPherson, box 51, LBJL.

41. Harry McPherson to LBJ, June 24, 1965, McPherson, box 52, LBJL.

42. McPherson, LBJL-OH, tape 3, 27-28. Harry McPherson to LBJ, "Thoughts on Bobby Kennedy and loyalty," June 24, 1965, McPherson, box 21, LBJL.

43. Harry McPherson to LBJ, "Thoughts on Bobby Kennedy and loyalty," June 24, 1965, McPherson, box 21, LBJL.

44. Harry McPherson to Bill Moyers, July 6, 1965, McPherson, box 51, LBJL. Harry McPherson to LBJ, July 7, 1965, McPherson, box 52, LBJL. Harry McPherson to Bill Moyers, August 3, 1965, McPherson, box 51, LBJL. Nelson Lichtenstein, ed., *Political Profiles: The Johnson Years* (New York, Facts on File, 1976), 443–444.

45. Valenti, *A Very*, 72. McPherson, LBJL-OH, tape 3, 22.

46. *Newsweek*, August 2, 1965, 20.

47. Goodwin, *Remembering*, 400–401.

48. Arthur M. Schlesinger, Jr., LBJL-OH, 21. Schlesinger, *Robert Kennedy*, 630–632, 689. Arthur Schlesinger to RFK, December 15, 1963, RFK-SF/PC, box 11, JFKL. See also Evans and Novak, *Lyndon B. Johnson*, 374.

49. Goldman, *Tragedy*, 86–91. See also Horace Busby to LBJ, May 4, 1964, Busby, box 52, LBJL. See also Theodore James Maher, "The Kennedy and Johnson Responses to Latin American Coups D'Etat," *World Affairs* 131 (3), 1968, 184–198.

50. Schlesinger, *Robert Kennedy*, 689–692. Merle Miller, *Lyndon: An Oral Biography* (New York, Putnam, 1980), 427.

51. *Public Papers, 1965*, 472. Lyndon Johnson, *The Vantage Point: Perspectives of the Presidency, 1963–1969* (New York, Holt, Rinehart and Winston, 1971), 197. RFK's reaction noted in Schlesinger, *Robert Kennedy*, 691. *Newsweek*, "Dominican Crisis: Help from OAS," 44. Tom Wicker, "The Kennedys and Johnson," *New York Times*, June 24, 1965, 16. *Newsweek* regarded the address as Kennedy's "first public criticism of the Administration." Wicker further noted that most observers considered the speech part of a concerted effort to establish liberal leadership. "[N]o one," he added, "least of all the White House, is losing sight of the fact that such a position is required of anyone who hopes to get anywhere at the Democratic National Convention." Further criticism noted in *Newsweek*, "Foreign Policy: Drift or Design?" May 17, 1965, 27–28. Wicker's observation noted in *Esquire*, 149. James Reston assessed Johnson's actions as a symptom of "disorderly policy making." Joseph Kraft cited "identifiable defects" in Johnson's application of foreign policy. The *London Times* noted that in Washington there were "snide suggestions that a man who gave the rebel yell in the Taj Mahal is ill-equipped to guide foreign policy." See James Reston, *New York Times*, November 10, 1965, 6.

52. Schlesinger, *Robert Kennedy*, 692–694. *Newsweek*, "Campaign Tour," November 22, 1965, 39–40, notes that the Vaughn meeting was "stormy, tense and unproductive."

53. *Newsweek*, "Two Senators Named Kennedy," January 17, 1966, 25. *Newsweek*, November 22, 1965, 39. Emmet John Hughes column, *Newsweek*, March 7, 1966, 21. See *New York Times*, November 22, 1965, 14, on RFK's support of LBJ in Latin America. Schlesinger, *Robert Kennedy*, 698.

54. Hugh Sidey, "He Makes a Truce . . . ," *Life*, November 18, 1966, 38–39.

55. Frederick Dutton to RFK, May 12, 1965, RFK-SF/PC, box 3, JFKL. *New York Times*, June 24, 1965, 1. Tom Wicker, *New York Times*, June 24, 1965, 16. *Newsweek*, "Myth-Busters," July 30, 1965, 32–33. See also Schlesinger, *Robert Kennedy*, 692.

56. Harry McPherson to LBJ, June 24, 1965, McPherson, box 21, LBJL. Hubert Humphrey to RFK, June 23, 1965, RFK-SF/PC, box 5, JFKL. *New York Times*, June 24, 1965, 1. *Time*, "Candor at the White House," July 30, 1965, 32–33. Goodwin, *Remembering*, 397.

57. Schlesinger, *Robert Kennedy*, 712–714, 727–728. RFK to LBJ, n.d., June 11, 1964, WHFN-RFK, box 6, LBJL. Johnson, *Vantage Point*, 99.

58. Kearns, *Lyndon Johnson*, 253, 259. Larry L. King, "Machismo in the White House: LBJ and Vietnam," *American Heritage* 27 (May 1976), 8–13, 98–101. Schlesinger, *Robert Kennedy*, 725.

59. Schlesinger, *Robert Kennedy*, 729–730. Johnson, *Vantage Point*, 136. Miller, *Lyndon*, 416. Tom Wicker, *New York Times*, June 24, 1965, 16.

60. RFK to Anthony Lewis, July 19, 1965, RFK-SF/PC, box 6, JFKL. Schlesinger, *Robert Kennedy*, 730–731. *Newsweek*, July 17, 1965, 18. RFK to Mr. President, Speech, July 9, 1965, Robert Kennedy–Senate Legislative Files, box 47, JFKL.

61. Lawrence O'Brien to RFK, April 6, 1965, RFK-SF/PC, box 8, JFKL. McGeorge Bundy to RFK, May 9, 1965, RFK-Senate Files, box 12, JFKL. A text of LBJ's July 28, 1965, press conference was sent by Lawrence O'Brien to RFK, August 3, 1965, RFK-SF/PC, box 8, JFKL. See also James Reston, *New York Times*, November 10, 1965, 6.

62. Douglass Cater to LBJ, May 14, 1965, Cater, box 13, LBJL. Horace Busby to LBJ, June 30, 1965, Busby, box 51, LBJL. See also Douglass Cater to LBJ, July 3, 1965, Cater, box 13, LBJL. Cater reported another conversation with European journalist Werner Imhoof, who assured him of "basic European support" for Johnson's policies in Vietnam. "He feels there is still an 'image' problem in Europe where there are comparisons with an idealized memory of JFK," Cater noted. "He concedes that correspondents haven't done a very good job of correcting this distortion."

63. Miller, *Lyndon*, 418. Horace Busby to LBJ, March 5, 1965, Busby, box 52, LBJL. For LBJ's use of Eisenhower to gain support for the war, see Henry William Brands, Jr., "Johnson and Eisenhower: The President, the Former President, and the War in Vietnam," *Presidential Studies Quarterly* 15 (Summer 1985), 589–601. See press conferences in *Public Papers, 1965* for March 13, April 27, June 1, July 13, July 28, and August 9.

64. McGeorge Bundy to LBJ, March 28, 1965, NSF:VN, box 15, LBJL. See also quotes on JFK in Statements, n.d., box 247, LBJL.

65. *Newsweek*, "A Path for Reasonable Men," April 19, 1965, 25–26. *Public Papers, 1965*, 394–399.

66. Schlesinger, *Robert Kennedy*, 685–686. Hayes Redmon to Bill Moyers, October 28, 1965, Moyers, box 11, LBJL. Redmon noted that if Johnson endorsed Beame and he won the election, Johnson would gain greater input into the gubernatorial race in 1966. He would also take "credit for victory away from RFK." Should Beame lose, however, Johnson would appear weak to liberal groups attracted to John Lindsay. If Johnson did not endorse Beame and Beame won, Kennedy would get "much credit for victory," and "much credit with Beame." If Johnson did not endorse Beame and he lost, "RFK would say 'Where was LBJ?' " The president endorsed Beame and Lindsay won.

67. Schlesinger, *Robert Kennedy*, 683–685. Johnson's instructions to Califano noted in Joseph A. Califano, Jr., *Governing America: An Insider's Report from the White House and the Cabinet* (New York, Simon and Schuster, 1981), 90. See also LBJ to RFK, September 24, 1964, RFK Senate Papers/1964 Campaign, box 9, JFKL.

68. Rivkin concerns noted in Schlesinger, *Robert Kennedy*, 686. Nickerson episode noted in Harry McPherson to LBJ, March 31, 1965, McPherson, box 52, LBJL. Harry McPherson to Bill Moyers, April 13, 1965, McPherson, box 51, LBJL. Harry McPherson to LBJ, April 14, 1965, McPherson, box 52, LBJL.

69. Harry McPherson to LBJ, June 18, 1965, McPherson, box 52, LBJL. *Newsweek*, March 15, 1965, 29.

70. Robert Hunter to Douglass Cater, November 12, 1964, PR18, box 367, LBJL.

71. Miller, *Lyndon*, 420–423.

72. Goldman, *Tragedy*, 518.

73. Douglass Cater to LBJ, May 13, 1965, Cater, box 13, LBJL. *Time*, "The Week," March 5, 1965, 20.

74. Goldman, *Tragedy*, 495–499. Busby had also recommended a "conference" for artists in January 1964.

75. Goldman, *Tragedy*, 498–499, 507, 529, 533, 545, 562. In the spring of 1965, for example, the first student teach-in was organized in Ann Arbor, Michigan. It gained media attention and was highly critical of Johnson's Vietnam policies. Valenti, LBJL-OH, part v, 32.

76. *New York Times*, June 12, 1965, 19. *New York Times*, June 16, 1965, 48. *Newsweek*, "Arts and the Man—and the State," June 28, 1965, 22–24. Goldman, *Tragedy*, 562. *Newsweek* noted, "No President in history, not even John F. Kennedy, with his hospitality to the arts, has ever played host" to such an event. The *New York Times* reported, "The Johnson Administration, following President Kennedy's lead, had begun doing something about [the arts' place in society]."

77. Goldman, *Tragedy*, 567. *New York Times*, June 27, 1965, 18. Horace Busby to LBJ, July 20, 1965, Busby, box 51, LBJL.

78. Bill Moyers to LBJ, May 10, 1966, Moyers, box 12, LBJL. *New York Times*, May 12, 1966, 1. *Newsweek*, "The Brain Pickers," September 19, 1966, 30. Delight in Goldman's resignation is noted in Hugh Sidey to Hal Pachios, September 30, 1966, FG11-8-1/Goldman, LBJL. Roche's hiring noted in Roche, LBJL-OH, 7. San Antonio speech noted in *Public Papers, 1966*, 404. Harry McPherson to Bill Moyers, May 21, 1966, McPherson, box 21, LBJL.

79. Harry McPherson to Bill Moyers, July 18, 1966, McPherson, box 32, LBJL.

80. Harry McPherson, LBJL-OH, tape 3, 23–25. Kenneth W. Thompson, ed., *The Johnson Presidency* (Lanham, Md., University Press of America, 1986), 213, notes that Johnson was wary of Katzenbach's affiliation with the "Georgetown crowd." Valenti, *A Very*, 125, describes his attraction for the Kennedys. Schlesinger, *Robert Kennedy*, 686–687.

81. McPherson, LBJL-OH, tape 3, 23–25. McPherson, *A Political*, 177.

82. McPherson, LBJL-OH, tape 3, 23–25. Charles Bartlett, LBJL-OH, 2, notes Johnson's relations with the press in the Senate. George Reedy, *Lyndon B. Johnson: A Memoir* (New York, Andrews and McMeel, 1982), 66–67, 138. Johnson's suspicions were not merely the result of his own insecurity. When his press problems climaxed in July 1965 the *New York*

Times confirmed that the president had been experiencing growing criticism, much of it privately expressed at Washington parties and gatherings. "The criticism is directed more at the President's personalities than his policies," it reported. "His critics say he is peremptory, demands dog-like loyalty from subordinates, is too sensitive to criticism and lacks the 'elegance of style' associated with President Kennedy."

83. For descriptions of LBJ's press problems, see *Newsweek*, February 15, 1965, 62–63; Walter Lippmann column, *Newsweek*, March 1, 1965, 17; *Time*, "Cold War in Washington," March 5, 1965, 38–39; *Time*, "No. 898," March 26, 1965, 38–39; *New York Times*, April 28, 1965, 18; *New York Times*, February 5, 1965. For a White House assessment, see Horace Busby to Bill Moyers, April 21, 1965, Busby, box 20, LBJL. Joseph Alsop wrote that "there are serious reasons to worry about Lyndon Johnson's frame of mind and approach to his heavy task." He noted that the president worried too much about "what has been said or may be said, not to mention plots in it. . . ." After the president had made a racist remark in private to Hugh Sidey of *Time*, the reporter confided to Goodwin. "He said there was an increasing worry about the President around town," Goodwin wrote in his diary. "A fear that his personal eccentricities are not affecting policy." Johnson's suspicions about spies are noted in Reedy, *Lyndon B. Johnson*, 64–65. Goodwin, *Remembering*, 401. See also Bartlett, LBJL-OH, 14.

84. *Newsweek*, "Accent on Style," July 19, 1965, 18. Douglass Cater to LBJ, July 14, 1965, Cater, box 13, LBJL. Walter Lippmann noted in March, "While I think that President Johnson has been quite right not to try to imitate the unique virtuosity of John F. Kennedy, I do not think he is providing a satisfactory alternative." See *Newsweek*, March 1, 1965, 17. *Time* noted on March 5, 1965, 38–39, "Reporters have begun to reminisce nostalgically about the Eisenhower and Kennedy years when press conferences were regularly scheduled well ahead of time and there were no rude surprises, no unventilated rooms without enough chairs to go around." Johnson's recent press conferences compared poorly with "Kennedy's skill at projecting the image of a man on top of his job. . . ."

85. *Newsweek*, February 15, 1965, 62–63. *Time*, March 26, 1965, 38.

86. "Various Editorials [for or from] the Press on President Kennedy's Press Conferences," April 9, 1965, PR18-2, box 375, LBJL. Horace Busby to LBJ, July 1, 1965, Busby, box 51, LBJL. Bob Oliver to LBJ, October 12, 1965, FG1, box 12, LBJL.

87. For samples of tabulations and comparisons of press conferences, see April 2, 1966, FG2, box 41, LBJL; April 22, 1966, PR19-2, box 375, LBJL. The number of respective press conferences was manipulated in May 25, 1966, PR18-2, box 375, LBJL. Johnson's message to Merriman Smith ("Smitty") noted on September 21, 1966, CF PR18, box 83, LBJL. For reports on criticism of JFK, see Fred Panzer to LBJ, February 24, 1967, FG2, box 38, LBJL. For credibility gap comparisons, see Fred Panzer to LBJ, January 21, 1967, Panzer, box 396, LBJL. For opening statements, see Fred Panzer to LBJ, February 21, 1967, FG1, box 14, LBJL; and Robert Kintner to LBJ, February 22, 1967, UT1-1, box 3, LBJL. For summary of criticisms of JFK, see Hayes Redmon to LBJ, June 20, 1966, FG2, box 41, LBJL.

88. For stories on the tension between Johnson and the press, see *New York Times*, July 8, 1965, 1; Tom Wicker, *New York Times*, July 9, 1965, 28: *Newsweek*, July 19, 1965, 18. Goodwin, *Remembering*, 395. According to Reedy, Johnson was "anguished" by the decision to escalate the war. Other aides observed that the president appeared "literally torn to pieces" and that his "puzzling outbursts became more frequent." That month Goodwin noted in his diary that he and Moyers had "another long discussion of Johnson in which we agreed on his paranoid condition."

89. Anderson, *President's Men*, 321–325. McPherson, *A Political*, 252–253. *Newsweek*, March 1, 1965, 28, 32. Goldman, *Tragedy*, 128. John Roche, LBJL-OH, 56.

90. Wicker, *New York Times Magazine*, May 3, 1964, 11ff. Goldman, *Tragedy*, 131. Anderson, *President's Men*, 325–327. Wicker noted that Moyers "has one vitally important, if unofficial function: as both an authentic Johnson man and an authentic New Frontiersman, he has the confidence of everybody on the White House staff and is a useful linchpin holding Kennedy and Johnson men together." Goldman noted, "President Johnson was happy to have an aide who was so close to him and yet had a real line into the Kennedy fortress." Roche believed that Moyers was "hypnotized" by the Kennedys. See Roche, LBJL-OH, 59. RFK's attraction to Moyers noted in Edwin O. Guthman and Jeffrey Shulman, eds., *Robert Kennedy in*

His Own Words: The Unpublished Recollections of the Kennedy Years (New York, Bantam, 1988), 412.

91. Horace Busby to LBJ, July 8, 1965, Busby, box 51, LBJL. Horace Busby to LBJ, July 13, 1965, Busby, box 51, LBJL. Harry McPherson to LBJ, July 17, 1965, McPherson, box 32, LBJL. Douglass Cater to LBJ, July 26, 1965, Cater, box 13. See also Horace Busby to LBJ, July 20, 1965, Busby, box 51, LBJL.

92. *Newsweek*, "An Interview with LBJ," August 2, 1965, 20–21.

93. State of the Union Message, January 4, 1965, RFK Senate Papers, box 5, JFKL; Mike Manatos to RFK, December 22, 1965, RFK Senate Papers, box 7, JFKL; LBJ to RFK, December 20, 1965, RFK Senate Papers, box 5, JFKL; LBJ to RFK, November 20, 1965, RFK Senate Papers, box 5, JFKL; LBJ to RFK, April 10, 1965, RFK Senate Papers, box 5, JFKL; LBJ to RFK, July 19, 1965, RFK-SF/PC, box 5, JFKL; Lawrence O'Brien to RFK, August 28, 1965, RFK-SF/PC, box 8, JFKL; Lawrence O'Brien to RFK, August 11, 1965, RFK-SF/PC, box 8, JFKL; RFK to LBJ, August 6, 1965, RFK Senate Papers, box 5, JFKL; RFK to LBJ, April 2, 1965, RFK Senate Papers, box 5, JFKL; RFK to LBJ, October 25, 1965, RFK Senate Papers, box 5, JFKL. Discussion over the Assassination Bill noted in Harry McPherson to Bill Moyers, August 24, 1965, McPherson, box 51, LBJL.

94. *Time*, August 6, 1965, 18–22. *Time*, "Letters," August 13, 1965, 10. *Newsweek*, "The Politics of Power," August 2, 1965, 18–19, 22, 25. Allen Otten, "Criticism of President's Style, Methods Mount Among Small But Important Group," *Wall Street Journal*, July 6, 1965, 16. Edwin O. Guthman sent the Otten article to RFK. See Edwin O. Guthman to RFK, July 17, 1965, RFK-SF/PC, box 4, JFKL.

CHAPTER IX
The Rupture, 1966–1967

1. In June 1965 Johnson's approval rating was 70 percent. By September 1966 his approval rating fell to 48 percent. See George Gallup, *The Gallup Poll: Public Opinion, 1935–1971* (New York, Random House, 1972), 1945, 2027.

2. *Newsweek*, "Two Senators Named Kennedy," January 17, 1966, 17–20, 25.

3. *Newsweek*, January 17, 1966, 17–20, 25. See also White House Famous Names (WHFN)—Edward Kennedy, box 5, Lyndon B. Johnson Library (LBJL). This file contains numerous greetings between LBJ and Edward. Assessing the Kennedys' past criticisms of the administration, *Newsweek* noted their "well-calculated sense of self-restraint," with Robert, who was first in line for the presidency, being more critical than Edward. They had established their independence, being "impeccably loyal to LBJ in the large, critical in detail often enough to make their presence felt." Johnson's assessment of Edward's political career noted in Joseph A. Califano, Jr., *Governing America: An Insider's Report from the White House and the Cabinet* (New York, Simon and Schuster, 1981), 90. Edward's regard for LBJ and the Vietnam War are noted in James MacGregor Burns, *Edward Kennedy and the Camelot Legacy* (New York, W. W. Norton, 1976), and Burton Hersh, *The Education of Edward Kennedy: A Family Biography* (New York, William Morrow, 1972).

4. Arthur M. Schlesinger, Jr., *Robert Kennedy and His Times* (Boston, Houghton Mifflin, 1978), 732–734. *Newsweek* noted that, though Kennedy did not criticize Johnson's policy in Vietnam, "somehow he always managed to leave behind the impression he would have handled the situation very differently from Mr. Johnson." RFK's shrugging off of criticism was evident in the lighthearted letters he exchanged with the press. See Edwin O. Guthman to RFK, November 9, 1965, Robert F. Kennedy–Senate Files/Personal Correspondences (RFK-SF/PC), box 4, John F. Kennedy Library (JFKL). When writing to William F. Buckley, Jr., RFK noted, "I enjoyed your article on Gore Vidal. I have changed my platform for 1968 from 'Let's give blood to the Viet Cong' to 'Let's give Gore Vidal to the Viet Cong.'" See RFK to William F. Buckley, Jr., April 4, 1967, RFK-SF/PC, box 2, JFKL.

5. *Newsweek*, January 17, 1966, 18. Bill Moyers to LBJ, January 24, 1966, Moyers, box 11, LBJL.

6. Merle Miller, *Lyndon: An Oral Biography* (New York, Putnam, 1980), 419–420. *Newsweek*, "Vietnam: The Pause Comes to an End," February 7, 1966, 16. Schlesinger, *Robert Kennedy*, 735. LBJ to RFK, January 27, 1966, FG2, box 41, LBJL.

7. *Newsweek*, February 7, 1966, 17. Schlesinger, *Robert Kennedy*, 735. Frederick Dutton to RFK, February 8, 1966, RFK-SF/PC, box 3, JFKL.

8. Schlesinger, *Robert Kennedy*, 735–736. *Newsweek*, "The Kennedy Caper," March 7, 1966, 24–25. For a draft of RFK's statement see Statement, February 19, 1966, RFK Senate Files/Legislative Subject Files, box 47, JFKL. On page 5 of this statement, RFK referred to LBJ's pacification program as "the most important and hopeful development in the recent history in that conflict." The passage was crossed out by RFK. RFK's expressed hope that the statement would not cause problems is noted in RFK to Robert McNamara, February 18, 1966, RFK-SF/PC, box 8, JFKL.

9. Schlesinger, *Robert Kennedy*, 736–737. *Newsweek*, March 7, 1966, 25. See also Kenneth Crawford column, *Newsweek*, March 7, 1966, 33. McGeorge Bundy to RFK, February 21, 1966, WHFN-RFK, box 6, LBJL. McGeorge Bundy to David Ginsburg, March 13, 1967, WHFN-RFK, box 6, LBJL. *Public Papers on the Presidents: Lyndon B. Johnson, 1966* (Washington, Government Printing Office, 1967), 213–214. RFK in "bed with the Communists" can be found in James A. Wechsler column, "LBJ and RFK," *New York Post*, February 24, 1966, 24. See also editorial, "The Kennedy-Johnson Debate," *New York Times*, February 27, 1966; David Lawrence column, "Key Phrases in Kennedy Proposal," *Washington Evening Star*, February 23, 1966, 23; "Kennedy Supports Johnson on Viet Nam But Still Differs," *Washington Evening Star*, February 23, 1966, 5.

10. Schlesinger, *Robert Kennedy*, 736–737. Victor Lasky, *Robert F. Kennedy: The Myth and the Man* (New York, Trident, 1968), 281. George Ball to RFK, February 21, 1966, RFK-SF/PC, box 1, JFKL. RFK to George Ball, February 24, 1966, RFK-SF/PC, box 1, JFKL. Transcript of *Today Show*, "Interview Senator Robert F. Kennedy," February 22, 1966, RFK-Senate Files/Legislative Subjects Files, box 48, JFKL.

11. Frederick Dutton to RFK, February 23, 1966, RFK-SF/PC, box 3, JFKL.

12. Harry McPherson to LBJ, February 28, 1966, McPherson, box 51, LBJL.

13. *New York Times*, April 28, 1966, 1. Robert Kintner to LBJ, April 28, 1966, UT1-1, box 3, LBJL.

14. *Newsweek*, "Counterattack," June 27, 1966, 31. Joseph Califano to George Smathers, January 22, 1966, FG2, box 41, LBJL. Robert Kintner to LBJ, April 28, 1966, UT1-1, box 3, LBJL.

15. *Public Papers, 1966*, 8, 518, 564. *New York Times*, February 24, 1966, 1.

16. Frederick Dutton to RFK, February 8, 1966, RFK-SF/PC, box 3, JFKL.

17. *Newsweek*, January 17, 1966, 17–20, 25. *Newsweek*, "The Bobby Phenomenon," October 24, 1966, 30, 35–38. Schlesinger, *Robert Kennedy*, 739. *Life*, "He Uses—and Deeply Feels—the Legend," November 18, 1966, 40. In February, when Kennedy tried to repair the damage of his call for a "compromise government," reporter Murray Kempton observed him sitting in the studio of the *Today Show*. Kempton was impressed by Robert's attempt to redefine himself in the manner of the late president. His "concentrated attempt to be his brother's interior, to talk not as John Kennedy did on the platform, but as he seems to have in private moments of crisis. . . . The most reckless and romantic of the Kennedys was deliberately reshaping himself according to the memory of the coolest and most detached of them." Goodwin's assessment noted in Richard Goodwin to RFK, n.d., 1967, RFK-SF/PC, box 4, JFKL.

18. *Newsweek*, "LBJ & RFK?" June 13, 1966, 35. *Newsweek*, October 24, 1966, 30, 35–38.

19. *Newsweek*, "Instant U," May 16, 1966, 34–35. *Newsweek*, October 24, 1966, 30, 35–38. Schlesinger, *Robert Kennedy*, 734, 739. Kennedy's "brain-pickers" included, among others, Theodore Sorensen, Arthur Schlesinger, Richard Goodwin, Carl Kaysen, Burke Marshall, John Kenneth Galbraith, Jerome Wiesner, Richard Neustadt, Patrick Moynihan, George McGovern, and Joseph Tydings. The effort to create a united front of Kennedy supporters among elite opinion-makers proved successful. By the fall Galbraith concluded that Robert "has a closer rapport with academics today than his brother did. . . . Academics in their majority

tend to be liberals, but they also respect a man who gets his back into the job." John Roche, Lyndon B. Johnson Library–Oral History (LBJL OH), 74. Kenneth Crawford column, *Newsweek*, May 9, 1966, 35. A particularly influential force was Schlesinger, who Roche characterized as "the *deus ex machina* in ADA." See Roche, LBJL-OH, 8.

20. Robert Kintner to LBJ, April 25, 1966, CF FG/RS/PR18, box 16, LBJL. He also noted gossip circulating at Washington parties in Robert Kintner to LBJ, July 25, 1966, Kintner, box 2, LBJL. Bill Moyers to LBJ, June 9, 1966, Moyers, box 12, LBJL. Alsop described himself to RFK as an "affectionate, admiring, and deeply concerned uncle." See Joseph Alsop to RFK, February 1, 1967, RFK-SF/PC, box 1, JFKL. David Brinkley once sent a handwritten note to RFK congratulating him on a speech. See David Brinkley to RFK, n.d., RFK-Senate Files, box 12, JFKL.

21. Bill Moyers to LBJ, September 10, 1966, Watson, box 25, LBJL.

22. Emmet John Hughes column, *Newsweek*, March 7, 1966, 21. In the fall of 1965 Tom Wicker noted the Kennedys' vast influence upon Washington. "[I]t is here," Wicker wrote, "in this self-transfixed company town of the American people, that the Golden Age counts its most passionate believers and it is here that the Johnson Administration is at its nadir of esteem." See Tom Wicker, "Lyndon Johnson vs. the Ghost of Jack Kennedy," *Esquire* 64 (November 1965). *Newsweek*, May 16, 1966, 34–35. Frederick Dutton to RFK, April 6, 1966, RFK-SF/PC, box 3, JFKL. For a list of those political and journalistic personalities who were invited to RFK's Hickory Hill parties, see AMN to RFK, August 9, 1966, and August 8, 1966, RFK-SF/PC, box 6, JFKL.

23. Robert Kintner to LBJ, April 25, 1966, CF FG/RS/PR18, box 16, LBJL. Liz Carpenter to LBJ, April 1, 1966, WHFN-RFK, box 6, LBJL.

24. Schlesinger, *Robert Kennedy*, 751.

25. Harry McPherson to LBJ, August 11, 1966, McPherson, box 52, LBJL.

26. *Newsweek*, October 24, 1966, 36. *Public Papers, 1966*, 445. Lasky, *Robert F. Kennedy*, 284.

27. Frederick Dutton to RFK, April 6, 1966, RFK-SF/PC, box 3, JFKL. Lasky, *Robert F. Kennedy*, 286, 316. Arthur Krock column, *New York Times*, May 26, 1966. *Newsweek*, "A Sympathetic Chord," June 20, 1966, 44A–44B. *Newsweek*, "A Favorite American," June 27, 1966, 53–54. Schlesinger, *Robert Kennedy*, 744. Kennedy "was speaking not only to Africans," *The Nation* concluded, "but to the liberals, intellectuals, progressive labor, and, in general, that part of America which is left of center."

28. Robert Kintner to LBJ, June 24, 1966, Kintner, box 1, LBJL.

29. *Public Papers, 1966*, 708. Robert Kintner to Bill Moyers, August 23, 1966, PR18-2, box 375, LBJL. *Public Papers, 1966*, 880.

30. Hugh Sidey, "He makes a truce ...," *Life*, November 18, 1966, 38–39. *Newsweek*, October 24, 1966, 30, 35–38. *Newsweek*, January 17, 1966, 17–20, 25. *Newsweek*, June 13, 1966, 35. *Newsweek*, "Making of the President, 1972?" 17–18. *Life* described them as having "purely a business relationship—proper, and almost affable." But tension was also apparent. "Robert Kennedy and Lyndon Johnson stare at each other uncomprehendingly across a generational and cultural chasm that gets wider each month," Hugh Sidey reported. "Johnson seems to be drifting on an island of time between Kennedys."

31. *Newsweek*, January 17, 1966, 25.

32. Roger Stevens to Bill Moyers, December 27, 1965, FG2, box 40, LBJL. *New York Times*, May 31, 1966, 1. Robert Kintner to LBJ, May 30, 1966, CF FG/RS/PR18, box 16, LBJL. Marvin Watson to LBJ, August 19, 1966, FG2, box 41, LBJL.

33. *Public Papers, 1966*, 232, 329, 364, 420, 427, 475, 529, 600, 841, 846, 943, 950, 1068, 1114, 1132, 1151, 1159, 1183. On 1016, LBJ refers to JFK as "beloved." On 796, LBJ refers to JFK as "our beloved, great late President." Johnson's most sentimental reference to JFK occurs on 869–874 while speaking at a dedication of the John F. Kennedy Memorial Park in Lewiston, Maine. "We have tried to carry forward his program," he noted, "and execute it as he would have had us do." But it was his only reference to JFK during the speech. *Newsweek*, September 5, 1966, 17.

34. *Newsweek*, "A Hopeful President Joins Debate," March 7, 1966, 23. *Newsweek*, "A

Word from Zephyr," May 16, 1966, 31. *Newsweek*, "The War Comes to the Campus," May 23, 1966, 29–30. *Gallup*, 1993.

35. Resignation of aides noted in *Newsweek*, "Revolving Door at 1600," May 9, 1966, 26–27. *Newsweek*, "Fresh Slant on Polls," June 20, 1966, 33–34. Hayes Redmon to Bill Moyers, July 11, 1966, Watson, box 25, LBJL. *Newsweek*, June 13, 1966, 35. *Newsweek*, "LBJ vs. RFK?" June 13, 1966, 35.

36. Schlesinger, *Robert Kennedy*, 741. *Newsweek*, October 24, 1966, 35. Roche, LBJL-OH, 60.

37. Louis Harris, "State of the LBJ Image," *Newsweek*, January 9, 1967, 18–19.

38. *Newsweek*, September 5, 1966, 17. *Gallup*, 2023. Lasky, *Robert F. Kennedy*, 315.

39. Wicker quoted in Lasky, *Robert F. Kennedy*, 321. The Kennedy organization collected clippings pertaining to LBJ's visit to New York in August 1966. See RFK 1968 Campaign/Press Division, box 11, JFKL. On the clipping from the *Buffalo Evening News*, August 20, 1965, an aide wrote, "Not Quite!" under a paragraph noting "the President was greeted by enthusiastic crowds and responded with Johnsonian enthusiasm."

40. Lasky, *Robert F. Kennedy*, 315. Kenneth Crawford column, *Newsweek*, September 5, 1966, 24. *Newsweek*, October 24, 1966, 30, 35–38. *Newsweek*, January 9, 1967, 18–19. *Newsweek*, September 5, 1966, 18. Harry McPherson to LBJ, September 22, 1966, McPherson, box 22, LBJL.

41. *Life*, November 18, 1966, 39. *Newsweek*, September 5, 1966, 18.

42. *Newsweek*, "Bridge Out," December 26, 1966, 18–19. Schlesinger, *Robert Kennedy*, 742. Some reporters speculated that the resignation was yet another example of the difficulty of working for Johnson. Others emphasized that Moyers resigned for personal reasons, mostly financial. Speaking with Schlesinger in December, Moyers expressed the futility of remaining with the administration: "You know, Arthur, I would not be leaving if I thought I could do any good by staying." Moyers's resignation had broad repercussions. Reporters lamented that he was one of the few staff members capable of bridging the "credibility gap." They further noted that Johnson had lost a valuable adviser, one who not only formulated important policy but did not hesitate to disagree with the president.

43. *Newsweek*, December 26, 1966, 18–19. Roche, LBJL-OH, 58.

44. The notion that the Kennedys had "sucked Bill away" was advanced by Kearns and is quoted in James Fallows, "Bill Moyers: His Heart Belongs to Daddy," *Washington Monthly*, July/August 1974, 45. Fred Panzer to LBJ, February 21, 1967, FG1, box 14, LBJL. Harry McPherson to LBJ, February 5, 1967, McPherson, box 53, LBJL. Moyers noted to McPherson that "Kennedy was, and his performance indicated that 'reasonable' men can't control 'unreasonable' forces. You have to have a gut reaction. You have to be 'unreasonable' to some extent." Harry McPherson to LBJ, June 20, 1967, McPherson, box 53, LBJL. See also McPherson, LBJL-OH, tape 4, 5. Moyers and RFK exchanged numerous personal greetings after he left the White House. See Bill Moyers to RFK, n.d., RFK-SF/PC, box 8, JFKL. RFK to Bill Moyers, July 20, 1967, RFK-SF/PC, box 8, JFKL. Bill Moyers to RFK, August 10, 1967, RFK-SF/PC, box 8, JFKL.

45. *Newsweek*, "Jacqueline B. Kennedy, Plaintiff . . . ," December 26, 1966, 39–43. *New York Times*, August 27, 1966, 27. *Newsweek*, "The Best Kennedy Book?" September 5, 1966, 211–212. Schlesinger, *Robert Kennedy*, 760–761. *Newsweek*, "Manchester's Own Story," January 30, 1967, 21–22. Lasky, *Robert F. Kennedy*, 367. See also William Manchester, *Controversy: And Other Essays in Journalism, 1950–75* (Boston, Little, Brown, 1976), 5–76.

46. Schlesinger, *Robert Kennedy*, 761. *Newsweek*, December 26, 1966, 43.

47. LBJ to Jacqueline Kennedy, December 16, 1966, WHFN—Mrs. JFK, box 5, LBJL.

48. Robert Kintner to LBJ, December 16, 1966, FG2, box 41, LBJL.

49. *Newsweek*, "Temporary Cease-Fire," January 9, 1967, 20. George Christian to LBJ, January 13, 1967, PU2-6/Manchester, box 84, LBJL.

50. *Newsweek*, "Jacqueline Kennedy's 'Victory,' " January 2, 1967, 16–19. *Newsweek*, "How to Lose a War," February 6, 1967, 34–35.

51. *Newsweek*, January 2, 1967, 18–19.

52. Popple to LBJ, December 29, 1966; Robert Kintner to LBJ, January 5, 1967; Jack

Valenti to LBJ, January 3, 1967; Marvin Watson to LBJ, October 21, 1967, all in PU2-6/ Manchester, box 84, LBJL. See also Robert Kintner to LBJ, December 30, 1966, CF PR19-2-1, box 84, LBJL. Johnson rejected a request to provide a reporter with material on the Manchester book in Robert Kintner to LBJ, February 9, 1967, CF PR18-2-1, box 84, LBJL.

53. *Newsweek*, "JFK Censored?" October 3, 1966, 65–66. Kenneth Crawford column, *Newsweek*, January 9, 1967, 25. *Newsweek*, December 26, 1966, 39–43.

54. *Newsweek*, December 26, 1966, 40. *Newsweek* quoted "one former admirer" saying, "I don't think that you can have deep, deep sympathy for a grieving widow who spends half her time at Ondine's and other places and appears in a mini-skirt and then expects privacy for herself and her children." Kenneth Crawford column, *Newsweek*, January 2, 1967, 22. *Newsweek*, February 6, 1967, 34. Emmet John Hughes column, *Newsweek*, February 6, 1967, 20. "The senator and the widow have profited little and suffered much," columnist Emmet John Hughes wrote. "In strictly political terms, the senator's enemies and critics sound more snappish and suspicious than ever . . . a buzzing chatter of doubt or distaste over the privileged place of the Kennedy family in American political life." *Gallup*, 2047–2048.

55. Schlesinger, *Robert Kennedy*, 762–763, 759, 764. Harris poll noted in Manchester, *Controversy*, 72–73. *Newsweek*, "Passing the Bug," December 26, 1966, 19–20. *Newsweek*, February 6, 1967, 34–35. *Newsweek* assessed it as "a week-long show of bugpassing that did little to credit either man." The *New York Times* concluded that neither man demonstrated that he "lay awake nights worrying about the dangers to civil liberties involved in wiretaps or 'bugging.' " RFK to Edward Lewis, January 17, 1967, RFK-SF/PC, box 7, JFKL.

56. Robert Kintner to LBJ, January 27, 1967, FG11-8-1/Kintner, LBJL. Harry McPherson to LBJ, February 5, 1967, McPherson, box 53, LBJL.

57. *Newsweek*, "Peace?—Hints, Signs, Hopes," February 13, 1967, 33–34. Schlesinger, *Robert Kennedy*, 764.

58. *Newsweek*, "Bobby Abroad," February 13, 1967, 34–35.

59. *Newsweek*, February 13, 1967, 34–35. Lasky, *Robert F. Kennedy*, 376.

60. Schlesinger, *Robert Kennedy*, 766–767.

61. *Newsweek*, "The Other War," February 20, 1967, 31–32. Kenneth Crawford column, *Newsweek*, February 20, 1967, 46. Schlesinger, *Robert Kennedy*, 767.

62. Nicholas Katzenbach, LBJL-OH, 27–29. David Wise, *The Politics of Lying: Government Deception, Secrecy, and Power* (New York, Random House, 1973), 85. Schlesinger, *Robert Kennedy*, 768.

63. Schlesinger, *Robert Kennedy*, 768–769. Lasky, *Robert F. Kennedy*, 383. *Time*, March 17, 1967. *Newsweek*, February 20, 1967, 31–32.

64. *Newsweek*, February 20, 1967, 32. Katharine Graham, LBJL-OH, 22. Lasky, *Robert F. Kennedy*, 385.

65. Lasky, *Robert F. Kennedy*, 385. Wise, *Politics*, 86.

CHAPTER X
End of the Ordeal

1. Lyndon B. Johnson, *The Vantage Point: Perspectives of the Presidency, 1963–1969* (New York, Holt, Rinehart and Winston, 1971), 252–257.

2. Johnson, *Vantage Point*, 257–258, 366–370.

3. Richard Goodwin to RFK, n.d., 1966, Robert F. Kennedy–Senate Files/Personal Correspondences (RFK-SF/PC), box 4, John F. Kennedy Library (JFKL). Although Goodwin makes it clear that he is presenting his views only for argument's sake, the undertone of the memorandum seems clearly intended to urge RFK to run for president in 1968.

4. Frederick Dutton to RFK, December 8, 1966, RFK-SF/PC, box 3, JFKL.

5. Victor Lasky, *Robert F. Kennedy: The Myth and the Man* (New York, Trident, 1968), 386. Arthur M. Schlesinger, Jr., *Robert Kennedy and His Times* (Boston, Houghton Mifflin, 1978), 769–770. *Newsweek*, "The Other War," February 20, 1967, 32. Harry McPherson to George Christian, February 9, 1967, McPherson, box 53, Lyndon B. Johnson Library (LBJL). Speech

and Press Release, February 8, 1967, Robert F. Kennedy Speeches and Press Releases, box 3, JFKL.

6. Lawrence O'Brien, *No Final Victories: A Life in Politics from JFK to Watergate* (Garden City, Doubleday, 1974), 215. John Roche to LBJ, February 9, 1967, Watson, box 29, LBJL.

7. John Roche to LBJ, February 20, 1967, Watson, box 29, LBJL. Joseph Bruce Gorman, *Kefauver: A Political Biography* (New York, Oxford University Press, 1971), 126–130.

8. John Roche, Lyndon B. Johnson Library—Oral History (LBJL-OH), 60. Lasky, *Robert F. Kennedy*, 392.

9. Frederick Dutton to RFK, December 8, 1966, RFK-SF/PC, box 3, JFKL. Schlesinger, *Robert Kennedy*, 769–770. John Roche to LBJ, March 15, 1967, Watson, box 29, LBJL.

10. Lasky, *Robert F. Kennedy*, 388. Schlesinger, *Robert Kennedy*, 770.

11. Lasky, *Robert F. Kennedy*, 388, 393. Schlesinger, *Robert Kennedy*, 771. *New York Times*, February 26, 1967, 8. Dave Powers sent RFK a clipping from the *Catholic Virginian* criticizing Farley's statement. See Dave Powers to Angie, March 22, 1967, RFK-SF/PC, box 9, JFKL.

12. *Newsweek*, "Men at War: RFK vs. LBJ," March 13, 1967, 33–34.

13. *New York Times*, March 3, 1967, 1. Schlesinger, *Robert Kennedy*, 772–773.

14. Mrs. Rowland Evans, Jr., March 10, 1967, RFK-SF/PC, box 3, JFKL. Hugh Sidey to RFK, March 4, 1967, RFK-SF/PC, box 10, JFKL. Schlesinger, *Robert Kennedy*, 770. George Gallup, *The Gallup Poll: Public Opinion, 1935–1971* (New York, Random House, 1972), 2063, 2074, 2054.

15. Schlesinger, *Robert Kennedy*, 772–774. *Newsweek*, March 13, 1967, 34. Lasky, *Robert F. Kennedy*, 390–391, 393. Emmet John Hughes column, *Newsweek*, March 20, 1967, 23. "The Bobby speech is bound to give [Hanoi] a shot in the arm," one unnamed aide remarked. "I read it carefully twice," another aide noted, "and I'm still wondering why he made the speech." Richard Nixon said Kennedy "had the effect of prolonging the war by encouraging the enemy. . . . Johnson is right and Kennedy is wrong." Journalist Marianne Means reported that party regulars in New York who once considered backing Kennedy in 1968 "are now irritated by his failure to join a united front behind President Johnson." Emmet John Hughes accused Kennedy of aiming his argument at "American politics rather than Asian politics." Javits used the opportunity to attack both Johnson and Kennedy, noting that the "political and emotional problems" between Kennedy and Johnson "cannot and should not be permitted to affect our national policy on Vietnam."

16. *New York Times*, March 9, 1967. Harry McPherson to LBJ, March 9, 1967, McPherson, box 53, LBJL.

17. Chalmers Roberts, *The First Rough Draft: A Journalist's Journal of Our Times* (New York, Praeger, 1973), 250. *Newsweek*, "'That Man' and 'That Boy,'" March 20, 1967, 25–26. "Press Briefing Paper," March 8, 1967, PR18-2, box 376, LBJL. Douglass Cater to LBJ, March 9, 1967, Cater, box 12, LBJL. Cater further noted that Elfin believed that the *New York Times* "seems to be embarked on a deliberate policy to needle you with the Kennedy dispute." He cited the *Times's* unwarranted front-page coverage of Schlesinger's news conference.

18. *Newsweek*, March 20, 1967, 25–26. Lasky, *Robert F. Kennedy*, 392.

19. Memorandum to the President, March 20, 1967, PR18-2, box 376, LBJL. Harry McPherson to George Christian, March 10, 1967, McPherson, box 32, LBJL. Lasky, *Robert F. Kennedy*, 394.

20. Lasky, *Robert F. Kennedy*, 392. *Newsweek*, March 20, 1967, 26. Schlesinger, *Robert Kennedy*, 774.

21. *Newsweek*, March 20, 1967, 25–26. RFK sent Senator Symington a letter and a news clipping from the *Buffalo Evening News* with the headline, "Criticism Is Closing In on Bobby." "This is another indication of what I am dealing with and which I have of course pointed out to you." See RFK to Senator Symington, February 23, 1967, RFK-SF/PC, box 10, JFKL. Frederick Dutton to RFK, March 15, 1967, RFK-SF/PC, box 3, JFKL. Milton Gwirtzman also advised RFK to "damp down the 'fued' [sic] again." See Milton Gwirtzman to RFK, March 20, 1967, RFK-SF/PC, box 4, JFKL.

22. Harry McPherson to George Christian, March 10, 1967, McPherson, box 32, LBJL. Memorandum to the President, March 20, 1967, PR18-2, box 376, LBJL. McPherson informed

Johnson of his talk with Novak. Kennedy had recently talked with Novak, confiding that he would not run for president. "I think it would destroy me and the Democratic Party," Kennedy told the columnist. When Novak asked Kennedy who should be president in 1968, Kennedy told him that Johnson "deserves to be." McPherson also noted, "Bartlett knows that Bobby is being fed steady streams of poison by the anti-LBJ men around Kennedy. It is Bartlett's theme that Bobby simply cannot allow this tragic, and deadly conflict with the President to gain any more momentum."

23. Schlesinger, *Robert Kennedy*, 776–777.

24. *Gallup*, 2058, 2062, 2063. Schlesinger, *Robert Kennedy*, 776. Robert Kintner to LBJ, May 8, 1967, FG1, box 14, LBJL. "I believe," Robert Kintner wrote in May, "the increases [in Johnson's public acceptance] came about from care of the President in exposure, Senator Kennedy's action, the Manchester book, etc." Edwin O. Guthman sent RFK results of a California state poll showing RFK ahead of LBJ. See Edwin O. Guthman to RFK, n.d., March 1967, RFK-SF/PC, box 4, JFKL. RFK also sensed that he had been hurt by recent political reversals, accounting for LBJ's rise in stature. See Richard Goodwin to RFK, n.d., 1967, RFK-SF/PC, box 4, JFKL. Frederick Dutton also listed for RFK the reasons for his decline in popularity. See Frederick Dutton to RFK, November 3, 1967, RFK-SF/PC, box 3, JFKL.

25. John Roche to LBJ, April 18, 1967, Watson, box 29, LBJL. One Kennedy faction consisted of "militant" followers who wanted Robert aggressively to proclaim his candidacy. A second faction wanted him to avoid any semblance of party division and urged him to "make the right acts of fealty. . . ." They were convinced that Johnson would self-destruct and that Robert could then win the presidency in 1972. Roche recommended that Martin Luther King be "disposed of first": "Essentially, the Communist origins of this operation must be exposed . . . by tough minded liberals." He advised that George Wallace be "contained in the North" by appeals to whites through "abstract, religious" arguments. The opposition party, meanwhile, generated little concern for Roche. "The Republicans we can beat," he wrote simply, "—if we can find the time to go after them."

26. John Roche to LBJ, February 1, 1967, Watson, box 29, LBJL. John Roche to LBJ, February 6, 1967, Watson, box 29, LBJL. Harry McPherson to LBJ, May 12, 1967, FG1, box 14, LBJL.

27. Ben Wattenberg to LBJ, January 6, 1967, McPherson, box 51, LBJL. Ben Wattenberg to LBJ, February 25, 1967, Wattenberg, box 22, LBJL.

28. John Roche to LBJ, January 30, 1967, FG11-8-1/Roche, box 110, LBJL.

29. Harry McPherson to LBJ, May 4, 1967, McPherson, box 53, LBJL. Harry McPherson to LBJ, May 17, 1967, McPherson, box 53, LBJL. McPherson also noted that Franklin Roosevelt had drawn intellectual strength from lawyers and that other presidents had tapped the ideas of the business community.

30. *Newsweek*, "LBJ and the Intellectuals," June 5, 1967, 27–28. John Roche memorandum is noted in Fred I. Greenstein, ed., *Leadership in the Modern Presidency* (Cambridge, Harvard University Press, 1988), 145. Harry McPherson to LBJ, December 2, 1967, McPherson, box 53, LBJL. Because the session contrasted to Johnson's known hostility toward the intellectuals, it received wide and generally favorable coverage. The occasion allowed some officials to disparage intellectual critics. One aide referred to them as "academic Liberaces." Another praised Johnson as "a pleasant intellectual, an exciting, challenging guy who knows when to ask the right question." Burns also noted, "It was just the sheer weight of courageous and correct decisions that made me a Johnson supporter." Assurances that JFK also suffered from a poor image with intellectuals and young adults noted in Joseph Califano to LBJ, May 25, 1967, FG2, box 41, LBJL, and John Criswell to Marvin Watson, May 8, 1967, Watson, box 25, LBJL. In May, Joseph Califano forwarded to Johnson "a precious clipping" from a 1961 article by James Reston that noted John Kennedy's "problems" with the intellectual community. An accompanying memorandum noted that "Jack Kennedy did go through a difficult period of adjustment with the 'intellectuals.' Looking back, everyone makes the easy comment that 'Kennedy was an intellectual and was respected by the intellectuals.' " Reston's column made clear that "[John] Kennedy had the same problems that Lyndon Johnson has in getting some liberals to understand that those who have responsibility must *act* and not just be liberal thinkers." Facing widespread student protest, Johnson was assured that his difficulties were

consistent with his predecessor's. An aide sent Johnson a copy of a 1963 *Time* article noting that John Kennedy had similarly suffered from an "image" problem with youth.

31. *Boston Globe* article, "Think Young Mr. President," February 5, 1967, FG1, box 13, LBJL. Tom Cronin to Harry McPherson, March 24, 1967, McPherson, box 18, LBJL. Other attempts to appeal to young adults noted in Robert Kintner to Marvin Watson, April 21, 1967, PR18-2, box 376, LBJL.

32. *New York Times*, March 16, 1967, 1.

33. Ben Wattenberg to LBJ, May 19, 1967, Wattenberg, box 22, LBJL.

34. Douglass Cater to LBJ, May 24, 1967, Cater, box 16, LBJL. Douglass Cater to LBJ, May 25, 1967, Cater, box 16, LBJL. *Newsweek*, "The John F. Kennedy," June 5, 1967, 26–27. *Public Papers of the Presidents of the United States: Lyndon B. Johnson, 1967* (Washington, Government Printing Office, 1968), 579–580. Lloyd Hackler to LBJ, June 2, 1967, FG2, box 40, LBJL, contains a clipping from the *Washington Daily News*. Hackler disputed the notion that there was tension.

35. Joseph Califano to LBJ, May 27, 1967, Namefile/Arthur M. Schlesinger, Jr., LBJL. Rose Kennedy to LBJ, June 28, 1967, White House Famous Names (WHFN)—Ambassador and Mrs. Joseph P. Kennedy, LBJL. *Public Papers, 1967*, 594. Schlesinger, *Robert Kennedy*, 776.

36. Schlesinger, *Robert Kennedy*, 776. Arthur Schlesinger to RFK, June 19, 1967, RFK-SF/PC, box 11, JFKL. Johnson, *Vantage Point*, 110–111.

37. For an appreciation of the Vietnam War as seen from the perspective of the summer of 1967, see *Newsweek*, July 10, 1967. *Newsweek*'s assessment quoted from 20. "Americans support Lyndon Johnson," *Newsweek* reported in July, "but they don't like him personally." That axiom became even more accurate as the summer progressed. The magazine quoted a number of private citizens assessing Johnson. A grandmother from Idaho remarked, "I'm beginning to hate that man." "Johnson's too clever," a New York executive told *Newsweek*. "He's always got something up his sleeve." A housewife from Los Angeles added, "I don't think I like Johnson now. I don't think he's an honest man."

38. *Newsweek*, "A New Sophistication," July 10, 1967, 20–22. *Newsweek*, "LBJ at a Low Ebb," August 21, 1967, 15–16. *Newsweek*, "A President in Trouble," September 4, 1967, 17–21.

39. *Newsweek*, "Tired Grandpa," August 14, 1967, 22. *Newsweek*, "LBJ at a Low Ebb," August 21, 1967, 15–16. Kenneth Crawford column, *Newsweek*, August 14, 1967, 27. "Having experienced the heady sense of power," columnist Kenneth Crawford observed, ". . . [the Kennedys in exile] are addicts. They make free with unsolicited advice and anger when it is not adopted. They complain that the successor to *their* President 'listens to the wrong people,'—meaning not to them. They are meddlers as well as critics."

40. Schlesinger, *Robert Kennedy*, 784, 789, 797. *Newsweek*, "Crest of the Wave," July 17, 1967, 24–25.

41. Tom Johnson to George Christian, July 10, 1967, PL/Kennedy, box 26, LBJL. Tom Johnson to George Christian, August 29, 1967, PL/Kennedy, box 26, LBJL. John Roche to LBJ, September 8, 1967, Watson, box 29, LBJL. In July Christian received word from Tom Johnson that the senator had recently gathered a group of reporters at his Hickory Hill home to discuss "What am I doing wrong." "[T]he reporters told Senator Kennedy that he was pushing too hard too fast. They said he was too obvious in his efforts to seek the Presidency and that his opposition to the President was doing him more harm than good." In early September Roche felt the administration had the upper hand in dealing with a Kennedy threat. Acknowledging that "we are going to have a real battle for survival next year," Roche nevertheless believed that Robert Kennedy understood that he needed the support of the administration in order to further his own ambitions. He assured Johnson that Kennedy's own presidential aspirations in 1972 required Johnson's election in 1968.

42. *Newsweek*, September 4, 1967, 17–21.

43. *Newsweek*, "Dump LBJ?" October 9, 1967, 24–25. Schlesinger, *Robert Kennedy*, 822. *Gallup*, 2083. Fred Panzer to LBJ, November 27, 1967, Panzer, box 398, LBJL. Marvin Watson to LBJ, October 24, 1967, FG1, box 15, LBJL.

44. *Newsweek*, September 4, 1967, 18–19.

45. Schlesinger, *Robert Kennedy*, 825, 829–830. Frederick Dutton to RFK, November 3, 1967, RFK-SF/PC, box 3, JFKL. Frederick Dutton to RFK, November 6, 1967, RFK-SF/PC, box 3, JFKL.

46. Roche, LBJL-OH, 77–78. Schlesinger, *Robert Kennedy*, 830. *Newsweek*, September 4, 1967, 21.

47. *Newsweek*, "Meet Candidate Lyndon Johnson," November 13, 1967, 31–32. *Newsweek*, "Outward Bound," November 20, 1967, 68.

48. Johnson, *Vantage Point*, 269. *Newsweek*, "Vietnam, 'Let's Not Be Children,'" October 23, 1967, 29–30. *Newsweek*, "Dissenting from the Dissenters," November 6, 1967, 25–26. Greenstein, ed., *Leadership*, 147. Marvin Watson to LBJ, September 6, 1967, FG1, box 15, LBJL.

49. Walter Rostow to LBJ, September 15, 1967, CF NSF:VN, box 97, LBJL.

50. *Public Papers, 1967*, 877, 912–913, 1082.

51. LBJ did not mention JFK's commitment to Vietnam during a highly publicized press conference on November 17 or during the December airing of "Conversation with the President." Memorandum to the President, November 1, 1967, FG2, box 41, LBJL, cites the letter from JFK to the sister of a dead soldier.

52. Mike Wallace and Gary Paul Gates, *Close Encounters: Mike Wallace's Own Story* (New York, William Morrow, 1984), 150–153.

53. *Newsweek*, "Live and in Color: The Real LBJ," November 27, 1967, 23–24. A video of the press conference is available for viewing at the Johnson Library. For a tabulation of responses, see Whitney Shoemaker to George Christian, November 20, 1967, PR19-2, box 367, LBJL. Of particular interest is Hugh Sidey's letter to LBJ, November 17, 1967, PR18-2, box 367, LBJL. He was moved to send a poignant letter to the president. "In my judgment, you broke through some kind of barrier that has been clouding your communication for four years," Sidey wrote. "...I suddenly sensed just how much I want you to succeed...." Also see Robert Kintner to LBJ, November 20, 1967, CF FG/RS/PR18, box 16, LBJL. "Morale booster" noted in Charles Maquire to LBJ, November 18, 1967, PR18-2, box 376. McPherson offers a more skeptical appraisal of the press conference in Harry McPherson, LBJL-OH, tape 5, 27. The Harris poll can be found in the *New York Times*, December 5, 1967, 18.

54. Robert A. Divine, ed., *The Johnson Years: Foreign Policy, the Great Society, and the White House* (Lawrence, University Press of Kansas, 1987), 231. The comparison with JFK during the Cuban missile crisis is noted in Greenstein, ed., *Leadership*, 152–153. *New York Times*, November 18, 1967, 1, 18.

55. *Newsweek*, "Life with Lyndon," January 1, 1968, 11–12. The White House circulated a transcript of Johnson's response to a possible Kennedy candidacy in George Christian to Jim Jones, December 27, 1967, PR18-2, box 376, LBJL. Nielsen rating noted in Jim Jones to George Christian, January 2, 1968, PR18-2, box 377, LBJL.

56. Kenneth Crawford column, *Newsweek*, November 13, 1967, 42. *Newsweek*, "Mc-Namara: Why Is He Leaving," December 11, 1967, 25–30. Schlesinger, *Robert Kennedy*, 823. Roche, LBJL-OH, 75–76. Doris Kearns, *Lyndon Johnson and the American Dream* (New York, Harper and Row, 1976), 320–321.

57. *Newsweek*, "TRL Himself," December 18, 1967, 33. George Christian to LBJ, December 4, 1967, PR18-2, box 367, LBJL.

58. Robert Kintner to LBJ, December 29, 1967, CF FG/RS/PR18, box 16, LBJL. Harry McPherson to LBJ, March 18, 1968, McPherson, box 53, LBJL.

59. *Newsweek*, November 20, 1967, 68.

60. *Newsweek*, "The Move to 'Dump' Johnson," November 27, 1967, 25–29. Schlesinger, *Robert Kennedy*, 827. Kenneth Crawford column, *Newsweek*, December 4, 1967, 32. Walter Lippmann column, *Newsweek*, December 18, 1967, 25.

61. Schlesinger, *Robert Kennedy*, 827, 833.

62. O'Brien, *No Final*, 215. He notes, "McCarthy's candidacy was not taken seriously by anyone around the President. It was regarded as a joke, an annoyance." *Newsweek*, "McCarthy or McCoy?" December 11, 1967, 30. Schlesinger, *Robert Kennedy*, 839. *Newsweek*, November 27, 1967, 26. Merle Miller, *Lyndon: An Oral Biography* (New York, Putnam, 1980), 506.

63. John Roche to LBJ, January 26, 1968, Watson, box 25, LBJL.

64. Ben Wattenberg to LBJ, November 21, 1967, Wattenberg, box 22, LBJL. James Rowe to LBJ, January 16, 1968, Watson, box 25, LBJL. John Roche to LBJ, December 18, 1967, Watson, box 29, LBJL. John Roche to LBJ, December 4, 1967, CF PL2, box 76, LBJL. Hoping to restrain Kennedy's impulsiveness, Rowe wanted to stress the need for party unity. Furthermore, it was to be implied to Kennedy that if he cooperated he would better assure his own election to the presidency in 1972. "This is the pitch," Rowe noted. "It should be made several times by several different people." Among those who should speak with Kennedy, Rowe recommended himself ("a recognized Johnson man") and "two or three Cabinet Members who are close to Bobby, and yet, I think, are loyal to you." "If I am wrong," he concluded, "—and he plans to run, as you sometimes suspect—what have we lost? Nothing. If I am right, and we do nothing about it, there is a very good chance his followers will push him over the brink."

65. Miller, *Lyndon*, 495–499. George Christian to LBJ, January 17, 1968, CF FG11-8-1, box 20, LBJL. While some aides tried to motivate Johnson, another faction recommended that he give in to his fears. They noted that the prospect of re-election looked bleak. His popular support was below 50 percent. Organizations were forming in an effort to "dump" him from the ticket. The press speculated that if progress in Vietnam continued to lag, Johnson might bow out of the campaign. They argued that he would gain only a "hollow victory" if re-elected. John Roche to LBJ, January 19, 1968, Watson, box 29, LBJL. Roche also informed LBJ that RFK had "hard" information that LBJ was not going to run for president. The "hard" evidence centered on separate conversations involving Johnson's son-in-law, the First Lady, and an intimate senator.

66. Johnson, *Vantage Point*, 429–430. *Newsweek*, "The State of LBJ," January 29, 1968, 16–17. *Newsweek*, "Bobby: To Be or Not to Be," January 29, 1968, 18–19.

67. Kearns, *Lyndon Johnson*, 335–336.

68. Kearns, *Lyndon Johnson*, 335. Schlesinger, *Robert Kennedy*, 842–844. "[Kennedy] put in nothing [in the speech]," Schlesinger recalled, "as he had done so often in the past, to preserve his relations with the administration." *Newsweek*, "Broadside," February 19, 1968, 24. Dutton's advice noted in Frederick Dutton to RFK, January 31, 1968, RFK-SF/PC, box 3, JFKL.

69. Harry McPherson to LBJ, February 13, 1968, McPherson, box 53, LBJL.

70. Iowa poll noted in Marvin Watson to LBJ, February 16, 1968, FG1, box 16, LBJL. John Roche to LBJ, February 13, 1968, PR18-1, box 368, LBJL. Johnson's use of polls noted in Bruce E. Altschuler, "Lyndon Johnson and the Public Polls," *Public Opinion Quarterly* 50 (Fall 1986), 285–299.

71. Evelyn Lincoln, *Kennedy and Johnson* (New York, Holt, Rinehart and Winston, 1968), 205–206.

72. *New York Times* and note from Marvin Watson, February 19, 1968, WHFN-JFK, box 4, LBJL. Marvin Watson to Horace Busby, February 20, 1968, FG2, box 41, LBJL. George Christian to LBJ, March 6, 1968, FG2, box 41, LBJL. See also Jack Valenti to Marvin Watson, January 24, 1968, WHFN-JFK, box 4, LBJL; Bob Fleming to LBJ, February 19, 1968, Namefile/Salinger, LBJL; Patrick Anderson, *The President's Men* (Garden City, Doubleday, 1968), 211.

73. *Newsweek*, "And from the White House—Silence," March 18, 1968, 45. Schlesinger, *Robert Kennedy*, 843–844.

74. *Newsweek*, March 18, 1968, 45. William Connell to John Criswell, Jim Rowe, and Marvin Watson, March 11, 1968, Watson, box 25, LBJL. Lloyd Hackler to Jim Jones, March 15, 1968, PL/Kennedy, box 26, LBJL.

75. Schlesinger, *Robert Kennedy*, 848.

76. Johnson, *Vantage Point*, 538.

77. RFK to Anthony Lewis, March 13, 1968, RFK-SF/PC, box 7, JFKL. *New York Times*, March 14, 1968, 1. *New York Times*, March 15, 1968, 1. Schlesinger, *Robert Kennedy*, 849. Memorandum to the President, March 14, 1968, WHFN-RFK, box 6, LBJL. Fred Panzer to Marvin Watson, March 15, 1968, FG1, box 17, LBJL.

78. Memorandum to the President, March 14, 1968, WHFN-RFK, box 6, LBJL. George Reedy to LBJ, March 14, 1968, Watson, box 28, LBJL.

79. Schlesinger, *Robert Kennedy*, 851–852. *Newsweek*, "The Deal Bobby Offered to Strike with LBJ," March 25, 1968, 25.

80. *Newsweek*, "We Want Camelot Again," March 25, 1968, 24–32. Goodwin's proposed declaration is noted in Goodwin, n.d., RFK-SF/PC, box 4, JFKL.

81. *Newsweek*, "How the Voters See the Issues," March 25, 1968, 26. *Newsweek*, March 25, 1968, 31.

82. Lloyd Hackler to LBJ, March 19, 1968, PL/Kennedy, box 26, LBJL. Liz Carpenter to LBJ and Lady Bird Johnson, March 19, 1968, FG1, box 17, LBJL. Bill Blackburn to George Christian, March 18, 1968, FG1, box 17, LBJL. Johnson was also informed that publisher Max Ascoli planned to use *The Reporter* "shamelessly" to promote his candidacy over Kennedy's.

83. Robert Storez to Marvin Watson, March 19, 1968, PL/Kennedy, box 26, LBJL. Barefoot Sanders to LBJ, March 25, 1968, FG1, box 17, LBJL. Tom Johnson to LBJ, March 28, 1968, PL/Kennedy, box 26, LBJL. William Crook to LBJ, March 28, 1968, FG1, box 18, LBJL. See also John Roche to Marvin Watson, March 26, 1968, Watson, box 29, LBJL, on Italian-American disdain for RFK. Fred Panzer to LBJ, March 26, 1968, Panzer, box 397, LBJL, notes the Kraft poll in New York in which LBJ defeated RFK: "This poll should be leaked—particularly the comparative LBJ-RFK portions." Another poll in which LBJ wins over RFK is noted in Fred Panzer to LBJ, March 31, 1968, FG1, box 19, LBJL.

84. Fred Panzer to LBJ, March 21, 1968, Panzer, box 397, LBJL. *Newsweek*, March 25, 1968, 26. *New York Times*, March 17, 1968. *Newsweek*, "Under Way with LBJ," April 1, 1968, 21.

85. Harry McPherson to LBJ, March 22, 1968, McPherson, box 30, LBJL. Charles Roche to LBJ, March 27, 1968, Watson, box 25, LBJL. Fred Panzer to LBJ, March 22, 1968, Panzer, box 397, LBJL.

86. *New York Post*, "Johnson Bides His Time in Kennedy Feud," March 20, 1968. *St. Louis Post-Dispatch*, "Johnson Plays Roosevelt's Wartime Role," March 23, 1968. *New York Times*, "Johnson Reassesses," March 24, 1968. Press clippings are located in RFK-1968 Presidential Campaign/Press Division, box 11, JFKL. *Newsweek*, April 1, 1968, 21.

87. *Newsweek*, "The Rivals," April 8, 1968, 35–36. *Newsweek* paralleled Johnson's 1968 campaign style with that of Franklin Roosevelt's in 1940, "behaving publicly as though politics didn't exist at all." Politically he remained in a passive state reminiscent of his response to John Kennedy during the spring of 1960. "Bobby draws eye-popping crowds everywhere," *Newsweek* reported, "while the President scarcely ventures out."

88. Harry McPherson to LBJ, March 18, 1968, McPherson, box 53, LBJL. Other aides forwarded similar aggressive advice. Wattenberg relayed a message from Democratic party organizer John Sharon urging Johnson to organize a group of campaign brainstormers. "He thinks that we ought to start nailing Bobby Kennedy—hard," Wattenberg wrote. Johnson checked "yes." Larry Temple urged Johnson to respond to a recent barrage of verbal attacks by Kennedy and McCarthy. He feared the consequences "if we don't nail them to these positions and point out the unfairness or inaccuracy of [the statements] as we should." Temple wanted "someone be assigned the responsibility of carefully reviewing every speech made by Kennedy and McCarthy," and that cabinet members be dispatched in a systematic counteroffensive. George Reedy, meanwhile, was alarmed about the Democratic Women's Convention in Washington. "This conference," he warned, "is the most perfect setup for trouble I have ever seen. . . . [I]t is inconceivable to me that the Kennedy people can let this one go by without an organized effort. . . . I cannot believe that Kennedy strategists will pass up this opportunity to create headlines that Democratic women repudiate the President." He feared that the wives and sisters of the Kennedys would receive "tremendous applause." Reedy recommended postponing the conference until after the convention, "regardless of any embarrassment." "I rather agree with that," Johnson wrote on the memorandum. "Look at it and talk to [campaign manager] Terry Sanford." For memoranda calling for a more aggressive campaign strategy, see Ben Wattenberg to LBJ, March 26, 1968, Wattenberg, box 22, LBJL. Larry Temple to LBJ, March 26, 1968, Watson, box 25, LBJL. George Reedy to LBJ, March 29, 1968, Watson, box 28, LBJL.

89. Memorandum to the President, March 16, 1968, CF PL/ST, box 77, LBJL.

90. Robert Storez to Marvin Watson, March 19, 1968, PL/Kennedy, box 26, LBJL. Roscoe

Drummond article, March 30, 1968, FG2, box 41, LBJL. See also Douglass Cater to LBJ, March 29, 1968, FG1, box 18, LBJL, noting the support of James MacGregor Burns.

91. Bill McSweeny to John Criswell, March 18, 1968, Watson, box 25, LBJL. Harry McPherson to LBJ, March 22, 1968, McPherson, box 21, LBJL. Bill Crook to Marvin Watson, March 27, 1968, PL/Kennedy, box 26, LBJL. Shortly after Robert declared his candidacy, Watson was informed that author Jim Bishop was concluding his book *The Day Kennedy Was Shot*. Bishop intended to include "a lot of material on how the Kennedys attempted to use JFK's death as a plan for the future," and the Kennedys subsequently denied him documents and reports. Told that exposure of this information "could seriously damage the RFK image," Watson wrote to Crook, "Please expedite suggestion." Another suggested ploy was to parallel Ambassador Joseph Kennedy's defeatist attitude during Hitler's rise to power in the 1930s with Robert's attacks on Vietnam policy. McPherson forwarded to Johnson a passage from a book, *The Founding Father*. It recalled Joe Sr.'s "innate pessimism" and noted that he "pushed the facts to the extreme" when he was Ambassador to Great Britain. "One shouldn't carry the analogy too far," McPherson wrote, "but as Joe once said, 'Bobby and I think alike.' " "Teenagers and students flipped over Frank Sinatra, Elvis Presley and the Beatles, too," Bill Crook wrote Watson, "but no one thought of nominating them for President."

92. For examples of RFK's TV advice, see Frederick Dutton to RFK, May 1, 1967, RFK-SF/PC, box 3, JFKL. Joe to RFK, May 15, 1967, RFK-SF/PC, box 3, JFKL. Frederick Dutton to RFK, November 3, 1967, RFK-SF/PC, box 3, JFKL. Frederick Dutton to RFK, November 6, 1967, RFK-SF/PC, box 3, JFKL.

93. George Reedy to LBJ, March 16, 1968, Watson, box 28, LBJL.

94. A summary of RFK's appearance at the University of Alabama noted that RFK was "emotional and preacherish." See Douglass Cater to LBJ, March 22, 1968, Watson, box 25, LBJL. Harry McPherson to George Christian, March 22, 1968, McPherson, box 30, LBJL. Lloyd Hackler to LBJ, March 25, 1968, PL/Kennedy, box 26, LBJL. By the fall of 1967 Robert Kennedy had mastered the television medium. In September 1967 Johnson was informed that the senator was conducting a monthly television program in New York. Robert Kintner told the president that "there is no question but that it was well done." Several days after Johnson's press conference, Kennedy appeared on *Face the Nation* and received glowing reviews. "Television has become the most effective medium for political persuasion," columnist Kenneth Crawford wrote, "and Senator Robert Kennedy has become one of its most effective users. He projects almost as well as Governor Ronald Reagan, the acknowledged professional master." Robert's capacity to convey an effective image was reinforced by a Harris poll forwarded to the president ten days after the November 1967 press conference. Johnson was told that Robert "benefits from the JFK memory, 54% believe he 'has many of the same outstanding qualities of JFK.' "

95. *Newsweek*, "Choosing Sides," April 8, 1968, 36–37. *Newsweek*, April 8, 1968, 35. Harry McPherson to Marvin Watson, March 18, 1968, McPherson, box 53, LBJL. John Roche to Marvin Watson, March 23, 1968, Watson, box 29, LBJL. The idea of using RFK to endorse LBJ was also noted in Ben Wattenberg to LBJ, December 2, 1967, Wattenberg, box 22, LBJL.

96. Douglass Cater to LBJ, March 25, 1968, FG11-8-1/Cater, box 77, LBJL. Walter Rostow to LBJ, March 22, 1968, McPherson, box 18, LBJL. George Reedy to LBJ, March 29, 1968, Watson, box 28, LBJL. The quality of the musical group was inconsequential. "I have seen enough of these groups," Reedy wrote, "to know that they bring young people out regardless of their political feelings and put them in an enthusiastic mood."

97. Douglass Cater to LBJ, March 28, 1968, FG1, box 18, LBJL.

98. Dallas speech noted in Ben Wattenberg to LBJ, February 25, 1968, Wattenberg, box 22, LBJL. *New York Times*, February 28, 1968, 1. Clippings noted in November 8, 1967, FG1, box 16, LBJL, and January 5, 1968, FG1, box 16, LBJL.

99. LBJ quoted in Drew Pearson column, *Washington Post*, April 3, 1968, 19. *Public Papers of the Presidents of the United States: Lyndon B. Johnson, 1968* (Washington, Government Printing Office, 1969), 475–476.

100. *Public Papers, 1968*, 477. *Newsweek*, "Why He Did It—What Now," April 15, 1968, 42–43.

101. Kearns, *Lyndon Johnson*, 343.

102. Miller, *Lyndon*, 510–513. Carl Rowan column, *Washington Evening Star*, April 3, 1968, 25.

103. James R. Jones, "Behind LBJ's Decision Not to Run in '68," *New York Times*, April 16, 1988, 17.

104. *New York Times*, April 2, 1968, 1. RFK to LBJ, April 1, 1968, WHFN-RFK, box 6, LBJL. Miller, *Lyndon*, 513. RFK's telegram is noted in "Statement of Robert F. Kennedy," April 1, 1968, Attorney General File, box 7, JFKL. Schlesinger, *Robert Kennedy*, 868–869.

105. The description of LBJ's meeting with RFK is based on a compilation of two summaries of the meeting found in the Johnson Papers. One was written by Walter Rostow on April 3, 1968, WHFN-RFK, box 6, LBJL. Another was written by Rostow and/or Murphy on April 4, 1968, WHFN-RFK, box 6, LBJL. LBJ published the April 3 version in *Vantage Point*, 539–542. Sorensen's recollection noted in Theodore C. Sorensen, *The Kennedy Legacy* (New York, Macmillan, 1969), 146–147. LBJ's comments to Pearson and Karr noted in Schlesinger, *Robert Kennedy*, 868–869. "Then my partner died," Johnson told them, "and I took over the partnership. I kept on the eleven cowhands [the cabinet]. Some of the tenderfeet left me. But I kept on." In a rambling monologue he reinvoked John Kennedy's heavenly presence and approval, held Robert Kennedy responsible for the Bay of Pigs, and declared that the roots of the credibility gap could be found in the failed invasion.

106. Johnson, *Vantage Point*, 539–542.

107. *Newsweek*, "The Democrats' New Ballgame," April 14, 1968, 44. Although Kennedy suspected that Johnson was quietly managing Humphrey, he lightened public criticism of the president. Earlier he had accused Johnson of "calling upon the darker impulses of the American spirit." In early April he told a campaign audience that "we take pride in President Johnson, who brought to final fulfillment the [party's] policies of 30 years. . . ." Various clippings about LBJ's ultimate intentions are noted in RFK-1968 Presidential Campaign/Research Division, box 56, JFKL and RFK-1968 Presidential Campaign/Press Division, box 11, JFKL.

108. Harry McPherson to LBJ, April 2, 1968, McPherson, box 21, LBJL. Transcript of "Issues and Answers" with Pierre Salinger, April 14, 1968, Namefile/Salinger, LBJL. Fred Panzer to LBJ, May 10, 1968, Panzer, box 397, LBJL. Memorandum to the President, April 23, 1968, PL/Kennedy, box 26, LBJL. George Reedy to LBJ, April 26, 1968, FG11-8-1/Reedy, box 106, LBJL. Fred Panzer to Jim Jones and Larry Temple, April 26, 1968, FG2, box 41, LBJL. "Charisma and style" noted in *Washington Sunday Star*, June 2, 1968, "Instant Elder" editorial located in RFK-1968 Presidential Campaign/Research Division, box 56, JFKL.

109. Mike Manatos to LBJ, June 5, 1968, FG1, box 18, LBJL. Harry McPherson to LBJ, June 5, 1968, WHFN-RFK, box 6, LBJL. Tom Johnson to LBJ, June 5, 1968, FG1, box 18, LBJL. Tom Johnson to LBJ, June 6, 1968, FG1, box 18, LBJL. Harry McPherson to LBJ, June 7, 1968, UT1-1, box 4, LBJL. Tom Johnson to LBJ, June 6, 1968, PR18-1, box 368, LBJL. Jim Jones memorandum, June 6, 1968, FG2, box 41, LBJL, wanted to include LBJ in a photograph with JFK, RFK, and Martin Luther King in a pamphlet.

110. *Public Papers, 1968*, 691–693. *New York Times*, June 9, 1968, 1. Claudia A. T. Johnson, *A White House Diary* (New York, Holt, Rinehart and Winston, 1970), 682–687. Mrs. Jacqueline Kennedy to LBJ, June 1968, WHFN-Mrs. JFK, box 5, LBJL. Ethel Kennedy to Jim Jones, June 19, 1968, WHFN-RFK, box 6, LBJL. Ethel Kennedy to LBJ, August 6, 1968, WHFN-RFK, box 6, LBJL. "I do thank you so much for your wire about Bobby," Jacqueline Kennedy wrote, "—and for all you did, in those sad days,—to make it possible for him to be laid to rest with all the love and care and nobility that meant so much to those who loved him. . . ." Debate over whether to invite LBJ to the funeral is noted in agenda of "Evening Meeting—8 p.m.," June 6, 1968, RFK-1968 Presidential Campaign/Youth-Student Division, box 5, JFKL.

111. McPherson, LBJL-OH, tape 5, 1. Johnson, *A White House Diary*, 679–681.

112. McPherson, LBJL-OH, tape 5, 1. Kearns, *Lyndon Johnson*, 350.

113. Michael W. Schuyler, "Ghosts in the White House: LBJ, RFK, and the Assassination of JFK," *Political Science Quarterly* 17 (Summer 1987), 516. Liz Carpenter to LBJ, June 9, 1968, FG1, box 18, LBJL. George Christian to LBJ, June 10, 1968, FG1, box 18, LBJL. "My guess is that the country CAN, with time, recover," Carpenter wrote, "but the Eastern seaboard and media cannot—without some drama of our own making." She recommended a

major policy change concerning Vietnam, a trip to the Soviet Union by the First Lady, an overseas trip by the President, or a strong stance on "gun control and law and order...."

114. Schuyler, "Ghosts," 515. Tom Johnson to Juanita Roberts, July 30, 1968, FG1, box 19, LBJL. Robert Kintner to LBJ, July 8, 1968. CF FG/RS/PR18, box 16, LBJL, notes the desire to link Humphrey with a vice-presidential candidate familiar with the Kennedys. He recommended to the president that Humphrey's running mate be "a person close to the Kennedy's, but not a Kennedy." Harry McPherson to LBJ, June 25, 1968, McPherson, box 32, LBJL, expresses continued resentment against the bias of the Kennedy press, "a phenomenon," McPherson wrote, "that has dogged the Administration since the beginning." Johnson, *A White House Diary*, 725. Califano's observations noted in Joseph A. Califano, Jr., *Governing America: An Insider's Report from the White House and the Cabinet* (New York, Simon and Schuster, 1981), 90.

115. Johnson, *Vantage Point*, 539. *Public Papers, 1968*, 938, 1044–1045, 964, 1026, 1089.

116. *Public Papers, 1968*, 1153. BK to Donna/Nell, November 21, 1968, FG2, box 41, LBJL, notes a message from Larry Temple to cancel the delivery of the president's wreath to Kennedy's graveside: "The President may want to deliver it himself." *New York Times*, November 23, 1968, 49, notes that Lt. Col. Hugh Robinson placed a wreath at JFK's grave for LBJ. *Public Papers, 1968*, 1204–1205, 1270.

117. Richard Harwood and Haynes B. Johnson, *Lyndon* (New York, Praeger, 1973), 137.

Epilogue

1. Walter Cronkite's interview with LBJ is noted in *New York Times*, May 3, 1970, 1, 79. Doris Kearns, *Lyndon Johnson and the American Dream* (New York, Harper and Row, 1976), 178. Lyndon B. Johnson, *The Vantage Point: Perspectives of the Presidency, 1963–1969* (New York, Holt, Rinehart and Winston, 1971), 19, 41. For relevant critiques of LBJ's memoir, see John Kenneth Galbraith, "Seeing Things Through for JFK," *Saturday Review of Books*, November 6, 1971, 37–42; Michael Janeway, "LBJ and the Kennedys," *Atlantic*, February 1972, 48–54. For a critique of LBJ's interview with Cronkite, see David Halberstam, "American Notes: Lyndon and Walter, Telling It Like It Is," *Harper's Magazine*, May 1979, 124ff.

2. *New York Times*, May 3, 1970, 1, 79. For LBJ's comment to Smith, see *New York Times*, June 25, 1976, 12. LBJ made a similar allusion to Cronkite, but he later asked for it to be edited. See *New York Times*, April 26, 1975, 12.

3. LBJ's comments about the Kennedy staff noted in *New York Times*, May 3, 1970, 1, 79. For LBJ's comments about Jacqueline and Edward Kennedy, see Bobby Baker, *Wheeling and Dealing: Confessions of a Capitol Hill Operator* (New York, W. W. Norton, 1978), 273–274. See also Burton Hersh, *The Education of Edward Kennedy: A Family Biography* (New York, William Morrow, 1972), 411.

4. Marshall Frady, "Cooling Off with LBJ," *Harper's Magazine*, June 1969, 65–72. Leo Janos, "The Last Days of the President: LBJ in Retirement," *Atlantic*, July 1973, 35–41.

5. Observations about the Johnson Library were based on my visit there in July 1987.

6. Observations about Washington, D.C., were based on my visit there in May 1990. Tom Wicker, *Kennedy Without Tears: The Man Beneath the Myth* (New York, William Morrow, 1964), 16.

7. Janos, "The Last Days," *Atlantic*, July 1973, 35–41. Arthur J. Snider, "Did LBJ Die from Power Hunger?" *Science Digest*, May 1974, 46–47.

8. *Time*, "Lyndon Johnson: 1908–1973," February 5, 1973. Hugh Sidey, "They Know When You Die," *Time*, February 5, 1973, 34. *Newsweek*, "Oh, Didn't He Live Well!" February 5, 1973, 30–36.

A NOTE ON SOURCES

Research for this work involved two areas of investigation. In the preliminary stages I synthesized the secondary literature pertaining to Lyndon Johnson's relationship with John and Robert Kennedy, consulting more than 125 books and approximately five hundred articles published in magazines, newspapers, and scholarly journals. Particularly helpful in gaining an understanding of the flow of events was *Newsweek*, from which I incorporated well over two hundred articles and columns. The *New York Times, Time,* and *U.S. News and World Report* were also vital in delineating Johnson's evolving struggle with the Kennedys.

After developing a general framework from this secondary literature, I examined primary evidence in the form of memoranda, letters, reports, speeches, and logs available at the Lyndon Baines Johnson Library in Austin, Texas, and the John F. Kennedy Library in Boston, Massachusetts. An archivist at the Johnson Library had informed me that the topic would be difficult to research. Although there were some name files associated with the Kennedys, I was told that there were few references to John and Robert Kennedy among the memoranda, and that these references were not indexed; I needed to search through each box of material in order to extract relevant documents. After examining about 160 boxes of material located largely in aides files, subject files, and confidential files, I was able to obtain just over a thousand pages of relevant documents. Although some of them had been published, their specific references to the Kennedys had often been overlooked or not placed in the context of Johnson's dilemma with the "mystique." I concentrated largely on the exchanges among aides and staff members. It should be noted that the portion of gleaned material is a small fraction of the extensive holdings at the Johnson Library, a building that houses four floors of documents containing more than fifty thousand boxes of materials. Some records remain closed to researchers, and the personnel at the Johnson Library, while extremely helpful, did not make all its data available despite requests for specific documents. David C. Humphrey, "Searching for LBJ at the Johnson Library," *SHARF Newsletter* 20 (June 1989), and Robert A. Divine, "President's Library," *Discovery: Research and Scholarship at the University of Texas at Austin* 10 (No. 1, 1985), offer commentaries on the usefulness of the Johnson Library.

The Kennedy Library yielded additional primary material. Research there involved cross-referencing the memoranda and letters obtained from the Johnson Library. About forty boxes of materials were examined, including John Kennedy's Pre-Presidency Papers, the President's Office Files, and White House Name Files, as well as Robert Kennedy's Attorney General Files, Senate Files, and Senate Papers. Theodore C. Sorensen's Papers were also useful. About five hundred pages of relevant documents at the Kennedy Library were obtained. In general, the Kennedy papers contain few references to Lyndon Johnson. Those memoranda and letters that refer to Johnson are remarkably different in nature from the memoranda that circulated among the Johnson aides in their references to the Kennedys. The exchanges among the Kennedy personnel were generally carefree and lacked the defensive tone that marked the Johnson memoranda. If the temperament of this book tends to stress the negative qualities of the Kennedys, it should be noted that this story of Lyndon Johnson's struggle with the Kennedy "mystique" is often told from the perspective of Lyndon Johnson and his aides, men who felt increasingly threatened by the Kennedys.

Introduction

The best book on Lyndon Johnson and the Kennedys is Tom Wicker, *JFK and LBJ: The Influence of Personality upon Politics* (New York, William Morrow, 1968). Wicker emphasizes the unique circumstances and the political environment under which each man struggled to win his policy objectives. The work focuses on Kennedy's inability to win his legislative goals with Congress and Johnson's loss of popular support for the Vietnam War. As with much of Wicker's work, *JFK and LBJ* is insightful, fresh, and ahead of its time. In a separate article, "Lyndon Johnson vs. the Ghost of Jack Kennedy," *Esquire* 64 (November 1965), Wicker astutely outlined the impressionistic impact of the Kennedy "mystique" on Johnson's presidency during his first year in office. Wicker has consistently provided the most revealing and evenhanded appraisals of Johnson and the Kennedys. See also "Bostonian vs. the Texan," *New York Times Magazine,* October 23, 1960, and "The Kennedys and Johnson," *New York Times,* June 24, 1965. A second book devoted exclusively to Johnson and the Kennedys is Evelyn Lincoln, *Kennedy and Johnson* (New York, Holt, Rinehart and Winston, 1968). This gossipy and politically motivated work by John Kennedy's personal secretary should not be taken seriously by historians.

Two essays have specifically examined the impact of the Kennedys on Johnson. Paul K. Conkin's biography, *Big Daddy from the Pedernales: Lyndon Baines Johnson* (Boston, Twayne, 1986) devotes a short but astute chapter to the subject. Michael Schuyler, "Ghosts in the White House: LBJ, RFK and the Assassination of JFK," *Presidential Studies Quarterly* 78 (Summer 1987) provides an excellent short essay on how John Kennedy's assassination was both a blessing and a burden for Johnson's presidency. Schuyler draws on unique primary evidence to describe the resulting rivalry between Johnson and Robert Kennedy.

Helpful works addressing the history of John Kennedy as a political symbol are Vincent L. Toscano, *Since Dallas: Images of John F. Kennedy in Popular and Scholarly Literature, 1963–1973* (San Francisco, Robert J. Reed, 1978), and Thomas Brown, *JFK: History of an Image* (Bloomington, Indiana University Press, 1988). Neither author examines the evolution of the Kennedy image as reflected through television, theatrical, or cinematic docudramas or documentaries. Important books dealing with other presidential images include William E. Leuchtenburg, *In the Shadow of FDR: From Harry Truman to Ronald Reagan* (Ithaca, Cornell University Press, 1983); Merrill D. Peterson, *The Jefferson Image in the American Mind* (New York, Oxford University Press, 1962); and John William Ward, *Andrew Jackson: Symbol for an Age* (New York, Oxford University Press, 1955).

Chapter I, Prologue: The Johnson Personality

The best critiques of the existing Johnson literature are available in Robert A. Divine's two essays, "The Johnson Literature," in Robert A. Divine, ed., *The Johnson Years: Foreign Policy, the Great Society, and the White House* (Lawrence,

University Press of Kansas, 1981), and "The Johnson Revival: A Bibliographical Appraisal," in Robert A. Divine, ed., *The Johnson Years, Volume Two: Vietnam, the Environment, and Science* (Lawrence, University Press of Kansas, 1987). An excellent comprehensive bibliography of the Johnson literature, *Lyndon B. Johnson: A Bibliography* (Austin, University of Texas Press, 1984), has been compiled by the staff of the Lyndon Baines Johnson Library and is invaluable to researchers.

Numerous works by scholars, journalists, and White House aides have addressed the topic of Johnson and the Kennedys, but they have generally treated the subject in a cursory fashion, without systematic analysis. Arthur M. Schlesinger, Jr., historian and John Kennedy's special assistant, has devoted two books to the Kennedys, *A Thousand Days: John F. Kennedy in the White House* (Boston, Houghton Mifflin, 1965), and *Robert Kennedy and His Times* (Boston, Houghton Mifflin, 1978). Within the context of a broad history of John and Robert Kennedy's political careers, Schlesinger discusses the evolution of the Kennedys' relationship with Johnson largely from the perspective of the Kennedys. Too often his interpretation seems slanted by his affection for the Kennedys. Important works by Kennedy aides are similarly tainted and include Theodore C. Sorensen, *Kennedy* (New York, Harper and Row, 1965); Pierre Salinger, *With Kennedy* (Garden City, Doubleday, 1966); Kenneth P. O'Donnell, *"Johnny, We Hardly Knew Ye"* (Boston, Little, Brown, 1972); and Richard Goodwin, *Remembering America: A Voice from the Sixties* (Boston, Little, Brown, 1988).

Several Johnson aides have also lightly addressed the topic. Eric Goldman, *The Tragedy of Lyndon Johnson* (New York, Dell, 1969) devotes particular attention to Johnson's frustration with the Kennedys' intellectual image. George Reedy, *Lyndon B. Johnson: A Memoir* (New York, Andrews and McMeel, 1982) offers a remarkably candid discussion of Johnson's frustration with the Kennedys' influence on the news media. Jack Valenti, *A Very Human President* (New York, W. W. Norton, 1976) provides a glowing appraisal of Johnson and is frank about the haunting presence of the Kennedys. Harry McPherson, *A Political Education* (Boston, Little, Brown, 1972) is an intelligent personal account of his career in the Johnson presidency and further illustrates Johnson's obsession. Booth Mooney, *LBJ: An Irreverent Chronicle* (New York, Crowell, 1976) adds information on the general tensions between Johnson and the Kennedys.

Many journalists have written about Johnson and have cited the strain between him and the Kennedys. Among the better books are Jack Bell, *The Johnson Treatment: How Lyndon B. Johnson Took Over the Presidency and Made It His Own* (New York, Harper and Row, 1965); Rowland Evans and Robert Novak, *Lyndon B. Johnson: The Exercise of Power (A Political Biography)* (New York, New American Library, 1966); Frank Cormier, *LBJ: The Way He Was* (Garden City, Doubleday, 1977); Robert Sherrill, *The Accidental President* (New York, Grossman, 1967); Hugh Sidey, *A Very Personal Presidency: Lyndon Johnson in the White House* (New York, Atheneum, 1968); and Michael Davie, *LBJ: A Foreign Observer's Viewpoint* (New York, Duell, Sloan, and Pearce, 1966). See also Nancy Dickerson, *Among Those Present: A Reporter's View of 25 Years in Washington* (New York, Random House, 1976); Chalmers Roberts, *The First Rough Draft: A Journalist's Journal of Our Times* (New York, Praeger, 1973); Tom Wicker, *On Press* (New York, Viking, 1978); and David Wise, *The Politics of Lying: Government Deception, Secrecy, and Power* (New York, Random House, 1973).

Major works that have analyzed Johnson's personality are Doris Kearns, *Lyndon Johnson and the American Dream* (New York, Harper and Row, 1976); Robert A. Caro, *The Years of Lyndon Johnson: The Path to Power* (New York, Alfred A.

Knopf, 1983) and, to a lesser degree, *The Years of Lyndon Johnson: Means of Ascent* (New York, Alfred A. Knopf, 1990); and Hyman Muslin and Thomas Jobe, "The Tragic Self of Lyndon Johnson and the Dilemma of Leadership," *Psychohistory Review* 15 (Spring 1987). See also the chapters dealing with active-negative personality types in James David Barber, *The Presidential Character: Predicting Performance in the White House* (Englewood Cliffs, Prentice-Hall, 1972). Works that augment the theories on which Muslin and Jobe drew their analyses are provided by Melanie Klein, *Contributions to Psychoanalysis, 1921–1945* (London, Hogarth Press, 1968); Hanna Segal, *Introduction to the Work of Melanie Klein* (New York, Basic Books, 1964, 1973); Heinz Kohut, *The Restoration of the Self* (New York, International Universities Press, 1977); and Alice Miller, *The Drama of the Gifted Child* (New York, Basic Books, 1981). See also David McCollough, "Mama's Boys: Relationships Between Famous Men and Their Mothers," *Psychology Today*, March 1983. A balanced collection of essays dealing with the validity of psycho-biography in general is Geoffrey Cocks and Travis L. Crosby, eds., *Psycho/History: Readings in the Method of Psychology, Psychoanalysis, and History* (New Haven, Yale University Press, 1987).

Chapter II, From Senate to White House

Books that effectively address Johnson's early career include Caro, *The Path to Power* and *Means of Ascent;* Kearns, *Lyndon Johnson and the American Dream;* Evans and Novak, *The Exercise of Power;* and Ronnie Dugger, *The Politician: The Life and Times of Lyndon Johnson* (New York: W. W. Norton, 1982). Merle Miller, *Lyndon: An Oral Biography* (New York, Putnam, 1980) pulls together a variety of oral history sources to describe Johnson's Senate career. Another helpful work is by Bobby Baker, with Larry King, *Wheeling and Dealing: Confessions of a Capitol Hill Operator* (New York, W. W. Norton, 1978). Two excellent works devoted to the early life and career of John Kennedy are Herbert S. Parmet, *Jack: The Struggles of John F. Kennedy* (New York, Doubleday/Dial, 1977), and Joan Blair and Clay Blair, *The Search for JFK* (New York, Berkeley, 1976). A good reference book dealing with the careers of Johnson and Kennedy is William A. DeGregorio, *The Complete Book of Presidents* (New York, Dembner Books, 1984).

Primary sources at the Johnson Library are helpful in reconstructing the relationship between Johnson and Kennedy in the Senate. The White House Famous Names files for John F. Kennedy and Joseph P. Kennedy contain numerous letters, telegrams, transcripts of conversations, and logs detailing the exchanges between Johnson and the Kennedy family during the 1950s. Augmenting this material are the letters and telegrams contained in Theodore Sorensen's papers, John Kennedy's Pre-Presidency Papers, and the President's Office Files available at the John F. Kennedy Library. Many documents contained in one library are not available in the other. See also numerous *Time* magazine articles cited in the notes.

Helpful in delineating the changing nature of presidential campaigns in 1960 is Leonard Baker, *The Johnson Eclipse: A President's Vice-Presidency* (New York, Macmillan, 1966), and an essay by Theodore C. Sorensen, "Election of 1960," in Arthur M. Schlesinger, Jr., ed., *History of American Presidential Elections: 1789–1968,* IV (New York, McGraw-Hill, 1971). In terms of general accounts of the 1960 election, Herbert S. Parmet, *JFK: The Presidency of John F. Kennedy* (New York, Doubleday/Dial, 1983) offers a concise and useful summary of events. Theodore White, *The Making of the President 1960* (New York, Atheneum, 1961) remains a timeless study. Important articles noting the contrasting styles of Kennedy and

Johnson include the *Wall Street Journal,* "The 'Regional' Candidate," July 10, 1959; *Time,* "The Men Who," November 24, 1958; and *Time,* "The Reverberating Issue," July 18, 1960. Miller's *Lyndon* offers pertinent comments from Johnson's staff on the pre-convention campaign. Books providing further insight include Doris Kearns Goodwin, *The Fitzgeralds and the Kennedys: An American Saga* (New York, Simon and Schuster, 1987); McPherson, *A Political Education;* Lester David and Irene David, *Bobby Kennedy: The Making of a Folk Hero* (New York, Dodd, Mead, 1986), Edwin O. Guthman and Jeffrey Shulman, eds., *Robert Kennedy in His Own Words: The Unpublished Recollections of the Kennedy Years* (New York, Bantam, 1988); Schlesinger, *A Thousand Days;* Salinger, *With Kennedy;* and Baker, *Wheeling and Dealing.* Several oral histories that touch on Johnson's mixed emotions about campaigning against Kennedy include George Reedy's interview for the Johnson Library and Peter Lisagor's oral history for the Kennedy Library.

Materials relevant to Johnson's later concern about depictions of the vice-presidential selection process include Lyndon B. Johnson, *The Vantage Point: Perspectives of the Presidency, 1963–1969* (New York, Holt, Rinehart and Winston, 1971); letters exchanged between Johnson and Joseph Alsop located in PL1, box 78, at the Johnson Library; Philip Graham's memorandum published in Theodore White, *The Making of the President 1964* (New York, Atheneum, 1965); and Katharine Graham's oral history at the Johnson Library. See also Hugh Sidey, "Boston-Austin Was an Accident," *Time,* July 25, 1988.

Chapter III, The Lost Frontiersman: Kennedy's Vice President

The one book devoted exclusively to Johnson's vice presidency is Leonard Baker, *The Johnson Eclipse.* Johnson's desire for power and his subsequent unhappiness as vice president are described in Baker, *Wheeling and Dealing,* and Kearns, *Lyndon Johnson and the American Dream.* Miller's *Lyndon* offers good firsthand observations about Johnson's tenure in the New Frontier. George Reedy offers pertinent material in his memoir, *Lyndon B. Johnson: A Memoir,* and provides further insight in Kenneth W. Thompson, ed., *The Johnson Presidency: Twenty Intimate Perspectives of Lyndon B. Johnson* (Lanham, Md., University Press of America, 1986). See also Ward Just, "Whatever Happened to Lyndon Johnson?" *Reporter,* January 17, 1963, and *Time,* "What Happened to LBJ," April 5, 1963. Robert Kennedy's negative perspective on Johnson's role is made clear by Guthman and Shulman, eds., *Robert Kennedy in His Own Words.* Benjamin C. Bradlee, *Conversations with Kennedy* (New York, W. W. Norton, 1975) also comments on John Kennedy's disappointment with Johnson.

Primary evidence pertaining to Johnson's role as vice president is difficult to obtain. The Johnson Library has yet to release documents that would shed more light on Johnson's compatibility with the Kennedy administration. The most relevant data is found in the White House Famous Names–John F. Kennedy and the Office Files of George Reedy. At the Kennedy Library the President's Office Files, box 30, contains letters and memoranda exchanged between Johnson and President Kennedy. In general, however, much of the material at the Johnson and Kennedy Libraries contains nebulous speeches, reports, and logs pertaining to the vice president's involvement with space and civil rights committees. Although these documents are useful in assessing Johnson's productivity in the Kennedy administration, they do not tell us much about Johnson's personal relationship with John and Robert Kennedy.

Among a number of oral histories at the Johnson Library that help round out the discussion of Johnson's vice presidency are Arthur M. Schlesinger, Jr., Charles Bartlett, Lee White, George Reedy, and Harry McPherson.

Chapter IV, The Caretaker:
President Johnson and the Kennedy Family

Johnson's reaction to John Kennedy's assassination is noted with considerable detail in William Manchester, *The Death of a President* (New York, Harper and Row, 1967). Manchester's interpretation, however, is severely biased against Johnson. Johnson's expressed insecurities after becoming president are noted in Kearns, *Lyndon Johnson and the American Dream*, and Miller, *Lyndon*. In Kearns's work and Johnson's own memoir, *The Vantage Point*, Johnson emphasized his determination to provide the country with leadership. The resulting conspiracy theories involving Johnson are offered by Joachim Joesten's highly prejudiced *The Dark Side of Lyndon Baines Johnson* (London, Dawnay, 1968). An article by Michael Schuyler, "The Bitter Harvest: Lyndon B. Johnson and the Assassination of John F. Kennedy," *Journal of American Culture* 8 (Fall 1985), provides a unique account of how Johnson was haunted by rumors that he had conspired in his predecessor's murder. Numerous White House aides have observed Johnson's rise to power. See George W. Ball, *The Past Has Another Pattern: Memoirs* (New York, W. W. Norton, 1982), and John Kenneth Galbraith, *Ambassador's Journal: A Personal Account of the Kennedy Years* (Boston, Houghton Mifflin, 1969).

Robert Kennedy's reaction to Johnson's rise is noted by Schlesinger, *Robert Kennedy and His Times;* Guthman and Schulman, eds., *Robert Kennedy in His Own Words;* and Goodwin, *Remembering America*. Details of Johnson's political feud with Robert Kennedy can also be found in Lawrence O'Brien, *No Final Victories: A Life in Politics from JFK to Watergate* (Garden City, Doubleday, 1974) as well as in such *Newsweek* articles as "The No. 2 Man," January 13, 1964; "A Vice Presidential Skirmish," March 16, 1964; "What's Bobby Going to Do?" July 6, 1964; and "LBJ and RFK," August 10, 1964. See also Edward T. Folliard, "Is an Austin-Boston Coalition Possible?" *America*, March 28, 1964.

Johnson's relationship with Jacqueline Kennedy is conveyed in the memoranda at the Johnson Library in the file White House Famous Names–Mrs. John F. Kennedy. Jacqueline Kennedy's oral history at the Johnson Library is also helpful in reconstructing their relationship. Other helpful files at the Johnson Library include PL/Kennedy as well as the papers of Douglass Cater and Horace Busby. At the Kennedy Library, Robert Kennedy Attorney General Files, box 3, and John Kennedy's President's Office File, box 30, are also of interest. For a breakdown of Johnson's effort to emphasize the Kennedy legacy in his speeches, see *Public Papers of the Presidents of the United States: Lyndon B. Johnson, 1963–64* (Washington, Government Printing Office, 1965).

Chapter V, Managing the White House:
Johnson and the New Frontiersmen

For a general discussion of Johnson's relationship with the Kennedy staff, see Kearns, *Lyndon Johnson and the American Dream;* Johnson, *The Vantage Point;* Goldman, *The Tragedy of Lyndon Johnson;* O'Brien, *No Final Victories;* Miller,

Lyndon; and Valenti, *A Very Human President.* An invaluable book denoting the careers and roles of members of the Kennedy and Johnson staffs is Patrick Anderson, *The President's Men: White House Assistants of Franklin D. Roosevelt, Harry S. Truman, Dwight D. Eisenhower, John F. Kennedy, and Lyndon B. Johnson* (Garden City, Doubleday, 1968). Further biographical information is available in Nelson Lichtenstein, ed., *Political Profiles: The Johnson Years* and *Political Profiles: The Kennedy Years* (New York, Facts on File, 1976). Also helpful is Richard T. Johnson, *Managing the White House: An Intimate Study of the Presidency* (New York, Harper and Row, 1974), and Emmett S. Redford and Richard T. McCulley, *White House Operations: The Johnson Presidency* (Austin, University of Texas Press, 1986).

The anxiety between the Kennedy staff and Lyndon Johnson is noted in Manchester, *The Death of a President,* and Schlesinger, *Robert Kennedy and His Times.* Two articles that consider the immediate consequences of the departure of Kennedy staff members from the Johnson White House are James Reston's and Anthony Lewis's columns in the March 22, 1964, *New York Times.* See also James Best, "Who Talked to the President When? A Study of Lyndon B. Johnson," *Political Science Quarterly* 103 (Fall 1988).

Primary documents dealing with the Kennedy staff are located at the Johnson Library in the following files: Cabinet Papers; PL2,FG/RS/PR18; Office Files of Bill Moyers; and the White House Famous Names files for Kenneth P. O'Donnell, Arthur Schlesinger, and Pierre Salinger. The Johnson Library oral histories for Arthur M. Schlesinger, Jr., John Roche, Clark Clifford, and Jack Valenti help round out the picture. The role of the Kennedy "loyalists" in creating John Kennedy's myth is discussed aptly in Andrew Logan's "The Stained Glass Image," *American Heritage,* August 1967; Brown, *JFK;* McGeorge Bundy, "The History-Maker," *Massachusetts Historical Society* 90 (December 1978); and Donald C. Lord, *John F. Kennedy: The Politics of Confrontation and Conciliation* (Woodbury, N.Y., Baron's, 1977).

The influence of the memory of John Kennedy on Johnson's decision to escalate the Vietnam War is noted by Reedy, *Lyndon B. Johnson: A Memoir,* and Thompson, ed., *The Johnson Presidency.* See also David M. Barrett, "The Mythology Surrounding Lyndon Johnson, His Advisers, and the 1965 Decision to Escalate the Vietnam War," *Political Science Quarterly* 103 (Winter 1988), and Kent M. Beck, "The Kennedy Image: Politics, Camelot, and Vietnam," *Wisconsin Magazine of History* 58 (Autumn 1974).

Chapter VI, "Let Us Continue": Johnson's Legislative Record and the Kennedy Shadow

Johnson's initial decision to draw on John Kennedy's legislative agenda is dealt with in Kearns, *Lyndon Johnson and the American Dream;* Reedy, *Lyndon B. Johnson: A Memoir;* and Miller, *Lyndon.* An interesting essay regarding Johnson's first address to Congress is Patricia D. Witherspoon, " 'Let Us Continue': The Rhetorical Initiation of Lyndon Johnson's Presidency," *Presidential Studies Quarterly* 17 (Summer 1987).

Johnson's political and personal feelings on civil rights are noted by Evans and Novak, *The Exercise of Power;* Goodwin, *Remembering America;* Miller, *Lyndon;* and Thompson, ed., *The Johnson Presidency.* Excellent short essays can be found in

Steven F. Lawson, "Civil Rights," in Robert A. Divine, ed., *The Johnson Years: Foreign Policy, the Great Society, and the White House,* and Monroe Billington, "Lyndon B. Johnson and Blacks: The Early Years," *Journal of Negro History* 62 (1) 1977. Carl M. Brauer, *John F. Kennedy and the Second Reconstruction* (New York, Columbia University Press, 1977) discusses John Kennedy's efforts on behalf of civil rights. A detailed account of the advice that Johnson offered President Kennedy on the Civil Rights Bill of 1963 can be found in Steven F. Lawson, " 'I Got It from the *New York Times*': Lyndon Johnson and the Kennedy Civil Rights Program," *Journal of Negro History* 67 (2), 1982. An argument that Kennedy followed Johnson's advice on civil rights is made by Michael P. Riccards, "Rare Counsel: Kennedy, Johnson, and the civil rights bill of 1963," *Presidential Studies Quarterly* 11 (Summer 1981). Johnson's determination to use civil rights as a means to win over liberal opinion is noted by Goodwin, *Remembering America,* and Kearns, *Lyndon Johnson and the American Dream.*

Robert Kennedy's reaction to the passage of the 1964 civil rights bill is described by Schlesinger, *Robert Kennedy and His Times,* and Guthman and Shulman, eds., *Robert Kennedy in His Own Words.* John Kennedy's endearing reputation among African Americans is noted in Bradley S. Greenberg and Edwin B. Parker, eds., *The Kennedy Assassination and the American Public: Social Communication in Crisis* (Stanford, Stanford University Press, 1965); Brown, *JFK;* Louis Heren, *No Hail, No Farewell* (New York, Harper and Row, 1970); and Alfred John Farrari, "Kennedy Assassinations and Political Detours (A Possibly Romantic Posthumous Speculation)," *Minority of One,* November 1968.

An excellent article on the origins of the War on Poverty is Nicholas Lemann, "The Unfinished War," *Atlantic* 262 (December 1988). Also informative and helpful is Mark I. Gelfand, "The War on Poverty," in Robert A. Divine, ed., The *Johnson Years: Foreign Policy, the Great Society, and the White House.* See also Carl M. Brauer, "Kennedy, Johnson, and the War on Poverty," *Journal of American History* 69 (June 1982). Important memoranda on Johnson's desire to separate himself legislatively from the Kennedy past can be found in FG1, box 10, and PR18, box 367, at the Johnson Library. Johnson's reputation for legislative success is noted in a variety of *Newsweek* articles from the summer of 1964, especially August 31. See also Milton C. Cummings, ed., *The National Election of 1964* (Washington, Brookings Institution, 1966), and Russell D. Renka, "Comparing Presidents Kennedy and Johnson as Legislative Leaders," *Presidential Studies Quarterly* 15 (Fall 1985). Johnson's references to John Kennedy are indexed in *Public Papers of the Presidents of the United States: Lyndon Baines Johnson, 1965* (Washington, Government Printing Office, 1966). His determination to measure himself against John Kennedy's legislative record is offered in numerous memoranda cited in the notes.

Chapter VII, Projecting the Johnson Image

Johnson's initial image-management strategies are the subject of several memoranda which Horace Busby sent to the president in the early months of 1964. Particularly important are Busby's memos to the president on January 14, 1964, located in Busby's Office Files, box 53; January 23, 1964 in FG/RS/PR18, box 9; an April 1964 memo in box 52; April 11, 1964, in box 53; April 29, 1964, in box 52; April 30, 1964, in box 53; and May 14, 1964, in box 52, all available at the Johnson Library. The memoranda by Jack Valenti, Bill Moyers, Douglass Cater, Eric Goldman, and others are also vital in reconstructing Johnson's earliest concerns for his image. Specific references to these memoranda can be found in the notes.

For a general understanding of Johnson's concern for and relationship with the press, see Reedy, *Lyndon B. Johnson: A Memoir;* Kathleen Turner, *Lyndon Johnson's Dual War: Vietnam and the Press* (Chicago, University of Chicago Press, 1985); Thompson, ed., *The Johnson Presidency;* David Culber, "Johnson and the Media," in Robert A. Divine, ed., *The Johnson Years: Foreign Policy, the Great Society, and the White House;* James E. Pollard, *The Presidents and the Press* (New York, Octagon, 1973); John Tebbel and Sarah Miles Watts, *The Press and the Presidency: From George Washington to Ronald Reagan* (New York, Oxford University Press, 1985); and Elmer Cornwell, Jr., *Presidential Leadership of Public Opinion* (Bloomington, Indiana University Press, 1965). Also helpful are several oral histories at the Johnson Library, including Jack Valenti's and George Reedy's. Numerous articles in magazines and newspapers discuss Johnson's concern for the press and are cited in the notes. For an understanding of how Johnson treated public opinion, see Bruce E. Altschuler, "Lyndon Johnson and Public Opinion Polls," *Public Opinion Quarterly* 50 (Fall 1986).

The social character types that impeded Johnson's ability to convey an effective image are proposed in David Riesman, *The Lonely Crowd: A Study of the Changing American Character* (New Haven, Yale University Press, 1950); William H. Whyte, *The Organization Man* (Garden City, Doubleday, 1957); Michael Maccoby, *The Gamesman: Winning and Losing in the Career Game* (New York, Simon and Schuster, 1976); and Milton Gordon, *Assimilation in American Life: The Role of Race, Religion, and National Origins* (New York, Oxford University Press, 1964)

The changing nature of journalism in the 1960s is considered in Wicker, *On Press;* William Rivers, "The Correspondents After 25 Years," *Columbia Journalism Review* 1 (Spring 1962); and Ben H. Bagdikian, "JFK to LBJ: Paradoxes of Change," *Columbia Journalism Review* 2 (Winter 1964). Several oral histories available at the Johnson Library lend further insight, including Charles Bartlett's and Katharine Graham's. At the Kennedy Library, oral histories by the Press Panel, Peter Lisagor, Henry Luce, Charles Roberts, and Hugh Sidey help explain how the press contrasted Johnson to John Kennedy. Johnson discussed his frustration in having to compete against John Kennedy's reputation in Kearns, *Lyndon Johnson and the American Dream;* in *The Vantage Point;* and in an interview for CBS News with Walter Cronkite, "LBJ: Tragedy and Transition," May 2, 1970.

Johnson's efforts to draw on John Kennedy's myth during the 1964 presidential campaign are indexed in *Public Papers of the Presidents of the United States: Lyndon Baines Johnson, 1963–64* (Washington, Government Printing Office, 1965) and in the *1964 New York Times Index*. His growing frustration about being shadowed by the Kennedy myth is expressed by Goldman, *The Tragedy of Lyndon Johnson;* Tip O'Neill, *Man of the House: The Life and Political Memoirs of Speaker Tip O'Neill* (New York, Random House, 1987); and Harry McPherson's and Jack Valenti's oral histories at the Johnson Library.

The degree to which the Kennedy myth helped Johnson in the 1964 election is noted in Milton C. Cummings, Jr., ed., *The National Election of 1964* (Washington, Brookings Institution, 1966). See also Harold Faber, ed., *The Road to the White House: The Story of the 1964 Election by the Staff of the New York Times* (New York, New York Times, 1965); Charles McDowell, Jr., *Campaign Fever: The National Folk Festival from New Hampshire to November, 1964* (New York, William Morrow, 1965); Theodore White, *The Making of the President 1964;* Kathleen Hall Jamieson, *Packaging the Presidency: A History and Criticism of Presidential Campaign Advertising* (New York, Oxford University Press, 1984); Stewart Alsop, "Only Johnson Can Beat Johnson," *Saturday Evening Post,* January

4, 1964, and "Uncle Lyndon," *Saturday Evening Post*, October 24, 1964; and Emmet John Hughes's column in *Newsweek*, February 24, 1964. Numerous memoranda and articles cited in the notes discussed Johnson's invocations of John Kennedy and his help in Robert Kennedy's senatorial campaign.

Chapter VIII, Emerging from the Kennedy Shadow

For discussions of Johnson's erratic personality change in 1965, see Kearns, *Lyndon Johnson and the American Dream;* Goodwin, *Remembering America;* John Roche's oral history for the Johnson Library; and Jack Valenti's letter to the *New York Times Magazine*, September 11, 1988.

Robert Kennedy's rise in political status and his use of the memory of John Kennedy are noted in numerous articles in *Newsweek, Time,* and the *New York Times* cited in the notes. Harry McPherson's June 24, 1965, memorandum to Johnson outlining Robert Kennedy's assumed political ambitions is remarkably astute and can be found in McPherson's Office Files, box 21, at the Johnson Library. Schlesinger, *Robert Kennedy and His Times* offers a detailed account of Robert's senatorial career, his hostile attitude toward Johnson, and his growing opposition to the president's policies.

Primary evidence on Johnson's relationship with Robert Kennedy is scattered among the office files of numerous aides, especially those of Jack Valenti, Horace Busby, and Harry McPherson. Exchanges between Johnson and Robert Kennedy are available in the White House Famous Names–Robert Kennedy folder at the Johnson Library. Numerous exchanges between Robert Kennedy and Johnson are also available in Robert Kennedy's Senate Papers, especially box 5, at the Kennedy Library. Johnson's drift away from associating himself with the memory of John Kennedy is expressed in numerous memoranda at the Johnson Library, and his desire to assert his own identity can be found in articles cited in the notes. Especially important is Horace Busby's December 4, 1964, memoranda to Johnson located in Busby's Office Files, box 52, at the Johnson Library. Johnson's references to John Kennedy are indexed in *Public Papers of the Presidents of the United States: Lyndon Baines Johnson, 1965* (Washington, Government Printing Office, 1966). Several memoranda encouraging Johnson to emulate John Kennedy's television presence are cited in the notes. An assessment of Johnson's television skills in 1965 is provided in "The Brand That's Being Burned in TV," *Broadcasting*, November 8, 1965. Criticism of Johnson's television presence is noted in *Time,* "Mover of Men," August 6, 1965.

The contrast between the Johnson and Kennedy staffs is noted by Tom Wicker, "Johnson's Men: 'Valuable Hunks of Humanity,' " *New York Times Magazine*, May 3, 1964; *Newsweek,* "Inside the White House," March 1, 1965; and *U.S. News and World Report,* "The Johnson Staff," December 2, 1963, and "How the White House Is Changing," December 23, 1963. See also the accounts by various aides, including Goldman, *The Tragedy of Lyndon Johnson;* Valenti, *A Very Human President;* McPherson, *A Political Education;* Joseph A. Califano, Jr., *Governing America: An Insider's Report from the White House and the Cabinet* (New York, Simon and Schuster, 1981); Liz Carpenter, *Ruffles and Flourishes* (Garden City, Doubleday, 1970); and memoranda from Harry McPherson, Bill Moyers, and Benjamin Wattenberg cited in the notes. McPherson's May and June memoranda to Bill Moyers and Lyndon Johnson are exceptionally revealing in terms of understanding Johnson's growing obsession with Robert Kennedy and his concern for loyalty. Especially critical are his two memoranda to Johnson on June 24, 1965, located in McPherson's

Office Files, boxes 21 and 52, at the Johnson Library. McPherson's oral history at the Johnson Library brings further light to the issue.

Johnson's early foreign policy departures on Latin America and Kennedy's reaction are aptly addressed in Schlesinger's *Robert Kennedy and His Times,* and Goodwin, *Remembering America.* See also Miller, *Lyndon,* and Theodore James Maher, "The Kennedy and Johnson Responses to Latin American Coups D'Etat," *World Affairs* 131 (3), 1968. Robert Kennedy's earliest criticisms are addressed in *Newsweek,* "Dominican Crisis," May 17, 1965, and Tom Wicker, "The Kennedys and Johnson," *New York Times,* June 24, 1965. See also Hugh Sidey, "He Makes a Truce...," *Life,* November 18, 1966. Frederick Dutton's memoranda to Kennedy, located in Robert Kennedy's Senate Files at the Kennedy Library, are extremely helpful in understanding Robert Kennedy's plotted course in undermining Johnson.

Johnson's evolving policy toward Vietnam as it relates specifically to Robert Kennedy is noted in Kearns, *Lyndon Johnson and the American Dream,* and Schlesinger, *Robert Kennedy and His Times.* Relevant here was Johnson's attempt to use the memory of John Kennedy as a shield to protect himself from Robert's criticism. Separate memoranda from McGeorge Bundy, Douglass Cater, and Horace Busby are especially important and are cited in the notes. See also Henry William Brands, Jr., "Johnson and Eisenhower: The President, the Former President, and the War in Vietnam," *Presidential Studies Quarterly* 15 (Summer 1985), and Walter Bunge, et al., "Johnson's Information Strategy for Vietnam: An Evaluation," *Journalism Quarterly* 45 (Autumn 1968).

Johnson's desire to hinder Robert Kennedy's political influence in New York is described in Schlesinger, *Robert Kennedy and His Times,* and augmented here by an account of Johnson's desire to keep Nassau County, New York, county executive Eugene Nickerson from traveling overseas. Harry McPherson's memoranda outline the Nickerson episode.

Johnson's battle with the intellectuals is detailed in Goldman, *The Tragedy of Lyndon Johnson,* and augmented by various articles and several memoranda cited in the notes. See also Hans J. Morgenthau, "Truth and Power: The Intellectuals in the Johnson Administration," *New Republic* (November 26, 1968); Henry Fairlie, "Johnson and the Intellectuals: A British View," *Commentary,* October 1965; and Eric F. Goldman, "The White House and the Intellectuals," *Harper's Magazine,* January 1969.

Johnson's hostility toward the "Georgetown Crowd" is addressed in Harry McPherson's oral history at the Johnson Library and in his book, *A Political Education.* Johnson's animosity toward the press is candidly noted in Reedy, *Lyndon B. Johnson: A Memoir;* Charles Bartlett's oral history for the Johnson Library; Goodwin, *Remembering America;* and in articles from the period cited in the notes. The Johnson staff compiled a number of studies comparing his press relations with John Kennedy's. See also Allen Otten, "Criticism of President's Style, Methods Mount Among Small but Important Group," *Wall Street Journal,* July 6, 1965. Johnson's relationship with his press secretary, Bill Moyers, is detailed in Patrick Anderson, *The President's Men.* A revealing interview with Moyers is provided by James Fallows, "Bill Moyers: His Heart Belongs to Daddy," *Washington Monthly,* July/August 1974. See also Bill Moyers, "Bill Moyers Talks About LBJ, Power, Poverty, War, and the Young," *Atlantic,* July 1968, and Michael Medved, *The Shadow Presidents: The Secret History of the Chief Executives and Their Top Aides* (New York, Times Books, 1979).

Chapter IX, The Rupture, 1966–1967

Robert Kennedy's heightened criticism of Johnson is detailed in Schlesinger, *Robert Kennedy and His Times*. Kennedy's Senate Files/Personal Correspondences in the John F. Kennedy Library contain numerous letters and memoranda from Johnson aides and Kennedy personnel relevant to his criticism of Johnson and are cited in the notes. Especially interesting are the memoranda from Frederick Dutton offering Kennedy advice intended to undermine Johnson and build Kennedy's political base for the 1968 presidential election. *Newsweek's* cover story on Robert and Edward Kennedy, "Two Senators Named Kennedy," January 17, 1966, is helpful in understanding the political environment that Robert sought to exploit in the early months of 1966. Other articles detailing Kennedy's criticism are cited in the notes. Reports from Johnson's staff concerning Kennedy's intentions were frequently sent to the president and are cited in the notes. See especially the memoranda from Harry McPherson, Bill Moyers, and Robert Kintner.

Robert Kennedy's attempt to exploit his brother's memory for his own purposes is noted in *Newsweek*, "Two Senators Named Kennedy," January 17, 1966; *Newsweek*, "The Bobby Phenomenon," October 24, 1966; and *Life*, "He Uses—and Deeply Feels—the Legend," November 18, 1966. For earlier demonstrations of this tactic, see *Newsweek*, "The Senators Kennedy," January 18, 1965; *Newsweek*, "The 99th Senator," March 15, 1965; *Newsweek*, "The Climber," April 5, 1965; and *Newsweek*, "Newsmakers," May 24, 1965. Schlesinger also remarks on Kennedy's emotional transformation in *Robert Kennedy and His Times*. Kennedy's success in building a political base is noted in Emmet John Hughes's column in *Newsweek*, March 7, 1966, and in Tom Wicker, "Lyndon Johnson vs. the Ghost of Jack Kennedy," *Esquire*. Johnson's subsequent distancing from the Kennedy "mystique" is noted in memoranda cited in the notes. His nebulous references to John Kennedy in 1966 are indexed in *Public Papers of the Presidents of the United States: Lyndon Baines Johnson* (Washington, Government Printing Office, 1967). Especially relevant is *Newsweek*, "LBJ President, 1972?" September 5, 1966, and Louis Harris, "State of the LBJ Image," *Newsweek*, January 9, 1967.

Johnson's growing "paranoia" about Robert Kennedy is cited in Schlesinger, *Robert Kennedy and His Times*, and in John Roche's oral history for the Johnson Library. See also newspaper clippings kept in Robert Kennedy's 1968 Campaign/ Press Division files at the Kennedy Library. Moyers's departure from the administration is noted in *Newsweek*, "Bridge Out," December 26, 1966; Schlesinger, *Robert Kennedy and His Times;* John Roche's and Harry McPherson's oral histories for the Johnson Library; Fallows, "Bill Moyers: His Heart Belongs to Daddy," *Washington Monthly;* and several memoranda listed in the notes. Articles and books have detailed the Manchester affair and are cited in the notes. Especially interesting is William Manchester, *Controversy and Other Essays in Journalism, 1950–75* (Boston, Little, Brown, 1976). See also the memoranda among Johnson aides cited in the notes.

Several books and articles helpful in reconstructing the February 6, 1967, confrontation between Johnson and Robert Kennedy are Schlesinger, *Robert Kennedy and His Times;* Victor Lasky, *Robert F. Kennedy: The Myth and the Man* (New York, Trident, 1968); David Wise, *The Politics of Lying; Newsweek,* "The Other War," February 20, 1967; and *Time,* March 17, 1967.

Chapter X, End of the Ordeal

Kennedy's political considerations after the February 6, 1967, confrontation with Johnson are noted in memoranda from Richard Goodwin and Frederick Dutton located in Robert Kennedy's Senate Files/Personal Correspondences at the Kennedy Library. Speculation among Johnson aides and planned counterattacks are expressed in the voluminous memoranda from John Roche, Harry McPherson, Robert Kintner, Benjamin Wattenberg, and Douglass Cater. See also O'Brien, *No Final Victories.* Johnson's attempt to undermine Robert Kennedy's March 2, 1967, Senate speech is noted in Victor Lasky, *Robert Kennedy;* Schlesinger, *Robert Kennedy and His Times; Newsweek,* "Men at War: RFK vs. LBJ," March 13, 1967; Emmet John Hughes's column in *Newsweek,* March 20, 1967; and *Newsweek,* "That Man and That Boy," March 20, 1967. Johnson's mounting political problems are noted in *Newsweek,* "Tired Grandpa," August 14, 1967; Kenneth Crawford's column in *Newsweek,* August 14, 1967; *Newsweek,* "LBJ at a Low Ebb," August 21, 1967; *Newsweek,* "A President in Trouble," September 4, 1967; and *Newsweek,* "Dump LBJ?" October 9, 1967.

Johnson's attempt to use the memory of John Kennedy in defense of his Vietnam policy can be found in a number of memoranda cited in the notes. See especially Walter Rostow's compilation of John Kennedy quotes located in Confidential Files, NSF:VN, box 97, at the Johnson Library. See also the index in *Public Papers of the Presidents of the United States: Lyndon Baines Johnson, 1967* (Washington, Government Printing Office, 1968) for Johnson's specific references to John Kennedy in 1968. Johnson's renewed television strategy is noted in *Newsweek,* "Live and in Color: The Real LBJ," November 27, 1967, and PR18-2, box 367, and PR18-2, box 376, located at the Johnson Library. Robert McNamara's resignation is detailed in *Newsweek,* "McNamara: Why Is He Leaving," December 11, 1967; Schlesinger, *Robert Kennedy and His Times;* John Roche's oral history at the Johnson Library; and Kearns, *Lyndon Johnson and the American Dream.* Eugene McCarthy's entrance into the race is observed by O'Brien, *No Final Victories;* Miller, *Lyndon;* and *Newsweek,* "McCarthy or McCoy?" December 11, 1967. Johnson staff reaction is noted in memoranda from John Roche, Benjamin Wattenberg, and James Rowe.

The political implications of the Tet Offensive, McCarthy's "victory" in the New Hampshire primary, and Robert Kennedy's announced candidacy are noted in Kearns, *Lyndon Johnson and the American Dream;* Schlesinger, *Robert Kennedy and His Times;* and memoranda from the Johnson staff and articles cited in the notes. Especially insightful are the memoranda from John Roche and Harry McPherson. See also Johnson, *The Vantage Point;* Marvin Barrett, "When LBJ Stunned the Experts," *Columbia Journalism Review* 7 (Summer 1968); and James R. Jones, "Behind LBJ's Decision Not to Run in '68," *New York Times,* April 16, 1988. See also John P. Roche, "February 29, 1968: A Day That Should Live in Irony," *National Review,* June 10, 1988, and "The Second Coming of RFK," *National Review,* July 22, 1988.

Johnson's last meeting with Robert Kennedy is described in Walter Rostow's summary written on April 3, 1968, and located in White House Famous Names–Robert F. Kennedy in the Johnson Library. See also Theodore C. Sorensen, *The Kennedy Legacy* (New York, Macmillan, 1969), and Schlesinger, *Robert Kennedy and His Times.* Articles and memoranda speculating about Johnson's and Kennedy's political futures are cited in the notes. Johnson's reaction to Robert Kennedy's assassination is discussed in Harry McPherson's oral history at the Johnson Library and in Claudia A. T. Johnson, *A White House Diary* (New York, Holt, Rinehart and

Winston, 1970). See also the memoranda cited in the notes. Johnson's final retreat to the Kennedy "mystique" is detailed in *The Vantage Point; Public Papers of the Presidents of the United States: Lyndon Baines Johnson, 1968–69* (Washington, Government Printing Office, 1969); Michael Janeway, "LBJ and the Kennedys," *Atlantic*, February 1972; John Kenneth Galbraith, "Seeing Things Through for JFK," *Saturday Review,* November 6, 1971; and in memoranda cited in the notes.

Epilogue

Two excellent articles depicting Johnson's years in retirement are Marshall Frady, "Cooling Off with LBJ," *Harper's Magazine*, June 1969, and Leo Jano, "The Last Days of the President: LBJ in Retirement," *Atlantic*, July 1973. Johnson's death is covered in *Time*, "Lyndon Johnson: 1908–1973," February 5, 1973; Hugh Sidey, "They Know When You Die," *Time*, February 5, 1973; and *Newsweek*, " 'Oh, Didn't He Live Well!' " February 5, 1973. See also Arthur J. Snider, "Did LBJ Die from Power Hunger?" *Science Digest*, May 1974.

INDEX

John F. Kennedy Education, Civic, and Cultural Center, 113, 138
John F. Kennedy Library, 70, 138, 199, 252
Johnson, Claudia Taylor (Lady Bird), 45, 52, 54, 55, 69, 88, 90, 133, 136, 138, 139, 195, 204, 248; and Kennedy "mystique," 249
Johnson, Lyndon—
CAREER: *as congressman and senator*, 6, 24–32, 111–112, 126, 128; World War II, 24, 31–32; campaign (1956), 25–28; support for JFK, 26–28; campaign (1960), 6, 26, 28, 30, 33–49, 50–52, 64, 95, 96, 97, 99, 102; Democratic National Convention, 6, 29, 30, 33–34, 37, 38–49, 64, 66, 245; debate with JFK, 41–43; selection as vice president, 43–49; *as vice president*, 52–64, 68, 112–113, 233–234; opinion of vice presidency, 59–60, 70; mimicks JFK style, 57–58; Bay of Pigs, 57, 164, 170; loyalty to JFK, 58–59, 245; relationship with New Frontiersmen, 55–56; possible removal from 1964 ticket, 3, 60, 62–63, 66, 157, 233–234; trips, 35, 51–52, 54–55, 57; *as president*, assassination of JFK, 3, 65–66, 86–87, 203–204, 250, 251; first cabinet meeting, 74–75, 93, 105–106; campaign (1964), 33, 72, 73, 76–91, 98, 99, 103, 120–121, 130, 142–150, 151, 245; eliminates RFK from 1964 ticket, 4, 76–85; Democratic National Convention, 79–80, 85–91, 143, 148, 156; inauguration, 73, 156–157; legislative skills, 53–54, 56–57, 66–67, 99, 103, 104, 110, 112–114, 116, 118, 119, 120, 121, 134–135, 153, 201, 225; Great Society, 14, 99, 109–122, 151–152, 157, 158, 175, 199–200, 211, 219, 224, 226, 253; civil rights, 54–55, 57, 61, 103, 109, 110, 111–115, 144, 152, 157, 161, 216, 223; tax reform, 72, 103, 109, 110, 117–118; war on poverty, 103, 115–122, 133, 157, 196, 219, 224, 254; Latin America, 169–171, 183; Dominican Republic crisis, 161, 169, 170, 171, 179; Panama crisis, 169–170; Vietnam, 99, 104–105, 107, 108, 151–152, 169, 172–175, 179, 187–193, 194, 195, 199–200, 201, 207–218, 222–223, 226–229, 232–233, 244, 247; decisions to escalate the war, 105–106, 172–173, 175, 183–184, 187, 189, 212, 234–235; Gulf of Tonkin Resolution, 106, 146; trips, 121, 133, 144, 147–149, 155, 171, 210, 241; White House staff, 84, 134, 204–205, 218–219; compared with JFK staff, 158, 161–169; need for staff loyalty, 75, 107, 165–169, 229–230; relationship with JFK holdovers, 66, 74, 84, 92–108, 158–159; opinion of LBJ staff, 84, 93, 163, 203; opinion of JFK staff, 57, 84, 93–94, 104, 105, 117, 157, 163, 251–252; campaign (1968), 99, 103, 154, 168, 171, 197, 198, 201, 212–214, 218, 219, 223–245, 249–250; "dump" LBJ movement (1968), 225, 237; withdrawal, 225–226, 232, 234, 242–244; Democratic National Convention, 247, 253; retirement, 251–254; memoirs, 12, 47–48, 84–85, 247, 249.
IMAGE MANAGEMENT: 110, 115, 116, 119–120, 121–122, 123–150, 155–161, 219–221, 241–242; intellectual image, 14–15, 113, 122, 134–139, 153, 154–155, 156, 158, 178–180, 219–221, 241; opinion of intellectuals, 135, 139, 180; image among young adults, 121, 139–140, 140–141, 221, 241; mimicks JFK style, 57–58, 126, 131, 139–141, 229; trend setter, 139–140; rejection of JFK image, 155–161, 180, 198–199; tributes to JFK, 70–71, 87–88, 90–91, 107, 109, 113, 114, 118,

318

A NOTE ON THE AUTHOR

Paul R. Henggeler is Assistant Professor of History at Bowling Green State University in Ohio. Born in Wantagh, New York, he grew up on Long Island. He studied at the State University of New York at Cortland and then taught social studies in high school before returning to graduate studies at Bowling Green, where he received a Ph.D. in history. This is his first book.